S0-CFK-546

Ithaca, Feb 2007.

Cells and Surveys

Should Biological Measures Be Included in Social Science Research?

Committee on Population

Caleb E. Finch, James W. Vaupel, and Kevin Kinsella, Editors

Commission on Behavioral and Social Sciences and Education

National Research Council

NATIONAL ACADEMY PRESS
Washington, D.C.

NATIONAL ACADEMY PRESS 2101 Constitution Avenue, N.W. Washington, D.C. 20418

NOTICE: The project that is the subject of this report was approved by the Governing Board of the National Research Council, whose members are drawn from the councils of the National Academy of Sciences, the National Academy of Engineering, and the Institute of Medicine. The members of the committee responsible for the report were chosen for their special competences and with regard for appropriate balance.

This study was supported by Task Order 49 under NIH Contract No. NOI-OD-4-2139 between the National Academy of Sciences and the Office of the Demography of Aging, National Institute of Aging, National Institutes of Health, U.S. Department of Health and Human Services. Additional funding was provided by the Office of the Director of the Behavioral and Social Research Program, National Institutes of Health, by the William and Flora Hewlett Foundation, and by the Andrew W. Mellon Foundation. Any opinions, findings, conclusions, or recommendations expressed in this publication are those of the author(s) and do not necessarily reflect the views of the organizations or agencies that provided support for the project.

Suggested citation: National Research Council (2000) *Cells and Surveys: Should Biological Measures Be Included in Social Science Research*? Committee on Population. Caleb E. Finch, James W. Vaupel, and Kevin Kinsella, eds. Commission on Behavioral and Social Sciences and Education. Washington, D.C.: National Academy Press.

Library of Congress Cataloging-in-Publication Data

Cells and surveys : should biological measures be included in social
science research? / Committee on Population ; Caleb E. Finch, James W.
Vaupel, and Kevin Kinsella, editors.
      p. cm.
Includes bibliographical references and index.
  ISBN 0-309-07199-2 (pbk.)
  1. Social medicine--Congresses. 2. Medical ethics--Congresses. 3.
Bioethics--Congresses. 4. Demography--Congresses. 5. Medical
genetics--Congresses. I. Finch, Caleb Ellicott. II. Vaupel, James W.
III. Kinsella, Kevin G. IV. National Research Council (U.S.). Committee
on Population. V. Title.
  RA418 .C45 2001
  300'.7'23--dc21
                          00-012155

Additional copies of this report are available from National Academy Press, 2101 Constitution Avenue, N.W., Lockbox 285, Washington, D.C. 20055; (800) 624-6242 or (202) 334-3313 (in the Washington metropolitan area); Internet, http://www.nap.edu

Printed in the United States of America

Copyright 2001 by the National Academy of Sciences. All rights reserved.

THE NATIONAL ACADEMIES

National Academy of Sciences
National Academy of Engineering
Institute of Medicine
National Research Council

The **National Academy of Sciences** is a private, nonprofit, self-perpetuating society of distinguished scholars engaged in scientific and engineering research, dedicated to the furtherance of science and technology and to their use for the general welfare. Upon the authority of the charter granted to it by the Congress in 1863, the Academy has a mandate that requires it to advise the federal government on scientific and technical matters. Dr. Bruce M. Alberts is president of the National Academy of Sciences.

The **National Academy of Engineering** was established in 1964, under the charter of the National Academy of Sciences, as a parallel organization of outstanding engineers. It is autonomous in its administration and in the selection of its members, sharing with the National Academy of Sciences the responsibility for advising the federal government. The National Academy of Engineering also sponsors engineering programs aimed at meeting national needs, encourages education and research, and recognizes the superior achievements of engineers. Dr. William A. Wulf is president of the National Academy of Engineering.

The **Institute of Medicine** was established in 1970 by the National Academy of Sciences to secure the services of eminent members of appropriate professions in the examination of policy matters pertaining to the health of the public. The Institute acts under the responsibility given to the National Academy of Sciences by its congressional charter to be an adviser to the federal government and, upon its own initiative, to identify issues of medical care, research, and education. Dr. Kenneth I. Shine is president of the Institute of Medicine.

The **National Research Council** was organized by the National Academy of Sciences in 1916 to associate the broad community of science and technology with the Academy's purposes of furthering knowledge and advising the federal government. Functioning in accordance with general policies determined by the Academy, the Council has become the principal operating agency of both the National Academy of Sciences and the National Academy of Engineering in providing services to the government, the public, and the scientific and engineering communities. The Council is administered jointly by both Academies and the Institute of Medicine. Dr. Bruce M. Alberts and Dr. William A. Wulf are chairman and vice chairman, respectively, of the National Research Council.

COMMITTEE ON POPULATION

JANE MENKEN *(Chair)*, Institute of Behavioral Sciences, University of Colorado, Boulder
CAROLINE H. BLEDSOE,* Department of Anthropology, Northwestern University
JOHN BONGAARTS, The Population Council, New York
ELLEN BRENNAN-GALVIN, Population Division, United Nations, New York
JOHN N. HOBCRAFT, Population Investigation Committee, London School of Economics
F. THOMAS JUSTER, Institute for Social Research, University of Michigan, Ann Arbor
CHARLES B. KEELY, Department of Demography, Georgetown University
DAVID I. KERTZER, Department of Anthropology, Brown University
DAVID A. LAM, Population Studies Center, University of Michigan, Ann Arbor
LINDA G. MARTIN,* The Population Council, New York
MARK R. MONTGOMERY,* The Population Council, New York, and Department of Economics, State University of New York, Stony Brook
W. HENRY MOSLEY, Department of Population and Family Health Sciences, Johns Hopkins University
ALBERTO PALLONI, Center for Demography and Ecology, University of Wisconsin, Madison
JAMES P. SMITH, RAND, Santa Monica, California
BETH J. SOLDO,* Population Studies Center, University of Pennsylvania
JAMES W. VAUPEL, Max Planck Institute for Demographic Research, Rostok, Germany
KENNETH W. WACHTER, Department of Demography, University of California, Berkeley
LINDA J. WAITE, Population Research Center, University of Chicago

BARNEY COHEN, *Director*
KEVIN KINSELLA, *Study Director*
BRIAN TOBACHNICK, *Project Administrative Coordinator*

---

*Through October 1999.

CONTRIBUTORS

JEFFREY R. BOTKIN, University of Utah
KAARE CHRISTENSEN, University of Southern Denmark
EILEEN M. CRIMMINS, University of Southern California
SHARON J. DURFY, University of Washington
DOUGLAS EWBANK, University of Pennsylvania
CALEB E. FINCH, University of Southern California
JEFFREY B. HALTER, University of Michigan
QUBAI HU, University of Washington
GEORGE M. MARTIN, University of Washington
GERALD E. McCLEARN, Pennsylvania State University
RICHARD A. MILLER, University of Michigan
DAVID B. REUBEN, University of California, Los Angeles
TERESA SEEMAN, University of California, Los Angeles
JAMES W. VAUPEL, Max Planck Institute for Demographic Research,
    Rostock, Germany
GEORGE P. VOGLER, Pennsylvania State University
KENNETH W. WACHTER, University of California, Berkeley
ROBERT B. WALLACE, University of Iowa
MAXINE WEINSTEIN, Georgetown University
ROBERT J. WILLIS, University of Michigan

Preface

In 1997 the Committee on Population published *Between Zeus and the Salmon: The Biodemography of Longevity*, a volume that drew on various disciplinary perspectives to take stock of what demography and biology could tell us about the trajectory of human longevity. One prescient chapter, written by Robert Wallace, noted the need to explore the potential usefulness of collecting biological (and especially genetic) data in the context of large, population-based surveys.

As the 1990s drew to a close, it became increasingly clear that advances in biodemography require a greater ability to analyze the interactions of genes, the environment, and behaviors, which in turn require linked data on all three domains. Recent technical developments in the collection and analysis of biological data have made it much more feasible to collect such information in nonclinical settings. Given the financial considerations created by researchers' appetites for ever more complex data, and the finite amount of public money that will ever be devoted to data collection, there is mounting pressure for multipurpose household surveys to collect biological data along with the more familiar interviewer-respondent question-and-answer type of information.

Many surveys to date have collected some biological and/or clinical data. Before the pressure to collect biological data in social surveys becomes broad-based and overwhelming, those who fund, design, and analyze survey data need to think through the rationale and potential consequences. Thus it was that the National Institute on Aging (NIA), which funds many of the cutting-edge social science surveys in the United

States, asked The National Academies to organize a series of planning meetings, culminating in a workshop on "Collecting Biological Indicators and Genetic Information in Household Surveys," held in Washington, D.C., in February 2000.

Committee on Population workshops are designed to be stimulating fora for researchers and policy makers from a wide range of disciplines. This meeting brought together demographers, economists, epidemiologists, ethicists, molecular biologists, physiologists, geneticists, pathologists, and sociologists, in addition to representatives of numerous government agencies. The workshop and this resultant volume sought to address a range of questions. What can social science, and demography in particular, reasonably expect to learn from biological information? Which genetic, pedigree, historical, and environmental data ought to be collected in order to be most useful to a wide range of scientists? Are there likely to be unintended side effects of amassing biological data (for example, what will attempts to collect bioindicators do to survey response rates, or to the quality of self-reported data)? How might ethical duties to research subjects change with the collection of bioindicators? How will confidentiality issues be handled? The methodological challenges for marrying large population surveys to genetic hypotheses are complex and not easily solved, in part because extant surveys have been structured and funded to address a set of important nongenetic scientific questions.

This report summarizes the workshop presentations. The chapters were enriched by the free-flowing workshop discussion that helped to sharpen key concerns and expand the breadth of several papers. A special note of thanks in this regard goes to Raynard Kington, director of the National Health and Nutrition Examination Survey, who shared his knowledge of and visions for future survey research. The chapters were then peer reviewed, and we owe a debt of gratitude to the many individuals who generously gave of their time to review and further strengthen the contents of this volume. For their insightful and constructive remarks, we would like to thank George Annas, Lisa Berkman, Ties Boerma, Charles Boult, Joy Boyer, Wylie Burke, James Carey, James Curtsinger, Ronald Freedman, Leonid Gavrilov, Noreen Goldman, Evan Hadley, Jennifer Harris, Richard Havlik, Wendy Mack, Scott Pletcher, Karen Swallen, Marc Tatar, Elizabeth Thomson, Martin Vaessen, and several anonymous reviewers.

Our greatest debt is to Caleb Finch and James Vaupel, who not only cochaired the workshop and edited the volume, but also were instrumental in developing the workshop framework, identifying a stellar cadre of authors and reviewers, and guiding authors in their revisions. We also would particularly like to thank Richard Suzman of the NIA who, as the prime motivator of this endeavor, shared his expertise and consistently challenged all involved to expand the boundaries of inquiry. The committee is grateful to a number of colleagues who worked with the cochairs and me on a steering committee to develop this project. These include demographers Douglas Ewbank, Beth Soldo, and Kenneth Wachter; three members of the National Research Council's Committee on National Statistics, William Kalsbeek, Thomas Louis, and Edward Perrin; and two members of The National Academies Board on Biology, Robert Sokal and Raymond White. Benjamin Wilfond of the National Human Genome Research Institute was especially helpful in providing initial guidance and information regarding ethical and legal issues that would need to be addressed.

Thanks are also due to staff and associates of the National Research Council. Brian Tobachnick coordinated the logistical and travel arrangements for the workshop and assisted with myriad aspects of manuscript preparation. Randi M. Blank edited the volume and made suggestions for the glossary. Christine McShane guided the manuscript through the publication process. Sally Stanfield and the Audubon team at the National Academy Press handled the technical preparation of the report. Kevin Kinsella directed the study and coordinated the review process. Development and execution of this project occurred under the general guidance of the committee's director, Barney Cohen.

Jane Menken
Chair, Committee on Population

Contents

xi

Cells and Surveys

1

Collecting Biological Indicators in Household Surveys

Caleb E. Finch and James W. Vaupel

In 1996, the Committee on Population of the National Research Council sponsored a novel workshop on the biodemography of aging, which resulted in the volume *Between Zeus and the Salmon: The Biodemography of Longevity* (National Research Council, 1997). The workshop and its report, which considered the continuing increases in human life span in a broad biological context, launched a new phase in studies of human aging at the population level. To no one's surprise, a mere four years later, we still lack basic understanding of why human life expectancies continue to increase at roughly similar rates around the world, despite huge differences in the patterns of disease and lifestyle.

The present volume, and its antecedent workshop in February 2000, was organized to pursue certain questions raised by *Zeus and the Salmon*. In particular we wanted to examine the issues and prospects for collecting biological data from individuals in household surveys. This volume, with its rich collection of essays, is a guide or a handbook to many emerging and portentous questions. The basic question remains open: Should large population-based household surveys consider instituting the collection of biological material (e.g., blood or urine), physiological measurements (e.g., blood pressure or handgrip strength), and environmental measurements (e.g., cadmium exposure or radon levels) in addition to the usual demographic, socioeconomic, and/or health data? This information would soon be integrated with the huge database from household surveys that describes many social, economic, educational, and even behavioral data on millions of individuals in the United States.

In the ensemble, the essays cover the questions of what, why, whether, who, and how. What kinds of biological materials, physiological measurements, and environmental measurements could and should be included in household surveys? Which researchers would be interested in this kind of information? Why should we or shouldn't we collect these data—what are the costs and disadvantages? What kind of personnel is needed for these new goals, with what kind of background and training? It is far from clear how to successfully include biological specimens and physiological and environmental measurements in household surveys. Collecting this information poses ethical concerns about privacy, confidentiality, and potential consequences for individuals and social groups.

The chapters are written by researchers and scholars with very differing perspectives. The topics addressed are diverse, as are the styles and structures of the essays. In exploring these new themes, each essay tackles multiple topics and sheds light on myriad questions. Several key issues are addressed in more than one essay, offering insights from different vantage points. The topics addressed in this volume are so new, and knowledge is evolving so rapidly, that it would be neither possible nor appropriate to expect the workshop to have produced a well-ordered set of concrete directions. Instead, readers will find much resonance across the diverse experience, values, and projections of the authors.

Household surveys have become a major research industry for demographers, economists, and other social and behavioral scientists. A prime example is the Health and Retirement Study (HRS), which is described and discussed in the chapter by Weinstein and Willis (see also Burkhauser and Gertler, 1995). This longitudinal study began in 1992 with a survey of 12,600 persons aged 51 to 61. In 1998 more than 22,000 persons were interviewed. Three further waves of the HRS are planned for 2000, 2002, and 2004. Besides this large, important study are scores of other studies of considerable size and significance. In the United States alone, there are at least ten other major population-based surveys with a focus on aging funded in full or in part by a single agency, the Behavioral and Social Science program of the National Institute on Aging (Wallace, 1997). Among other major surveys with an emphasis on specific age groups or the entire age range are the U.S. Panel Study of Income Dynamics and the German Socio-Economic Panel.

WHICH INDICATORS?

What kind of bioindicators can be gathered in household surveys? The chapter by Wallace is valuable in providing experienced, judicious guidance about practical issues. Weinstein and Willis, Christensen, and Crimmins and Seeman give helpful practical information in particular contexts for incorporating bioindicators into surveys. The chapters by Christensen and Ewbank focus on DNA, which can be sampled in many ways, including from blood samples, blood dry spots obtained by the prick of a finger, cheek swabs, hair follicles, and urine. It is portentous that usable amounts of DNA might be gathered from the minute numbers of cells left unwittingly when a stamp is licked, or even when an envelope is handled during its return to an agency. Even if DNA is not available, studies of twins, siblings, and other relatives and studies of adopted children can be used to shed some light on genetic factors and their interaction with specific environmental factors. Several chapters, especially the one by Vogler, consider gene-environment issues.

Other authors focus on various physiological measurements. Wachter considers the evocative example of height as a very simple physiological measure. Halter and Reuben survey a wide range of function indicators. Indeed, they consider measures of functioning from the levels of molecules, cells, and organs up to the level of the whole organism. Crimmins and Seeman also consider an array of measurements about function, with emphasis on measures that capture aspects of the cumulative stress—the allostatic load—an organism has suffered. Several chapters mention performance tests. Lung capacity, for instance, can be simply measured by asking respondents to blow into a spirometer. Handgrip strength can be measured. Respondents can be asked to get up from a chair without using their arms. Performance testing is common in household surveys when information is needed on cognitive functioning: respondents are quizzed and their mental status assessed on the basis of how well they can remember and respond.

In some household surveys, administrative data from official records can be linked to respondents. The Health and Retirement Study obtains Social Security earnings and benefit histories from the Social Security Administration. Medical costs and diagnoses are obtained from Medicare records. In Denmark, a broad array of information can be garnered from administrative records. This means that considerable vital and personal information is on reserve for 100 percent of the population surveyed, even those who refuse to be interviewed.

Environmental measures that might be obtained in household surveys are considered by Wallace in his thought-provoking discussion. Here we briefly note some remarkable technical developments in miniaturized sensors that will soon enable characterization of local environments in unprecedented detail. In general, these devices are referred to as microelectromechanical systems, or MEMS. Miniaturized sensors on the scale of microns or even less (nanoscale) that can reside unobtrusively in a household are being developed for specific environmental parameters. Arrays of sensors ("electronic noses"), for example, can sample the local atmosphere continuously for trace metals or specific organic toxins (Kovacs, 1998; Gardner and Bartlett, 1999). Even airborne microorganisms can be sampled and their DNA characterized through enzymatic amplification of DNA by polymerase chain reactions. Forthcoming generations of gene machines will be miniaturized, with mixing chambers, valves, and pumps as small as several microns. Nanoscale MEMS could be implanted in human volunteers, giving real-time correlations between environmental factors and their long-term health effects. Wireless technology will soon allow the possibility of collecting the most intimate information on body functions and activities, transmitted from within each household-based MEMS on a community basis. This technology could reveal the widely sought basis for the wide local variations in the incidence of cancers and vascular disease.

WHAT BENEFITS?

Genes, siblings, height, handgrip, air pollution, autopsies: this summary list conveys the broad range of bioindicators that can be added to household surveys. But why would a researcher want this kind of information? The chapters that describe the information that can be gathered also consider the reasons for gathering this information. For instance, Ewbank gives a penetrating discussion of the kind of genetic information that might be of use to a demographer. Vogler explains why data on siblings can shed valuable light on both genetic and environmental factors that determine health and behavior. Chapters by Christensen, Crimmins and Seeman, and Weinstein and Willis illustrate what can be learned from surveys that include genetic, physiological, and environmental information. In particular, Weinstein and Willis differentiate several themes: (1) obtaining population-representative data from nonclinical samples; (2) calibrating self-reports with other measures of health and disease; (3) explicating pathways and elaborating causal linkages between social environment and health; and (4) linking genetic markers with survey materials. The three chapters by Martin and Hu, McClearn, and Miller provide an accessible introduction to the needed conceptual framework. Wachter argues persuasively that social scientists should more actively consider bioindicators in tempering overly enthusiastic interpretations of genetic information that sometimes lead to crude biological determinism.

Autopsies are increasingly rare, and Martin and Hu make a cogent plea for their great value. An important precedent is the Nun Study, directed by David Snowdon at the University of Kentucky, which is yielding major insights into early indicators of Alzheimer disease (see, for example, Riley et al., 2000). Most of the Catholic sisters in this study have agreed to allow their brains to be autopsied. In general, funds for postmortem studies are difficult to obtain through the peer review process. It might be possible to ask survey respondents to allow autopsies at their demise as well as preservation of certain organs.

As the genome juggernaut grinds on, data sets with information on both an individual's genes and his or her physiology and environment will become more and more valuable. Soon we will know the location of all the human genes, which may tally 100,000, from which are transcribed even more types of messenger RNA. Rapidly advancing technology will then allow comprehensive analysis of genetic variations. We expect a huge number of individual gene differences, because each person's DNA code differs at intervals of about 100 to 1000 bases.

But getting to know the DNA variations, gene by gene, in different human populations will confront us with the next huge step in human genetics: the need to identify the *functional* significance of gene variations to the individual gene carrier. It is likely that most gene differences are neutral, with little-to-no tangible impact during development or aging. However, as we understand more about gene architecture, certain DNA variations may be predicted to be sensitive to the external environment. Present discussions of gene-environment interactions that alter aging are fundamental to the central problem in human biology during the 21st century: *to identify environmental factors that evoke harmful traits from particular sets of genes.*

We anticipate that ascertaining the adverse gene-environment interactions during development may be much easier than determining which have adverse impacts on health at later ages. Progress in these hugely complex problems of gene-environment interactions will synergize with the new field of functional genomics, which is addressing the functions of the huge number of new genes being discovered. With the fully detailed human gene map soon to be at hand, we may now consider the far more complex problem of *environmental maps* that will be needed to optimize individual health throughout the life course.

In the most general terms, three types of environmental factors can influence human health during aging: physical, chemical, and biological. Physical factors include temperature and solar radiation. Chemical factors from natural and biological sources include trace toxins (asbestos, lead, tobacco smoke), but also trace morphogens that can cause subtle abnormalities in development. Biological factors include diet and infectious organisms, but also stress from social interactions. We know little about the concentrations of a vast number of bioactive substances that may be present sporadically in the environment. It seems fair to say that our concept of the environment will evolve rapidly with new technical developments and may come to include multigenerational effects. For example, in the case of diabetes, the maternal physiological state existing before pregnancy can influence fetal growth. Moreover, the ovary acquires its full stock of eggs in the fetus: thus, the egg cell from which all of our cells stem was exposed to the environment of our maternal grandmother (Finch and Loehlin, 1998). The depth of the transgenerational environment is a completely obscure aspect of human experience.

The huge number of variables being considered in this discussion calls for new statistical approaches to integrate all of these different kinds of parameters. Wachter discusses strategies of dimensionality reduction and new statistical models that consider whole sequences of life-course events or experiences as predictor variables, in place of the one-by-one predictor variables familiar in linear regression.

WHAT COSTS?

Given all the cogent reasons to add bioindicators to household surveys, what are the counter-arguments, what are the costs, the drawbacks, the disadvantages? In their insightful discussion, Weinstein and Willis consider three major categories of cost: (1) respondent burden, (2) financial and logistic constraints, and (3) the potential to compromise research objectives. The burden on respondents can be heavy, involving many hours of physical testing or uncomfortable invasions such as those required to draw blood. As a result, some people may refuse to participate in part or all of a survey. Additionally, some respondents who endured one survey round may decide not to participate in the next, which can be very disruptive to longitudinal analysis. Surveys in Denmark and in Taiwan suggest that respondent dropout may be modest. This concern, however, is so large that survey researchers may be wise to pilot test the collection of bioindicators on a subset of subjects before they risk challenging their entire population with the procedures. Moreover, bioindicator sampling can be expensive and logistically difficult, as conveyed by Wallace. Finally, research objectives may be compromised by some kinds of bioindicators if, as Weinstein and Willis put it, "the research process itself affects behaviors that we wish to study." In particular, providing respondents with information about their health and about their genetic risks may cause them to alter their behavior.

Throughout this volume lurk a number of ominous questions regarding ethical and legal issues that confront biological data collection, and data collection and use more generally. As one obvious example, the outfitting of households or people with arrays of wireless sensors raises enormous concerns about loss of privacy and the dissemination of lifestyle information. In addition to understanding how conceptually to add bioindicators to household surveys, researchers need to understand how ethically to do so.

Theoretical and practical questions about the ethics of biodemography and genetic research are changing as rapidly as the research methodologies themselves, if not more so. Seminars, workshops, and entire conferences are devoted to discussions of these multifaceted concerns, and the latter could easily constitute the focus of an entire volume. The chapters by Botkin and by Durfy provide practical, judicious guidance to the complicated ethical issues that face survey researchers who attempt to incorporate bioindicators. Botkin focuses on key factors in the area of informed consent. Durfy probes issues associated with the nature of, access to, and ownership of genetic information, and considers potential psychological and group-harm risks that may accrue to participation in research studies.

There are deep connections between demography as a discipline and both the broader social sciences and the biological sciences. The branch of demography known as biodemography continues to grow rapidly. Demographers are involved in many of the major household surveys, in part because of their training in statistics and their knowledge of concepts useful in studying large populations. It seems natural that demographers will be among the first who are able to design, run, and analyze surveys with bioindicators. Many other fields are likely to join these efforts. Although not strongly represented here, economists have begun to show an interest in biology and may be receptive to broadening their knowledge in ways that would help incorporate bioindicators into household surveys. Economists assume that people make decisions based on their preferences. Economists are now giving some thought to where preferences come from, including the childhood environment.

Lastly, we point out the need to consider training. If bioindicators are to be included in household surveys, then new kinds of personnel will be needed to conduct such surveys and to analyze the data collected. Training of field workers will be important in the success of adding bioindicators to field studies. Special skills are needed to explain the significance of complex tests for environmental factors or for particular gene variations. The shortage of a new generation of well-trained autopsy pathologists is also of great concern. Detailed postmortem histopathology is needed to adequately characterize morbid conditions, which are *always at some level the outcome of gene-environment interactions*. An expanded mindset, a broader vision, and enhanced biological thinking are needed for successful incorporation of bioindicators into household surveys. On a larger front, we state the obvious: A new approach to transdisiplinary training programs is needed to prepare future generations of scientists for charting the human life course on the emerging gene-environment maps.

REFERENCES

Burkhauser, R.V., and P.J. Gertler
   1995   The health and retirement study. Data quality and early results. *The Journal of Human Resources*. 30, Supplement 1995.
Finch, C.E., and J. Loehlin
   1998   Environmental influences that may precede fertilization: A first examination of the prezygotic hypothesis from maternal age influences on twins. *Behavior Genetics* 28:101-106.
Gardner, J.W., and P.N. Bartlett
   1999   *Electronic Noses*. New York: Oxford University Press.
Kovacs, G.T.A.
   1998   *Micromachined Transducers Sourcebook*. Boston: McGraw-Hill.
National Research Council
   1997   *Between Zeus and the Salmon: The Biodemography of Longevity*. Committee on Population. K.W. Wachter and C.E. Finch, eds. Commission on Behavioral and Social Sciences and Education. Washington, DC: National Academy Press.
Riley, K.P., D.A. Snowdon, A.M. Saunders, A.D. Roses, J.A. Mortimer, and N. Nanayakkara
   2000   Cognitive function and Apolipoprotein-E in the very old: Findings from the Nun Study. *Journal of Gerontology: Social Sciences* 55B(2):S69-S75.
Wallace, R.B.
   1997   The potential of population surveys for genetic studies. Pp. 234-244 in *Between Zeus and the Salmon: The Biodemography of Longevity*. Committee on Population. K.W. Wachter and C.E. Finch, eds. Commission on Behavioral and Social Sciences and Education. Washington, DC: National Academy Press.

2

Integrating Biology into Demographic Research on Health and Aging (With a Focus on the MacArthur Study of Successful Aging)

Eileen M. Crimmins and Teresa Seeman

Information on bioindicators can lead to a better understanding and clearer implications of the well-established relationships of demographic factors to health-related outcomes. The history of demographic analysis of health has been one of refining and widening the outcomes examined and clarifying the mechanisms through which demographic factors operate to affect health. Mechanisms now common in demographic analyses include social, economic, psychological, behavioral, and biological factors. The unique approach of demographic analysis is the use of large, representative samples of the population in order to understand and project trends and differences in health outcomes. Models of health outcomes currently used by demographers build heavily on a variety of interdisciplinary approaches. Recent epidemiological results indicate a clear role for the inclusion of additional bioindicators in demographic models of health outcomes at older ages. Such development would both specify the way that traditional demographic factors operate and point to places for intervention. Inclusion of the collection of biological data in representative surveys will be required to link population health outcomes to individual social, economic, and psychological characteristics and better understand and address the policy issues linked to questions about trends and differentials in population health.

This chapter outlines the current demographic approach to the study of health outcomes among older populations and concludes by arguing that the inclusion of bioindicators as proximate determinants of health outcomes is now appropriate. The second section of the chapter clarifies the potential of specific bioindicators in answering demographic questions about health outcomes. Building on results from a number of epidemiological studies, but emphasizing results from the MacArthur Study of Successful Aging, we emphasize the links between major demographic variables of interest such as socioeconomic status and race, a set of bioindicators indicating physiological status, and important health outcomes in aging populations. The third section of the chapter introduces the details of biological data collection for the MacArthur Study. This study is an example of a completed, multiple-community study in the United States with extensive biological information of the type which can be useful in augmenting current demographic approaches toward health in aging populations. Details on the methods of data collection, sources of biological information, and use of this information from the MacArthur study, which are relevant to the collection of bioindicators in household surveys, are provided.

BACKGROUND

Incorporation of additional information on bioindicators will represent a continuation of a long-term trend toward widening the scope of outcomes and explanatory variables in demographic research on health outcomes. In the last three decades the scope of analysis has consistently been expanded because of theoretical, analytical, and data developments in demography and related fields (Crimmins 1993; Hummer, 1996; Mosley and Chen, 1984; Preston and Taubman, 1994; Rogers et al., 2000). The expansion of the scope of survey-based demographic analysis in the health area has occurred both in the outcomes examined and in the complexity and type of independent variables included in explanatory models. This proliferation of outcomes is related to improved understanding of the multidimensional aspects of health outcomes and of mechanisms through which health is affected (Verbrugge and Jette, 1994). This increased complexity of the conceptual model employed in demographic approaches to health has built on theoretical developments and empirical research in demography and related fields. For instance, the economic model of health has emphasized the role of economic pathways as well as the development of formal models (Grossman, 1972; Preston and Taubman, 1994). Epidemiological models have incorporated more emphasis on biological as well as social pathways (Howe, 1998; Mosley and Chen, 1984). Empirical results linking a large number of independent variables to health outcomes from targeted epidemiological studies such as the Framingham Heart Study (Kannel et al., 1987) or from nationally representative samples such as the National Health and Examination Survey (NHANES) have provided a solid epidemiological basis for further model development.

As epidemiological knowledge has increased, the possibilities of clarifying the mechanisms through which traditional demographic differences in health outcomes arise and the interventions one might use to influence population health have also grown. The inclusion of bioindicators in demographic models of health outcomes adds an additional level of mechanisms through which traditional socio-demographic variables affect health outcomes. Inclusion of a set of biological proximate determinants in models of health outcomes among the older population represents a model expansion similar to that occurring over the last two decades in demographic models of fertility or of child health (Bongaarts, 1978; Mosley and Chen, 1984). Demographic analyses in these fields have moved toward specifying the biological mechanisms through which final outcomes are determined.

Health Outcomes

While demographic research once concentrated on mortality, as noted above, many additional indicators of health status are now included in demographic analyses. Clarification of the dimensions of health and their potential relationships to causal factors has been important in expanding demographic research to nonmortal outcomes (Verbrugge and Jette, 1994). Health outcomes now regularly investigated in population studies include disability, physical functioning loss, and the presence of specific diseases and conditions (Smith and Kington, 1997a, 1997b). The newest generation of national surveys has also included mental health and cognitive functioning among the domains investigated (Colsher and Wallace, 1991; Herzog and Wallace, 1997). These dimensions of health and examples of specific health outcomes investigated are shown in Figure 2-1.

The number of analytical health outcomes has grown with the recognition that population health disparities at any point in time can vary across dimensions of health, and can change over time as well (Crimmins, 1996; Verbrugge and Jette, 1994). We have also clarified that trends in mortality and other health outcomes are not necessarily closely related in populations where death is dominated by chronic conditions (Crimmins et al., 1994). One reason for this is that among older populations nonfatal health outcomes like arthritis and cognitive loss are major causes of functioning loss and disability yet they are not important causes of mortality. Another reason is that mortality decline may occur because people with diseases and disabilities survive longer than in the past, resulting in an increase in people with disease and disability.

Specification of health outcomes has been important in joining demographic research models to results derived from medicine and epidemiology. It has made clear the need to develop explanatory models tailored to

A. Dimensions of Health

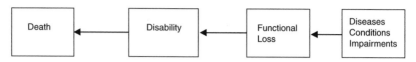

B. Specific Examples of Dimensions

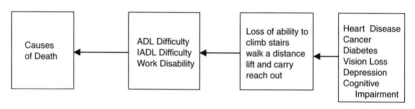

FIGURE 2-1 Health outcomes included in contemporary demographic surveys.

the health outcomes investigated. Some health outcomes are affected only by what happens "within the skin" of individuals; others are affected by the environment outside the skin as well as within the skin. For instance, the onset of heart disease may be affected primarily by an individual's characteristics and behaviors. On the other hand, disability due to heart disease may be affected by the environment in which a person functions, i.e., the presence of steps, the characteristics of transportation, or the characteristics of the workplace may influence whether a person with heart disease can live alone or work. Other outcomes such as how long a person survives after a heart attack may be partially explained by the use and availability of medical care.

A hallmark of the current demographic approach is the use of longitudinal data to investigate change in health status or onset of health problems rather than static health state. This approach is necessary for assessing the effect of causal mechanisms from an earlier point in time on subsequent health outcomes (Rogers et al., 2000). In an older population where health status has been achieved over a life span, the study of health change is particularly important in identifying current health processes and the relationship of independent variables to outcomes.

Information on most of the health outcomes identified in Figure 2-1, other than mortality, is usually collected in population surveys through self or proxy report; however, performance testing of mental functioning has been incorporated in recent national surveys (Herzog and Wallace, 1997), and a number of more localized epidemiological studies have also incorporated performance measures for physical functioning (Berkman et al., 1993; Seeman et al., 1994b). In addition to self-reports, links to administrative data such as Medicare files can provide more detailed information on inpatient and outpatient medical diagnoses and treatments. Information on causes of death from the National Death Index can also be used to supplement knowledge of health experiences reported in surveys.

Models of Health Outcomes

It is not only the health outcomes or dependent variables that have expanded in demographic approaches to health in recent years. While the demographic approach to health outcomes for most of the last century has continued to emphasize differences by age, sex, race/ethnicity, and socioeconomic status (SES) (Figure 2-2), in recent years demographers have increasingly employed a more model-based approach to explain health outcomes, with greater emphasis on developing fully specified models of health outcomes. This approach has led to incorporating addi-

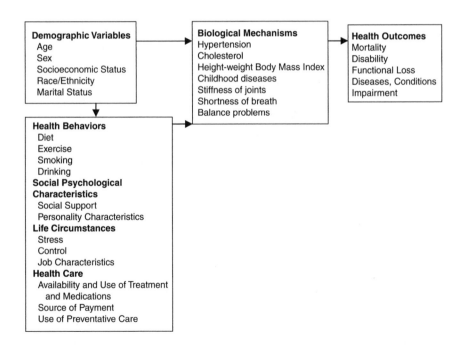

FIGURE 2-2 Model of health outcomes employed with contemporary demographic surveys.

tional independent influences as well as a clarification of the mechanisms through which demographic variables work. Following developments in other demographic areas of research, there is increasing interest in understanding the social, economic, psychological, and behavioral mechanisms causing health change and health differences.

Developments in the field of economics have emphasized the role of individual choice in determining health outcomes (Preston and Taubman, 1994). Social psychological approaches have emphasized the role of social networks and personality characteristics in determining health outcomes (Taylor et al., 1997). Epidemiological research has emphasized the role of personal health practices, while medical research has focused on the role of differential care. These developments have led to the incorporation in demographic models of indicators of health behaviors (e.g., diet, weight, drinking, smoking, exercise), social-psychological characteristics (e.g., social support and demands, personality characteristics), life circumstances (e.g., stress, control, and job characteristics), and health care usage and availability (e.g., source of payment, use of preventive care, use of prescription and nonprescription drugs) (Figure 2-2).

In addition to including a wider range of psychosocial and behavioral factors as explanatory factors of health outcomes, current research has incorporated a lifecycle approach and recognized the value of including circumstances surrounding birth and childhood as well as a time component to later lifecycle influences (Barker, 1998). Childhood and early life exposure to infectious disease or toxic substances has also been related to health outcomes in old age (Blackwell et al., in press; Kuh and Ben-Shlomo, 1997).

Finally, the bidirectionality of many relationships in Figure 2-2 has been recognized (Ettner, 1996). Particularly with regard to the role of SES, the potential for reverse causation has been investigated. It is also possible that psychological states can be affected by health outcomes, or that functional loss could affect social support, or that even marital status could be linked to health status. The potential for reverse causation is another reason for the emphasis on longitudinal study, which allows the timing of health events and changes in independent variables to be noted.

Bioindicators in the Demographic Approach

The demographic approach to health analysis currently includes some indicators of "biology" which can be thought of as either biological risk factors for the onset of disease, precursors of disease outcomes, or additional biological outcomes. The development of models clearly specifying the role of biological factors in determining health outcomes in old age has been less formal than in other areas of demographic research. In the areas of fertility (Bongaarts, 1978) and child health (Mosley and Chen, 1984), the role of biological indicators as proximate determinants of fertility and child health have been well integrated both theoretically and empirically. In both of these areas, biological factors have been introduced into models to clarify the mechanisms through which differentials and trends arise and the paths through which other variables work. Better specification of the biological paths relevant to health outcomes in older age will be an important addition to future demographic work.

Currently employed biological indicators have usually been indicators of increased risk for poor health outcomes. For instance, the presence of high cholesterol and hypertension are generally asked in current surveys, reflecting the increase in both professional and informant knowledge of these health indicators as risk factors for poor health outcomes. Height and weight combined into a body mass index is often included as an additional risk factor. Information on symptoms and precursors to disease is sometimes collected through questions on symptoms such as stiffness in joints, balance problems, and pain. Information is also solicited on childhood diseases and occupational exposure to toxic substances.

It is important to realize that some traditional demographic variables are often interpreted as representing a mixture of biology and other influences. For instance, age often has been seen as having largely biological effects. The demographic emphasis on the similarity of age curves of mortality across societies and across species relates to the underlying biological mechanisms of aging (Ricklefs and Finch, 1995). While chronological age may be related to the biological "aging" of an organism, social and other lifestyle factors are known to influence the age at which health outcomes occur. With social and behavioral factors controlled, however, age is often assumed to represent a biological effect.

Sex or gender also combines both biology and other influences. Over the life cycle, sex differences in life expectancy are thought to be approximately evenly divided between behavior and biology (Verbrugge, 1983; Waldron, 1986). The biological basis of sex differences in population-based studies has generally not been directly measured; rather, it has been assumed to be indicated by residual effects after gender, behavioral differences, and other lifestyle factors are controlled.

Observed differences in health by SES are generally assumed to have little to do with innate biological differences, instead being due to a difference in resources, knowledge, and opportunity resulting in differences in behavior and life situations (Adler et al., 1993, 1994; Kaplan and Keil, 1993; Link and Phelan, 1995; Marmot et al., 1997). Race and ethnic differences are also regarded as arising from a combination of SES differences and behavioral differences, which are, in turn, socioeconomically determined. Some biological differences between racial groups are acknowledged, however, especially with regard to specific health outcomes like stroke or diabetes. The emphasis of much demographic research has been an attempt to eliminate effects of race and SES through the statistical control of behavioral and social variables; evidence to date, however, suggests that these factors do not wholly account for race or SES differences in health. Recent analyses have indicated that the inclusion of biological variables is an important addition in explaining health outcomes in these models (Luoto et al., 1994).

We argue that more insight could be gathered into the paths by which demographic, social, economic, psychological, and behavioral variables affect health outcomes by clarifying the biological pathways through which variables of interest produce varying health outcomes. A better understanding of biological pathways will allow us to develop effective policies and interventions to improve health outcomes and reduce health inequalities within populations. Ultimately, social, psychological, and behavioral factors must work through biological mechanisms; that is, they must get "under the skin" in order to affect health outcomes. We need to clarify how this occurs. There is a significant body of research linking demographic variables to biological indicators and bioindicators to health outcomes important in aging populations that will allow the development of a set of biological proximate determinants of health outcomes relevant to older populations. Of course, while all health outcomes have biological components, development of models relevant to specified health outcomes is appropriate. For instance, models specific to physical functioning, mental functioning, and mortality from specified causes may differ in the biological components emphasized.

Collection of Data in Household Surveys

Our aim in this chapter is to clarify the potential for developing demographic approaches incorporating bioindicators that can be collected from large nationally representative samples of the population. The content of these surveys has grown in recent years in conjunction with the developments described above. Before proceeding to discuss specific biological indicators that would require the collection of biological materials in addition to questionnaire responses, we briefly discuss data quality relevant to health measurement using survey-based responses. Most surveys have relied heavily on the ability of people to accurately self-report information to an interviewer in a limited amount of time. This has contributed to the nature of biologically relevant measures included and excluded from population surveys.

Demographic surveys have generally used self-reports of disease presence, functioning, and disability as analytic outcomes. Some information has been shown to be relatively reliably reported among older persons, although certainly other sources of information would result in different assessments of health status for some individuals. For instance, self-reports of having had a heart attack have 75 percent agreement with medical records (Bush et al., 1989), and the sensitivity of self-reports of hypertension has been shown to be about 80 percent reliable (Brownson et al., 1994; Giles et al., 1995). Self-reports of diabetes also appear to be highly reliable while those of arthritis are somewhat less so (Kehoe et al., 1994), and the reliability of cancer reporting varies by site (Schrijvers et al., 1994). Health behaviors and health care usage have also been shown to be relatively reliably reported (Brownson et al., 1994).

Demographic researchers must realize that even with accurate reporting to questions on the part of respondents, it can be difficult to use survey responses to set up groups with similar biological profiles. For instance, while respondents are able to self-report whether they have ever been told that they have hypertension by a medical professional, this information often groups people who are currently very heterogeneous with respect to health risks. Comparing self-reports and measured blood pressure and having knowledge of medication usage in the MacArthur sample indicates that among those who report they are not hypertensive, only approximately half are truly nonhypertensive. The other half includes people who do not know they have measured high blood pressure as well as people who are taking medication that lowers blood pressure, even though they report they were never told that they were hypertensive (Lu et al., 1998). There is also variability in measured blood pressure and current drug usage among those who have been told they are hypertensive. For instance, many persons who are currently using medication still have elevated measured blood pressure, while some who have been hypertensive in the past measure as normotensive even though they are not under treatment.

THE INCORPORATION OF ADDITIONAL BIOLOGICAL INDICATORS

Biological indicators can appropriately be included in demographic analysis if they represent biological states that are reasonably prevalent in the general population and states that have been linked both to major population health outcomes and to demographic, social, or psychological mechanisms affecting health outcomes. Biomarkers have been increasingly introduced into epidemiologic studies (Howe, 1998), and there has been a long history of the study of biomarkers of aging (Sprott, 1999). Both of these areas provide a foundation on which to further develop demographic approaches.

Development of specific models including biological indicators as proximate determinants of health outcomes needs to be tailored to the outcomes studied. As an example, some biological indicators known as Syndrome X are relevant for cardiovascular conditions. Other indicators like balance and strength may be more important factors in determining functioning ability. Some biological measures indicate initial biological capacity, resiliency, or resistance of an organism, while others indicate later physiological status resulting from an organism's initial capacity and consequent lifecycle influences. In epidemiological terms, biomarkers represent susceptibility to health outcomes, exposure to health-affecting events, or the presence of adverse health outcomes (Schulte and Rothman, 1998).

Biological characteristics indicating initial resiliency or susceptibility of an organism include genetic profiles. As noted above, genetic markers need to have a high prevalence in the population and have a reasonably strong effect on common population health outcomes, or have an inter-action effect with other health-affecting mechanisms, to be candidates for inclusion in population studies. At the moment, the only known genetic marker of clear value in a population survey is the apolipoprotein E gene (APOE), although this is likely to change in the very near future. APOE allele status is clearly related to a number of major health outcomes in older populations which are reasonably well measured in population surveys: mortality, heart disease, and cognitive functioning (Albert et al., 1995b; Corder et al., 1993; Evans et al., 1997; Ewbank, 1997; Hofman et al., 1997; Hyman et al., 1996; Luc et al., 1994; Saunders et al., 1993). Both the prevalence of alleles indicating higher risk and the size of the effect are large enough to be of importance in explaining variability in currently studied health outcomes. APOE allele status has been shown to have independent effects on health outcomes and to interact with other life circumstances such as sex and race in its effect on health outcomes (Jarvik et al., 1995; Maestre et al., 1995; Payami et al., 1992). Incorporation of information on this genetic indicator could lead to increased knowledge of the interactive mechanisms of this genetic marker and other social and behavioral variables and thus clarify some of the mechanisms leading to population differentials in cognition, heart disease, and mortality.

We suggest that other bioindicators appropriate for current demo-graphic surveys include those that represent the physiological status of major regulatory systems and processes through which demographic, social, psychological, and behavioral variables work to affect health. These measures would indicate current biological status, which would be determined by some combination of genetic and lifetime environmental factors. In this discussion we limit ourselves to indicators that can be collected in a household survey with current technology and trained staff.

These indicators have all been shown to have relationships to demographic variables and to health outcomes in older populations. Currently, some of these indicators are obtained from blood samples, some from urine samples, and some from examinations of the survey respondent.

Biological parameters which meet the criteria for inclusion in population health surveys include measures of cardiovascular health, metabolic processes, markers of inflammation and coagulation, indicators of musculoskeletal health, and respiratory function (Seeman et al., 1997b). We also believe that inclusion of markers of activity in the hypothalamic-pituitary-adrenal (HPA) axis and the sympathetic nervous system (SNS) represent important biological indicators that are related to demographic, social, and psychological factors, and their inclusion will clarify how population health differences and trends arise. These systems, potential biological measures, and sources of information are included in Box 2-1.

Cardiovascular System

Blood pressure is an indicator of the health of the cardiovascular system, which has been linked in numerous studies to age, race, sex, and SES and a range of poorer health outcomes including higher death rates, the onset of cardiovascular disease, and the loss of both physical and cognitive functioning (Kaplan and Keil, 1993; Seeman et al., 1994b; Zelinski et al., 1999). Blood pressure is also related to health behaviors, social-psychological factors, life circumstances, and the use of health care. Among the older population systolic blood pressure appears to be the best predictor of these outcomes, and measuring both systolic and diastolic blood pressure would be an important addition to current surveys. As noted above, questions on hypertension are asked in population surveys, but measurement would provide valuable supplemental information on actual blood pressure and its components.

Metabolic Processes

Metabolic processes have usually been indicated by levels of obesity and presence of reported high cholesterol. Higher total serum cholesterol and higher relative weight have been shown to be risk factors for poor health outcomes including mortality, cardiovascular disease, and functioning loss and to be related to race, sex, age, and SES (Adler et al., 1994; Benfante et al., 1985; Bucher and Ragland, 1995; Kaplan and Keil, 1993; Lynch et al., 1996; Marmot et al., 1997; Winkleby et al., 1992). While information has been gathered in surveys on the presence of high total cholesterol, recent medical practice emphasizes the importance of knowing the components of cholesterol—high density (HDL) and low density

BOX 2-1
Biological Measures that are Related to Demographic, Social,
Psychological and Behavioral Influences and Health Outcomes

	Source
Cardiovascular System	
Systolic blood pressure	Exam
Diastolic blood pressure	Exam
Metabolic System	
Body-mass index/waist-hip ratio	Self-report/exam
Total cholesterol	Blood
HDL/LDL cholesterol	Blood
Homocysteine	Blood
Glycosylated hemoglobin	Blood
Inflammation and Coagulation Factors	
IL-6, CRP, low cholesterol	Blood
Albumin	Blood
Fibrinogen	Blood
Antioxidant Profiles	Blood
Hypothalamic Pituitary Adrenal Axis	
Cortisol	Urine
DHEAS	Blood
Sympathetic Nervous System	
Norepinephrine	Urine
Epinephrine	Urine
Renal Function	
Creatinine clearance	Blood/urine
Lung Function	
Peak flow rate	Exam

(LDL)—and their ratio. Measurement of the components of cholesterol could be productively included in population studies where blood samples are drawn. Comparison of total levels of cholesterol and levels of high density cholesterol in the MacArthur study indicates that using an indicator of total cholesterol or one of high-density cholesterol will stratify the population differently according to risk. Among those in the most risky quartile of the distribution of total cholesterol, only 22 percent are in the highest risk category of HDL cholesterol.

Indicators of glucose metabolism could also be important in clarifying some of the population differences in health by both race and SES as well as the trend toward an increasing prevalence in diabetes now being experienced. Elevated glucose levels, which are common among minority group members and poorer people, have been related to heart disease risk (Reaven, 1988), to higher mortality (Fried et al., 1998), and to poorer cognitive function (Craft et al., 1993; Gradman et al., 1993; Manning et al., 1990; Reaven et al., 1990). Analyses using the MacArthur data have shown that functional decline in older persons is related to a history of diabetes and poorer glucose metabolism (Seeman et al., 1994b). Levels of glycosylated hemoglobin provide an indicator of glucose metabolism and can be determined using blood samples.

Homocysteine has garnered recent attention because of its importance in predicting many of the major health outcomes common in aging populations: cardiovascular, cerebrovascular, peripheral vascular disease, and poorer cognitive function (Arnesen et al., 1995; Jacques and Riggs, 1995; Riggs et al., 1996; Verhoef et al., 1996). Other cofactors involved in homocysteine metabolism, specifically vitamins B6, B12, and folic acid, have also been related to a lower incidence of such problems (Verhoef et al., 1996). These same cofactors are also required for synthesis of dopamine (Kruk and Pycock, 1983), suggesting the possibility that levels of these factors might be related to motor/physical functioning as well. Homocysteine is linked to age and likely to race and SES because homocysteine metabolism is strongly influenced by diet and deficiencies in some vitamins. Homocysteine levels are potentially more easily modified than those of other risk factors and are likely to change in the U.S. population in the near future with folic acid supplementation of flours and cereals. Therefore, changing homocysteine levels have the potential for explaining time change or cohort differences in population health.

Inflammation and Coagulation

Markers of the inflammation and coagulation processes have been linked to negative health outcomes and to some demographic, social, and psychological factors. Recent research using population-based studies has indicated that inflammation markers such as levels of C-reactive protein (CRP), interleukin 6 (IL-6), and albumin may be predictors of heart attack, stroke, functioning loss, and death among older persons (Cohen et al., 1997; Kannel et al., 1987; Kuller et al., 1991, 1996; Mendall et al., 1996; Reuben et al., 2000a; Ridker et al., 1997; Tracy et al., 1995, 1997). Data from the MacArthur study have related levels of IL-6 and C-reactive protein to increased mortality risks and physical and cognitive decline (Reuben et al., 2000a; Weaver et al., 2000). Evidence for the influence of albumin levels and low cholesterol on functional decline and death has also been found in the MacArthur data (Reuben et al., 1999). Albumin has also been related to cognitive impairment (Cattin et al., 1997).

These markers have proven to be relatively strong risk factors for major health outcomes. In fact, high levels of CRP appear to increase the risk for cardiovascular disease as much as adverse levels of HDL cholesterol (de la Serna, 1994; Kannel et al., 1987; Ridker et al., 1997). Low albumin also has been found to be one of the stronger biological indicators, predicting mortality and coronary heart disease within a few years (Corti et al., 1995; Fried et al, 1998; Gillum, 1993; Gillum et al., 1994).

Many of the social and psychological mechanisms through which SES is expected to affect health outcomes also appear to show association with markers of inflammation. Thus, for example, levels of CRP and IL-6 have been linked to indicators of social integration such as participation in religious activities (Koenig et al., 1997). Higher SES has been found to correlate negatively with IL-6 (S. Cohen, unpublished data). There is also strong evidence from animal studies that IL-6 is related to stress (LeMay et al., 1990; Morrow et al., 1992; Takaki et al., 1994; Zhou et al., 1993), and similar relationships are expected in humans (Sternberg et al., 1992).

Fibrinogen levels, a marker of coagulation processes, have been included in analyses of SES differences in Finland and Great Britain, but such relationships have not been examined for a representative sample of the U.S. population (Markowe et al., 1985; Wilson et al., 1993). Fibrinogen has been shown to be strongly predictive of both mortality (Fried et al., 1998) and the onset of cardiovascular disease (Kannel et al., 1987; Patel et al., 1994, 1995; Ridker et al., 1997; Tracy et al., 1995). Indeed, fibrinogen is as important as low levels of HDL cholesterol in predicting cardiovascular disease (de la Serna, 1994). The well-established relationship between SES and fibrinogen levels (in European data) has been suggested as the mechanism linking low social status and stress to cardiovascular disease (Brunner et al., 1996; De Boever et al., 1995; Markowe et al., 1985; Wilson et al., 1993).

Hypothalamic Pituitary Adrenal (HPA) Axis

The HPA axis plays a central role in the ongoing homeostatic regulatory processes of the body (McEwen and Stellar, 1993; Meites, 1982). Levels of cortisol and dehydroepiandrosterone sulfate (DHEAS) are indicators of axis activity. As an individual interacts with his/her environment, the stimuli encountered can serve as challenges or stressors that elicit responses from the HPA axis as well as other internal homeostatic regulatory systems. A number of the mechanisms through which race and SES are thought to affect health have also been shown to be related to cortisol levels (Seeman et al., 1994a; Seeman and McEwen, 1996). Recent data suggest that individuals from lower SES environments exhibit higher cortisol levels (Epel et al., 1998). Health consequences of exposure to elevated cortisol include increased cardiovascular risk (Henry, 1983), poorer cognitive functioning (Lupien et al., 1994; Seeman et al., 1997a), and increased risks for fractures (Greendale et al., 1999). Higher levels of urinary catecholamine excretion have also been shown to predict functional disability and mortality (Reuben et al., 2000b).

DHEAS has been hypothesized to serve as a functional antagonist to HPA axis activity and thus is an important indicator of overall activity in the HPA axis (Kimonides et al., 1998; Svec and Lopez, 1989). DHEAS is negatively related to a history of heart disease and mortality (Barrett-Connor and Goodman-Gruen, 1995; Beer et al., 1996; Feldman et al., 1998) as well as to physical functioning (Ravaglia et al., 1997). DHEAS is thought to be protective against heart disease because of its anticlotting and antiproliferative properties (Beer et al., 1996; Jesse et al., 1994).

Sympathetic Nervous System (SNS) Activity

SNS activity can be indicated by levels of norepinephrine and epinephrine. SNS activity is another mechanism through which racial, SES, and a variety of social/psychological mechanisms are assumed to affect population health outcomes. While these mechanisms play a major role in theories of why some race and SES groups have poor health outcomes, the relationship between SNS activity and life circumstances or health outcomes has not been clarified in the general population. However, levels of neuroendocrine functioning have been shown to relate to stress and challenge (Seeman and McEwen, 1996; Uchino et al., 1996), and endocrine patterns and cardiovascular reactivity have been related to self-efficacy and control (Gerin et al., 1995; Houston, 1972; Lundberg and Frankenhaeuser, 1978; Naditch, 1974; Rodin, 1986). Like the HPA axis, the SNS is one of the body's central regulatory systems, assisting in maintaining the body's overall physiological integrity in the face of changing environmental stimuli. Along with the HPA axis, the SNS is mobilized in response to challenge and serves a critical role in providing the body with the physiologic substrate needed for what have been termed "fight or flight" responses. Again, the problem is that activation of the HPA and SNS systems, while beneficial in the short-term, has been associated with increased risks for health problems such as hypertension and heart disease if activation is excessive or prolonged (Eliot et al., 1982; Krantz and Manuck, 1984; Matthews et al., 1986; Troxler et al., 1977; Williams, 1985).

Antioxidants

Antioxidants protect the body against the DNA damage that can be caused by free radicals (Marx, 1987). Low levels of antioxidants have been related to the likelihood of experiencing a heart attack or stroke (Gaziano, 1996; Gey, 1993), and have been shown to be related to hypertension (Kendall et al., 1994). Antioxidants may work to inhibit the oxidation of low density lipoproteins and thus reduce the onset of atherosclerosis (Kohlmeier et al., 1997). Higher levels of antioxidants have also been related to greater longevity (Gey, 1993), and they have been shown to protect against cognitive (Balanzs and Leon, 1994; Schmidt et al., 1996) and physical decline (Snowdon et al., 1996). Antioxidants are expected to be influenced by diet and may be related to the ingestion of vitamin supplements; through these mechanisms antioxidant levels would be hypothesized to show an association with SES and race and possibly age and gender.

Renal Function

The kidney performs several essential physiological functions, including regulation of the excretion of sodium and water, maintenance of extracellular fluid volume, regulation of acid-base homeostasis, and excretion of toxins and medications. In addition it has an important role as an endocrine organ. Although renal function, on average, declines with age, there are wide variations in the amount of decline for any individual (Lindeman et al., 1985). Lower SES has been found to predict greater renal dysfunction over time (Klahr, 1989; Rostand et al, 1989), and even mild decline in renal function has been associated with increased five-year mortality among community-dwelling older persons (Fried et al., 1998). There are a variety of possible indicators of renal function that can be gathered from either blood or urine samples, including creatinine clearance.

Lung Function

Lung function can be measured to provide an indicator of the functioning of the respiratory system. It has been measured in household surveys by the peak-flow rate. In the MacArthur sample it has been linked to both cognitive (Albert et al., 1995a) and physical decline (Seeman et al., 1994b) and has been shown to be related to both five-year mortality and SES within older populations (Cook et al., 1989, 1991). Reduced lung function is likely to be more common among those of lower SES and those with poor health behaviors.

Allostatic Load

In addition to the links between specific, individual biological parameters and health outcomes described above, analysts using the MacArthur
data have been actively pursuing analyses deriving from a more integrative model of biological risk which focuses on the combined effects of
multiple biological parameters as they impact on risks for various health
outcomes. Much of this work is based on the concept of allostatic load,
first proposed by McEwen and Stellar (1993) and further developed in
McEwen (1998). Allostatic load represents the cumulative physiological
toll of dysregulation across multiple systems over time, reflecting both a
multisystem and life-span orientation, and is hypothesized to affect subsequent mortality, disease pathology, and aging. Recent research has
established a link between allostatic load and socioeconomic status (Singer
and Ryff, 1999).

Analyses based on the MacArthur data have shown a link between a
summary measure of allostatic load and patterns of change in both physical
and cognitive functioning, cardiovascular disease, and mortality (Seeman
et al., 1997b). The first operational measure of allostatic load included
information on 10 biological parameters that reflect functioning of four of
the systems discussed above: the hypothalamic-pituitary-adrenal axis,
sympathetic nervous system, cardiovascular system, and metabolic processes. Parameters included in initial measures of allostatic load included:
systolic and diastolic blood pressure, waist-hip ratio, serum HDL and
total cholesterol, blood plasma levels of glycosylated hemoglobin,
DHEAS, 12-hour urinary cortisol excretion, and 12-hour urinary norepinephrine and epinephrine excretion levels. The summary measure of
allostatic load was also shown to be a significantly better predictor of
outcomes than the individual component factors, providing evidence that
risk for these outcomes is related to the overall impact of dysregulation
across the various regulatory systems. Comparison of the explanatory
power of the index of allostatic load to an indicator of Syndrome X also
demonstrated the value of the multisystem allostatic load approach to
health outcomes.

Other related analyses using summary biological risks scores similar
to allostatic load have focused on risks associated with low albumin and
cholesterol and on a combined index of inflammation based on high IL-6
and C-reactive protein in combination with low albumin and cholesterol.
Results of these analyses have indicated that higher scores on these summary indices are associated with increased risks for functional disability
and mortality (Reuben et al., 1999, 2000a).

In the preceding section, we have listed a number of bioindicators
that we feel are appropriate for inclusion in population surveys because

of evidence of their role in causing the health differences that are the focus in demographic approaches to health. In addition, some of these factors are likely to be important in explaining both current differences and future trends in health. We believe, however, that a comprehensive approach to indicators of the health of bodily systems related to demographic factors, major health outcomes, and social, behavioral, and psychological factors remains to be completed. Most epidemiologic and demographic analysis has been limited to the inclusion of bioindicators representing cardiovascular and metabolic states. Epidemiological and medical results regularly add to the group of potential indicators linked to both demographic variables and health outcomes. We also believe that while a myriad of research results indicate the potential of such an approach, it has yet to be comprehensively documented with empirical data for the United States.

The issue of measurement error is relevant to the biological data as well as the self-report data. Measurement error is one factor that prevents the collection of some data as part of home-based protocols where collection and processing methods make it difficult, if not impossible, to collect certain data with any reasonable accuracy. Thus, for example, data on additional bioindicators such as plasma adrenocorticotropic hormone (ACTH) or catecholamines would be extremely difficult to collect due to the need for rapid processing and cold storage of these samples. Likewise, data that require large and complex instrumentation are likely to be difficult to collect in home-based protocols both because of the difficulty in transporting such instruments as well as the standardization of the instruments after moving them. Examples of such limitations would include current instrumentation needed to collect heart rate variability data, which is not easily transportable, and MRI instrumentation, which is large, extremely complex, and not at all transportable at this time. With respect to those protocols that are possible (e.g., saliva sampling, blood samples for certain parameters, urine collection), assays performed based on these samples should always include standard laboratory tests for reliability and validity of the assays (e.g., intra-assay coefficient of variation, sensitivity of the assay).

COLLECTION OF BIOLOGICAL INFORMATION
IN THE MacARTHUR STUDY

Many of the findings cited above have been derived from or replicated in the MacArthur Study of Successful Aging with which Seeman has long been associated (see Rowe and Kahn, 1998, for an overview). We use the MacArthur Study as an illustrative example of the type of bioindicator approach that is possible with existing data. The data collection effort for this study was designed in the mid-1980s and used then-available technology and epidemiological knowledge. This study was among the first to explicitly design protocols for collection of biological data in subjects' homes, including not only blood collections but overnight urine sampling as well. The home-based approach to collection of biological material used in MacArthur, however, is similar to that used in other studies including the National Institute on Aging's Established Populations for Epidemiologic Studies of the Elderly (EPESE) studies and the Taiwan Study described by Weinstein and Willis (2000). The home-based nature of the data collection has important implications for the use of this approach with larger, more geographically dispersed samples.

There are numerous other community-based surveys that have collected biological data using a clinic setting for collection of bioindicators. These include the long-running Framingham Study, a study that began in the 1950s as a representative sample of adults living in the town of Framingham, Massachusetts. Data collection for the original cohort as well as their offspring has continued to this day and has largely, if not solely, been done through clinic-based protocols. Similar clinic-based data collection has been used for multisite, community-based studies such as the Cardiovascular Health Study (Newman et al., 1999), the Atherosclerosis Risk in Communities study (Brancati et al., 2000), CARDIA (Iribarren et al., 2000), the Study of Women's Health Across the Nation, as well as the nationally representative NHANES surveys (Wu et al., 1999). In each case, data on biological characteristics have been collected for large cohorts of individuals through clinic-based data collection.

While all of the studies listed above provide important background relevant to the inclusion of bioindicators in demographic surveys, we describe the home-based data collection procedures used in the MacArthur study. The MacArthur Study of Successful Aging is a three-site longitudinal study of 1,189 persons aged 70-79 years at baseline. MacArthur subjects were interviewed three times: 1988, 1991, and 1996. Respondents were originally selected on the basis of age and both high physical and cognitive functioning from three community-based cohorts of the EPESE in Durham, NC, East Boston, MA, and New Haven, CT (Cornoni-Huntley et al., 1986). While this sample has better cognitive and physical functioning than a national sample of the same age, comparison of the MacArthur sample and the Longitudinal Study of Aging (LSOA) respondents from 1984 indicates that this sample is actually fairly similar to the total U.S. population aged 70-79. While it is an initially healthier sample, the sample has similar social and economic variation to the national LSOA sample. In addition, there is a large (19 percent black) minority component of the sample.

Initial data collection included a 90-minute, face-to-face interview covering detailed self and performance-based assessments of physical and cognitive performance, health status, social and psychological characteristics, and other lifestyle characteristics. This included standard sociodemographic characteristics plus extensive information from the following domains: psychological characteristics (e.g., self-efficacy and personal mastery beliefs, depression, happiness, life satisfaction), social ties and support, and health behaviors (e.g., smoking and alcohol consumption as well as extensive data on physical activities). In addition, subjects were asked to provide blood samples and 12-hour, overnight urines. Wave 2 data collection included reassessment of all measures included in the baseline interview and collection of blood samples and 12-hour urines. In the third wave only interview data were collected; no blood or urine samples were gathered.

Biomedical Assessments

While most population surveys get self-reports on some biological indicators, the MacArthur study included measurement of seated and postural blood pressure, pulmonary function, and waist/hip ratio as part of the biomedical protocol. Systolic and diastolic pressures were calculated as the average of three readings (Hypertension Detection and Follow-up Program Cooperative Group, 1978). Waist/hip ratio was assessed by measuring the waist at its narrowest point between the ribs and iliac crest, and the hips at the iliac crest (Lohman et al., 1988). A second hip circumference was also taken at the maximal buttocks level. Pulmonary function was assessed by the peak flow rate of subjects using a mini-Wright meter. Subjects were asked to exhale at maximal effort through the meter. Measures are based on the average of three attempts (Cook et al., 1991). Physical functioning was assessed using a series of performance tests as well as being self-reported by subjects; cognitive functioning was also directly assessed with a series of tasks covering major aspects of cognition.

Physiological Measures from Blood and Urine Specimens

As noted above, both blood and urine samples were collected from MacArthur subjects. These were collected by phlebotomists and laboratory personnel who were sent to subjects' homes the morning after the home interview to collect a blood sample and the overnight urine. The development of standardized urine collection procedures for almost 1,200 elderly across three geographic sites represented a major effort. Twelve-hour samples (from 8 PM until 8 AM) rather than 24-hour samples were used in this study to optimize participation and complete collection. Pilot data for this study indicated that a 24-hour schedule would result in higher refusal and incidence of incomplete collection. Pilot tests also showed that 12-hour specimens and 24-hour specimens were highly correlated for epinephrine, norepinephrine, and cortisol. The overnight collection protocol has a further advantage in that it serves to minimize the potential confounding effects of physical activity as subjects generally spent this time at home (and much of that time in bed). As a result, individual differences in overnight excretion of cortisol as well as norepinephrine and epinephrine may well reflect differences in "steady state" operating levels of their HPA axis and SNS (i.e., estimates of "basal," non-stimulated levels of activity).

Insulated cooler packs were designed in order to permit optimal urine temperature to be maintained to preserve the specimens in the respondents' homes. A bottle within each cooler pack contained 12 ml of 6 N HCL to acidify and preserve the urine during collection. Upon collection, the mean temperature of the specimens was 14.6°C with a pH of 2-3. A 60-ml aliquot of urine was then sent to Nichols Laboratories for assays of cortisol, epinephrine, norepinephrine, dopamine, and creatinine content. Results for each of the three outcomes are reported as "micrograms (NE, E, or C) per gram creatinine" in order to adjust for body size. Urinary free cortisol was assayed by high-performance liquid chromatography (HPLC) (Caldrella et al., 1982; Canalis et al., 1982). Urine catecholamines were extracted via column chromatography and also determined by HPLC (Krsulovic, 1983).

A phlebotomist was sent to each respondent's home to draw blood. Although subjects were not required to fast, most blood samples were taken early in the morning before subjects had eaten. Samples were processed and frozen within eight hours of blood drawing. Nine cm^3 of blood were drawn in serum-separator tubes and another 10 cm^3 of blood were drawn into heparinized tubes. Blood in the serum-separator tubes was allowed to clot and the tube was centrifuged at 1,500 RCF for ten minutes in a refrigerated (4°C) centrifuge. The sera were then sent to Nichols Laboratories for standard assessments including a CBC and an SMAC and measurements of HDL and total cholesterol, dehydroepiandrosterone sulfate (DHEAS), and serum glutamic-oxaloacetic transaminase (SGOT). Two cm^3 of blood from the heparinized tubes were removed after mixing for assays of glycosylated hemoglobin (HbA). This measure provides an assessment of integrated long-term blood glucose concentrations and was assayed using affinity chromatography methods (Little et al., 1983). The remainder was centrifuged and the plasma and cell pellet were frozen for future analyses. From each of the first two interviews, three vials of plasma (1 cm^3 each) and a cell pellet for DNA were obtained and stored for future use. The stored samples have proven to be a valuable resource for examining biological factors whose importance was not yet recognized when the samples were first collected. From the stored samples assays for homocysteine (and cofactors involved in its metabolism—folic acid, B12), IL-6, and C-reactive protein have been completed using plasma samples, and APOE genotyping is in process using DNA from the cell pellets; assays for fibrinogen and antioxidants are currently being obtained.

Most of the subjects in this study agreed to provide blood and urine samples. Eighty percent (80.3%) agreed to provide blood samples and 85.8 percent consented to provide urine samples at the first interview. This resulted in baseline biological data for over 900 subjects, of whom 765 provided complete blood *and* urine data. Comparison of the refusers to the complete cohort suggests that they do not have distinctive characteristics (Seeman et al., 1997a). The collection of specimens does not appear to have made the sample prone to attrition. At the second interview only 4 percent of the sample interviewed at the first wave refused to participate; 5 percent refused at the third. Among those who gave blood and urine at the first interview and who were interviewed at the second wave, 91 and 93 percent, respectively, provided a second sample. About half of those who refused to provide blood and urine samples at the first interview agreed to do so at the second. This experience indicates that the request for blood and urine samples had little effect on survey response.

SUMMARY AND CONCLUSIONS

We argue that the current demographic approach to health incorporates a limited set of biological explanatory mechanisms into models containing a variety of social, economic, psychological, behavioral, and environmental indicators that must eventually affect biology. The variables included to date have been limited to those that can be self-reported in either a personal interview or telephone interview rather than those that will best clarify the mechanisms through which health differences and health changes arise. In order to clarify the mechanisms through which health trends arise and to reduce health differentials in the U.S. population, we should develop sets of proximate biological factors related to health outcomes based on our knowledge of biology and the relationship between bioindicators, demographic variables, and health outcomes. The value of population surveys addressing health issues will increase markedly when additional biological information is collected which can be used to clarify how demographic factors get under the skin to produce health outcomes.

As outlined above, studies such as the MacArthur Study of Successful Aging, which have included demographic information along with information on a range of social, psychological, behavioral, and biological parameters, have demonstrated the value of this information in linking traditional demographic variables and health outcomes. There are strong relationships between all of the biological parameters described and what are usually considered demographic variables. There are also relationships between the major health outcomes of interest in aging populations and these biological indicators. Evidence such as this clearly points to the potential value of developing more comprehensive data collection strategies in our efforts to better understand inequalities in health outcomes in populations. It is only through efforts to build more comprehensive models of health and aging that we will gain the requisite knowledge to develop effective policies and interventions to promote health and reduce health disparities in populations.

The value of stored specimens for continuing to augment sample information as science progresses is also evident in the MacArthur data. Planning ahead for appropriate storage of samples can allow the data from a survey that is well underway to be used to address new scientific questions. Of course, scientific advances in the methods of collecting biological data are imminent. Less invasive and cumbersome means of scanning are being developed that will allow for noninvasive collection of biological information on the health of the cardiovascular system, the skeletal system, and other organs. Potentially, information once gathered from blood and urine samples can be gathered in some less invasive manner in the future; however, at the moment the technology for household collection of urine and blood is manageable.

We have not discussed the ethical issues that arise when a survey adds the collection of biological information to its protocols; other chapters in this volume comprehensively address these issues. We should recognize that asking respondents to provide biological samples does place additional burden on respondents. Both respondent cost as well as potential gain need to be considered in making this request. While respondent burden is greater, collecting biological information creates an opportunity for respondent gain by potentially providing participants with information on a set of individual bioindicators that could personally be useful.

REFERENCES

Adler, N., T. Boyce, M. Chesney, S. Cohen, S. Folkman, R. Kahn, and L. Syme
    1994   Socioeconomic status and health. *American Psychologist* 49:15-24.
Adler, N., T. Boyce, M. Chesney, S. Folkman, and L. Syme
    1993   Socioeconomic inequalities in health. *Journal of American Medical Association* 269(24):3140-3145.

Albert, M., C. Graffagnino, C. McClenny, D. DeLong, W. Strittmatter, A. Saunders, and A. Roses
   1995a ApoE genotype and survival from intracerebral hemorrhage. *Lancet* 346:575.
Albert, M., K. Jones, C. Savage, L. Berkman, T. Seeman, D. Blazer, and J. Rowe
   1995b Predictors of cognitive change in older persons: MacArthur Studies of Successful Aging. *Psychology and Aging* 10:578-589.
Arnesen, E., et al.
   1995 Serum total homocysteine and coronary heart disease. *International Journal of Epidemiology* 23:704-709.
Balanzs, L., and M. Leon
   1994 Evidence of an oxidative challenge in the Alzheimer's brain. *Neurochemical Research* 19:1131.
Barker, D.
   1998 *Mothers, Babies, and Health in Later Life*. 2nd Edition. London: Churchill Livingstone.
Barrett-Connor, E., and D. Goodman-Gruen
   1995 The epidemiology of DHEAS and cardiovascular disease. *Annals of the New York Academy of Sciences* 774:259-270.
Beer, N., D. Jakubowicz, D. Matt, R. Beer, and J. Nestler
   1996 Dehydroepiandrosterone reduces plasma plasminogen activator inhibitor type I and tissue plasminogen activator antigen in men. *American Journal of the Medical Sciences* 311:205-210.
Benfante, R., D. Reed, and J. Brody
   1985 Biological and social predictors of health in an aging cohort. *Journal of Chronic Diseases* 28:385-395.
Berkman, L., T. Seeman, M. Albert, D. Blazer, and R. Robert
   1993 High, usual and impaired functioning in community-dwelling older men and women: Findings from the MacArthur Foundation Research Network on Successful Aging. *Journal of Clinical Epidemiology* 46:1129-1140.
Blackwell, D., M. Hayward, and E. Crimmins
   in   Does childhood health affect chronic morbidity in later life? *Social Science and*
   press *Medicine*.
Bongaarts, J.
   1978 A framework for analyzing the proximate determinants of fertility. *Population and Development Review* 4:105-132.
Brancati, F. L., W.H.L. Kao, A.R. Folsom, R.L. Watson, and M. Szklo
   2000 Incident type 2 diabetes mellitus in African American and white adults: The Atherosclerosis Risk in Communities Study. *Journal of American Medical Association* 283:2253-2259.
Brownson, R.C., J. Jackson-Thompson, J.C. Wilkerson, and F. Kiani
   1994 Reliability of information on chronic disease risk factors collected in the Missouri behavioral risk factor surveillance system. *Epidemiology* 5:545-549.
Brunner, E., G. Smith, M. Marmot, R. Canner, M. Beksinska, and J. O'Brien
   1996 Childhood social circumstances and psychosocial and behavioural factors as determinants of plasma fibrinogen. *Lancet* 347:1008-1013.
Bucher, H., and D. Ragland
   1995 Socioeconomic indicators and mortality from coronary heart disease and cancer: A 22 year follow-up of middle-aged men. *American Journal of Public Health* 85:1231-1236.
Bush, T., S. Miller, A. Golden, and W. Hale
   1989 Self-report and medical record agreement of selected medical conditions in the elderly. *American Journal of Public Health* 85:1231-1236.

Caldrella A., G. Reardon, and E. Canalis
    1982   Analysis of cortisol in serum by liquid chromatography. *Clinical Chemistry* 28:538-
            543.
Canalis E., G. Reardon, and A. Caldrella
    1982   A more specific, liquid chromatography for free cortisol in urine. *Clinical Chemis-
            try* 28:2418-2420.
Cattin, L., P. Bordin, M. Fonda, C. Adamo, F. Barbone, M. Bovenzi, A. Manto, C. Pedone,
and M. Panor
    1997   Factors associated with cognitive impairment among older Italian inpatients. *Jour-
            nal of American Geriatrics Society* 45:1124-1130.
Cohen, H., C. Pieper, T. Harris, K.M. Rao, and M. Currie
    1997   Plasma IL-6: An indicator of functional disability in community dwelling elderly.
            Journal of Gerontology: Medical Sciences 52A:M201-M208.
Colsher, P., and R. Wallace
    1991   Longitudinal application of cognitive function measures in a defined population
            of community-dwelling elders. *Annals of Epidemiology* 1:215-230.
Cook, N., D. Evans, P. Scherr, F. Speizer, et al.
    1989   Peak expiratory flow rate in an elderly population. *American Journal of Epidemiol-
            ogy* 130:66-78.
Cook, N.R., D.A. Evans, P.A. Scherr, F.E. Speizer, J.O. Taylor, and C.H. Hennekens
    1991   Peak expiratory flow rate and 5-year mortality in an elderly population. *American
            Journal of Epidemiology* 133:784-794.
Corder, E.H., A. Saunders, W. Strittmatter, D. Schmechel, P. Gaskell, G. Small, A. Roses, J.
Haines, and M. Pericak-Vance
    1993   Gene dose of apolipoprotein-E type 4 allele and the risk of Alzheimer's disease in
            late-onset families. *Science* 261:921-923.
Cornoni-Huntley, J., D.M. Brock, A. Ostfeld, J.O. Taylor, and R.B. Wallace, eds.
    1986   *Established Populations for Epidemiological Studies of the Elderly, Resource Data Book.*
            NIH Pub. No. 86-2443. Bethesda, MD: National Institutes of Health.
Corti, M., J.M. Guralnik, M.E. Salive, T. Harris, T.S. Field, R.B. Wallace, L.F. Berkman, T.E.
Seeman, R.J. Glynn, C.H. Hennekens, and R.J. Havlik
    1995   HDL cholesterol predicts coronary heart disease mortality in older persons. *Jour-
            nal of American Medical Association* 274(7):539-544.
Craft, S, S. Dagogo-Jack, B. Wiethop, C. Murphy, R. Nevins, S. Fleischman, V. Rice, J.
Newcomer, and P. Cryer
    1993   Effects of hyperglycemia on memory and hormone levels in dementia of the
            Alzheimer type: A longitudinal study. *Behavioral Neuroscience* 107:926-940.
Crimmins, E.
    1993   Demography: The past 30 years, the present, and the future. *Demography* 30(4):579-
            591.
    1996   Mixed trends in population health among older adults. *Journal of Gerontology:
            Social Sciences* 51B(5):S223-S225.
Crimmins, E., M. Hayward, and Y. Saito
    1994   Changing mortality and morbidity rates and the health status and life expectancy
            of the older U.S. population. *Demography* 31:159-175.
De Boever, E., D. De Bacquer, L. Braeckman, G. Baele, M. Rosseneu, and G. De Backer
    1995   Relation of fibrinogen to lifestyles and to cardiovascular risk factors in a working
            population. *International Journal of Epidemiology* 24(5):915-921.
de la Serna, G.
    1994   Fibrinogen: A new major risk factor for cardiovascular disease: A review of the
            literature. *Journal of Family Practice* 39:468-477.

Eliot, R.S., J.C. Buell, and T.M. Dembroski
    1982   Bio-behavioral perspectives on coronary heart disease, hypertension, and sudden cardiac death. *Acta Medica Scandinavica* 13(suppl. 660):203-219.
Epel, E., B. McEwen, and J. Ickovics
    1998   Embodying psychological thriving: Physical thriving in response to stress. *Journal of Social Issues* 54:301-322.
Ettner, S.
    1996   New evidence in the relationship between income and health. *Journal of Health Economics* 15:67-86.
Evans, D., L. Beckett, T. Field, M. Albert, D. Benneett, B. Tycko, and R. Mayeux
    1997   Apolipoprotein E epsilon 4 and incidence of Alzheimer disease in a community population of older persons. *Journal of American Medical Association* 277:822-824.
Ewbank, D.
    1997   The genetic make-up of population and its implications for mortality by cause of death: Links between Alzheimer's and ischemic heart disease. Symposium on Health and Mortality, Brussels, Belgium.
Feldman, H., C. Johannes, J. McKinlay, and C. Longcope
    1998   Low dehydroepiandrosterone sulfate and heart disease in middle-aged men: Cross-sectional results from the Massachusetts Male Aging Study. *Annals of Epidemiology* 8:217-228.
Fried, L., R. Kronmal, A. Newman, D. Bild, M. Mittelmark, J. Polak, J. Robbins, and J. Gardin
    1998   Risk factors for 5-year mortality in older adults: The Cardiovascular Health Study. *Journal of American Medical Association* 279:585-592.
Gaziano, M.
    1996   Antioxidants in cardiovascular disease: Randomized trials. *Nutrition* 12:584-588.
Gerin W., M. Litt, J. Deich, and T. Pickering
    1995   Self-efficacy as a moderator of perceived control effects on cardiovascular reactivity: Is enhanced control always beneficial? *Psychosomatic Medicine* 57:390-397.
Gey, K.
    1993   Prospects for the prevention of free radical disease, regarding cancer and cardiovascular disease. *British Medical Bulletin* 49:679-699.
Giles, W., J. Croft, N. Keenan, M. Lane, and F. Wheeler
    1995   Validity of self-reported hypertension and correlates of hypertension awareness among blacks and whites within the stroke belt. *American Journal of Preventive Medicine* 11:163-169.
Gillum, R.F.
    1993   The association between serum albumin and HDL and total cholesterol. *Journal of the National Medical Association* 85(4):290-292.
Gillum, R.F., and D. Ingram
    1994   Relation between serum-albumin concentration and stroke incidence and death: the NHANES-I epidemiological follow-up study. *American Journal of Epidemiology* 140(10):876-888.
Gradman, T., A. Laws, L. Thompson, and G. Reaven
    1993   Verbal learning and/or memory improves with glycemic control in older subjects with non-insulin-dependent diabetes mellitus. *Journal of American Geriatrics Society* 41:1305-1312.
Greendale, G., J.B. Unger, J.W. Rowe, and T. Seeman
    1999   The relation between cortisol excretion and fractures in healthy older peope: Results from the MacArthur Studies of Successful Aging. *Journal of American Geriatrics Society* 47(7):799-803.

Grossman, M.
   1972   *The Demand for Health: A Theoretical and Empirical Investigation.* New York: National Bureau of Economic Research.
Henry, J.
   1983   Coronary heart disease and arousal of the adrenal cortical axis. Pp.365-381 in *Biobehavioral Bases of Coronary Heart Disease*, T. Dembroski, T. Schmidt, and G. Blumchen, eds. Basel: Karger.
Herzog, R., and R. Wallace
   1997   Measures of cognitive-functioning in the AHEAD study. *Journal of Gerontology: Psychological Sciences* 52B:293-293.
Hofman, A., A. Ott, M. Breteler, M. Bots, A. Slooter, F. Harskamp, C. Dujin, C. Broeckhoven, and D. Brobbee
   1997   Atherosclerosis, apolipoprotein E, and prevalence of dementia and Alzheimer's disease in the Rotterdam Study. *Lancet* 349:151-154.
Houston, B.
   1972   Control over stress, locus of control, and response to stress. *Journal of Personality and Social Psychology* 21:249-255.
Howe, G.
   1998   Practical uses of biomarkers in population studies. Pp. 41-49 in *Biomarkers: Medical and Workplace Applications*, M. Mendelsohn, L. Mohr, and J. Peeters, eds. Washington, DC: Joseph Henry Press.
Hummer, R.
   1996   Black-white differences in health and mortality: A review and conceptual model. *The Sociological Quarterly* 37:105-125.
Hyman, B., T. Gomez-Isla, M. Briggs, H. Chung, S. Nichols, F. Kohour, and R. Wallace
   1996   Apolipoprotein E and cognitive change in an elderly population. *Annals of Neurology* 40:55-66.
Hypertension Detection, and Follow-up Program Cooperative Group (HDFP)
   1978   Variability of blood pressure and results of screening in HDFP program. *Journal of Chronic Diseases* 31:651-667.
Iribarren, C., S. Sidney, D.E. Bild, K. Liu, J.H. Markovitz, J.M. Roseman, and K.P. Matthews
   2000   Association of hostility with coronary artery calcification in young adults: The Cardia Study. *Journal of American Medical Association* 283(19):2546-2551.
Jacques, P., and K. Riggs
   1995   B vitamins as risk factors for age-related diseases. In *Nutritional Assessment of Elderly Populations: Measure and Function*, I.H. Rosenberg, ed. New York: Raven Press.
Jarvik, G., E. Wijsman, W. Kukull, G. Schellenberg, C. Yu, and E. Larson
   1995   Interactions of apolipoprotein E genotype, total cholesterol level, age, and sex in prediction of Alzheimer's disease: A case-control study. *Neurology* 45:1092-1098.
Jesse, R., et al.
   1994   Dehydroepiandrosterone inhibits human platelet aggregation *in vitro* and *in vivo*. *Annals of the New York Academy of Sciences* 774:281-290.
Kannel, W., P. Wolf, W. Castelli, and R. D'Agostino
   1987   Fibrinogen and risk of cardiovascular disease: The Framingham Study. *Journal of American Medical Association* 258:1183-1186.
Kaplan, G., and J. Keil
   1993   Socioeconomic factors and cardiovascular disease. *Circulation* 88:1973-1998.
Kehoe, R., S. Wu, C. Leske, and L. Chylack, Jr.
   1994   Comparing self-reported and physician-reported medical history. *American Journal of Epidemiology* 139(8):813-818.

Kendall. M., I. Rajman, and S. Maxwell
    1994   Cardioprotective therapeutics: Drugs used in hypertension, hyperlipidaemia, thromboembolism, arrhythmias, the postmenopausal state and as anti-oxidants. *Postgraduate Medical Journal* 70:329-343.
Kimonides, V., N. Khatibi, M. Sofroniew, and J. Herbert
    1998   Dehydroepiandrosterone (DHEA) and DHEA-sulfate (DHEAS) protect hippocampal neurons against excitatory amino acid-induced neurotoxicity. *Proceedings of the National Academy of Sciences of the United States of America* 95:1852-1857.
Klahr, S.
    1989   The kidney in hypertension—villain and victim. *New England Journal of Medicine* 320:731-733.
Koenig. H., H. Cohen, L. George, J. Hays, D. Larson, and D. Blazer
    1997   Attendance at religious services, interleukin-6, and other biological parameters of immune function in older adults. *International Journal of Psychiatry in Medicine* 27:233-250.
Kohlmeier, L., J. Kark, E., E. Gomezgarcia, B. Martin, S. Steck, A. Kardinaal, J. Ringstad, M. Thamm, V. Masaev, R. Riemersma, J. Martin-Moreno, J. Huttunen, and F. Kok
    1997   Lycopene and myocardial infarction risk in the Euramic Study. *American Journal of Epidemiology* 146:618-626.
Krantz, D.S., and S.B. Manuck
    1984   Acute psychophysiological reactivity and risk of cardiovascular disease: A review and methodologic critique. *Psychological Bulletin* 96:435-464.
Krsulovic, A.M.
    1983   Investigations of catecholamine metabolism using high performance liquid chromatography: Analytical methodology and clinical applicators. *Journal of Chromatography* 9:1-34.
Kruk, Z., and C. Pycock
    1983   *Neurotransmitters and Drugs.* Baltimore: University Park Press.
Kuh, D., and B. Ben-Shlomo
    1997   *Life Course Approach to Chronic Disease Epidemiology.* Oxford: Oxford University Press.
Kuller, L., J. Eichner, T. Orchard, G. Grandits, L. McCallum, and R. Tracy
    1991   The relation between serum albumin levels and risk of coronary heart disease in the Multiple Risk Factor Intervention Trial. *American Journal of Epidemiology* 134:1266-1277.
Kuller, L., R. Tracy, J. Shaten, and E. Meilahn
    1996   Relation of C-reactive protein and coronary heart disease in the MRFIT nested case-control study. *American Journal of Epidemiology* 144:537-547.
LeMay, L., A. Vander, and M. Kluger
    1990   The effects of psychological stress on plasma interleukin-6 activity in rats. *Physiology and Behavior* 47:957-961.
Lindeman, R., J. Tobin, and N. Shock
    1985   Longitudinal studies on the rate of decline in renal function with age. *Journal of American Geriatrics Society* 33:278-286.
Link, B.G., and J. Phelan
    1995   Social conditions as fundamental causes of disease. *Journal of Health and Social Behavior* 36 (extra issue):80-94.
Little, R.R., J. England, H. Wiedmeyer, and D. Goldstein
    1983   Effects of whole blood storage on results of glycosolated hemoglobin as measured by ion exchange chromatography, affinity chromatography and colorimetry. *Clinical Chemistry* 29:1080-1082.

Lohman, T.G., A.F. Roche, and R. Martorell
    1988   *Anthropometric Standardization Reference Manual.* Champaign, IL: Human Kinetics Books.
Lu, R., E. Crimmins, and T. Seeman
    1998   Measurement of Hypertension in Sample Surveys of the U.S. Elderly Population. Paper presented at the annual meeting of the Gerontological Society of America, Philadelphia. PA.
Luc, E., J. Bard, D. Arveiler, A. Evans, J. Cambou, A. Bingham, P. Amouyel, P. Schaffer, J. Ruidavets, and F. Cambien
    1994   Impact of apolipoprotein E polymorphism on lipoproteins and risk of myocardial infarction: The ECTIM study. *Arteriosclerosis and Thrombosis* 14:1412-1419.
Lundberg, U., and M. Frankenhaeuser
    1978   Psychophysiological reactions to noise as modified by personal control over stimulus intensity. *Biological Psychology* 6:51-59.
Luoto, R., J. Pekkanen, A. Utela, and J. Tuomilehto
    1994   Cardiovascular risks and socioeconomic status: Differences between men and women in Finland. *Journal of Epidemiology and Community Health* 48:348-354.
Lupien, S., A. LeCours, I. Lussier, G. Schwartz, N. Nair, and M. Meaney
    1994   Basal cortisol levels and cognitive deficits in human aging. *Journal of Neuroscience* 14:2893-2903.
Lynch, J., G. Kaplan, R. Cohen, J. Tuomilehto, and J. Salonen
    1996   Do cardiovascular risk factors explain the relation between socioeconomic status and risk of all-cause mortality, cardiovascular mortality, and acute myocardial infarction? *American Journal of Epidemiology* 144:934-942.
Maestre, G., R. Ottman, Y. Stern, B. Gurland, M. Chun, M. Tang, M. Shelanski, B. Tycko, and R. Mayeux
    1995   Apolipoprotein-E and Alzheimer's disease: Ethnic variation in genotype risks. *Annals of Neurology* 37:254-259.
Manning, C., J. Hall, and P. Gold
    1990   Glucose effects on memory and other neuropsychological tests in elderly humans. *Psychological Science* 5:307-311.
Markowe, H., M. Marmot, M. Shipley, C. Bulpitt, T. Meade, Y. Stirling, M. Vickers, and A. Semmence
    1985   Fibrinogen: A possible link between social class and coronary heart disease. *British Medical Journal* 291:1312-1314.
Marmot, M., C. Ryff, L. Bumpass, M. Shipley, and N. Marks
    1997   Social inequalities in health: Next question and converging evidence. *Social Science and Medicine* 44:901-910.
Marx, J.
    1987   Oxygen free radicals linked to many diseases. *Science* 235:529-531.
Matthews, K., S. Weiss, T. Detre et al.
    1986   *Handbook of Stress, Reactivity, and Cardiovascular Disease.* New York: John Wiley & Sons.
McEwen, B.
    1998   Protective and damaging effects of stress mediators. *New England Journal of Medicine* 338:171-179.
McEwen, B., and E. Stellar
    1993   Stress and the individual: Mechanisms leading to disease. *Archives of Internal Medicine* 153:2093-2101.

Meites, J.
    1982   Changes in neuroendocrine control of anterior pituitary function during aging. *Neuroendocrinology* 34:151-156.
Mendall, M., P. Patel, L. Ballam, D. Strachan, and T. Northfield
    1996   C-reactive protein and its relation to cardiovascular risk factors: A population based cross sectional study. *British Medical Journal* 312:1049-1050.
Morrow, L.E., J.L. McClellan, C.A. Conn, and M.J. Kluger
    1992   Glucocorticoids alter fever and IL-6 responses to psychological stress and to lipopolysaccharide. *American Journal of Physiology* 264:R1010-R1016.
Mosley, W.H., and L.C. Chen
    1984   An analytical framework for the study of child survival in developing countries. *Population Development Review* 10(Suppl):25-45.
Naditch, M.
    1974   Locus of control, relative discontent and hypertension. *Social Psychiatry* 9:111-117.
Newman, A.B., P. Enright, M. McBurnie, V. Bittner, R. Tracy, and R. McNamara
    1999   Predictors of 6 minute walk distance in a community-based cohort: The Cardiovascular Health Study. *Journal of American Geriatrics Society* 47:S79.
Patel, P., D. Carrington, D. Strachan, E. Leatham, P. Goggin, T. Northfield, and M. Mendall
    1994   Fibrinogen: A link between chronic infection and coronary heart disease. *Lancet* 343(8913):1634-1635.
Patel, P., M. Mendall, D. Carrington, D. Strachan, E. Leatham, and N. Molineaux
    1995   Association of helicobacter pylori and chlamydia pneumonia infections with coronary heart disease and cardiovascular risk factors. *British Medical Journal* 311:711-714.
Payami, H., et al.
    1992   Apolipoprotein E polymorphism and Alzheimer's disease. *Lancet* 342:697-699.
Preston, S., and P. Taubman
    1994   Socioeconomic differences in adult mortality and health status. Pp. 279-318 in *Demography of Aging*, L. Martin and S. Preston, eds. Washington, DC: National Academy Press.
Ravaglia, G., P. Forti, F. Maioli, F. Boschi, A. Cicognani, M. Bernardi, L. Pratelli, A. Pizzoferrato, S. Porcu, and G. Gasbarrini
    1997   Determinants of functional status in healthy Italian nonagenarians and centenarians: A comprehensive functional assessment by the instruments of geriatric practice. *Journal of American Geriatrics Society* 45(10):1196-1202.
Reaven, F.
    1988   Banting lecture 1988: Role of insulin resistance in human disease. *Diabetes* 37:1595-1607.
Reaven, G., L. Thompson, D. Nahum, and E. Haskins
    1990   Relationship between hyperglycemia and cognitive function in older NIDDM patients. *Diabetes Care* 13:16-21.
Reuben, D., J. Ix, G. Greendale, and T. Seeman
    1999   The predictive value of combined hypoalbuminemia and hypocholesterolemia in high functioning community-dwelling older persons. *Journal of American Geriatrics Society* 47:402-406.
Reuben, D., A. Chen, T. Harris, and T. Seeman
    2000a Peripheral blood markers of inflammation predict mortality and functional decline among high functioning community-dwelling older persons: MacArthur Studies of Successful Aging (submitted).

Reuben, D., S. Talvi, and T. Seeman
  2000b High urinary catecholamine excretion predicts mortality and functional decline in high functioning community-dwelling older persons: MacArthur Studies of Successful Aging (submitted).
Ricklefs, R., and C. Finch
  1995 *Aging: A Natural History*. New York: Scientific American Library.
Ridker, P., M. Cushman, M. Stampfer, R. Tracy, and C. Hennekens
  1997 Inflammation, aspirin, and the risk of cardiovascular disease in apparently healthy men. *New England Journal of Medicine* 336:973-979.
Riggs, K.M., A. Spiro, K. Tucker, and D. Rush
  1996 Relations of vitamin B-12, vitamin B-6, folate and homocysteine to cognitive performance in the Normative Aging Study. *American Journal of Clinical Nutrition* 63:306-314.
Rodin J.
  1986 Health, control, and aging. Pp. 139-161 in *The Psychology of Control and Aging*, M. Baltes, and P. Baltes, eds. Hillsdale: Lawrence Erlbaum.
Rogers, R., R. Hummer, and C. Nam
  2000 *Living and Dying in the USA: Behavioral, Health, and Social Differentials of Adult Mortality*. San Diego: Academic Press.
Rostand, S., G. Brown, K. Kirk, E. Rutsky, and H. Dustan
  1989 Renal insufficiency in treated essential hypertension. *New England Journal of Medicine* 320:684-688.
Saunders, A., W. Strittmatter, D. Schmechel, P. George-Hyslop, and M. Pericak-Vance
  1993 Association of apolipoprotein E allele e4 with late-onset familial and sporadic Alzheimer's disease. *Neurology* 43:1467-1472.
Schmidt, R., M. Hayn, F. Fazekas, P. Kapeller, and H. Esterbauer
  1996 Magnetic resonance imaging white matter hyperintensities in clinically normal elderly individuals: Correlations with plasma concentrations of naturally occurring antioxidants. *Stroke* 27:2043-2047.
Schrijvers, C., K. Stronks, D. van de Mheen, J. Coebergh, and J. Mackenbach
  1994 Validation of cancer prevalence data from a postal survey by comparison with cancer registry records. *American Journal of Epidemiology* 139(4):408-414.
Schulte, P., and Rothman, N.
  1998 Epidemiological validation of biomarkers of early biological effect and susceptibility. Pp. 23-32 in *Biomarkers: Medical and Workplace Applications*, M. Mendelsohn, L. Mohr, and J. Peeters, eds. Washington, DC: Joseph Henry Press.
Seeman, T., L. Berkman, D. Blazer, and J. Rowe
  1994a Social ties and support and neuroendocrine function: MacArthur Studies of Successful Aging. *Annals of Behavioral Medicine* 16:95-106.
Seeman, T., P. Charpentier, L. Berkman, M. Tinetti, J. Guralnik, M. Albert, D. Blazer, and J. Rowe
  1994b Predicting changes in physical performance in a high functioning elderly cohort: MacArthur studies of successful aging. *Journal of Gerontology* 49:M97-M108.
Seeman, T., and B. McEwen
  1996 Social environment characteristics and neuroendocrine function: The impact of social ties and support on neuroendocrine regulation. *Psychosomatic Medicine* 58:459-471.
Seeman, T., B. McEwen, B. Singer, M. Albert, and J. Rowe
  1997a Increase in urinary cortisol excretion and declines in memory: MacArthur Studies of Successful Aging. *Journal of Clinical Endocrinology and Metabolism* 82:2458-2465.

Seeman, T., B. Singer, R. Horwitz, and B. McEwen
    1997b The price of adaptation—allostatic load and its health consequences: MacArthur Studies of Successful Aging. *Archives of Internal Medicine* 157:2259-2268.
Singer, B. and C. Ryff
    1999 Hierarchies of life histories and associated health risks. *Annals of the New York Academy of Sciences* 896:96-115.
Smith, J., and R. Kington
    1997a Demographic and economic correlates of health in old age. *Demography* 34(1):159-170.
    1997b Race, socioeconomic status, and health in late life. Pp. 106-162 in *Racial and Ethnic Differences in the Health of Older Americans*, L. Martin and B. Soldo, eds. Washington, DC: National Academy Press.
Snowdon, D., M. Gross, and S. Butler
    1996 Antioxidants and reduced functional capacity in the elderly: Findings from the Nun Study. *Journal of Gerontology: Medical Science* 51A:M10-M16.
Sprott, R.
    1999 Biomarkers of aging. *Journal of Gerontology: Biological Sciences* 54:B464-B465.
Sternberg, E., G. Chrousos, R. Wilder, and P. Gold
    1992 The stress response and the regulation of inflammatory disease. *Annals of Internal Medicine* 117:854-866.
Svec, S., and A. Lopez
    1989 Antiglucocorticoid actions of dehydroepiandrosterone and low concentrations in Alzheimer's disease. *Lancet* 2:1335-1336.
Takaki A., Q.H. Huang, V.A. Somogyvari, and A. Arimura
    1994 Immobilization stress may increase plasma interleukin-6 via central and peripheral catecholamines. *Neuroimmunomodulation* 1:335-342.
Taylor, S., R. Repetti, and T. Seeman
    1997 Health psychology: What is an unhealthy environment and how does it get under the skin? *Annual Review of Psychology* 48:s411-447.
Tracy, R., E. Bovill, D. Yanez, B. Psaty, L. Fried, G. Heiss, M. Lee, J. Polak, P. Savage, and the Cardiovascular Health Study investigators
    1995 Fibrinogen and Factor VIII, but not Factor VII, are associated with measures of subclinical cardiovascular disease in the elderly: Results from the Cardiovascular Health Study. *Arteriosclerosis, Thrombosis and Vascular Biology* 15:1269-1279.
Tracy, R., R. Lemaitre, B. Psaty, D. Ives, R. Evans, M. Cushman, E. Meilahn, and L. Kuller
    1997 Relationship of C-reactive protein to risk of cardiovascular disease in the elderly: Results from the Cardiovascular Health Study and the Rural Health Promotion Project. *Arteriosclerosis, Thrombosis and Vascular Biology* 17:1121-1127.
Troxler, R.G., E.A. Sprague, R.A. Albanese, R. Fuchs, and A.J. Thompson
    1977 The association of elevated plasma cortisol and early atherosclerosis as demonstrated by coronary angiography. *Atherosclerosis* 26:151-162.
Uchino, B., J. Cacioppo, K. Kiecolt-Glaser
    1996 The relationship between social support and physiological processes: A review with emphasis on underlying mechanisms and implications for health. *Psychological Bulletin* 119:488-531.
Verbrugge, L.
    1983 The social roles of the sexes and their relative health and mortality. Pp. 221-245 in *Sex Differentials in Mortality: Trends, Determinants and Consequences*, A. Lopez and L. Ruzicka, eds. Canberra: Australian National University Press.

Verbrugge, L., and A. Jette
  1994   The disablement process. *Social Science and Medicine* 38(1):1-14.
Verhoef, P., M. Stampfer, J. Buring, J. Gaziano, R. Allen, S. Stabler, R. Reynolds, F. Kok, C. Hennekens, and W. Willett
  1996   Homocysteine metabolism and risk of myocardial infarction: Relation with vitamins B$_6$, B$_{12}$, and folate. *American Journal of Epidemiology* 143:845-859.
Waldron, I.
  1986   What do we know about causes of sex differences in mortality? A review of the literature. *Population Bulletin of the United States* 8:59-76.
Weaver, J.D., M. Albert, T. Harris, J.W. Rowe, and T.E. Seeman
  2000   Interleukin-6 as a predictor of cognitive function and cognitive decline (submitted).
Weinstein, M., and R. Willis
  2000   Stretching Social Surveys to Include Bioindicators: Possibilities for the Health and Retirement Study, Experience from the Taiwan Study of the Elderly. Paper prepared for the Workshop on Collecting Biological Indicators and Genetic Information in Household Surveys, National Research Council, Washington, DC, February 10-11.
Williams Jr., R.
  1985   Neuroendocrine response patterns and stress: Biobehavioral mechanisms of disease. Pp. 71-101 in *Perspectives on Behavioral Medicine: Neuroendocrine Control and Behavior*, v.2, R. Williams Jr., ed. Orlando, FL: Academic Press, Inc.
Wilson, T., G. Kaplan, J. Kauhanen, R. Cohen, M. Wu, R. Salonen, and J. Salonen
  1993   Association between plasma fibrinogen concentration and five socioeconomic indices in the Kuopio Ischemic Heart Disease Risk Factor Study. *American Journal of Epidemiology* 137(3):292-300.
Winkleby, M., D. Jatulis, E. Frank, and S. Fortmann
  1992   Socioeconomic status and health: How education, income and occupation contribute to risk factors for cardiovascular disease. *American Journal of Public Health* 82:816-820.
Wu, T., M. Trevisan, R. Genco, J. Dorn, K. Falkner, and C. Sempos
  1999   Periodontal disease as a risk factor for CVD, CHD, and stroke: The first National Health and Nutrition Examination Survey (NHANES I) and its follow-up study. *Circulation* 99(8):1109.
Zelinski, E., E. Crimmins, S. Reynolds, and T. Seeman
  1999   Do medical conditions affect cognition in older adults? *Health and Psychology* 17(6):504-512.
Zhou D., A. Kusnecov, M. Shurin, M. DePaoli, and B. Rabin
  1993   Exposure to physical and psychological stressors elevates plasma interleukin 6: Relationship to the activation of hypothalamic-pituitary-adrenal axis. *Endocrinology* 133:2523-2530.

3

Biological Material in Household Surveys: The Interface Between Epidemiology and Genetics

Kaare Christensen

Many traits—from health outcomes to behavior and wealth—have a tendency to run in families. Families share not only environment (including sociological and socialization factors), but also genetic factors. Epidemiologists have traditionally looked for environmental causes for variations in health outcome and behavior, while geneticists have focused on tracing genetic factors of importance. The interaction between these two research traditions has been surprisingly slow in emerging (e.g., the International Genetic Epidemiology Society was founded in 1991), although many researchers in both areas agree that the determinants of most health outcomes and behaviors are to be found in the interaction between genes and environment. Not only are both genes and environment etiological factors, but the effect of an environmental factor depends on the genetic background upon which it acts and vice versa. One of the major obstacles to conducting gene-environment interaction studies is that it usually requires large sample sizes to get reasonable statistical power to detect an interaction. The collection of biological material in sizeable household surveys could provide a sound basis for future gene-environment interaction studies.

The inclusion of biological material in household surveys can also improve information about environmental factors usually studied by epidemiologists, such as diet and exposure to heavy metal compounds and pesticides. Biological material in household surveys can be collected in many ways (e.g., blood, cheek brushes, saliva, urine, sperm, hair, and nails) for many purposes. For the interface between epidemiology and genetics, however, the genetic material—the DNA—is of the greatest interest, and due to technological developments DNA can now be obtained from very small samples of body fluids or tissues.

Genetic factors obviously play a central role in a broad range of monogenic diseases (i.e., diseases caused by mutation in one gene), from cystic fibrosis to Huntington disease to early-onset dementia. Most common diseases, however, are not monogenic, and are more likely to be influenced by a large number of environmental and genetic factors and their interactions. The first part of this chapter will consider the evidence for the impact of genetic factors on variations in survival, reproduction, health, and behavior—traits which are central to demographers and social scientists. The second part will describe examples of gene-environment interaction, point towards design options suitable for studying gene-environment interaction within the framework of a household survey, and provide estimates of required sample sizes. Finally, the feasibility of collecting biological material in household surveys will be evaluated based on a series of recent Danish surveys among middle-aged and elderly persons and the oldest-old, including such aspects as the methods for and the costs of, both monetary and in terms of potential response rate decrease, sampling biological material.

DO GENETIC FACTORS PLAY A SIGNIFICANT ROLE IN THE VARIATION IN SURVIVAL, REPRODUCTION, HEALTH, AND BEHAVIOR?

This is a central question when considering whether demographers and social scientists should include genetic material in household surveys. If there is no strong evidence that genetic factors play a role in the variation in a number of important traits, there seems to be little reason to undertake the logistic and ethical challenge of including genetic material in household surveys. Twin and adoption studies can estimate the overall genetic influence on a given trait, while other kinds of family studies are not very well suited to disentangle the effects of genes and common environment.

Adoption Studies

For logistical reasons adoption studies are much fewer and smaller than other kinds of family studies. Nevertheless, adoption studies have had a major impact on the nature-nurture debate concerning a number of traits, because these studies have produced remarkable results and their designs are easily understood and interpreted. Adoption studies use the fact that adoptees share genes but not environment with their biological families, and environment but not genes with their adoptive families. Among the most notable findings from adoption studies is one from Heston (1966), which showed that among 47 children who had schizophrenic mothers and who were adopted away, 5 developed schizophrenia, while none of the 50 control adoptees developed schizophrenia. Although the sample size is small, the study convincingly demonstrated that schizophrenia has a strong genetic component. Another intriguing finding that surprised many nongenetically oriented researchers comes from a Danish adoption study of body-mass index (weight in kilos divided by height in cm squared), which is a measure of body composition (obesity). This study showed that the body-mass index of adoptees correlated more with the body-mass index of their biological relatives than their adoptive relatives, indicating a strong genetic component to variation in body composition in settings with no shortage of food supply (Stunkard et al., 1986). An investigation of early-adult life mortality in the same study population similarly showed a genetic component to premature death (Sørensen et al., 1988). The adoption studies, however, are not without weaknesses. In particular, a bias can be introduced by selective placement of adoptees (i.e., the adoptees are preferably placed with adoptive parents who resemble the birth parents in some ways). This bias tends to overestimate the effect of both genetic and shared family environment.

Twin Studies

In humans two types of twinning occur: monozygotic (identical) twins, who share all their genetic material, and dizygotic (fraternal) twins, who on average share 50 percent of their genes, like ordinary siblings. A twin study of a condition/disease in its simplest form is based on a comparison of monozygotic and dizygotic concordance rates (i.e., the probability that a twin has the condition under study given that the co-twin has it). A significantly higher concordance rate in monozygotic than in dizygotic twins indicates that genetic factors play a role in the etiology. For continuous traits, intraclass correlations are used instead of concordance rates. The twin study does not identify specific genes that affect a given trait, but rather, assesses the overall effect of genetic factors: the degree to which differences in the phenotype are attributable to genetic differences between people. To estimate the heritability of a trait (i.e., the proportion of the population variance attributable to genetic variation), twin data can be analyzed using standard biometric models (Neale and Cardon, 1992).

A number of recent developments in twin methodology have taken place based on the incorporation of measured genotype information. This enables twin models to estimate how much of the genetic variation is due to variation in a specific gene. Gene-environment interaction studies, linkage analyses, and association studies can also be performed within a twin population.

As with adoption studies, twin studies are not without weaknesses. Of particular concern has been the "equal environment assumption," that is, the assumption that the degree of intrapair environmental similarity is the same in monozygotic and dizygotic pairs. If, in fact, the degree of environmental similarity is greater in monozygotic twins, then the heritability is overestimated.

Plomin et al. (1994) have made a comprehensive review of twin studies of a number of important medical and behavior disorders as well as personality traits (Figures 3-1, 3-2, and 3-3). Below is a description of recent twin studies of particular interest to demographers and social scientists.

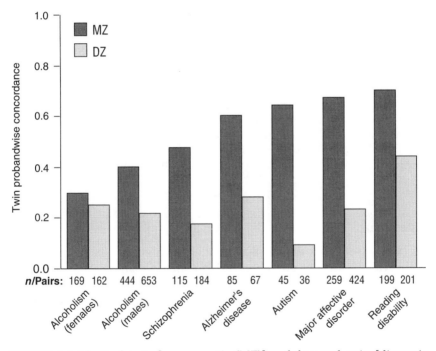

FIGURE 3-1 Identical twin [monozygotic (MZ)] and fraternal twin [dizygotic (DZ)] probandwise concordances for behavioral disorders. Average weighted concordances were derived from a series of studies. SOURCE: Reprinted with permission from R. Plomin, M.J. Owen, and P. McGuffin. 1994. The genetic basis of complex human behaviors. *Science* 264(5166):1733-1739. Copyright 1994, American Association for the Advancement of Science.

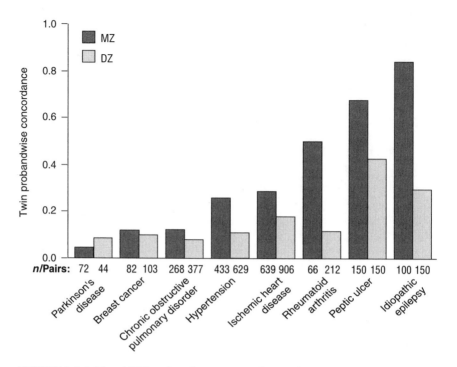

FIGURE 3-2 MZ and DZ probandwise concordances for common medical disorders. Average weighted concordances were derived from series of studies. SOURCE: Reprinted with permission from R. Plomin, M.J. Owen, and P. McGuffin. 1994. The genetic basis of complex human behaviors. *Science* 264(5166):1733-1739. Copyright 1994, American Association for the Advancement of Science.

Life Span

During the last decade a variety of twin studies have shown that approximately 25 percent of the variation in life span is caused by genetic differences. This seems to be a rather consistent finding in various Nordic countries in different time periods and even so among other species not living in the wild (Herskind et al., 1996; Iachine et al., 1999; Finch and Tanzi, 1997).

Reproduction

Kohler et al. (1999) studied the genetic dispositions influencing fertility and fertility-related behavior using Danish twins born in the period 1870-1964. It was found that genetic influences on fertility exist, and that

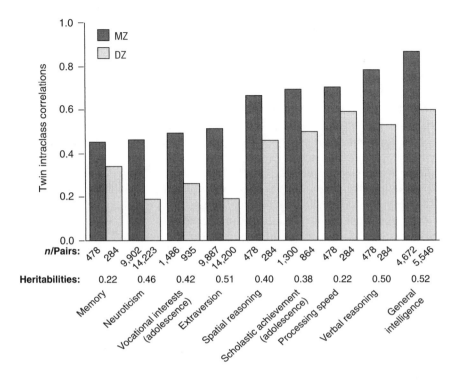

FIGURE 3-3 MZ and DZ twin intraclass correlations for personality (neuroticism and extraversion), vocational interests in adolescence, scholastic achievement in adolescence (combined across similar results for English usage, mathematics, social studies, and natural science), specific cognitive abilities in adolescence (memory, spatial reasoning, processing speed, verbal reasoning), and general intelligence. Average weighted correlations were derived from series of studies. SOURCE: Reprinted with permission from R. Plomin, M.J. Owen, and P. McGuffin. 1994. The genetic basis of complex human behaviors. *Science* 264(5166):1733-1739. Copyright 1994, American Association for the Advancement of Science.

their relative magnitude and pattern depend on sex and on the socioeconomic environment experienced by successive birth cohorts. Genetic effects were most pronounced in periods with consciously controlled fertility, suggesting that the genetic disposition primarily affects fertility behavior and motivation for having children. Analyses of fertility motivation in some of the more recent twin cohorts, measured by age at first attempt to have children, supported this interpretation.

Health and Diseases

For a number of diseases which occur in early or midlife, such as insulin-dependent diabetes and schizophrenia, twin studies have demonstrated the existence of a significant genetic component (Kyvik et al., 1995; Plomin et al., 1994). Genetic factors also influence cardiovascular diseases which occur in early or midlife, while for cardiovascular diseases occurring late in life there is little evidence of a genetic effect (Marenberg et al., 1994). Dementia has a very strong genetic component, not only with regard to early-onset monogenic types but also to late-onset dementia (Breitner et al., 1993; Gatz et al., 1997). Alternatively, twin studies provide little evidence of genetic factors in the etiology of Parkinson disease (Tanner et al., 1999). Twin studies of general physical functioning such as strength (younger individuals) or functional abilities (elderly individuals) show evidence of a considerable genetic influence, an influence that seems to increase with age (Christensen et al., 2000b).

Psychology and Behavior

The genetic component of physical abilities and diseases is usually broadly accepted. Similar claims regarding psychological and behavioral phenotypes often meet resistance, although a very large body of evidence suggests that heritabilities consistently range from 30 to 50 percent for personality, vocational interests, general intelligence, and scholastic achievement (Plomin et al., 1994). Depression symptomatology (Kendler et al., 1987; McGue and Christensen, 1997) and even proclivity to divorce (McGue and Lykken, 1992) have also been shown to have substantial genetic contributions to their etiology.

Summary: Phenotypes and Heritability

Twin and adoption studies suggest that a wide variety of phenotypes have a genetic component to their etiology. Naturally, it should be recognized that the heritability estimates are time- and population-specific, i.e., the overall influence of genetic factors depends on the amount of environmental variance in the study population and vice versa. If, for example, more equal access to favorable living conditions and health care is introduced in a population, this is likely to decrease the environmental variance and hence increase the proportion of the total variation attributable to genetic factors (i.e., the heritability). At the same time, an increase in environmental variance as seen in modern societies may also provide the opportunity for genetic effects to be expressed.

A substantial heritability for a trait suggests that it may be possible to identify specific genetic variants that influence the trait. The chance of identifying, through genetic association or family studies, gene variants affecting a trait depends on the number of gene variants and the size of their effect. At this point in time few important specific gene variants affecting variation in survival, fertility, health, and behavior are known, but this is likely to change within the next few years. Therefore, including genetic material in household surveys is not so much for immediate use as to ensure that the survey will be valuable in a future scenario where genetic covariates are likely to play an important role in the understanding of variations in traits. The most promising aspect emerging from the identification of specific genes influencing various traits is that this may be the basis for insight into the underlying biological processes and, in particular, how genes interact with the environment. An understanding of such gene-environment interactions can lead to environmentally based prevention or treatment of unwanted conditions or diseases with a strong genetic component, as described in the next section.

GENE-ENVIRONMENT INTERACTIONS

The classic example of gene-environment interaction is phenylketonuria, an inborn error of metabolism. This disease is caused by a mutation in a gene on chromosome 12 (coding for the enzyme phenylalanine hydroxylase). If a child inherits a mutated gene from both the father and the mother, the child will be severely mentally retarded if it consumes an ordinary diet during childhood. However, a child with two copies of this mutation can have a normal development if he or she gets a diet low in phenylalanine and supplemented with tyrosine, thereby bypassing the lack of enzyme problem. Most countries in the industrialized world screen for this defect among newborns, which makes it possible to prevent the effects of a genetic defect through modification of the environment, in this case the diet.

Another example is Smith-Lemli-Opitz syndrome (SLOS), first described in 1964. SLOS also requires two mutated copies to develop in a fetus. Craniofacial anomalies are predominant, in addition to limb and genital anomalies, failure to thrive, and mental retardation. SLOS is thought to be the second most common autosomal recessive disorder among white North Americans after cystic fibrosis, with a carrier frequency of 1 to 2 percent. Molecular research has shown that SLOS results in an error in cholesterol synthesis. Insight into the etiology of this genetically determined disease has induced a medical treatment that may reduce some of the postnatal symptoms. The treatment is a diet high in cholesterol (Tint et al., 1994).

The two diseases described above are very rare. However, common genetic variants with a moderate or even small effect on prevalent diseases are likely to be of great importance on a population level, although at present few such genetic variants have been documented. The best example is the gene coding for apolipoprotein E (APOE), a protein that ferries cholesterol through the blood stream. Three common variants of this gene (APOE e2, APOE e3 and APOE e4) are found, which are slightly different forms of the protein. Despite the small differences, the e4 variant has been consistently associated with a moderately increased risk of both cardiovascular diseases and Alzheimer disease (Corder et al., 1993).

Not only has APOE e4 been shown to be a risk factor for cardiovascular diseases and Alzheimer disease per se, but several studies have found that the e4 variant is involved in gene-environment interaction, making the e4 carrier more susceptible to environmental exposures. For example, an increased risk of chronic brain injury after head trauma has been observed for individuals who carry the e4 gene variant, compared to non-e4 carriers (Jordan et al., 1997). APOE e4 also seems to modulate the effect of other risk factors for cognitive decline. Individuals with APOE e4 in combination with atherosclerosis, peripheral vascular disease, or diabetes mellitus have a substantially higher risk of cognitive decline than those without APOE e4 (Haan et al., 1999). The APOE genotype has also been found to influence the effect of alcohol on blood pressure in middle-aged men (Kauma et al., 1998) and to increase the risk of neurological diseases after HIV infection (Corder et al., 1998). It seems likely that APOE e4 is just one of many common genetic variants in the estimated 50,000 to 100,000 genes in the human genome that increase susceptibility for environmental exposures.

Design Options for Gene-Environment Interaction Studies Within Household Surveys

Within the framework of a household survey, there are two major design options for studying gene-environment interactions: the cohort study and the so-called "nested case-control study."

Cohort Studies

This design uses the entire study population of persons at risk for the outcome of interest and follows this cohort over time. The cohort study design is feasible if the cost of genotyping (e.g., of APOE variants) is inexpensive. In this case, the APOE genotype can be determined for all participants who have provided a biological sample, and all outcomes studied can be stratified not only on sex and age but also on APOE genotype. For example, if one wanted to study cardiovascular diseases, survey participants within a reasonable age range and free of cardiovascular diseases at intake would be genotyped and followed over time. Traditional survival analysis could then be used to assess the effect of the different APOE genotypes on cardiovascular disease risk. In cohort studies, the assessment of gene-environment interactions can be done by comparing the disease-free survival of individuals stratified on genotype (e.g., +/- APOE e4) and exposure to the environmental factor (+/-), or by using standard techniques such as Cox regression analysis.

Nested Case-Control Studies

This design is an attractive option if the outcome of interest is a rare disease/condition or if the assessment of the gene variant is expensive (which today is often the case, but this is likely to change within a few years). In the nested case-control study, all new cases of the phenotype of interest (e.g., cardiovascular diseases) are included as well as one to four controls selected from the study base. Including more than four controls results in a limited increase in statistical power (Rothman, 1986). The method for selection of controls from the survey population is essential, and must include consideration of factors such as the ethnic background of the cases and the controls (for more details, see Rothman and Greenland, 1998, and Khoury et al., 1993).

Only the biological samples from the cases and the one to four controls per case are analyzed for the gene variants of interest. From the frequencies of the gene variants in the case and the control group, the odds ratio can be estimated, which is approximately equal to the relative risk associated with an allele if the outcome studied is not too common (i.e., less than 5 percent of the population studied will get the disease/ condition). Gene-environment interactions are assessed by stratifying on genotype; i.e., the relative risk associated with the exposure is estimated for each genotype separately—most often using a multivariate logistic regression analysis with interaction terms (Hosmer and Lemeshow, 1989). However, as seen in Figure 3-4, several hundred cases and controls are required to detect modest interaction terms, and some researchers argue that in some scenarios the estimated sample size requirement in Figure 3-4 may be underestimated (Garcia and Lubin, 1999). Household surveys, therefore, will often be one of the best methods to fulfill sample size requirements.

Problems in Gene-Environment Studies within Household Surveys

Household surveys are most often conducted with lay interviewers, which places certain constraints on which phenotypes can be studied. For

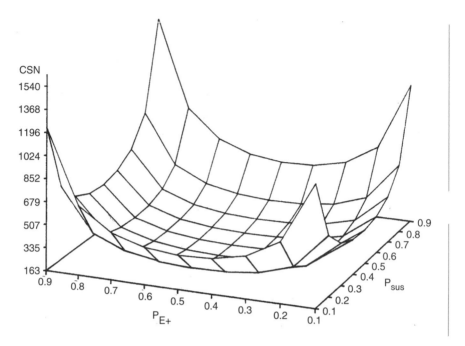

FIGURE 3-4 Number of cases required for 80 percent power at a 5 percent Type I error in a case-control study designed to detect gene-environment interaction with two controls per case over a series of frequencies of exposure (e.g., head trauma) and proportions of susceptibility (e.g., proportion of ApoE-4 carriers). The proposed odds ratio of interaction equals 4 (i.e., the exposure is associated with a four times higher risk among susceptibles compared to nonsusceptibles). SOURCE: Reprinted with permission from S.-J. Hwang, T.H. Beaty, et al. 1994. Minimum sample size estimation to detect gene-environmental interaction in case-control designs. *American Journal of Epidemiology* 140(11):1029-1037. Copyright 1994, Oxford University Press.

example, in medically oriented surveys, cognitive abilities and depression symptomatology can be assessed, but a dementia or depression diagnosis according to internationally recognized criteria can be obtained only in follow-up studies with the assessment done by specialists.

The biggest challenge to gene-environment interaction studies in the years to come will probably be a multiple comparison problem. With 50,000-100,000 genes being identified, many of which are likely to have several variants, an enormous number of possible gene-environment interactions can be studied. To choose a significance level in statistical testing of gene-environment interaction seems difficult. The most reasonable strategy probably will be testing of biologically plausible interactions and verification of positive findings in large studies, which again points towards the important role that household surveys can play in future gene-environment studies.

FEASIBILITY OF COLLECTING BIOLOGICAL MATERIAL IN HOUSEHOLD SURVEYS

The Danish 1995-1999 Experience

Since 1995 our group at The Aging Research Center at the University of Southern Denmark and the Danish Center for Demographic Research has conducted six major surveys: The Longitudinal Study of Aging Danish Twins (three waves in 1995, 1997, and 1999, respectively: LSADT-95, LSADT-97, LSADT-99), The Longitudinal Study of Middle-Aged Twins, The Danish 1905-Cohort Survey, and The Danish Centenarian Study, together comprising more than 10,000 individuals. These surveys provide an opportunity to evaluate the logistic impact of including biological material in ongoing household surveys with lay interviewers in populations of middle-aged and elderly persons and the oldest-old, and to compare such surveys with smaller scale studies done by medically trained persons. Table 3-1 gives an overview of the size of the surveys and their participation rates.

The Longitudinal Study of Aging Danish Twins (LSADT)

In 1995, LSADT began by assessing all cooperating Danish twins aged 75 years and older (a sample of nearly 2,500 individuals). The assessment

TABLE 3-1 Surveys Conducted at the Aging Research Center at the University of Southern Denmark and the Danish Center for Demographic Research in the Period 1995-1999

	Mean Age	Age Range	Participants	Interview Response Rate %
LSADT-95	81	75-102	2,401	77
LSADT-97	77	73-102	2,172	79
LSADT-99	76	70-101	2,709	72
Middle-aged twins	57	46-67	4,314	83
The 1905-cohort	92	92-93	2,262	63
The Centenarian Study	100	100	207	75

was repeated in 1997 by including all twins who participated in 1995 as well as a sample of previously unassessed twin pairs who were between 73 and 76 years old in 1997. In 1999, we included all Danish twins aged 70 years and older. By 1999, over 5,000 individuals aged 70 years and older had completed the LSADT intake assessment, nearly 3,500 individuals had completed a two-year follow-up assessment, and nearly 1,000 individuals had completed both a two- and four-year follow-up assessment. Additional assessments are planned for 2001 and 2003.

The first two waves (1995 and 1997) included anthropometric measures and questions on sociodemographic factors, lifestyle habits, self-rated health, diseases, sensory deficit, symptoms, medications, physical abilities, depression symptomatology, family history, and social life. Cognitive abilities were assessed using the Mini Mental State Examination (Folstein et al., 1975) and a number of other tests. The 1997 wave used the same survey instrument. In the 1999 wave, the survey instrument was expanded to include physical performance tests, measurement of lung functioning (spirometry), and sampling of DNA by self-administered finger prick or cheek brushes (see details about DNA sampling in a later section of this chapter) (Christensen et al., 1996, 1998, 1999, 2000a, 2000b; Yashin et al., 1998; Andersen-Ranberg et al., 1999; Kohler et al., 1999).

The Longitudinal Study of Middle-Aged Twins

To complement the LSADT studies with a twin study of middle-aged twins, we identified a random sample of twin pairs born between 1931 and 1952 through the Danish Twin Registry (Kyvik et al., 1996; Skytthe et al., 1998). In 1999, more than 5,000 twins aged 46-67, including monozygotic twins and fraternal twins of same and opposite sex, were invited to participate in an extensive face-to-face interview conducted by lay interviewers, which included tests of physical and cognitive function. The questionnaire, which was based on the LSADT questionnaire, included items on the twins' current and childhood socioeconomic status, social network, self-rated health, diseases, use of medications, lifestyle habits, physical activity at work and during leisure time, reproductive history, and a brief food frequency questionnaire (Gaist et al., 2000). The same procedure used in LSADT was implemented for DNA sampling.

The Danish 1905-Cohort Survey

In order to study nonagenarians, all Danes born in 1905 were invited in 1998 to participate in a home-based two-hour multidimensional interview that included cognitive and physical performance tests. The interview instrument was similar to the LSADT instrument and carried out by the same lay interviewers. Population-based registers were used to evaluate representativeness. Participants and nonparticipants were highly comparable with regard to marital status, institutionalization, and hospitalization patterns, but men and rural residents were more likely to participate than women and urban residents. Despite the known difficulties of conducting surveys among the very old, the study showed that it was possible to conduct a nationwide survey of more than 2,000 fairly representative nonagenarians using lay interviewers. Again, the LSADT procedure was used for DNA sampling (Nybo et al., in press).

The Longitudinal Danish Centenarian Study

This study is a nationwide survey of all persons living in Denmark who celebrated their 100th birthday during the period April 1, 1995, to May 31, 1996. The residence of all centenarians in the study population was identified through the Civil Registration System by the personal identification number of each centenarian. Approximately two weeks after their 100th birthday, all centenarians received a letter explaining the study, and their permission was sought to allow a geriatrician and a geriatric nurse to visit in order to interview them and carry out a physical examination including phlebotomy. More than 200 centenarians participated (Andersen-Ranberg et al., 1999).

What Does Inclusion of Biological Material Cost in Terms of Interview Participation Rate?

The LSADT studies have response rates of 72-79 percent, which many regard as very good for extensive surveys among the elderly (Table 3-1). The best way to estimate the participation cost of including biological material in an ongoing survey is to compare the 1997 (no biological sampling) response rate for LSADT-95 participants with the 1999 (biological sampling) response rate for individuals who participated for the first time in LSADT-97. For these two subgroups the participation rates were 81 and 80 percent, respectively, indicating that the costs in terms of decrease in interview participation rate in this setting are minimal. It should be noted, though, that Denmark has a free, national health care system, which may enhance participation because insurance and out-of-pocket costs are of less importance compared to the United States, for example. Although the participants in the studies do not receive any information about their health, the surveys are conducted by a medical school, which in itself may make the participants more willing to provide a biological sample.

More disappointing was the survey of the 1905-cohort, which had only a 63 percent participation rate, although analyses of register data on all eligible nonagenarians indicated that the responders were fairly representative. There are several probable reasons for the lower response rate in the 1905-cohort. The group is uniformly very old, and it may not be obvious to people born in 1905 (or their relatives) that they could be of interest to science; hence they may be less committed to participating. The centenarian study showed a considerably higher response rate compared to The Danish 1905-Cohort Survey. This is probably due to the "celebrity status" of centenarians and to the fact that the survey was done by a geriatrician and a geriatric nurse.

How to Obtain DNA from the Participants by Means of a Finger Prick and Cheek Brushes

The same procedure for DNA sampling was used in The Danish 1905-Cohort Study, The Danish Middle-Aged Twins Study, and LSADT-99 without any notable logistic problems. In these investigations, participants were asked to donate a DNA sample in the form of a blood spot or, if they disliked the idea of blood spots, by means of cheek brushes. A full blood sample of approximately 20 ml would have been preferable because the amount and analytical options are much greater, but this would require a second visit to the participants by a trained phlebotomist (usually a hospital technician) and would approximately double the survey expenses. DNA could also have been obtained by other methods such as mouth lavage or urine (see Wallace in this volume), but we found these methods logistically less appealing.

Finger Prick

The blood spots were made by the participants themselves, guided by the interviewer, using a sterile automated incision device (Tenderfoot®) with a standardized incision depth of 1.0 mm and length of 2.5 mm. This device has a safety clip, which prevents the premature release of the blade, and a retracting blade, which improves safety by protecting both participant and interviewer from injury due to an exposed blade contaminated with blood (Figure 3-5). The participant chose one of the three lateral fingers on either the right or left hand, and the chosen finger was warm, dry, and clean. The Tenderfoot safety clip was removed and the device was positioned longitudinally at the site of the distal part of the chosen finger and triggered. The first drop of blood was wiped away and the next blood drops distributed to the blood spot card. On the blood spot card there are five roundels, and we aimed at collecting three or four drops of blood on each roundel (in total 5 cm^2) (Figure 3-6). The blood spot card was air dried and sent to a laboratory the same day, after being

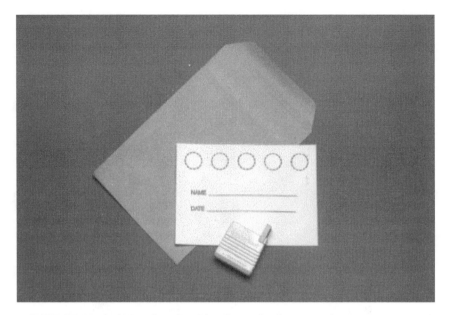

FIGURE 3-5 Utensils for obtaining blood spots by finger prick in connection with household surveys. The blood spots can be made by the participants guided by the interviewer using the sterile automated incision device (e.g., Tenderfoot[R]) with a standardized incision.

marked with the date, the interview subject number, and the number of the interviewer. Only the blood spot was sent to the laboratory, so that the identity of the participant was unknown to the laboratory, ensuring that all analyses and genotyping were done blinded. To avoid catastrophic sample loss, the blood spots were divided in two and are kept in two locked locations. The blood spot cards are stored in boxes at room temperature. The utensil cost was $2-3 per person and the interview time averaged 5-10 minutes depending on age, but with large variation.

Cheek Brushes

Alternatively, the DNA sample was taken by means of cheek brushes (Figure 3-7). Three cheek brushes were used for each subject. Again the samples were self-collected by the participant, guided by the interviewer. The brush was inserted in the mouth and twirled firmly against the inner cheek for 30 seconds. This process collects cells from which to obtain the DNA. The brush was placed in the original tube and the cap replaced. A

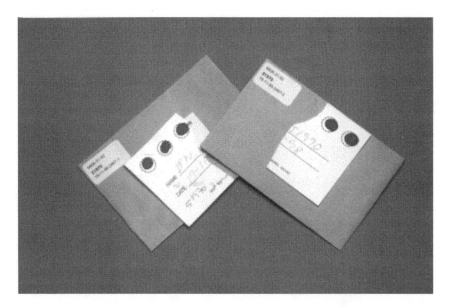

FIGURE 3-6 To avoid sample loss, the blood spots are divided in two and kept in two different locations.

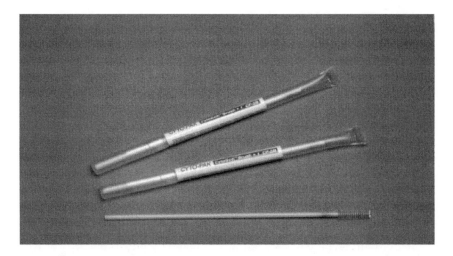

FIGURE 3-7 Brushes used to obtain biological samples from the inner cheek in connection with household surveys. The samples can be collected by the participant guided by the interviewer. The brush is inserted in the mouth and twirled firmly against the inner cheek for 30 seconds. This process collects cells from which to obtain the DNA.

new place on the inner side of the cheek was chosen for each brush. Every brush was labeled with the date, the participant number, and the number of the interviewer, and sent to the laboratory the same day (arrived the next day). In the laboratory the brush head was placed in a tube and kept at –80° C until the isolation of DNA took place (within one month). The utensil cost was $3-4 per person and the interview time averaged 2-5 minutes depending on age, but with large variation.

Participation in DNA Sampling

Naturally, the respondents in these surveys could choose to participate only in the interview and not the biological sampling (Table 3-2). The reason for lower participation in the DNA sampling among the oldest participants is proxy interviews: when a person in the study population was unable to participate (most often due to dementia), we tried to identify a relative who could answer on behalf of that person (a proxy interview). For ethical reasons we did not sample DNA from the participant in connection with proxy interviews.

For nonproxy participants, the difference in participation rate between the surveys was modest: 97 percent in the survey of middle-aged twins (mean age 57) versus 90 percent in both LSADT-97 (mean age 76) and the 1905-Cohort Study. As seen in Table 3-2, the percentage of cheek brush samples is highly dependent on age: nearly all middle-aged participants provided DNA by finger prick, while among the oldest-old a fifth of the DNA samples were cheek brushes.

TABLE 3-2 Surveys Conducted at the Aging Research Center at the University of Southern Denmark and the Danish Center for Demographic Research in the Period 1998-1999, Which Included Collection of Biological Material by a Finger Prick or Cheek Brush

		Biological Samples				
	Participants	No.	% of Participants	% of Nonproxy Participants	Blood Spots %	Cheek Brushes %
The 1905-cohort	2,262	1,632	72	90	80	20
LSADT-99	2,709	2,319	86	90	91	9
Middle-aged twins	4,314	4,171	97	97	95	5
TOTAL	9,285	8,122	87	93	93	7

Storage and DNA Quality Control

The success of any data-intensive project is dependent on the ability to store and retrieve data. It is important to have a facility that is used to handling large numbers of biological samples. In the surveys mentioned above, the Department of Clinical Biochemistry at Odense University Hospital takes care of the registration, storage, and retrieval of the samples. This department handles 3 million biochemical analyses each year, and therefore an addition of some 10,000 samples did not impose major logistic problems. As mentioned, the biological samples are kept anonymously and apart from the information obtained during the interview, but the information is linkable through the participants' ID numbers. For quality control we have determined APOE gene variants on a subsample of the blood spots and the cheek brushes with a success rate of 99 percent. Based on our experience, the DNA isolated from cheek brushes is of a sufficient quantity and quality to perform at least 200 genotypings for each brush, while each blood spot card can provide DNA for approximately 2,000 genotypings. DNA can be obtained from blood spot cards stored for decades at room temperature (Strobel et al., 1998; Makowski et al., 1996). Although experiences with storing cheek brushes for longer time periods are few, it seems likely that storage at –80° C will preserve the DNA for decades.

CONCLUSION

Collecting biological material in household surveys is feasible. From the perspective of the interface between epidemiology and genetics, collection of genetic material is valuable because genetic factors do play a role in many traits of interest to demographers and social scientists. The identification of genes of importance and their interaction with the environment can provide the basis for prevention and treatment of unwanted conditions through modification of environmental factors.

ACKNOWLEDGMENT

This research was supported by a grant from the Danish National Research Foundation and the National Institute of Aging (P01-AG08761). David Gaist, M.D., Ph.D., Hanne Nybo, M.D., and Karen Andersen-Ranberg M.D. coordinated the surveys, and Lise Bathum, M.D., Ph.D., established the biobank. Bernard Jeune, Matt McGue, and James W. Vaupel played a major role in planning these studies.

REFERENCES

Andersen-Ranberg, K., K. Christensen, B. Jeune, A. Skytthe, L. Vasegaard, and J.W. Vaupel
    1999   Declining physical abilities with age: A cross-sectional study of older twins and centenarians in Denmark. *Age and Ageing* 28:373-377.
Breitner, J.C., M. Gatz, A.L. Bergem, J.C. Christian, J.A. Mortimer, G.E. McClearn, L.L. Heston, K.A. Welsh, J.C. Anthony, M.F. Folstein, et al.
    1993   Use of twin cohorts for research in Alzheimer's disease. *Neurology* 43(2):261-267.
Christensen, K., D. Gaist, B. Jeune, and J.W. Vaupel
    1998   A tooth per child? *Lancet* 352:204.
Christensen, K., N.V. Holm, M. McGue, L. Corder, and J.W. Vaupel
    1999   A Danish population-based twin study on general health in the elderly. *Journal of Aging and Health* 11:49-64.
Christensen, K., N.V. Holm, and J.W. Vaupel
    1996   Alzheimer's disease in twins. *Lancet* 347:976.
Christensen, K., M. Kristiansen, H. Hagen-Larsen, A. Skytthe, L. Bathum, B. Jeune, K. Andersen-Ranberg, J.W. Vaupel, and K.H. Ørstavik
    2000a   X-linked genetic factors regulate hematopoietic stem-cell kinetics in females. *Blood 2000* 95(7):2449-2451.
Christensen, K, M. McGue, A.I. Yashin, I.A. Iachine, N.V. Holm, and J.W. Vaupel
    2000b   Genetic and environmental influences on functional abilities among Danish twins aged 75 years and older. *Journals of Gerontology: Medical Sciences* 55A(8):M446-M452.
Corder, E.H., K. Robertson, L. Lannfelt, N. Bogdanovic, G. Eggertsen, J. Wilkins, and C. Hall
    1998   HIV-infected subjects with the E4 allele for APOE have excess dementia and peripheral neuropathy. *Nature Medicine* 4:1182-1184.
Corder, E.H., A.M. Saunders, W.J. Strittmatter, D.E. Schmechel, P.C. Gaskell, G.W. Small, A.D. Roses, J.L. Haines, and M.A. Pericak-Vance
    1993   Gene dose of apolipoprotein E type 4 allele and the risk of Alzheimer's disease in late onset families. *Science* 261:921-923.
Finch, C.E., and R.E. Tanzi
    1997   Genetics of aging. *Science* 278(5337):1996-1998.
Folstein, M.F., S.E. Folstein, and P.R. McHugh
    1975   "Mini-mental state." A practical method for grading the cognitive state of patients for the clinician. *Journal of Psychiatric Research* 12:189-198.
Gaist, D., L. Bathum, A. Skytthe, T.K. Jensen, M. McGue, J.W. Vaupel, and K. Christensen
    2000   Strength and anthropometric measures in identical and fraternal twins: No evidence of masculinization of females with male co-twins. *Epidemiology* 11(3):340-343.
Garcia, C.M. and J.H. Lubin
    1999   Power and sample size calculations in case-control studies of gene-environment interactions: Comments on different approaches. *American Journal of Epidemiology* 149:689-692.
Gatz, M., N.L. Pedersen, S. Berg, B. Johansson, K. Johansson, J.A. Mortimer, S.F. Posner, M. Viitanen, B. Winblad, and A. Ahlbom
    1997   Heritability for Alzheimer's disease: The study of dementia in Swedish twins. *Journal of Gerontology: Medical Sciences* 52(2):M117-125.
Haan, M. N., L. Shemanski, W.J. Jagust, T.A. Manolio, and L. Kuller
    1999   The role of APOE epsilon 4 in modulating effects of other risk factors for cognitive decline in elderly persons. *Journal of the American Medical Association* 282:40-46.

Herskind, A.M., M. McGue, N.V. Holm, T.I. Sorensen, B. Harvald, and J.W. Vaupel
  1996 The heritability of human longevity: A population-based study of 2872 Danish twin pairs born 1870-1900. *Human Genetics* 97:319-323.
Heston, L.L.
  1966 Psychiatric disorders in foster home reared children of schizophrenic mothers. *British Journal of Psychiatry* 112:819-825.
Hosmer, D.W., and S. Lemeshow
  1989 *Applied Logistic Regression.* New York: John Wiley and Sons.
Hwang, S.J., T.H. Beaty, K.Y. Liang, J. Coresh, and M.J. Khoury
  1994 Minimum sample size estimation to detect gene-environment interaction in case-control designs. *American Journal of Epidemiology* 140(11):1029-1037.
Iachine, I.A., N.V. Holm, J.R. Harris, A.Z. Begun, M.K. Iachina, M. Laitinen, J. Kaprio, and A.I. Yashin
  1999 How heritable is individual susceptibility to death? The results of an analysis of survival data on Danish, Swedish and Finnish twins. *Twin Research* 1(4):196-205.
Jordan, B.D., N.R. Relkin, L.D. Ravdin, A.R. Jacobs, A. Bennett, and S. Gandy
  1997 Apolipoprotein E epsilon 4 associated with chronic traumatic brain injury in boxing. *Journal of the American Medical Association* 278:136-140.
Kauma, H., M.J. Savolainen, A.O. Rantala, M. Lilja, K. Kervinen, A. Reunanen, and Y.A. Kesaniemi
  1998 Apolipoprotein E phenotype determines the effect of alcohol on blood pressure in middle-aged men. *American Journal of Hypertension* 11:1334-1343.
Kendler, K.S., A.C. Heath, N.G. Martin, and L.J. Eaves
  1987 Symptoms of anxiety and symptoms of depression: Same genes, different environments? *Archives of General Psychiatry* 44:451-457.
Khoury, M.J., T.H. Beaty, and B.H. Cohen
  1993 *Fundamentals of Genetic Epidemiology.* New York/Oxford: Oxford University Press.
Kohler, H.P., J.L. Rodgers, and K. Christensen
  1999 Is fertility behaviour in our genes? Findings from a Danish twin study. *Population and Development Review* 25:253-288.
Kyvik, K.O., K. Christensen, A. Skytthe, B. Harvald, and N.V. Holm
  1996 The Danish twin register. *Danish Medical Bulletin* 43:467-470.
Kyvik, K.O., A. Green, and N.H. Beck
  1995 Concordance rates of insulin dependent diabetes mellitus: A population based study of young Danish twins. *British Medical Journal* 311:913-917.
Makowski, G.S., E.L. Davis, and S.M. Hopfer
  1996 The effect of storage on Guthrie cards: Implications for deoxyribonucleic acid amplification. *Annals of Clinical and Laboratory Science* 26:458-469.
Marenberg, M.E., N. Risch, L.F. Berkman, B. Floderus, and U. de Faire
  1994 Genetic susceptibility to death from coronary heart disease in a study of twins. *New England Journal of Medicine* 330:1041-1046.
McGue, M., and K. Christensen
  1997 Genetic and environmental contributions to depression symptomatology: Evidence from Danish twins 75 years of age and older. *Journal of Abnormal Psychology* 106:439-448.
McGue, M. and D.T. Lykken
  1992 Genetic influence on risk of divorce. *Psychological Science* 3:368-373.
Neale, M.C., and L.R. Cardon
  1992 *Methodology for Genetic Studies of Twins and Families.* Dordrecht: Kluwer Academic Publisher.

Nybo, H., D. Gaist, B. Jeune, L. Bathum, M. McGue, J.W. Vaupel, and K. Christensen
in   The Danish 1905-Cohort. A genetic-epidemiological nationwide survey. *Journal*
press   *of Aging and Health.*
Plomin, R., M.J. Owen, and P. McGuffin
    1994   The genetic basis of complex human behaviors. *Science* 264:1733-1739.
Rothman, K.J.
    1986   *Modern Epidemiology.* Boston/Toronto: Little, Brown and Company.
Rothman, K.J., and S. Greenland
    1998   *Modern Epidemiology.* Second Edition. Philadelphia: Lippincott-Raven Publishers.
Skytthe, A., N.V. Holm, J.W. Vaupel, and K. Christensen
    1998   Establishing a population-based register of middle-aged twins in Denmark (abstract). *Twin Research* 1(2):110.
Sørensen, T.I., G.G. Nielsen, P.K. Andersen, and T.W. Teasdale
    1988   Genetic and environmental influences on premature death in adult adoptees. *New England Journal of Medicine* 318(12):727-732.
Strobel, E., C. Emminger, G. Mayer, J. Eberle, and L. Gurtler
    1998   Detection of HIV 1 infection in dried blood spots from a 12 year old ABO bedside test card. *Vox Sanguinis.* 75:303-305.
Stunkard, A.J., T.I. Sorensen, C. Hanis, T.W. Teasdale, R. Chakraborty, W.J. Schull, and F. Schulsinger
    1986   An adoption study of human obesity. *New England Journal of Medicine* 314:193-198.
Tanner, C.M., R. Ottman, S.M. Goldman, J. Ellenberg, P. Chan, R. Mayeux, and J. Langston
    1999   Parkinson disease in twins: An etiologic study. *Journal of the American Medical Association* 281:341-346.
Tint, G.S., M. Irons, E.R. Elias, A.K. Batta, R. Frieden, T.S. Chen, and G. Salen
    1994   Defective cholesterol biosynthesis associated with the Smith-Lemli-Opitz syndrome. *New England Journal of Medicine* 330:107-113.
Yashin, A.I., I.A. Iachine, K. Christensen, N.V. Holm, and J.W. Vaupel
    1998   Genetic component of discrete disability traits: Liability models with age dependent thresholds. *Behaviour Genetics* 28:207-214.

4

Demography in the Age of Genomics: A First Look at the Prospects

Douglas Ewbank

The popular consensus seems to be that genetics is the wave of the future. Information technology was the driving force that changed our economy and our society during the late twentieth century. Genetics is expected to have similar effects on medicine and the social sciences during coming decades. The 1980s and 1990s produced numerous developments in molecular biology, statistics, and computer technology. These developments make it easier to associate observed traits (e.g., diseases, risk factors for disease, personality traits, or differences in protein structures) with specific genes. The resulting changes in our understanding of genetics are so profound that Weiss (1996) has suggested they may amount to a paradigm shift. A few examples suggest the speed of change.

- The first *positional cloning* (identification of a gene by virtue of its location in the genome rather than by its biochemical function) occurred in 1986. By 1990, when the Human Genome Project (HGP) began, only a handful of genes had been identified this way. The discovery of the gene for Huntington's chorea came in 1993, ten years after it was learned that it had to be near one end of chromosome 4. Improvements in molecular biology have greatly speeded up this process. By 1997 the number of genes identified by positional cloning was close to 100 (Collins et al., 1997).
- The development of new statistical techniques for studying complex traits was marked in 1993 by the publication of three textbooks in

genetic epidemiology (Weiss, 1993; Khoury, 1993; Schulte and Perera, 1993). This development continued through the 1990s with improved computer programs and estimation procedures. Recent developments have reopened the debate about the best way to find genes associated with complex traits (Risch and Merikangas, 1996; Long et al., 1997; Bell and Taylor, 1997; Gambaro et al., 2000).

• The HGP's first five-year plan, for 1993-1998, was to map the human genome using marker loci. By 1994, they had already published a map with about three times the resolution that they had planned for 1998. They have now sequenced and checked over 50 percent of the genome thus providing a complete description of the genome of a "consensus" individual. This was accomplished well ahead of the goal set for 2003.

The revolution in genetic epidemiology was just becoming apparent in 1989 when there was a meeting of geneticists and demographers to discuss "convergent issues in genetics and demography" (Adams et al., 1990). Reading the resulting volume, it is clear that in 1989 there really were no issues pulling demographers and geneticists together. Genetics was just getting to the point where it could begin to address the kinds of questions that interest demographers. Now, more than ten years later, the nature of the revolution in genetics is clearer and we can begin to consider how it might affect demography.

For demographers, and for social scientists in general, there are several options for dealing with genetics. The first is simply to ignore it. Since we are primarily interested in the social and behavioral factors affecting demographic variables, there is a temptation to ignore genetic differences. This may be a reasonable option as long as ignoring genetics doesn't distort our estimates of the effects of social and behavioral factors. A second option is to use samples of twins (or other related individuals) to control for unobserved heterogeneity associated with genetics. However, samples of twins are hard to collect, especially when there is a need for twins raised apart in different environments. In addition, twin studies don't allow us to directly address questions about the importance of specific genes. This makes it difficult to understand differences between populations and to forecast the potential impact of developments in genetic medicine.

The third strategy is to include in our analyses data on the genetics of individuals or gene frequencies for populations. Adding genetic information to our analyses could reduce the amount of unobserved heterogeneity and produce estimates of the contribution of specific genes to variations among individuals or across populations. This is not yet a real option. As long as most of the genes that have been identified are associated with rare diseases (like Huntington's chorea or sickle cell anemia), the potential impact of genetics on demographic research is very limited. However, genetic epidemiologists are now searching for genes that have large effects on common conditions. During the next ten years this might lead to discoveries that will substantially alter demographic research.

This paper examines how future research on complex traits made possible by the HGP will affect demography. There are two ways in which demographic research might change. First, research on the genetic basis for common diseases and mortality will benefit from applications of demographic multistate modeling. Eventually, this could change epidemiology more than demography. Second, research on the determinants of health and behaviors could expand to include controls for genetic differences. As more genes are linked to common diseases and behaviors, adding genetic data into statistical analyses will become more attractive. However, it is important to be realistic about what we can expect from genetics. In particular, demographers need to think about what kinds of genetic associations will be useful for our purposes.

Before turning to the implications for demography of new development in genetics, it is useful to examine the developments in genetic epidemiology during the past 15 years. This review provides a framework within which to discuss the likely developments in genetics in the next five to ten years.

AN OUTLINE OF GENETIC EPIDEMIOLOGY

The revolution in genetics has been driven largely by developments in molecular biology. However, for demographers the important changes can be more easily described through developments in genetic epidemiology.[1] *Genetic epidemiology* is study of the relationship between *genotypes* (the particular combination of genes carried by an individual) and *phenotypes* (observable traits). The choice of statistical methods depends on whether the trait is *quantitative* (i.e., a continuous variable like body weight) or *qualitative* (i.e., a discrete variable such as being overweight or a case of diabetes). Genetic variation results from errors in chromosome

---

[1]Ridley's popular book *Genome: The Autobiography of a Species in 23 Chapters* (1999) provides a fascinating review of the history of genetics and an exceptionally clear discussion of the complexity of inheritance revealed by recent research. Weiss (1996) provides a summary of how the developments of the 1980s and early 1990s have moved genetics away from a simple Mendelian view. Lander and Schork (1994) provide a nonstatistical discussion of the basic approaches in genetic epidemiology. Weiss (1993) presents the basic statistical methods and an excellent overview of human evolution. A brief overview of the molecular biology that makes the HGP possible can be found in a series of articles by Ellsworth and Manolio (1999a, 1999b, and 1999c) which include excellent glossaries of important terms.

duplication which lead to different forms of a gene (termed *alleles*). The most common difference among alleles is single base-pair differences called *single-nucleotide polymorphisms* (SNPs). Some mutations render the gene completely incapable of performing its intended function, but most alleles have no noticeable effect on gene functioning. Most genes have only one allele with high frequency and many (often hundreds) rare alleles (Weiss, 1993).

An individual's genotype is defined by the particular combination of alleles he or she carries. Relatively common alleles (found in 1 percent or more of a population) are termed *polymorphisms*. A gene is not apt to explain much of the variation in risk in a population unless it has common polymorphisms or numerous different alleles that are all associated with substantial excess risk. *Major* genes or *oligogenes* for quantitative traits are usually defined as those for which the mean values for two genotypes differ by at least 2.5 times the standard deviation within genotypes (Weiss, 1993).

Most variables of interest to demographers are what genetic epidemiologists call *complex traits*. They are traits that are affected by numerous genes as well as the environment and interactions between environment and genotype. Variables like mortality, health status, and limitations of activities of daily living are extreme cases of complex traits. However, even the individual health problems that demographers consider as components of health and mortality are very complex.

The genetics revolution started with breakthroughs that increase the ability of genetic epidemiology to link specific genes with individual traits. The identification of the genes responsible for specific traits then forms the basis for all of the other aspects of the genetic revolution including the promises of medical genetics and the potential future use of genetic information in demographic research. Recent developments will greatly increase the rate of discovery of genes associated with complex traits.

It is useful to distinguish four areas of research in genetic epidemiology in humans. The first two examine the role of genetic factors without reference to specific genes. The third area involves research to identify relevant genes by determining their position on individual chromosomes. The fourth area uses genetic differences between populations to study the origin of populations.[2]

---

[2]Genetic research in nonhuman populations often involves cross-breeding which enables researchers to increase the frequency of a trait (and therefore the associated genes). It can also be used to increase genetic heterogeneity.

Twin and Family Studies of the Contribution of Genetics to Observed Differences Among Individuals

Genetic epidemiologists have long relied on studies of twins and other related individuals to estimate the relative importance of genetics in determining various traits. They apply variance component models to decompose differences in quantitative traits (like blood pressure) into components associated with genetics, family environment, individual unshared traits, and interactions among these factors. Different sample designs give information about different factors. For example, comparisons of *monozygotic* (identical) and *dizygotic* (fraternal) twins provide estimates of the contribution of genetics. Comparisons of monozygotic twins raised apart provide estimates of the contribution of shared environment. One outcome of these studies is estimates of *heritability*, the proportion of the variation in the distribution of a quantitative trait that is explained by genetics.[3] For example, a study of Danish twins estimated that about 25 percent of the variation in life span is genetically determined (Herskind et al., 1996). Twin studies have produced estimates of heritability for a wide range of traits. For example it has been estimated that genes explain 25 percent to 50 percent of the variation in the risk of cancer, IQ scores, risk-taking behavior, and sexuality. Estimates of heritability are responsible for much of the excitement (and anxiety) surrounding recent developments in genetics.

Demographers and economists have occasionally applied variance component models to twin data (e.g., Behrman et al., 1994). However, they have also used data on twins as controls for genetics to improve estimates of the effects of other variables. For example, they have used data on twins to control for genetic endowments and improve estimates of the economic returns to education (Miller et al., 1995; Behrman et al., 1996).

Inheritance Patterns for Genetically Determined Traits

Studies of families to determine inheritance patterns use *segregation analysis*. By examining the proportions of siblings (or more distant relatives) that exhibit a trait, it is possible to distinguish various genetic patterns (e.g., a single recessive gene) and to estimate the rate of *penetrance* (the probability of developing the trait given a specific genotype). Until the late 1980s this research was primarily focused on *Mendelian models*, that is, qualitative traits caused by single genes with a high rate of penetrance. This research led to an expansion of genetic counseling. It was

---

[3]The equivalent measure for qualitative traits is a relative risk.

generally most successful for diseases associated with clearly defined outcomes with high penetrance and young ages at onset. Recently, the focus has shifted to the search for genes associated with variation in quantitative traits. Quantitative traits are generally *multifactorial* and *polygenic*, that is, they are determined by the interaction of several genes or between genes and environment.[4] Individual genes contributing to a quantitative trait are called *QTLs* (quantitative trait loci).

The inheritance patterns of traits associated with multiple genes are much more difficult to discern. During the 1980s advances in statistical techniques and computer speed led to the development of QTL models. These models assume that a trait is controlled by one or two important genes with moderate to large effects (termed *oligogenes*) and numerous other genes with much smaller effects (jointly termed *polygenes*). These models require strong assumptions about the distributions of the relative importance of these genes including the number of oligogenes. A brief overview of segregation models is provided by Weiss (1990). His textbook on genetic epidemiology (1993) provides a more complete discussion.

Segregation studies are complicated by gene-environment interactions. For example, segregation studies in families that exhibit large variation in relevant environmental variables may fail to identify oligogenes. Also, segregation analyses performed in populations with different environments may lead to very different conclusions because the genetic effects may be masked by the environment.

The Search for Genes Responsible for Specific Traits

The study of inheritance patterns only provides evidence that there are genes associated with a given trait. The next step is to identify the specific *loci* (i.e., locations on chromosomes) that contain these genes. There are two approaches to locating the loci associated with specific traits.

The first is *association studies*. The simplest association studies compare a trait to the presence of known alleles of a *candidate gene*.[5] For quantitative traits this involves samples of cases and controls. Studies of quantitative traits test for differences in means among genotypes. Candidate genes are often associated with a known protein. For example, the

---

[4]However, see Weiss (1993) for a discussion of the quantitative variability caused by different alleles of a single gene (PAH) associated with PKU, phenylketonuria, a well-known genetic disease.

[5]Gambaro et al. (2000) discuss the difficulties in selecting candidate genes. They note that association studies are actually based on candidate *alleles*, which are even more difficult to identify than candidate *genes*.

vitamin D receptor gene was a logical candidate for involvement in osteo-porosis (Ralston, 1997). Alternatively, genes identified through rare alleles can be tested for the effects of more common alleles. For example, rare mutations of the genes encoding type I collagen (COLIA1 and COLIA2) lead to a severe osteoporotic condition. Therefore, a more common poly-morphism is a candidate for explaining the more common osteoporosis (Ralston, 1997). The list of candidate genes will probably expand rapidly once the human genome is completely sequenced (Guo and Lange, 2000).

In the absence of a candidate gene, it is possible to do a *whole-genome scan* to look for genes associated with a trait. Testing correlations at many loci raises the problem of multiple comparisons. However, recent analyses have demonstrated that whole-genome scans can be efficient methods for identifying genes associated with specific traits even after adjusting for multiple comparisons (van den Oord, 1999). However, whole-genome scans require a large number of candidate alleles or SNPs, not just candi-date genes. The HGP and other groups are beginning to address this need (see below). The availability of a large number of known alleles may make association studies the method of choice for identifying the genes associated with complex traits.

Association studies are prone to two common problems that can lead to spurious correlations. First a gene may show a close correlation with the trait because it is very close to the true causal gene on the same chromosome (see the discussion of linkage below).[6] This can lead to close associations in one population that are not replicable in other populations since the correlations among neighboring genes will differ among popu-lations. A second problem is *population admixture*. In a population, a trait that is more common in one ethnic group will appear to be correlated with any allele that also happens to be more common in that group. Therefore, association studies should be performed in relatively homoge-neous populations like Finland and Iceland and in small populations of individuals descended from a small number of ancestors.[7]

The second approach, involving techniques such as *linkage analysis, fine mapping,* and *positional cloning,* has been the predominant method used for genetic research during the past decade. It enables researchers to identify first a region of a chromosome, and then a gene based solely on

---

[6]With incomplete mapping of SNPs, it is also possible to find a spurious correlation with an SNP in a noncoding region, which cannot affect a trait. In this way, SNPs can act like marker loci to identify the neighborhood within a gene in which a relevant allele is located (Collins et al., 1997).

[7]Another solution to this problem is to use a sample of affected individuals and their parents to control for differences in allele frequencies among populations (van den Oord, 1999).

the position of the gene without any knowledge of its function. Linkage takes advantage of the fact that the chromosomes inherited from your parents are not always passed on to your children intact. Instead, the two copies of the chromosome sometimes exchange segments (called *recombination*). Because of recombination, it is possible to associate the inheritance of a trait with the inheritance of a segment of a chromosome. Loci that are physically close to each other on a chromosome are more apt to remain together after recombination. Loci that are very close will be in *linkage disequilibrium*.[8] It is therefore possible to examine the frequency of the trait in relation to the occurrence of *genetic markers* (known sequences of nucleotides that occur at specific locations on chromosomes). The relevant gene probably lies between the two markers that are most highly correlated with the presence of the trait. The more markers that are available, the smaller the area identified by linkage analysis. The first goal of the HGP was to produce a finer genetic map to improve the precision of linkage studies.

Linkage analysis leads to a candidate region of a chromosome. For example, linkage analysis suggested that there was a gene associated with the risk of Alzheimer's disease (AD) in the long arm of chromosome 19 (labeled 19q).[9] The gene can then be identified within this region through fine mapping based on positional cloning (Ellsworth and Manolio, 1999b). The gene for AD turned out to be the gene for apolipoprotein E (Corder et al., 1993), which is described below. Fine mapping is a time consuming process since there can be hundreds of genes between markers. This process will be eased by the complete sequencing of the human genome.

Linkage studies require large *pedigrees* (i.e., families in which the trait in question is unusually common). Linkage can be very difficult for traits that don't follow Mendelian inheritance (i.e., a single gene with few alleles). It is also difficult in the case of common alleles. When the risky allele is common, many individuals will be homozygous for the risky allele. Since the two copies of the allele may be linked with different markers, inheritance may not always be associated with the same marker. This problem complicated early linkage studies of Alzheimer's disease and the identification of a linkage to chromosome 19 (Lander and Schork, 1994; Corder et al., 1993).

---

[8]If the two loci were not linked, the inheritance of an allele of one gene would be independent of the inheritance of an allele of the other gene. Independent inheritance is associated with equilibrium when there is random mating. Therefore, correlated risks of joint inheritance of two alleles constitute disequilibrium.

[9]The short arm of each chromosome is labeled p and the long arm is q.

Studies of the Origins of Human Populations

A third area of research applies knowledge about the geographic distribution of a few dozen alleles (often including genes for blood type) or markers of genotype (e.g., lactose intolerance) to infer historical relationships among populations (Cavalli-Sforza et al., 1994). When combined with archeological and linguistic evidence, these maps provide important insights into the origin of man, ancient migration streams (Owens and King, 1999), and the role of evolution in human history. An excellent example of the use of mapping is research on the geographic distribution of lactose malabsorption (Simoons, 1978; Weinberg, 1999).

The Human Genome Project

The HGP will significantly increase the speed of discovery of genes associated with specific traits. Linkage analysis and genome-wide scans depend on the availability of numerous markers and maps of the genes that lie between them. The mapping of the human genome will provide a very detailed map, thereby increasing the ability to narrow in on the specific loci associated with a given trait. This development, combined with improved statistical methods and expanded computer power, makes possible large-scale searches for the genes associated with complex traits. The full sequencing will also expand the identification of candidate genes based on an understanding of the functioning of genes (Guo and Lange, 2000).

Weiss (1998) points out that the HGP was originally designed to produce a map for an "average" individual. To social scientists it is genetic diversity that is important. Heterogeneity is also central to genetic epidemiology research on humans. The only way we can study the action of a gene is by observing mutations which alter gene functioning. The study of diversity was added to the goals of the HGP in 1998. The goal is mapping 100,000 polymorphisms involving SNPs by 2003 (Collins et al., 1998), taking advantage of the diversity of the U.S. population. Although this is a huge number, it is estimated that there are about 200,000 SNPs in protein-coding regions (cSNPs) which are apt to be most important for understanding disease (Collins et al., 1997). A second project involving the Wellcome Trust and ten international pharmaceutical partners was formed in 1999 to identify 300,000 DNA variants (Cardon and Watkins, 2000).

DEMOGRAPHY AND THE GENETICS OF COMPLEX TRAITS

Developments in genetic epidemiology during the past fifteen years have greatly expanded the opportunities for identifying the genes associated with variation in complex quantitative traits. As more genes are identified, the potential gain from incorporating genetic information into demographic research will increase dramatically.

Measured genotypes associated with common traits are in some ways ideal variables for the kinds of research conducted by demographers and other social scientists. The reason is simple: genotype is fixed at birth. This has two implications for the relationship between genetics and demography. First, demographic models are ideally suited to the study of fixed traits. Second, we can add genetic information to our statistical models and improve the fit without introducing complex correlations associated with joint causation.

The following sections discuss potential applications of demographic models to the study of complex traits, and the use of genetic information in research on standard demographic variables. These are the two areas where developments in genetic epidemiology are apt to have the biggest impact on demography and demography is apt to have the biggest impact on epidemiology.

Demographic Models for Studying Major Genes Affecting Common Diseases

Once a gene for a common, complex condition has been identified, there will be numerous questions about its effect in populations. These problems are apparent in research on the only known gene like this, the apolipoprotein E gene (APOE). APOE is so unique and so heavily studied that few discussions of genetics can avoid using it as an example. It is a major risk factor for both ischemic heart disease (IHD) (Wilson et al., 1996) and Alzheimer's disease (AD) (Corder et al., 1993; Farrer et al., 1997). The APOE gene has three common polymorphisms labeled e2, e3, and e4.[10] Therefore, individuals have one of six possible genotypes, e2/2, e2/3, e2/4, e3/3, e3/4, or e4/4. The e3/3 is the most common genotype, comprising about 60-70 percent in all populations. The e3/4 and e4/4 genotypes are associated with increased risk of both IHD and AD. The e2/2 and e2/3 genotypes are associated with reduced risk of AD.

One issue raised by the discovery of major genes involves differences in the amount of excess risk at different ages. For example, the effect of APOE e4 on the risk of AD increases with age up to about age 60 and declines at the oldest ages (Farrer et al., 1997). Similarly, a segregation analysis of the risk of lung cancer suggests that there is a major gene that

---

[10]Numerous very rare mutations of the APOE gene have also been discovered. However, there has been little research examining the effects of these mutations.

has a very large effect on the risk under age 60, but only marginal effects after age 80 (Gauderman and Morrison, 2000). The genetic effects on breast cancer also change with age (see discussion below). These changes might be the result of unobserved heterogeneity in the risks of disease, cohort trends in risk (e.g., Colilla et al., 2000), or changes in the nature of the disease with age. For example, very early onset AD might involve a very different natural history than AD at later ages.

A second complication arises when a gene is associated with more than one disease. For example, the gene for the vitamin D receptor appears to affect bone density. Alleles that reduce bone density might increase the risk of osteoporosis but reduce the risk of osteoarthritis (Uitterlinden et al., 1997). Most epidemiologic research examines individual diseases. For example, almost all of the research on APOE examines only its relationship with AD or with IHD. One reason for this is that few studies include both a thorough examination for dementia and precise diagnoses of cardiac events or measures of serum lipids. Case-control studies in particular are designed to study one well-defined condition.

A third set of issues arises when two or more major genes are identified as being associated with the same disease. Since most epidemiologic research focuses on the effects of single genes, there may be little direct evidence of the combined effects of several genes. If the effects of different genes are not additive, estimates of the effects of alleles of one gene might differ between populations because of unobserved differences at other loci. The interactions of the two genes can be very complex especially if the gene frequencies differ across populations or the effects of each gene change with age. For example, mutations of the PS-1 and PS-2 genes are associated with very early onset AD (Lendon et al., 1997). It appears that the increase in the relative risks of AD under age 60 associated with the e4 allele of APOE are due to complications introduced by PS-1 and PS-2 (Ewbank, unpublished results).

Combining Disparate Studies

These problems complicate research on mortality differences by APOE genotype. The APOE e4 allele is clearly associated with increased risk of death due to both IHD and AD, at least in males (Ewbank, 1999). There are numerous studies that suggest the importance of APOE for mortality, but few provide direct evidence of mortality differentials by genotype. No single study is large enough to provide solid evidence of the effect of APOE on mortality at various ages. Therefore, it is necessary to combine studies to understand the effects of APOE genotype on the level and age pattern of mortality at the oldest ages.

The process of comparing and combining studies is complicated by the fact that published analyses present different types of data. For example, the published analysis of data from the Kungsholmen Project in Sweden provides estimates of excess risk of death over a seven-year period by APOE genotype for a cohort (Corder et al., 1996). Eichner et al. (1993) provide data from a case-control study showing excess risk associated with the e4 allele. Stengård et al. (1995) provide data on the APOE allele frequencies (i.e., the proportion of alleles, not individuals, that are of each APOE type) for survivors and decedents over a five-year period. Several studies document that the e4 allele is less common among centenarians than among octogenarians, which suggests excess mortality (Schächter et al., 1994; Asada et al., 1996; Louhija et al., 1994). Each of these studies provides evidence of excess risk of death associated with the e4 allele. However, the measures provided by the studies are not comparable.

Demographic multistate models are ideally suited to dealing with these issues. Since genotype is a fixed trait, it is possible to develop a basic multistate model and apply it separately to each genotype with different risks. Early efforts in this regard include work by Yashin et al. (1999). The model can easily incorporate multiple causes of death, age patterns of onset of disease that incorporate heterogeneity, and, if necessary, duration of disease. If two or more major genes are involved, the multistate model can be applied separately to each combination of genotypes. If there are subgroups in the population defined by nongenetic characteristics (e.g., race/ethnicity or sex), these can be incorporated as well. The effects of different combinations of risk by genotype on the total population can be studied by merely summing the l_x or $_nL_x$ columns for the subgroups to get a multistate table for the whole population.

Genetic epidemiology has developed most of the tools necessary for identifying the genes associated with common complex diseases. However, once those genes have been identified demographers and epidemiologists will have to develop the tools to study their joint impact on health and mortality. Demographic multistate models will become increasingly important for sorting out the interactions between multiple genes and diseases.

POTENTIAL USES OF GENETIC INFORMATION IN DEMOGRAPHIC RESEARCH

The recent revolution in genetic epidemiology means that demographers will increasingly have the option of including measured genotypes in their data collection and analyses. Several areas of demographic research are particularly ripe for including information on the genotypes of individuals.

The following sections discuss various applications. The first is the use of genes in demographic research on the social correlates of health status, mortality, and other demographic events. This discussion examines the potential impact of genetic information on analyses based on linear regression, logistic regression, or survival analysis. The second section discusses the potential value to studies of the age pattern of mortality or onset of ill health at older ages, i.e., the potential contribution of genetic information to understanding heterogeneity in frailty. The third area is the potential value of genetic information in research on differences between populations, including cross-national comparisons and differences by race and ethnicity. The fourth section considers how the discovery of genes associated with behavior might change demographic research. The fifth section discusses the potential importance to demography of longevity genes, or "gerontogenes." The final section discusses a few examples of epidemiologic surveys that include genetic information. Data from these surveys might be useful for the development of methods for incorporating genetics into demographic research.

These discussions lead to the concept of "demogenes." These genes have a sufficiently large impact that their effects are important at the population level. The number of demogenes discovered in the next decade will determine how much impact genetics has on demography during the next twenty years.

Genetic Information in Studies of Differences Among Individuals

To understand what demography would gain from genetic information, we have to consider the range of analytical approaches that constitute the bulk of current demographic research. Much demographic research is based on regression-type statistical methods. The outcome of interest, y, might be death, the onset of disability, savings behavior, or retirement. This is generally related to a vector of social and behavioral variables, X. We are now considering what would be gained by adding a vector of genetic characteristics, G. The resulting generalized linear model is:

$$f(y_i) = \alpha + \beta \mathbf{X}_i + \Gamma \mathbf{G}_i + n \mathbf{X}_i \mathbf{G}_i. \tag{1}$$

The choice of the functional form for $f(y)$ determines whether the model is a simple linear regression; a logistic, probit, or Poisson regression; or some other model. The following paragraphs examine how genetic information might be utilized in linear regression, logistic regression, and survival analysis to study the effect of social, economic, and behavioral characteristics on demographic variables. Each type of analysis highlights different issues.

Predicting Status or Explaining Variance

Segregation analyses of numerous traits, including longevity, suggest that we will not explain more than 60-90 percent of the variance in many outcomes if we ignore genetics. However, sample sizes in the largest surveys are too small to capture all of the variance attributable to genetic variation in standard regression-type analyses. We will generally have to focus on a small number of genes that are most relevant to our research. For a gene to be useful for statistical analysis it would have to have common alleles associated with large differences in the dependent variable. An allele (or a group of alleles) found in only 0.01 percent of the population, or that increased risk by only 0.01 percent, contributes very little to understanding the distributions of demographic variables.

An alternative is to develop ways of combining data from multiple sources to control for the effects of rare genotypes. For example, we might combine data from a demographic survey with data from case-control studies. The case-control samples would provide power for estimating the effects of rare genotypes but they include very few social and behavioral variables. Therefore, we would need methods for combining data sets that do not include all of the same variables. A simple method is to impose estimates of the effects of the genotypes from epidemiologic studies on the analysis of data from a demographic survey. For example, we could adjust observed blood pressure measurements for known differences between genotypes. Similarly, we could use offsets in Poisson regressions to incorporate the combined effect of many genotypes. This approach would be relatively easy to implement, would allow controls for even the rarest genotypes, and could make use of published estimates from the case-control studies or from meta-analyses.

However, using point estimates from case-control surveys would exaggerate the precision of the resulting estimates. Even the largest case-control studies produce estimates with large confidence intervals. Fully utilizing external sources of information to inform adjustments would require maximizing the joint likelihood of observing the data reported in different data sets. Methods for imputing missing data could be adapted to this problem.

Genes as Controls to Improve Estimates of the Effects of Other Variables

In some cases excluding genetic variables, the $\Gamma \mathbf{G}_i$ term in equation (1), might lead to biased estimates of the effects of social and behavioral variables, the β. In linear regression, excluding a relevant variable from the analysis does not bias the estimates of the parameters of interest unless that variable is highly correlated with the independent variable of interest. However, this is not apt to be the case. A genotype that is associated with a health outcome (e.g., a gene associated with cancer) is not apt to also be highly correlated with behavioral risk factors (e.g., diet, smoking, etc.).[11] In particular, since genotype is not determined by choice, we don't have the problem of joint determination that often causes problems in social research.[12]

The problem is somewhat different in logistic regression. Omitting a variable biases the estimates of the other coefficients even if there is no correlation between the omitted variable and the variable of interest. However, in the absence of interaction effects the magnitude of the bias is related to the magnitude of the effect of the omitted variable. To have a noticeable effect, an omitted genotype would have to be an important determinant of the probability of the event in question. Therefore, excluding genetic determinants from analyses of differences in health and behavior is not apt to be a frequent source of significant error.

Genes as Effect Modifiers

Recent developments in the methodologies for linkage analysis and association studies have increased the power of genetic epidemiology to study gene-environment interactions (Yang and Khoury, 1997; van den Oord, 1999). For demographers, controlling for genotype is potentially important when it interacts with social or behavioral variables. In equation (1), effect modifiers are shown as the interaction term $n\,X_i\,G_i$, which genetic epidemiologists often refer to simply as GxE. The full effect of the behavioral variables is misspecified if the interaction term is omitted. Gene-environment interactions would cause serious biases only if alleles associated with significant interactions with environmental variables were very common.

For example, there are two common alleles that probably have significant interactions with a high-fat diet. Carriers of the APOE e4 allele may be more susceptible to the effects of high-fat diets on the risk of death due

---

[11]An exception would be genes that are risk factors for behaviors. An example would be genotypes that increased the risk of addiction to alcohol or nicotine. In these cases the intermediate-variables model is actually inverted. The effect of such a genotype on health would work through the intermediate behavior variable. However, if demographers are only interested in the link between the behavior and the outcome, there may be little gained by incorporating the genetic risk factors for the behavior since the selectivity associated with the genotype is not apt to be correlated with other behaviors of interest to demographers.

[12]There is a chance that some genes that cause ill health at early ages might affect social status variables determined at young ages, such as education or marital status.

to ischemic heart disease. Similarly, the 825T allele of the gene for the G protein β3 subunit (GNB3) appears to be associated with obesity (Siffert et al., 1999). If the relationship of the 825T allele to obesity is replicated, understanding the effect of diet on health might require interaction terms between diet and the APOE and GNB3 genotypes. Understanding these interactions might also be important for predicting future trends in mortality. In particular, African populations have high allele frequencies for the risky genotypes of both genes (allele frequencies of about 20 percent for the e4 allele of APOE and about 80 percent for the 825T allele of GNB3) and may therefore be particularly susceptible to the health and mortality risks associated with a high-fat diet (Zekraoui et al., 1997; Corbo et al., 1999; Siffert et al., 1999).

Genes as Instrumental Variables

Research on the relationship between health and social status variables is complicated by the fact that social, economic, and health variables are so intertwined. For example, we might want to control for health status when studying the economic correlates of labor force participation. However, we will never be able to measure all of the determinants of participation rates. If some of the unmeasured determinants are also correlated with health status (for example, psychological variables, family history, or personal circumstances), then the regression estimates will be biased. This would affect the estimates of all of the coefficients, not just the coefficient of health status. One approach to this problem is the use of instrumental variables. This involves replacing the health status variable with variables that are highly correlated with health status but not correlated with the unobserved variables. Although this approach is good in theory, it is generally very difficult to find appropriate instrumental variables.

Genetic information might be useful as instrumental variables. Since genotype is determined at birth, it is not affected by any aspects of life history. If sufficient genetic information were available to identify a substantial fraction of those with high risks of health problems, we could replace actual health status with measures of genetic risk of health problems. However, we are rarely interested in controlling for specific health conditions, and overall health status is determined by a large number of genes. Therefore, the value of genes as instrumental variables for health status will depend on the number of common genotypes associated with excess risk of the most common health problems.

Genes as Sources of Heterogeneity in Survival Analysis

In introducing a 1990 volume edited by Adams, Hermalin, Lam, and Smouse entitled *Convergent Issues in Genetics and Demography*, Julian Adams suggested that

> [p]erhaps the most striking difference in approach and paradoxically the best hope for a convergence of the two fields can be seen in the way in which the fields view within-population variation (p. 10).

A third of the book is devoted to the section entitled "Heterogeneity, Phenotypic Variation, and Frailty." Demographers are primarily interested in studying the variation associated with social and behavioral variables. However, other sources of variation cannot be safely ignored in survival analyses and multistate models. In Trussell and Rodrigues's (1990) review of statistical approaches to handling "unobserved" heterogeneity they conclude that:

> The methods proposed to correct for unobservable heterogeneity deliver less than is commonly assumed, particularly because of an inherent non-identifiability involved when the analyst must rely on observables to assess goodness-of-fit (p. 129).

Incorporating genetic information into large demographic surveys would reduce the amount of heterogeneity that is unobserved. This would reduce the importance of the mathematical assumptions about the distribution of unobserved frailty.

The next section discusses the effects of unobserved heterogeneity in a different context. The conclusions from that discussion apply here as well. In summary, it is not likely that we will be able to use standard regression techniques to control for many genotypes. Therefore, the contribution of genetic information to controlling for heterogeneity will depend on the discovery of a few genes associated with a large fraction of the unobserved heterogeneity.

Genetic research also might provide evidence of the functional form for the distribution of risks (Weiss, 1990). This would improve our controls for unobserved heterogeneity even if demographic surveys did not collect genetic information for individuals. This possibility was suggested by several of the authors in *Convergent Issues in Genetics and Demography*. However, several notes of caution are in order. First, genetics is only one of the sources of unobserved heterogeneity. Unobserved differences in behavior (e.g., attitudes toward health care, disease prevention behaviors) and in personal history (previous illnesses, accidents, etc.) have a significant impact on the health of the elderly. Therefore, firm estimates of the distribution of genetic risk factors would not completely solve the problem of choosing a functional form for unobserved heterogeneity.

Second, genetic epidemiology is focused on gene finding. Their study designs and research agendas may not lead to useful information on the overall distribution of genetic risk. If demographers want to use genetic information to derive functional forms for the distribution of genetic frailty, we may have to tackle that question ourselves. Estimating the distribution of genetic frailty would require combining information on the co-occurrence of risky genotypes, the relative risks of each genotype, and information on how those risks are combined to form total risk. Large-scale demographic surveys could provide data for examining the distribution of risk associated with both genetic and behavioral variables.

Genes and Demographic Models of the Age Pattern of Mortality

The rate of increase in mortality at the oldest ages can be thought of as the result of two factors: (1) the increase in risk with age for individuals, and (2) variation in risk among individuals. We only observe the way mortality increases with age in a population, not the risks for individuals or the distribution of risks across individuals. However, we want to understand how individuals age. To do this, we either have to explain most of the variation among individuals or model the effects of unobserved variation on the rates for a population.

This problem can be illustrated using a simple simulation. We assume that the age pattern of mortality for white males in the United States results from averaging two hypothetical subgroups: one with low risk and one with elevated risk. We assume that at birth half of the population has low risk and half has high risk. We assume that the high-risk subgroup has a mortality rate three times that of the low-risk subgroup at every age. At age 50, the population composition is essentially the same as at birth and the risk for the population is close to the average of the risks for the subgroups. However, only about 0.2 percent of the high-risk subgroup survives to age 100, compared to 12 percent of the low-risk subgroup. Therefore, at age 100 the average risk in the population is very close to the risk in the low-risk subgroup.

If we ignored the existence of two subgroups, we would guess that the risk for an individual increases by a factor of 7.5 between ages 70 and 90. However, this increase is based on the overall population, which is 39 percent high risk at age 70 and 3.4 percent high risk at age 90. In fact, within each subgroup the risk increases by a factor of 9.5. Thus by ignoring heterogeneity we get a distorted picture of the effects of age and aging on individuals. Vaupel has stated that this is the "fundamental problem . . . for analyses of age-trajectories of mortality" (1997:25).

We rarely know anything about the number of subgroups that comprise the total population or about the variation in mortality among them.

We can estimate the age pattern of risk in individuals from population data if we assume functional forms for the age pattern for individuals and for the distribution of risks in the population (Manton et al., 1986). However, since the risks for individuals are unobservable and the distribution of risks across individuals is unknown, it is not possible to test the plausibility of our assumptions. We can improve our understanding of aging by reducing the amount of heterogeneity that is unobserved. Much of the unobserved variation in mortality risks is due to genetic variation. If a few genes were responsible for a large part of the variation in the risk of death, we could reduce the problem of unobserved heterogeneity by modeling mortality separately for subgroups defined by their genotype.

The model described above of a population composed of two subgroups provides insight into the types of genes that will be useful for reducing unobserved heterogeneity in mortality. The changing composition of the population is a result of the differences in survival rates. The proportion surviving to age x in a subgroup is equal to:

$$e^{-\int \mu_x dx}$$

The relative size of two groups at age y with mortality rates ${}^1\mu_x$ and ${}^2\mu_x$ is:

$$\frac{B_2 e^{-\int {}^2 u_x dx}}{B_1 e^{-\int {}^1 u_x dx}} = \frac{B_2}{B_1} e^{-\int ({}^2 u_x - {}^1 u_x) dx}$$

where the B_i are the numbers born into the two groups and the integration is over ages 0 to y. We see from this that the change in the relative size of the two groups depends on the absolute difference between the age-specific mortality rates in the two subgroups. Therefore, heterogeneity does not have much effect on the hazard rate unless the subgroups have very different risks.[13]

For genetic information to explain much heterogeneity, the relative risk associated with the risky genotypes must be large enough to cause a sufficient difference in the absolute risks. In addition, the risky genotypes must be sufficiently common to have a noticeable effect on overall mortal-

---

[13]This ignores changes in functional form associated with averaging hazards functions for the two subgroups. For example, the weighted average of two Weibull functions for the risk of repeatable events is a Weibull function only if the two subpopulations have the same exponent on age.

ity. Therefore, to be useful for understanding heterogeneity, a gene would have to have common polymorphisms associated with relatively large differences in risk.

This leads to three conclusions about the potential gain from genetic research for understanding the effects of heterogeneity. First, it is not likely that any single genotype will explain much of the heterogeneity in mortality under age 80. Before age 80, overall mortality rates are low enough that it would take exceedingly large differences in relative mortality between genotypes to cause noticeable heterogeneity. For example, with equal size subgroups of U.S. white males at birth, it takes a relative risk of 1.5 to cause a noticeable change in population composition by age 80.[14] A less equal split between subgroups would require a much larger relative risk. To put this into perspective, I estimate that the APOE e4/4 genotype is associated with a relative risk of death at age 80 of about 2 relative to the most common genotype, e3/3. Less than 5 percent of the population has the e4/4 genotype.

Second, even at the oldest ages only very common genotypes associated with large differences in risk are apt to be useful in demographic modeling of mortality. Third, since single genes are not apt to have a big enough impact, explaining a substantial fraction of the effects of heterogeneity will probably require the use of complex genotypes that combine information on several genes.

The situation is similar if we look at individual causes of death or chronic diseases instead of total mortality rates. Although there are probably genes with larger relative risks for specific diseases, the incidence rates are much lower than the overall risk of death. Therefore, to get sufficiently large absolute differences in rates would require even larger relative risks. For example, we can simulate two equal-sized subgroups at birth which differ only in their mortality due to ischemic heart disease, the most common cause of death. To get noticeable signs of heterogeneity by age 70 requires that the high-risk subgroup have IHD mortality rates 3 times the low risk subgroup. Common genotypes for common conditions are not apt to have relative risks anywhere near this high. A relative risk for IHD mortality of 1.5 doesn't lead to a noticeable effect of heterogeneity until after age 90. Therefore, reducing the amount of unobserved heterogeneity will usually require several common risk factors that are each associated with large relative risks.

---

[14]A noticeable change in population composition was taken to be a drop in the percent in the high-risk subgroup from 50 percent at birth to 40 percent.

Studies of Differences Among Populations

Research on differences among populations always confronts the possibility that the differences are partly due to genetics. Without controls for genetic differences it is difficult to estimate the relative importance of various social, economic, and cultural factors.[15] Gene information can only help explain variation across populations if there are significant differences in allele frequencies across populations, or there are important gene-environment interactions. These two criteria are often related. Large differences in allele frequencies are often the result of current or historical differences in environment. Polymorphisms can arise in situations where there are advantages of different alleles. For example, the sickle cell mutation provides some protection against falciparum malaria to those who are heterozygous (i.e., have only one copy of the mutation). However, those who are homozygous suffer life-threatening anemia (Weiss, 1993). In populations that historically lived in malarious areas, the frequency of the mutation was determined by the balance between the survival advantage of being heterozygous and the disadvantage of being homozygous. In populations that emerged in areas free of malaria, the sickle cell mutation is very rare.

Genetic variation within populations does not guarantee differences among populations, so genes that are useful for explaining variation within populations may not explain variation across populations. This has one important implication for identifying genes that might be useful for demographic research. To this point, I have not differentiated between genes that have a few very common polymorphisms and genes that have numerous rare alleles. If there are many rare mutations that are associated with increased risk, it is not likely that those mutations will cluster in the same populations.[16] An example of this is the genes for breast cancer, which are discussed below.

For comparisons of populations, the relevant index is the sum of the frequencies of all of the risky mutations.[17] If there are numerous risky

---

[15]Sokal et al. (1997) have performed an interesting analysis of cancer mortality rates in Europe without examining the effects of individual alleles. They found that cancer mortality rates are more closely correlated with a measure of ethnohistorical distance between populations than with a measure of genetic distances. This was true of rates for many cancer sites as well as overall cancer mortality. It was also true in both Western and Central Europe, suggesting that cultural practices may be more important than genetic differences in determining cancer mortality. This research strategy is an interesting alternative to research using allele frequencies for individual genes.

[16]This applies to naturally occurring populations, not populations defined by risk factors for an accelerated rate of mutation, such as exposure to radiation or occupational hazards that might increase the rate of mutations in germ cells.

[17]For simplicity, I assume that risky alleles are associated with the same amount of excess risk.

alleles, a surplus of one risky allele in one population might be counter-balanced by a surplus of a second allele elsewhere. It is reasonable to assume that mutations occur with similar frequency in all populations and selection keeps each risky allele rare in all populations. In that case, there might be differences in the frequencies of individual risky alleles, but little variation in the total frequency of risky alleles.

This is not the case if there are one or more common polymorphisms associated with substantial risk. If one or two mutations become common in at least one population (say at least 5 percent of all alleles), there is no reason to believe that the same mutation will be equally common in all populations. For example, differences in the frequency of common alleles can be due to founder effects[18] or differences in environment. Therefore, polymorphisms will be more useful for explaining variation across populations than will differences in the frequencies of numerous rare mutations.

Gene-environment interactions, including interactions with behavior, might be very important for understanding differences among populations. This is especially true since large differences in gene frequencies may reflect current or historical differences in environment. Therefore, differences in gene frequencies between populations may indicate that gene-environment interactions are potentially important.

Gene-gene interactions may also be important. The effects of a mutation of one gene might be counterbalanced by the effects of mutations of other genes. Therefore, an allele may not have the same effect in all populations even given the same current environment. This complicates studies of the contribution of genetics to race/ethnic differences in health. For example, we cannot assume that the effect of APOE genotype on serum cholesterol levels is exactly the same in all ethnic groups since numerous genes affect serum lipid levels. The effects must be documented in different ethnic groups (i.e., genetic environments) as well as in different social/behavioral environments.

Genes and Behavior

Genes associated with basic personality traits or susceptibility to addictions could help to explain differences in behaviors like risk taking, diet, and use of health services. The potential importance of behavioral genetics, which combines genetics and psychology, is suggested by the fact that an estimated 30 percent of all human genes are expressed primarily in the

---

[18]Founder effects occur when migration leads to a population that is descended from a small number of ancestors. Weiss (1993) provides an excellent discussion of the factors that lead to genetic heterogeneity within and between populations.

brain. Much of the brief summary that follows is based on recent reviews by Gilger (2000) and Merikangas and Swendsen (1997).

Twin and family studies provide intriguing insights into the possible role of genetics in personality and behavior. Numerous behavioral traits of interest to demographers have often been shown to have heritability in the range of 45 to 50 percent (Gilger, 2000). This includes variables associated with personality (e.g., risk-taking behavior, harm avoidance, self-control), cognition (IQ, memory, speed of processing information), and social status variables associated with achievement (occupation and years of education). For example, one study of female twins suggested that about half of the variance in several measures of perceived social support from friends, family, and confidants is attributable to genetics (Kendler, 1997).

Although these results are intriguing, genetic information might not provide much insight into behaviors of interest to demographers in the next ten to twenty years. First, even narrowly defined aspects of behavior are polygenic so it might be necessary to control for dozens of genes to add much to our understanding of differences in complex behaviors (like savings decisions). However, it may also turn out that some genes have widespread effects on numerous aspects of behavior. For example, research in behavioral genetics suggests there may be some genes that affect multiple dimensions of cognition (Gilger, 2000).

The second issue is that it will be exceedingly difficult to identify the specific genes that affect behavior even with QTL models and dense maps of the human genome. This is even true for severe psychiatric disorders such as schizophrenia, major mood disorders, and panic disorder, which have very high estimates of heritability. The evidence suggests that the genetic causes of these diseases are very complex and often involve gene-environment interactions. The use of linkage and association studies has produced a number of candidate genes for these disorders, but there have been problems of consistency and replicability of results (Merikangas and Swendsen, 1997).

One area of interest to demographers studying health and behavior is genetic research on addictive behaviors, including smoking and alcohol consumption. Despite newspaper headlines, little is known for sure about specific genetic markers for addiction. Merikangas and Swendsen concluded that "although several investigations have replicated significant associations between alcoholism and [several genetic] markers, the majority of investigations are either preliminary, nonconfirmatory, or have revealed potential sampling biases that may independently explain observed associations" (1997:153).

Thus far, the most successful case in behavioral genetics is the study of dyslexia. Even there, the specific genes and alleles are uncertain. Only the identification of a region of chromosome 6 is definite (Gilger, 2000). Therefore, despite the HGP and numerous developments in genetic epidemiology, it may be decades before much is known about specific genes that affect behavior.

A third issue is that associations between genes and behavior might differ substantially by age, sex, ethnic groups, and social environment. For example, numerous genes on the X chromosome have alleles associated with very low intelligence. It is possible that other alleles have less dramatic effects. Since women have two copies of the X chromosome and men only have one, the effects of genes associated with intelligence on the X chromosome might differ substantially by sex. This might explain the fact that men are more likely to be at the extremes of intelligence than women (Gécz and Mulley, 2000). The effects of genes on intelligence also vary by age. Estimates of heritability of IQ increase from about 15 percent among young children to about 40 percent among adolescents to about 80 percent among older adults (Gilger, 2000). Similarly, the relative role of genetics in antisocial and criminal behavior is probably very different among teenagers than among adults (Lyons et al., 1995). Social and ethnic differences in gene action attributable to gene-environment and gene-gene interactions are especially difficult problems for the use of genetics in nationally representative samples. Behaviors or health conditions that vary by ethnic group (for example, between northern and southern European heritage) could be falsely linked to polymorphisms that also differ by ethnicity.

When behavioral genetics does discover specific genes associated with behaviors, demographic surveys might prove invaluable for putting the results into a social context. Associations between genes and personality traits are especially prone to exaggeration and misunderstanding in public discussions. Individual genes probably explain little of the variation in complex behaviors. However, preliminary reports of genetic factors affecting behavior are so intriguing that they invite speculation far beyond the actual research findings. It is possible to combine case-control data and gene frequencies to estimate how much variation is attributable to a particular genotype. However, this will always be less convincing than a head-to-head comparison of genetic effects and social, behavioral, and economic effects using a single data set. Large-scale demographic surveys that measure numerous complex behaviors like saving rates, family caregiving, and health practices could provide invaluable tests of the relative importance of genetics for common behaviors.

Longevity Genes—A Special Case

Demographers are fascinated by the possibility that one or more genes might determine the rate of decline in multiple organ systems. Several such genes have been identified in other species (Vaupel et al., 1998). These genes are sometimes called *gerontogenes* or *longevity genes*. The discovery of one or more genes that act as aging "clocks" in humans would be a major breakthrough for genetics. However, the mere existence of such genes would not have a major effect on demographic research. For example, a mutation in a longevity gene that was present in 0.1 percent of the population would still be rare (probably less than 1 percent) among centenarians.[19] Such a genotype would not explain much about survival to the oldest ages. Therefore, in order to be important for demographic research, there would have to be common polymorphisms associated with large differences in survival. Vaupel has estimated that there could be hundreds of genotypes with frequencies of 5-10 percent that lower death rates by 5-10 percent (Vaupel, personal communication).

Any discovery about the biological determinants of the rate of aging raises the possibility of therapies to slow aging. Therefore the discovery of a gerontogene with even very rare mutations that increased longevity would cause speculation about future trends in mortality. However, the discovery of such a gene would be relevant only to long-term (and, therefore, very speculative) projections.

Prospective Epidemiologic Surveys that Include Genetic Information

Some epidemiologic cohort studies of populations have collected genetic information that could be used for demographic research. It is instructive to examine a few examples of data on the APOE gene collected in population-based epidemiologic studies. One recent example is the Helsinki Ageing Study, a prospective study of a sample of individuals born in 1904, 1909, and 1914. The study began in 1989 and included blood samples that were tested for APOE. Tilvis et al. (1998) present five-year survival rates by the presence or absence of an e4 allele. Carriers of the e4 allele had a mortality rate between ages 75 and 80 that was 1.85 times that of the rest of the population. Between ages 80 and 85, the risk ratio was 1.52. There was no evidence of excess mortality between 85 and 90 (risk ratio of 0.98). A Cox regression controlling for age and sex showed a risk ratio of 1.61 associated with the e4 allele. The authors do not present results controlling for any other variables, so we don't know whether controlling for APOE changes the estimates of the effects of social and economic variables that are of interest to demographers.

---

[19]If the rare genotype was associated with a tenfold increase in the chance of surviving to age 100, the gene frequency at age 100 would be slightly less than 10 times the frequency at birth.

This study is typical of epidemiologic studies that include APOE genotyping. Other studies in the United States that provide similar data include a subsample of the MRFIT study (Eichner et al., 1993), the Framingham study (Myers et al., 1996), the Framingham Offspring Study (Schaefer et al., 1994; Wilson et al., 1994), the NHANES III (National Center for Health Statistics, 2000), the Iowa EPESE study (Ferrucci et al., 1997), several epidemiologic studies of AD (e.g., Evans et al., 1997), and studies of other conditions such as osteoporotic fractures (Vogt et al., 1997). Population-based European studies include the Kungsholmen Study in Sweden (Corder et al., 1996) and the Rotterdam Study (Slooter et al., 1998). The research from these studies is generally limited to the association of APOE genotypes with one outcome. Most of them control only for age and sex, although they rarely provide data by sex unless the differences are statistically significant.[20] Many of these studies could be used to study the relative importance of APOE genotype and other risk factors in determining mortality risks.

IDENTIFYING GENES THAT MIGHT BE IMPORTANT FOR DEMOGRAPHY

Genes that might be of interest to demographers can be termed *demogenes*. Their defining characteristic is that they have a noticeable effect at the population level. This simple criterion excludes virtually all genes that have been identified to date. However, this could change in coming years as a result of the rapid developments in genetic epidemiology, especially the HGP and progress in methods for identifying QTLs. Given the rapid pace of developments, it is useful to have criteria for identifying the genes that are most apt to be useful for demographic research.

The preceding discussion suggests several criteria for demogenes. The first is that they must be associated with one or more common conditions or behaviors. This screens out most known genotypes since they affect characteristics that are rare. Most of the diseases for which genetic causes or risk factors have been proven are not major causes of death or disability. The second criterion for demogenes is that many individuals carry alleles that are associated with substantial variations in risk. In other words, they must be major genes or oligogenes with common poly-

---

[20]This presents problems for meta-analytic studies since few studies have adequate sample sizes to detect moderate sized differences by sex (or many other variables). Consistent differences between the sexes observed in several studies could be lost when the studies don't even report the direction of differences by sex if the differences are not significant.

morphisms. As a rule, we should look for risky (or protective) genotypes that have frequencies of at least 5 percent.

These two criteria for demogenes determine the *attributable fraction*, the proportion of cases of a disease that are associated with a given risk factor. For example, about 20-25 percent of individuals with Alzheimer's disease have at least one copy of the APOE e4 allele.[21] Demogenes must be associated with a large attributable fraction of deaths, cases of disease, or variation in other variables of interest to demographers.

Each of these criteria eliminates a large number of genes identified to date, but the combination of the two criteria eliminates almost all known genes. Alleles associated with large effects on major causes of death are generally very rare due to natural selection. Most of the major diseases are complex traits whose heritability results from the effects of numerous, relatively rare mutations (the polygenes in segregation analysis). Therefore, only a very small proportion of genes are likely to meet these first two criteria for demogenes.

Research on differences between populations leads to a third criteria for demogenes: the frequency of genotypes should vary substantially across populations. Founder effects and differences in environment can lead to very large differences in the frequency of polymorphisms. On the other hand, it is not likely that large numbers of rare mutations of a single gene will cumulate in specific populations without becoming common in any population. Therefore, genes associated with common polymorphisms are much more apt to be useful for explaining variation across populations.

Fourth, interactions with social or behavioral variables of interest to demographers enhance the value of genes for demographic research. Research on gene-environment interactions is not as advanced as the search for single genes. This is an area of research that might benefit from collaboration between demographers and genetic epidemiologists.

Finally, many of the mutations recently linked to diseases are somatic mutations, i.e., mutations that occur in a single cell of the body and are not inherited. This is particularly true of much of the genetic research on cancer. It is not feasible to screen for somatic mutations in population surveys since they are often localized in individual organs or certain cell types. Although somatic mutations might play a role in demographic models of aging and disease in individuals (Manton and Stallard, 1979),

---

[21]Attributable risk is often confused with the concept of causation. This is especially true of genetic risk factors. Since many cases of disease are associated with multiple risk factors, the simple association of a risk factor with a case does not mean that that risk factor caused the case. For example, it is not appropriate to state that 20-25 percent of cases of Alzheimer's disease are caused by APOE e4.

germinal (i.e., inherited) mutations are apt to be more useful for demographic research based on large surveys.

An Illustrative Comparison: BRCA Genes and APOE

A comparison of three genes illustrates these criteria. The APOE gene is associated with the risk of both ischemic heart disease (IHD) and Alzheimer's disease (AD). The genes BRCA1 and BRCA2 both are associated with the risk of breast and ovarian cancers. All three of these genes may prove to be very important to biomedical research and may play a role in future demographic work. However, APOE is much better suited to incorporation into demographic research.

The six common polymorphisms of the APOE gene (e2/2, e2/3, e2/4, e3/3, e3/4, and e4/4) are described above. The e3 allele is the most common form in all populations, but e2 and e4 are common polymorphisms. More than 200 mutations of BRCA1 and more than 100 mutations of BRCA2 have been associated with cancer susceptibility (Rahman and Stratton, 1998). None of these BRCA1 and BRCA2 mutations is sufficiently common to be termed a polymorphism. We can define a BRCA genotype in terms of the presence of one or two mutations of either BRCA1 or BRCA2 that are associated with increased risk.

We can apply the four criteria for demogenes to compare the potential usefulness of these genes to demographic research.

APOE is Associated with More Common Causes of Death and Disability than the BRCA Genes

Table 4-1 shows the associations between polymorphisms of APOE and the risk of IHD mortality and the incidence of AD. IHD is the leading cause of death and AD is the third or fourth leading cause (Ewbank, 1999). The range of risks for AD is especially large, with the e4/4 genotype having an odds ratio of more than 20 relative to the low risk e2/3

TABLE 4-1 Odds Ratios by APOE Genotype for the Risk of Death Due to Ischemic Heart Disease and the Incidence of Alzheimer's Disease

	Odds Ratio by APOE Genotype			
	e3/3	e3/4	e4/4	e2/3
IHD mortality (at age 65)	1.0	1.71	2.82	0.97
AD incidence (at age 85)	1.0	3.34	7.87	0.33

genotype (i.e., 7.87 ÷ 0.33 or 23.8). When the risks of IHD and AD are combined, white males in the United States with the e3/4 genotype have a risk of death at age 80 that is about 20-25 percent higher than those with the e3/3 genotype. The e4/4 have a risk of death almost twice that of the e3/3 (Ewbank, unpublished results).

Although cancer is the second leading cause of death, the BRCA genes are associated only with the risks of breast and ovarian cancers, which account for 21.5 percent of cancer deaths in women (Hoyert et al., 1999). For the total population, breast and ovarian cancers are responsible only for about 9 percent as many deaths as IHD and AD combined. For women, this rises to about 17 percent. It is more difficult to compare the morbidity burden of AD with that of breast and ovarian cancers. However, all three are associated with substantial disability. It would be easier to control for BRCA genotype in demographic analyses if all of the known mutations were associated with similar amounts of excess risk. We could then simply include a binary variable indicating women with one or more BRCA mutations. However, the mutations are so rare that it will never be possible to get accurate estimates of relative risks for each allele. Almost all of the known mutations of BRCA1 are protein-truncating (i.e., mutations that prevent the gene from producing copies of the complete protein molecule), and, therefore, they are associated with substantial increases in risk (Rahman and Stratton, 1998) and have high rates of penetrance.

Polymorphisms and Rare Alleles

Table 4-2 (from Gerdes et al., 1992) shows the APOE gene frequencies in several populations. In these populations at least 11 percent of the population carries one or more copies of the e4 allele and at least 5 percent carries one or more copies of the e2 allele. The frequency of the e4 allele is correlated with IHD in high income countries (Luc et al., 1994). For example, the rate among men aged 65-69 is more than twice as high in

TABLE 4-2 APOE Gene Frequencies in Five Populations

	APOE Genotype			
	e3/3 or e2/4	e3/4	e4/4	e2/3 or e2/2
U.S. whites	65%	21%	2%	13%
Italy	71%	17%	1%	11%
Finland	59%	31%	4%	6%
China	72%	11%	0.4%	16%
Nigeria	47%	40%	9%	5%

Finland as in Italy (United Nations, 1993). The differences in APOE gene frequencies explain some of the variation in IHD mortality at ages 65-69 and in total mortality at ages 80-84 (Ewbank, 1999; Stengård et al., 1998). These large differences in APOE gene frequencies also may be associated with differences in the prevalence of AD within Europe. However, variations in the prevalence of AD are not well documented.

The frequencies of mutations of BRCA1 and BRCA2 have not been determined in many populations. It is more difficult to determine BRCA frequencies since hundreds of mutations of BRCA1 and BRCA2 have been identified. An indirect estimate for Britain suggests that only about 0.6 to 0.12 percent carry a BRCA1 or BRCA2 mutation (Rahman and Stratton, 1998). The previous discussion suggests that the variations across populations are probably not as large as the variation in the frequency of the APOE e4 allele. The proportions carrying BRCA1 or BRCA2 mutations are very high in Icelandics and Ashkenazim, about 0.5 percent and 2.5 percent. These high rates are probably due to founder effects and small population sizes (Rahman and Stratton, 1998). Mutations of BRCA1 or BRCA2 will not explain much of the variation in breast and ovarian cancer mortality rates across populations.

The APOE e4 Allele Is Associated with Larger Attributable Risks than the BRCA Genes

The high frequency of the APOE e4 allele combined with high relative risks for IHD and AD leads to a high attributable risk of death. The e4 allele is associated with about 20-25 percent of cases of AD among U.S. whites (Evans et al., 1997), and I estimate that it is associated with about 10-11 percent of IHD deaths among white males in the United States. The associations of APOE e4 with IHD and with mortality are probably smaller among women (Wilson et al., 1994; Vogt et al., 1997). However, AD is slightly more common among women then men. The combined effects of e4 on IHD and AD lead to the large variations in mortality (e.g., Tilvis et al., 1998; Corder et al., 1996).

In contrast, BRCA1 and BRCA2 are associated only with about 6-7 percent of cases of breast cancer and probably a smaller proportion of ovarian cancers (Rahman and Stratton, 1998). This proportion changes with age. About 30-35 percent of breast cancer cases at ages 20-29 are associated with BRCA mutations as opposed to about 2 percent over age 70 (Rahman and Stratton, 1998). In addition, breast and ovarian cancers are only responsible for 5 percent of deaths in women in the United States (Hoyert et al., 1999). Therefore, the fraction of total deaths in women that is attributable to BRCA1 and BRCA2 is less than 1 percent.

The Risk Associated with APOE e4 Probably Differs Across Environments

There is some evidence of gene-environment interactions that increase the importance of APOE for demographic research. In particular, APOE appears to interact with dietary consumption of fats to determine the levels of serum lipids (Lopez-Miranda et al., 1994; Lehtimäki et al., 1995; however, see Lefevre et al., 1997). Therefore, the e4 allele may carry less risk of IHD in populations that consume low levels of fats. This is consistent with the finding that IHD does not appear to be as significant a cause of death in Nigeria and other areas of Africa where APOE e4 is very common. There may be a similar interaction at work with AD since it appears that the prevalence of AD is low in Nigeria but high in African-Americans (Hendrie et al., 1995). Similarly, a study of AD in Japanese-Americans living in Hawaii found a higher prevalence than seen in prevalence studies in Japan (White et al., 1996). All of these findings are consistent with an important interaction between environment (probably including dietary lipids) and the effect of the e4 allele. This increases the potential value of the e4 allele to demographic research. There may also be interactions between environment and the BRCA genes. There is as yet little research on gene-environment interactions involving BRCA genes. However, given the high rate of penetrance, it is unlikely that gene-environment interactions affect much more than the age at onset.

HOW MANY DEMOGENES ARE THERE AND HOW SOON WILL WE FIND THEM?

This is the million dollar question for demographers interested in genetics. If there are apt to be a dozen demogenes discovered in the next ten years, then we have to begin planning for the collection of genetic information in demographic surveys. If APOE is apt to be the only true demogene for the next ten years, then genetic information collected in demographic surveys will not have much impact on demographic research in the next ten to twenty years.

It is useful to consider the evidence for likely demogenes from genetic epidemiology. The previous discussion of behavioral genetics provided a summary of the current state of knowledge about genes affecting behavior. The following paragraphs review the evidence for five other traits of interest to demographers. Body mass index (BMI) and blood pressure are biomarkers that would be relatively easy to add to demographic surveys. They are important risk factors for death and disability and have been the focus of social, economic, and behavioral research. Osteoporosis is a major chronic disease that plays an important role in disability at older ages, and coronary artery disease is a major cause of death. There is substantial evidence that all four of these traits have high rates of heritability. The fifth trait is exceptional longevity in the form of survival to age 90 or 100.

Body Mass Index

There is substantial evidence from segregation analyses for major gene effects on BMI in numerous populations (Ginsburg et al., 1998; Colilla et al., 2000). Although the estimates vary across studies, it is common to find estimates of a single gene with alleles that have a frequency of 20-30 percent that explain 15-50 percent of the variation in BMI. A few notes of caution are important. First, even if BMI is largely controlled by a single major gene in each population, it is theoretically possible that it is not the same gene or the same alleles in each population. Second, segregation studies use significance tests to select among models with different assumptions about the number of major genes. It is often difficult to determine whether heritability is due only to numerous polygenes or whether there are one or two major genes. This is one reason for different conclusions from different studies. Third, BMI is especially difficult because of gene-environment interactions and the possibility of assortative (i.e., nonrandom) mating, although segregation analyses attempt to control for these complications.

Siffert et al. (1999) present evidence for men in two populations linking the 825T allele of the G protein β3 subunit (GNB3) with the risk of obesity as defined by BMI.[22] They also show that the frequency of the 825T allele varies substantially across populations, with values of about 30 percent in much of Europe and 85 percent in Africa (Siffert et al., 1999). If their findings are replicated by other labs in additional populations, this allele might be valuable for demographic research on body weight and obesity.

Hypertension

Twin studies and pedigree studies suggest that the heritability of blood pressure is probably in the range of 25-50 percent (Williams et al., 1994). However, it is still not clear whether there are one or more major genes for blood pressure. Livshits et al. (1999) reviewed previous segregation analyses and genetic studies of blood pressure before presenting

---

[22]They present significant findings for German men and Chinese men. Results for Zimbabwean men were similar but not significant, possibly due to the small number of obese men in the sample and to strong environmental (urban/rural) differences.

their own results. They find only two conclusions that can be drawn unequivocally. First, blood pressure is closely tied to other variables (especially body mass), so the genetic effects on blood pressure may be largely indirect. Second, genetics does affect blood pressure, but it is not clear whether this includes a major gene with a direct effect.

One possibility is that the genetic influences on blood pressure are dominated by different genes in different populations. Schork (1997) provides an excellent discussion of the possible effects of gene interactions, migration, population size and subdivision, inbreeding, and stochastic factors on the genetics of blood pressure. He concludes that

> [s]ince there are so many physiological and biochemical pathways that mediate blood pressure regulation and the human species is relatively old . . . there are quite likely to be, on a worldwide scale, different mutations and gene combinations contributing to [hypertensive cardiovascular disease] (1997:147).

Coronary Artery Disease

There is a clear genetic component to the risk of death from coronary artery disease (Peyser, 1997). However, this is the result of numerous genes that affect many of the common risk factors for coronary artery disease. For example, heritability estimates from a study of Mexican-Americans in San Antonio, Texas (Peyser, 1997), ranged between 18 and 69 percent for ten major risk factors for coronary artery disease, including total cholesterol, systolic blood pressure, and body mass index. None of these risk factors appears to be controlled by a single gene, although segregation analyses suggest that there are major unidentified genes for several of these traits. Most of these genes have not been identified. Some reports of alleles associated with heart disease have not yet been adequately replicated. Those genes that have been identified for measures of lipids, lipoproteins, and apolipoproteins generally explain less than 10 percent of the observed variation (Peyser, 1997). APOE is the only gene that has been consistently associated with coronary artery disease (Peyser, 1997), and even its association with mortality due to coronary artery disease is not clear in females (e.g., Vogt et al., 1997). In summary, variation in the risk of coronary artery disease is the result of numerous risk factors that are themselves complex traits for which few genes have been identified.

Osteoporosis

Reduced bone mass and fracture are major health problems in the elderly. Genetics appears to explain about 75 to 85 percent of the variation in bone mass (Ralston, 1997). However, segregation analyses suggest that there are several genes with relatively small effects rather than one or two major genes with common alleles (Ralston, 1997; Zmuda et al., 1999). In addition, genetics may explain little of the risk for fractures in the elderly (Kannus et al., 1999), which is only partially determined by bone density.

The main candidate for a major gene associated with osteoporosis is the vitamin D receptor gene (VDR). Several studies of alleles at the BsmI site of VDR have found significant differences in bone mass, although these findings have not been universal (Ralston, 1997; Zmuda et al., 1999). There are numerous other candidate genes. For example, Zmuda et al. (1999) discuss research on six candidate genes (including APOE), mention several more candidates, and refer to several linkage studies that have identified promising regions. There are also alternative candidate alleles for some of the genes that have been studied. The pace of research on this topic is suggested by the fact that Zmuda et al. (1999) reference 12 important association studies published in 1997 alone.

Exceptional Longevity

One approach to identifying genes associated with low mortality is to examine the genes of those who survive to the oldest ages. Several studies have examined gene frequencies among centenarians or nonagenarians and compared them with frequencies at younger ages. Since changes in gene frequencies are more rapid when mortality rates are high, cross-sectional comparisons must be adjusted for differences in mortality among cohorts.

Yashin et al. (1999) provide models for estimating the relative risks of death associated with various genotypes. These models could easily be extended to incorporate genetic effects on one or more causes of death. Toupance et al. (1998) present models based on Gompertz-Makeham models. These have the advantage of incorporating the possibility that the relative risks of death associated with each genotype can change with age. Many genes are *pleiotropic*, that is, they affect several phenotypes. With *antagonistic pleiotropy*, a gene can have opposing effects at different ages. For example, a genotype associated with strong immune responses can protect against infectious disease at the youngest ages. However, strong immune responses can cause excessive stress that could be associated with high mortality at the oldest ages.

The model for studies of changes in gene frequencies is several studies of changes in APOE gene frequencies with age (Asada et al., 1996; Kervinen et al., 1994; Louhija et al., 1994; Panza et al., 1999; Rebeck et al., 1994; Schächter et al., 1994). Several other candidate genotypes have been tested for evidence of association with exceptional longevity. These include ACE (Schächter et al., 1994; Bladbjerg et al., 1999), APOB (Kervinen et al., 1994), and numerous other genes (e.g., Bladbjerg et al., 1999; Bonafé et al., 1999; Brattström et al., 1998). Mitochondrial DNA[23] has also been examined for changes in gene frequencies (De Benedictis et al., 1999).

Few studies of changes in gene frequencies have been replicated in diverse populations. There are several reasons why changes in gene frequencies with age can vary across populations. First is the possibility that some of the findings are spurious. Second, if the effect of the gene on survival varies by environment, populations with different environments (or histories of environmental change) could have very different associations between genotype and longevity. Third, it is possible that the gene being studied is not actually the gene that is associated with longevity but is in linkage disequilibrium with the true gene. If the linkage association differs between populations, the associations between the observed gene and longevity can vary substantially. Finally, studies of exceptional longevity could be sensitive to sample selection and phenotype definitions. For example, gene frequencies could be very different in samples of "healthy" centenarians, centenarians living in institutions, and random samples of centenarians.

Prospects for Demogenes

These five conditions are indicative of the state of research on the genetics of complex conditions. Segregation analyses sometimes suggest major genes that would be potential candidates for demogenes. However, locating the genes, characterizing the alleles, and replicating the results in different populations will require extensive research. Documenting allele frequencies for different populations is relatively easy, but generally requires work by numerous researchers. Unraveling gene-environment interactions and documenting differences in results across populations will require additional years of research. However, the rate of progress on complex diseases is increasing steadily. More labs have genetic samples appropriate for research on specific conditions and are geared up for rapid assessments of candidate genes. Some of the associations that have already been found in single studies will prove to be important, and the consensus of opinion on individual genes could change rapidly. In addition, the rate of discovery will continue to increase as the

---

[23]Mitochondria are present in every cell of the body. They have a separate DNA structure, MtDNA, that is not part of the 23 pairs of chromosomes. They are generally only inherited from the maternal line.

HGP completes the sequencing of the human genome and begins to catalogue SNPs.

SUMMARY AND RECOMMENDATIONS

Social and behavioral researchers have always been intrigued by genetics, but the exciting developments in the study of rare genetic diseases have found little application in demography. This could change as genetic epidemiology discovers genes associated with common conditions. However, in the short run, the flood of new genetic research has led to a more complicated view of the genetics of complex traits. Genetic epidemiology has demonstrated that genetic variation in humans does not fit the simple Mendelian model of diseases associated with a small number of genes each with a few alleles (Weiss, 1996). The amount of genetic variation in human populations is much greater than many experts expected twenty years ago. This diversity results from historical differences in environment, population migrations of small groups of related individuals, and numerous random events (Weiss, 1993). The diversity is staggering. For example, research on cystic fibrosis, a "simple genetic" disease, has uncovered more than 800 mutations of the cystic fibrosis gene that are associated with the disease (Kaprio, 2000).

This review has examined how future research in the genetic epidemiology of complex diseases might affect demographic research, which provides insight into the characteristics of the types of genes that are most apt to be useful to demographers. Demogenes are those that:

1. are associated with the most common diseases, causes of death, or other variables of interest to demographers;
2. have common polymorphisms associated with substantial variation in risk;
3. have large variations in allele frequencies across populations; and
4. interact with environmental or behavioral characteristics being studied by demographers.

APOE is the only gene that has been proven to meet all of these criteria. The impact of genetic research on demography during the next ten to fifteen years will depend on how many additional demogenes are discovered. Demographic research on mortality would be significantly altered if genetic epidemiologists discovered two or three additional genes with impact on overall mortality as large as APOE. Research on functional disability would benefit greatly from four to six genes associated with large attributable fractions for the most common chronic conditions.

It is hard to predict how many demogenes there are and how soon they will be discovered. One expert (Kaprio, 2000) recently predicted that during the next five to ten years "genetic dissection of complex traits will continue to yield specific genes, each accounting for only a relatively small fraction of cases." This seems to be the general consensus. On the other hand, Peyser (1997) predicted that "within a few years, most of the risk factors [for coronary artery disease], both established and proposed, will be found to be associated with specific measured genes." Predicting the future is complicated by the recent acceleration of research. The Human Genome Project is completing the sequencing of the human genome and is just starting its search for SNPs, and there are still disagreements over the relative advantages of association studies and linkage methods for studying complex traits.

The Potential Role of Large-Scale Demographic Surveys in Genetic Research

We will almost certainly decide to add the collection of genetic material to large-scale demographic surveys. The question is, should we begin designing supplements to current surveys, or is it premature to collect genetic material before genetic epidemiology has identified more demogenes? There are a few conclusions that follow from the preceding review:

1. Surveys of diverse populations are not useful for identifying the genes associated with specific conditions. Spurious correlations associated with population diversity would completely overwhelm genome-wide scans in nationally representative samples of unrelated individuals.

2. Large-scale surveys may have a role to play in replicating studies of the effect of previously identified genes. In this case the diversity in nationally representative samples could be an advantage if the data were analyzed properly. However, demographic surveys would only be useful for replicating findings for phenotypes that are carefully measured in those surveys. Studies of a few measures, like body mass index, might rely on self-reported measures. Others, like blood pressure and insulin levels, might be added to large surveys. However, errors in defining phenotypes severely complicate replication in genetic research.

3. Perhaps the biggest potential for demographic surveys in the next ten years is putting genetic research into a social or public health context. This will certainly be true of genetic effects on behavior. In many cases this might involve demonstrating that individual genes contribute little to understanding complex behaviors. However, given the likelihood of misperceptions about the generalizability of findings in behavioral genetics to everyday life, negative findings could be very important.

4. There is a long time lag between the first plans for a major survey and the availability of useful data. For example, if genetic material was collected in 2002, two more biannual rounds of data collection would provide reasonable follow-up data by 2006. Most of the data analysis would occur after 2007 and would probably have to rely on genes first identified by 2005. If data collection continues until 2020, most of the research would involve genes discovered by 2015. It will take several years to plan the collection and analysis of nationally representative samples and determine the best approach to testing them for a wide range of candidate genes. Given the speed of progress in genetic epidemiology, it would be wise to begin work on the design of appropriate strategies for demographic surveys.

5. Currently available data from epidemiologic surveys could be used to develop models for incorporating genetic information into demographic research. For example, a number of data sets already include APOE genotype, basic social and economic indicators, and prospective data on survival. Some of these surveys probably have additional data on health such as functional health and nursing home placement.

6. It is useful to remember that even if genetic information does not become important for demography until after 2010, this is well within the time horizon of our current graduate students. Ten years from now they will be the young associate professors who will determine how genetics ultimately affects demography.

Genes and Demography—A Broader View

The preceding discussion started from the perspective of demography by asking what genetic information will add to our current research and what new demographic research it might stimulate. An alternative approach is to ask what demographic questions will be raised by the accelerated pace of discoveries in genetics. Will public discussions of genetics pose demographic questions that we are not currently able to address?

Clinicians are already feeling pressure from the public for further information. Patients whose parents had Alzheimer's disease are asking whether they should get tested for APOE or for rare mutations of the Presenilin genes (Mayeux et al., 1998). Women with familial risk of breast cancer are interested in testing for BRCA1 and BRCA2 mutations (Coughlin et al., 1999). Those who carry these mutations are looking for appropriate prevention strategies. Therefore, while biomedical researchers study how individual mutations cause disease, clinical researchers are struggling to understand what these findings already mean for their patients.

As the steady stream of new genetic findings cumulates into a flood, social scientists will be under pressure to figure out what this all means for society. We will face new questions that need to be answered and common perceptions that need to be tested. For example, does the higher prevalence of APOE e4 in African-Americans explain much of the differential in mortality by race? How important can tobacco advertising be if it turns out there is a gene associated with addiction to nicotine? If there is a gene for caution or risk taking, does it explain differences in savings or income? How much of the relationship between poverty and poor health is "simply" due to bad genes? What would be the implications of genes associated with "intelligence?"

Newly discovered genes will lead to new thinking about who we are as individuals and what we are as a society. It is almost certain that speculation will outpace evidence. Popular perceptions will stray beyond what has been demonstrated by scientists. The old aphorism about "seeing the forest for the trees" may be replaced by "seeing the person (or the ethnic group) for the genes." We will be faced with the problem of putting the flood of genetic information into a social and demographic context.

Epidemiology will respond to some of these challenges. However, the perspective of most epidemiologists is a desire to understand the causes of specific disease. Demographers, including social demographers and economic demographers, have always concentrated on the bigger picture. To demographers, the social and economic context of health is more than mechanisms complicating disease rates. We are also interested in nonhealth behaviors such as retirement decisions, savings behavior, and caregiving.

Adding genetic and bioindicator data to large demographic surveys may be useful to epidemiologists. However, these data will be crucial to demographers if we are to put genes into a wider social context. It is difficult to predict where genetic research will lead us as a society in the next 20 years. For that reason it is difficult to predict what social, economic, and demographic questions will arise and what new avenues of research will open up. However, if the current promises of new genetic discoveries are even partially realized, they could change the questions demographers study and how we study them.

REFERENCES

Adams, J., D.A. Lam, A.I. Hermalin, and P.E. Smouse, eds.
   1990 *Convergent Issues in Genetics and Demography.* New York: Oxford University Press.
Asada, T., Z.Ymagata, T. Kinoshita, A. Kinoshita, T. Kariya, A. Asaka, and T. Kakuma
   1996 Prevalence of dementia and distribution of apo E alleles in Japanese centenarians: An almost-complete survey in Yamanashi Prefecture, Japan. *Journal of the American Geriatrics Society* 44:151-155.

Behrman, J.R., M.R. Rosenzweig, and P. Taubman.
  1994 Endowments and the allocation of schooling in the family and in the marriage market: The twins experiment. *Journal of Political Economy* 102(6):1131-1174.
  1996 College choice and wages: Estimates using data on female twins. *Review of Economics and Statistics* 73(4):672-685.
Bell, D.A., and J.A. Taylor
  1997 Genetic analysis of complex disease. *Science* 275(5304):1327-1328.
Bladbjerg, E.M., K. Andersen-Ranberg, M.P. de Maat, S.R. Kristensen, B. Jeune, J. Gram, and J. Jespersen
  1999 Longevity is independent of common variations in genes associated with cardiovascular risk. *Thrombosis & Haemostasis* 82(3):1100-1105.
Bonafé, M., F. Olivieri, D. Mari, G. Baggio, R. Mattace, M. Berardelli, P. Sansoni, G. De Benedictis, M. De Luca, F. Marchegiani, L. Cavallone, M. Cardelli, S. Giovagnetti, L. Ferrucci, L. Amadio, R. Lisa, M. G. Tucci, L. Troiano, G. Pini, P. Gueresi, M. Morellini, S. Sorbi, G. Passeri, C. Barbi, S. Valensin, and others
  1999 P53 codon 72 polymorphism and longevity: Additional data on centenarians from continental Italy and Sardinia. *American Journal of Human Genetics* 65(6): 1782-1785.
Brattström, L., Y. Zhang, M. Hurtig, H. Refsum, S. Östensson, L. Fransson, K. Jonés, F. Landgren, L. Brudin, and P.M. Ueland
  1998 A common methylenetetrahydrofolate reductase gene mutation and longevity. *Atherosclerosis* 141:315-319.
Cardon, L.R., and H. Watkins
  2000 Waiting for the working draft from the human genome project: A huge achievement, but not of immediate medical use. *British Medical Journal* 320:1223-1224.
Cavalli-Sforza, L. L., P. Menozzi, and A. Piazza
  1994 *The History and Geography of Human Genes.* Princeton, NJ: Princeton University Press.
Colilla, S., C. Rotimi, R. Cooper, J. Goldberg, and N. Cox
  2000 Genetic inheritance of body mass index in African-American and African families. *Genetic Epidemiology* 18:360-376.
Collins, F.S., M.S. Guyer, and A. Chakravarti
  1997 Variations on a theme: Cataloging human DNA sequence variation. *Science* 278(5343):1580-1581.
Collins, F.S., A. Patrinos, E. Jordan, A. Chakravarti, R. Gesteland, L. Walters, and members of the DOE and NIH planning groups
  1998 New goals for the U.S. Human Genome Project: 1998-2003. *Science* 282:682-689.
Corbo, R.M., R. Scacchi, O. Rickards, C. Martinez-Labarga, and G.F. De Stefano
  1999 An investigation of human apolipoproteins B and E polymorphisms in two African populations from Ethiopia and Benin. *American Journal of Human Biology* 11:297-304.
Corder, E.H., A.M. Saunders, W.J. Strittmatter, D.E. Schmechel, P.C. Gaskell, G.W. Small, A.D. Roses, J.L. Haines, and M.A. Pericak-Vance
  1993 Gene dose of apolipoprotein E type 4 allele and the risk of Alzheimer's disease in late onset families. *Science* 261(5123):921-923.
Corder, E.H., L. Lannfelt, M. Viitanen, L.S. Corder, K.G. Manton, B. Winblad, and H. Basun
  1996 Apolipoprotein E genotype determines survival in the oldest old (85 years or older) who have good cognition. *Archives of Neurology* 53(5):418-422.
Coughlin, S.S., M.J. Khoury, and K.K. Steinberg
  1999 BRCA1 and BRCA2 gene mutations and risk of breast cancer. Public health perspectives. *American Journal of Preventive Medicine* 16(2):91-98.

De Benedictis, G., G. Rose, G. Carrieri, M. De Luca, E. Falcone, G. Passarino, M. Bonafe, D. Monti, G. Baggio, S. Bertolini, D. Mari, R. Mattace, and C. Franceschi
  1999   Mitochondrial DNA inherited variants are associated with successful aging and longevity in humans. *FASEB Journal* 13(12):1532-1536.
Eichner, J.E., L.H. Kuller, T.J. Orchard, G.A. Grandits, L.M. McCallum, R.E. Ferrell, and J.D. Neaton
  1993   Relation of apolipoprotein E phenotype to myocardial infarction and mortality from coronary artery disease. *American Journal of Cardiology* 71:160-165.
Ellsworth, D.L., and T.A. Manolio
  1999a The emerging importance of genetics in epidemiologic research I. Basic concepts in human genetics and laboratory technology. *Annals of Epidemiology* 9(1):1-16.
  1999b The emerging importance of genetics in epidemiologic research II. Issues in study design and gene mapping. *Annals of Epidemiology* 9(2):75-90.
  1999c The emerging importance of genetics in epidemiologic research III. Bioinformatics and statistical genetic models. *Annals of Epidemiology* 9(3):207-224.
Evans, D.A., L.A. Beckett, T.S. Field, L.Feng, M. Albert, D.A. Bennett, B. Tycko, and R. Mayeux
  1997   Apolipoprotein E4 and incidence of Alzheimer disease in a community population of older persons. *Journal of the American Medical Association* 277:822-824.
Ewbank, D.C.
  1999   The genetic make-up of population and its implications for mortality by cause of death: Links between Alzheimer's and ischemic heart disease. Pp. 344-356 in *Health and Mortality Issues of Global Concern*, J. Chamie and R. L. Cliquet, eds. Brussels, Belgium: Population and Family Study Centre and Population Division, United Nations.
Farrer, L.A., L.A. Cupples, J.L. Haines, B. Hyman, W.A. Kukull, R. Mayeux, R.H. Myers, M.A. Pericak-Vance, N. Risch, C.M. van Duijn, and APOE and Alzheimer Disease Meta Analysis Consortium
  1997   Effects of age, sex, and ethnicity on the association between apolipoprotein E genotype and Alzheimer disease. *Journal of the American Medical Association* 278:1349-1356.
Ferrucci, L., J.M Guralnik, M. Pahor, T. Harris, M.C. Corti, B.T. Hyman, R.B. Wallace, and R.J. Havlik
  1997   Apolipoprotein E epsilon 2 allele and risk of stroke in the older population. *Stroke* 28(12):2410-2416.
Gambaro, G., F. Anglani, and A. D'Angelo
  2000   Association studies of genetic polymorphisms and complex disease. *Lancet* 355(9200):308-311.
Gauderman, W.J., and J.L. Morrison
  2000   Evidence for age-specific genetic relative risks in lung cancer. *American Journal of Epidemiology* 151(1):41-49.
Gécz, J., and J. Mulley
  2000   Genes for cognitive function: Developments on the X. *Genome Research* 10:157-163.
Gerdes, L.U., I.C. Klausen, I. Sihm, and O. Færgeman
  1992   Apolipoprotein E polymorphism in a Danish population compared to findings in 45 other study populations around the world. *Genetic Epidemiology* 9:155-167.
Gilger, J.W.
  2000   Contributions and promise of human behavioral genetics. *Human Biology* 71(1):229-255.

Ginsburg, E., G. Livshits, K. Yakovenko, and E. Kobyliansky
1998 Major gene control of human body height, weight and BMI in five ethnically different populations. *Annals of Human Genetics* 62(4):307-322.

Guo, S.-W., and K. Lange
2000 Genetic mapping of complex traits: Promises, problems, and prospects. *Theoretical Population Biology* 57:1-11.

Hendrie, H.C., B.O. Osuntokun, K.S. Hall, A.O. Ogunniyi, S.L. Hui, F.W. Unverzagt, O. Gureje, C.A. Rodenberg, O. Baiyewu, B.S. Musick, A. Adeyinka, M.R. Farlow, S.O. Oluwole, C.A. Class, O. Komolafe, A. Brashear, and V. Burdine
1995 Prevalence of Alzheimer's disease and dementia in two communities: Nigerian Africans and African Americans. *American Journal of Psychiatry* 152(10):1485-1492.

Herskind, A.M., M. McGue, N.V. Holm, T.I.A. Sørnsen, B. Harvald, and J.W. Vaupel
1996 The heritability of human longevity: A population-based study of 2872 Danish twin pairs born 1870-1900. *Human Genetics* 97(3):319-323.

Hoyert, D.L., K.D. Kochanek, and S.L. Murphy
1999 Deaths: Final data for 1997. *National Vital Statistics Reports* 47(19).

Kannus, P., M. Palvanen, J. Kaprio, J. Parkkari, and M. Koskenvuo
1999 Genetic factors and osteoporotic fractures in elderly people: Prospective 25 year follow up of a nationwide cohort of elderly Finnish twins. *British Medical Journal* 319(7221):1334-1337.

Kaprio, J.
2000 Genetic epidemiology. *British Medical Journal* 320:1257-1259.

Kendler, K.S.
1997 Social support: A genetic-epidemiologic analysis. *American Journal of Psychiatry* 154(10):1398-1404.

Kervinen, K., M.J. Savolainen, J. Salokannel, A. Hynninen, J. Heikkinen, C. Ehnholm, M.J. Koistinen, and Y.A. Kesäniemi
1994 Apolipoprotein E and B polymorphisms—longevity factors assessed in nonagenarians. *Atherosclerosis* 105(1):89-95.

Khoury, M.J., T.H. Beaty, and B.H. Cohen
1993 *Fundamentals of genetic epidemiology.* New York: Oxford University Press.

Lander, E.S., and N.J. Schork
1994 Genetic dissection of complex traits. *Science* 265(5181):2037-2048.

Lefevre, M., H.N. Ginsberg, P.M. Kris-Etherton, P.J. Elmer, P.W. Stewart, A. Ershow, T.A. Pearson, P.S. Roheim, R. Ramakrishnan, J. Derr, D.J. Gordon, and R. Reed
1997 Apo E genotype does not predict lipid response to changes in dietary saturated fatty acids in a heterogeneous normolipidemic population. *Arteriosclerosis, Thrombosis & Vascular Biology* 17(11):2914-2923.

Lehtimäki, T., T. Moilanen, K. Porkka, H.K. Åkerblom, T. Rönnemaa, L. Räsänen, J. Viikari, C. Ehnholm, and T. Nikkari
1995 Association between serum lipids and apolipoprotein E phenotype is influenced by diet in a population-based sample of free-living children and young adults: The cardiovascular risk in young Finns study. *Journal of Lipid Research* 36(4):653-661.

Lendon, C.L., F. Ashall, and A.M. Goate
1997 Exploring the etiology of Alzheimer disease using molecular genetics. *Journal of the American Medical Association* 277(10):825-831.

Livshits, G., E. Ginsburg, and E. Kobyliansky
1999 Heterogeneity of genetic control of blood pressure in ethnically different populations. *Human Biology* 71(4):685-708.

Long, A.D., M.N. Grote, and C.H. Langley
    1997   Genetic analysis of complex diseases. *Science* 275(5304):1328.
Lopez-Miranda, J., J.M. Ordovas, P. Mata, A.H. Lichtenstein, B. Clevidence, J.T. Judd, and
E.J. Schaefer
    1994   Effect of apolipoprotein E phenotype on diet-induced lowering of plasma low
           density lipoprotein cholesterol. *Journal of Lipid Research* 35(11):1965-1975.
Louhija, J., H.E. Miettinen, K. Kontula, M.J. Tikkanen, T.A. Miettinen, and R.S. Tilvis
    1994   Aging and genetic variation of plasma apolipoproteins. Relative loss of the
           apolipoprotein E4 phenotype in centenarians. *Arteriosclerosis & Thrombosis*
           14(7):1084-1089.
Luc, G., J.-M. Bard, D. Arveiler, A. Evans, J.-P. Cambou, A. Bingham, P. Amouyel, P.
Schaffer, J.-B. Ruidavets, F. Cambien, J.-C. Fruchart, and P. Ducimetiere
    1994   Impact of apolipoprotein e polymorphism on lipoproteins and risk of myocardial
           infarction. The ECTIM study. *Arteriosclerosis & Thrombosis* 14(9):1412-1419.
Lyons, M.J., W.R. True, S.A. Eisen, J. Goldberg, J.M. Meyer, S.V. Faraone, L.J. Eaves, and
M.T. Tsuang
    1995   Differential heritability of adult and juvenile antisocial traits. *Archives of General
           Psychiatry* 52(11):906-915.
Manton, K.G., and E. Stallard
    1979   Maximum likelihood estimation of a stochastic compartment model of cancer
           latency: Lung cancer mortality among white females in the U.S. *Computers and
           Biomedical Research* 12:313-325.
Manton, K.G., E. Stallard, and J.W. Vaupel
    1986   Alternative models for the heterogeneity of mortality risks among the aged. *Jour-
           nal of the American Statistical Association* 81(395):635-644.
Mayeux, R., A.M. Saunders, S. Shea, S. Mirra, D. Evans, A.D. Roses, B.T. Hyman, B. Crain,
M.X. Tang, and C.H. Phelps
    1998   Utility of the apolipoprotein E genotype in the diagnosis of Alzheimer's disease.
           Alzheimer's Disease Centers Consortium on Apolipoprotein E and Alzheimer's
           Disease. *New England Journal of Medicine* 338(8):506-511.
Merikangas, K.R., and J.D. Swendsen
    1997   Genetic epidemiology of psychiatric disorders. *Epidemiologic Reviews* 19(1):144-
           155.
Miller, P., C. Mulvey, and N. Martin
    1995   What do twins studies tell us about the economic returns to education? A com-
           parison of U.S. and Australian findings. *American Economic Review* 85:586-599.
Myers, R.H., E.J. Schaefer, P.W.F. Wilson, R. D'Agostino, J.M. Ordovas, A. Espino, R. Au,
R.F. White, J.E. Knoefel, J.L. Cobb, K.A. McNulty, A. Beiser, and P.A. Wolf
    1996   Apolipoprotein E4 association with dementia in a population-based study: The
           Framingham Study. *Neurology* 46:673-677.
National Center for Health Statistics
    2000   http://www.cdc.gov/nchs/nhanes.htm
Owens, K., and M. C. King
    1999   Genomic views of human history. *Science* 286(5439):451-453.
Panza, F., V. Solfrizzi, F. Torres, F. Mastroianni, A. Del Parigi, A.M. Colacicco, A.M. Basile,
C. Capurso, R. Noya, and A. Capurso
    1999   Decreased frequency of apolipoprotein E,4 allele from Northern to Southern Eu-
           rope in Alzheimer's disease patients and centenarians. *Neuroscience Letters* 277:53-
           56.
Peyser, P.A.
    1997   Genetic epidemiology of coronary artery disease. *Epidemiologic Reviews* 19(1):80-
           90.

Rahman, N., and M.R. Stratton
    1998   The genetics of breast cancer susceptibility. *Annual Review of Genetics* 32:95-121.
Ralston, S.H.
    1997   The genetics of osteoporosis. *Quarterly Journal of Medicine* 90(4):247-251.
Rebeck, G.W., T.T. Perls, H.L. West, P. Sodhi, L.A. Lipsitz, and B.T. Hyman
    1994   Reduced apolipoprotein ,4 allele frequency in the oldest old Alzheimer's patients
            and cognitively normal individuals. *Neurology* 44:1513-1516.
Ridley, M.
    1999   *Genome: The Autobiography of a Species in 23 Chapters*. New York: Harper Collins
            Publishers.
Risch, N., and K. Merikangas
    1996   The future of genetic studies of complex human diseases. *Science* 273:1516-1517.
Schächter, F., L. Faure-Delanef, F.G. Guenot, H. Rouger, P. Froguel, L. Lesueur-Ginot, and
D. Cohen
    1994   Genetic associations with human longevity at the APOE and ACE loci. *Nature
            Genetics* 6(1):29-32.
Schaefer, E.J., S. Lamon-Fava, S. Johnson, J.M. Ordovas, M.M. Schaefer, W.P. Castelli, and
P.W. Wilson
    1994   Effects of gender and menopausal status on the association of apolipoprotein E
            phenotype with plasma lipoprotein levels. Results from the Framingham Off-
            spring Study. *Arteriosclerosis and Thrombosis* 14(7):1105-1113.
Schork, N.J.
    1997   Genetically complex cardiovascular traits: Origins, problems, and potential solu-
            tions. *Hypertension* 29(1):145-149.
Schulte, P.A., and F.P. Perera, eds.
    1993   *Molecular Epidemiology: Principles and Practices*. New York: Academic Press, Inc.
Siffert, W., P. Forster, K.H. Jockel, D.A. Mvere, B. Brinkmann, C. Naber, R. Crookes, A. Du
P. Heyns, J.T. Epplen, J. Fridey, B.I. Freedman, N. Muller, D. Stolke, A.M. Sharma, K. Al
Moutaery, H. Grosse-Wilde, B. Buerbaum, T. Ehrlich, H.R. Ahmad, B. Horsthemke, E.D. Du
Toit, A. Tiilikainen, J. Ge, Y. Wang, D. Yang, J. Hüsing, and D. Rosskopf
    1999   Worldwide ethnic distribution of the G protein beta3 subunit 825T allele and its
            association with obesity in Caucasian, Chinese, and Black African individuals.
            Journal of the American Society of Nephrology 10(9):1921-1930.
Simoons, F.J.
    1978   The geographic hypothesis and lactose malabsorption: A weighing of the evi-
            dence. *American Journal of Digestive Diseases* 23(11):963-980.
Slooter, A.J., M. Cruts, S. Kalmijn, A. Hofman, M.M. Breteler, B.C. Van, and C.M. van Duijn
    1998   Risk estimates of dementia by apolipoprotein E genotypes from a population-
            based incidence study: The Rotterdam Study. *Archives of Neurology* 55(7):964-968.
Sokal, R.R., N.L. Oden, M.S. Rosenberg, and D. DiGiovanni
    1997   Ethnohistory, genetics, and cancer mortality in Europeans. *Proceedings of the Na-
            tional Academy of Sciences of the United States of America* 94(23):12728-12731.
Stengård, J.H., K.M. Weiss, and C.F. Sing
    1998   An ecological study of association between coronary heart disease mortality rates
            in men and the relative frequencies of common allelic variations in the gene cod-
            ing for apolipoprotein E. *Human Genetics* 103(2):234-241.
Stengård, J.H., K.E. Zerba, J. Pekkanen, C. Ehnholm, A. Nissinen, and C.F. Sing
    1995   Apolipoprotein E polymorphism predicts death from coronary heart disease in a
            longitudinal study of elderly Finnish men. *Circulation* 91:265-269.
Tilvis, R.S., T.E. Strandberg, and K. Juva
    1998   Apolipoprotein E phenotypes, dementia and mortality in a prospective popula-
            tion sample. *Journal of the American Geriatrics Society* 46(6):712-715.

Toupance, B., B. Godelle, P.-H. Gouyon, and F. Schächter
  1998   A model for antagonistic pleiotropic gene action for mortality and advanced age. *American Journal of Human Genetics* 62:1525-1534.
Trussell, J., and G. Ròdríguez
  1990   Heterogeneity in demographic research. Pp. 111-132 in *Convergent Issues in Genetics and Demography*, J. Adams, D.A. Lam, A.I. Hermalin, and P.E. Smouse, eds. New York: Oxford University Press.
Uitterlinden, A.G., H. Burger, Q. Huang, E. Odding, C.M. van Duijn, A. Hofman, J.C. Birkenhager, J. P.U.M. van Leeuwen, and H.A.P. Plis
  1997   Vitamin D receptor genotype is associated with radiographic osterarthritis at the knee. *Journal of Clinical Investigation* 100(2):259-263.
United Nations
  1993   *Demographic Yearbook; Special Issue: Population Aging and the Situation of Elderly Persons.*, ST/ESA/STAT/SER.R./22. New York: United Nations.
van den Oord, E.J.C.G.
  1999   Method to detect genotype-environment interactions for quantitative trait loci in association studies. *American Journal of Epidemiology* 150(11):1179-1187.
Vaupel, J.W., J.R. Carey, K. Christensen, T.E. Johnson, A.I. Yashin, N.V. Holm, I.A. Iachine, V. Kannisto, A.A. Khazaeli, P. Liedo, V.D. Longo, Y. Zeng, K.G. Manton, and J.W. Curtsinger
  1998   Biodemographic trajectories of longevity. *Science* 280(5365):855-860.
Vaupel, J.W.
  1997   Trajectories of mortality at advanced age. Pp. 17-37 in *Between Zeus and the Salmon: The Biodemography of Longevity*, K.W. Wachter and C.E. Finch, eds. Washington, DC: National Academy Press.
Vogt, M.T., J.A. Cauley, and L.H. Kuller
  1997   Apolipoprotein E phenotype, arterial disease, and mortality among older women: The study of osteoporotic fractures. *Genetic Epidemiology* 14(2):147-156.
Weinberg, R.B.
  1999   Apolipoprotein A-IV-2 allele: Association of its worldwide distribution with adult persistence of lactase and speculation on its function and origin. *Genetic Epidemiology* 17:285-297.
Weiss, K.M.
  1990   The biodemography of variation in human frailty. *Demography* 27(2):185-206.
  1993   *Genetic Variation and Human Disease.* Cambridge: Cambridge University Press.
  1996   Is there a paradigm shift in genetics? Lessons from the study of human diseases. *Molecular Phylogenetics and Evolution* 5(1):259-265.
  1998   In search of human variation. *Genome Research* 8:691-697.
White, L., H. Petrovitch, G.W. Ross, K.H. Masaki, R.D. Abbott, E.L. Teng, B.L. Rodriguez, P.L. Blanchette, R.J. Havlik, G. Wergowske, D. Chiu, D.J. Foley, C. Murdaugh, and J.D. Curb
  1996   Prevalence of dementia in older Japanese-American men in Hawaii: The Honolulu-Asia Aging Study. *Journal of the American Medical Association* 276(12):955-960.
Williams, R.R., S.C. Hunt, P.N. Hopkins, S.J. Hasstedet, L.L. Wu, and J.M. Lalouel
  1994   Tabulations and expectations regarding the genetics of human hypertension. *Kidney International* 45(Suppl. 44):S57-S64.
Wilson, P.W., R.H. Myers, M.G. Larson, J.M. Ordovas, P.A. Wolf, and E.J. Schaefer
  1994   Apolipoprotein E alleles, dyslipidemia, and coronary heart disease. The Framingham Offspring Study. *Journal of the American Medical Association* 272(21):1666-1671.
Wilson, P.W.F., E.J. Schaefer, M.G. Larson, and J.M. Ordovas
  1996   Apolipoprotein E alleles and risk of coronary disease: A meta-analysis. *Arteriosclerosis, Thrombosis & Vascular Biology* 16:1250-1255.

Yang, Q., and M.J. Khoury
    1997   Evolving methods in genetic epidemiology. III. Gene-environment interaction in epidemiologic research. *Epidemiologic Reviews* 19(1):33-43.

Yashin, A.I., G. De Benedictis, J.W. Vaupel, Q. Tan, K.F. Andreev, I.A. Iachine, M. Bonafe, M. DeLuca, S. Valensin, L. Carotenuto, and C. Franceschi
    1999   Genes, demography and life span: the contribution of demographic data in genetic studies of aging and longevity. *American Journal of Human Genetics* 65:1178-1193.

Zekraoui, L., J.P. Lagarde, A. Raisonnier, N. Gérard, A. Aouizérate, and G. Lucotte
    1997   High frequency of the apolipoprotein E ,4 allele in African Pygmies and most of the African populations in sub-Saharan Africa. *Human Biology* 69(4):575-581.

Zmuda, J.M., J.A. Cauley, and R.E. Ferrell
    1999   Recent progress in understanding the genetic susceptibility to osteoporosis. *Genetic Epidemiology* 16:356-367.

5

The Value of Sibling and Other "Relational" Data for Biodemography and Genetic Epidemiology

George P. Vogler

A fundamental characteristic of many traits in human populations is that variability occurs. This is true for qualitative traits such as presence or absence of disease as well as for quantitative traits that are characterized by a continuous range of variability in the population. From the perspective of evolutionary theory, it is desirable to maintain the broadest range of opportunities to respond to varying environmental circumstances in order to optimize the likelihood of survival in the face of potentially rapid fluctuations in environmental circumstances. From the perspective of public health policy, individual differences resulting from genetically based sources of variability make it desirable to move towards a more individual-based perspective on recommendations or intervention strategies, in contrast to a focus on the potential effect on the population mean. While an intervention may impact the population at large in a desirable direction, its impact on individuals might consist of nonrandom variability in response, with some individuals responding in a positive direction, other individuals not being influenced by the intervention, and other individuals actually being harmed. Individual differences in response are expected to be generally observed in a variety of contexts of environmental agents, including social or pharmacological interventions, nutritional factors, or exposure to toxicological substances. Research that advances this perspective can best be approached using study designs that are a hybrid between population-based survey methods and those that are informative from a genetic perspective.

Individual variability results, at a minimum, from environmental factors (the focus of epidemiologists) and genetic factors (the focus of geneticists). An important step in the process of developing an understanding of the impact of risk factors on traits of health relevance is to identify the individual environmental and genetic risk factors. The approaches taken by epidemiologists to detect effects of exposure to environmental risk factors and by geneticists to detect the effects of genetic loci are very different. Yet an integrated approach is required to be able to examine the impact of multiple effects, genetic and environmental, in a comprehensive manner.

Genetic epidemiology incorporates the perspective of several different disciplines. However, much research that is considered to be genetic epidemiology is geared towards characterizing genetic effects in the context of a complex system rather than fully integrating information about the effects of both genetic and environmental influences on health-related outcomes. While a number of definitions of the field of genetic epidemiology have been advanced (summarized by Khoury et al., 1993), a sense of this emphasis on genetics is evident in the statement on the overleaf of each issue of the journal *Genetic Epidemiology*, the official publication of the International Genetic Epidemiology Society:

> A peer-reviewed record and forum for discussion of research on the distribution and determinants of human disease, with emphasis on possible familial and hereditary factors as revealed by genetic, molecular, and epidemiological investigations.

More complete integration of genetically informative study designs with designs that address issues of interest in epidemiology and demography can be useful from several perspectives. To address questions about specific risk factors, an integrated design can permit some degree of control over other sources of variability that exist in a population-based sample. Certain issues of bias that arise because of sampling can be addressed using within-family controls. Large-scale survey data can be used to select an optimally powerful subsample for undertaking detailed molecular studies that focus on highly specific research issues (such as a particular disease or trait). And perhaps most significantly, a truly integrated approach would provide the opportunity to model genetic and environmental influences as they co-act and interact to produce the trait as it exists as a complete phenotype rather than focusing on isolated subsystems.

Because the traits of interest in aging research are observed in late life, options for incorporating genetically informative extensions to survey research are limited. Family study designs that use parent-offspring information are impractical because parents of index cases are likely to be deceased and children of index cases may not yet be old enough to express age-related traits of interest. Extended pedigrees and adoption studies that rely on the contrast between adoptees and biological and/or adoptive parents have a similar limitation. Twin studies are useful when a study is designed at the outset as a twin study, but are less useful when the base sample is not specifically composed of twins.

Study designs that incorporate measures on siblings have emerged as a very useful tool, particularly in genetic designs for detection of the influence of specific genes. This is encouraging for considering hybrid designs for incorporating genetic information into survey research designs in aging since siblings are the most practical group to consider for recruitment into extensions of population-based surveys. In the following sections, sources of variability are considered in the context of genetic and environmental influences. The informativeness of sibling data in addressing issues of variability in this context is explored.

SOURCES OF VARIABILITY FOR QUANTITATIVE TRAITS

The theoretical basis of genetic and environmental influences on a trait was developed from a number of perspectives, with Fisher (1918) being arguably among the most influential. The basic model is that the trait, or phenotype (P), is a function of genetic (G) and environmental (E) influences. These may consist of major factors—major genes that follow a Mendelian pattern of inheritance in the case of genetic factors or major qualitative exposure to risk factors in the case of environment. Alternatively, a quantitative model can be considered in which there are multiple genetic and environmental influences, each of which has a vanishingly small impact on the phenotype. These result in a quantitative distribution of a trait. Models of major factors are generally most applicable in the case of diseases that occur at a relatively low frequency in the population. The quantitative model is generally more applicable to complex traits such as relatively common chronic disease or variability that falls within the normal range for a quantitative trait.

The theory underlying the quantitative model is based on the assumption that there are an infinitely large number of individual factors affecting the trait. In reality, a quantitative distribution is approached relatively quickly with a finite number of factors (even as few as seven, for example) of modest impact. Consequently, much work in study design is now focused on the identification of specific factors, such as individual genetic loci, that impact a trait but only account for a relatively small proportion of the total variance. Identification of specific measurable genetic and environmental factors opens up new opportunities to develop models of interacting influences among the multiple influences.

Genetic Variance

Major Effects

Mendelian inheritance of major gene effects has played a significant role in medical genetics. As of January 24, 2000, there were 11,123 entries catalogued in Online Mendelian Inheritance in Man (OMIM, 2000). In general, study designs that are appropriate for survey research are not optimal for investigating major gene effects because such traits tend to occur at a very rare frequency in the population. As a result, major gene effects can be more efficiently investigated using sampling strategies that sample through ascertainment of probands and their relatives in studies that are designed for the purpose of exploring specific traits. Some sampling strategies that are designed to optimize the ability to identify major genes are not designed to address population parameters of interest to demographers and epidemiologists. In general, traits that are relevant for aging-related research are likely to exhibit genetic influences that are more complex than single major genes or are likely to occur at too rare a frequency to be a major focus of population-based survey research.

Polygenic Variance

Extensive theoretical development has occurred in quantitative genetics over nearly a century. Summaries of this work are very accessible (e.g., Falconer and Mackay, 1996 and earlier editions; Lynch and Walsh, 1998). The basis of the quantitative genetic model is that variability in traits arises from the cumulative action of an infinitely large number of influences of vanishingly small effect. A wide assortment of sophisticated models has been developed to decompose a population's phenotypic variance into its components. These models permit the distinction between genetic components and environmental components. Classical approaches in animal studies use patterns of means and variances in inbred strains and derived generations primarily to investigate polygenic influences (additive, dominant, and epistatic effects). Classical approaches in human studies use models of covariance among relatives (twins, families, extended pedigrees, and adoptions) to investigate both genetic effects and, in some designs, cultural transmission effects (Cloninger et al., 1979a, 1979b; Rice et al., 1978). It is important to note that these models consider latent, unobserved components of variance that are not directly measurable, although a recent trend is to merge these approaches with gene mapping studies to incorporate the effect of individual quantitative trait loci (QTLs). There is no theoretical reason why such approaches cannot also be extended to incorporate the effect of individual measured environmental factors.

A Compromise Approach

For any given trait, the true genetic architecture may consist of a finite number of genes, each of which accounts for a modest percent of the variation in the trait (modest might be as low as a few percent or as great as perhaps twenty percent). Recognition that this is likely to be the true state of affairs for many complex phenotypes drives one current thrust in human genetics to emphasize the development of new sampling procedures and statistical techniques and the initiation of large-scale data collection. These efforts are designed to permit detection of loci of relatively small individual impact on complex traits, especially chronic disease traits.

Latent Effects

Variance decomposition models conceptualize genetic effects as latent, unobservable factors that are assessed as components of variation within a population. This approach is useful for addressing the initial question of whether there are indeed genetic influences worth pursuing at a more molecular level for a phenotype. Even in many of the more refined models that are designed to detect the influence of QTLs, the gene itself is not necessarily directly measured but rather is detected as a factor linked to a DNA marker that is not likely to be part of a functional gene. Variance decomposition models still have an important role in genetic investigations. However, the power of such approaches is limited in the ability to adequately include effects such as epistatic interactions, gene-environment correlation or interaction, loci of small effect, developmental effects, and numerous other effects that might be operating in the context of genetic influences in a complex system.

Measurable Effects

The idea of incorporating measured genotypic effects into models of complex traits is not new (Boerwinkle et al., 1986; 1987). However, the explosion of information that is becoming available regarding molecular markers and specific genes, along with the acceleration of available information on specific loci from the Human Genome Project, has intensified interest in this area. There has been a rapid increase in interest in general models of complex traits that explicitly incorporate information on individual loci (Almasy and Blangero, 1998; Amos, 1994; Fulker and Cherny, 1996; Vogler et al., 1997). We are beginning to see application of such an approach to diverse phenotypes such as Alzheimer's disease (reviewed by Lovestone, 1999), gene-environment interactions in asthma (Cookson,

1999), and risk for colorectal cancer (Le Marchand, 1999). Further research along these lines will result in an enhanced ability to incorporate measurable influences into a complex-system model that includes more detailed models of specific genetic effects interacting with other genetic and environmental effects.

Shared Genetic Effects

One feature of quantitative genetic theory is the provision of detailed expectations regarding the resemblance of genetic factors among various pairs of relatives. This underlying theory provides the basis for using patterns of covariation among relatives to infer the existence of genetic influences. Features of common study designs that exploit this approach are outlined in a later section.

Environmental Variance

It is beyond the scope of this chapter to provide a detailed summary of environmental sources of variance. This section provides a synopsis of environmental effects as they are conceptualized and incorporated into quantitative genetic models.

Major Effects

Major environmental influences can be characterized as qualitative variables such as exposure or nonexposure to an environmental risk factor. This kind of major environmental factor can be readily incorporated into quantitative genetic models either as a covariate or as a variable that distinguishes among multiple subgroups that can be compared for differences in covariance structure (e.g., Sörbom, 1974). It is important to ensure that stratification by a major environmental factor is not confounded with stratification on genetic factors for this approach to work. It can be used to address questions of genotype-environment interaction (see Kang and Gauch, 1995, for an overview).

Polyenvironmental Variance

The term *polyenvironmental influence* is not common but is used here to draw attention to the analogy between polygenic variance and environmental variance that is due to the impact of numerous small environmental effects. In this model, environmental influences can result in continuous quantitative variability in phenotypic expression. In quantitative genetic models, the "environment" includes systematic environmental effects that are shared by family members to varying degrees; true environmental influences that are unique to the individual; and random effects including true random variability, measurement error, and other sources of error (Falconer and Mackay, 1996; Fisher, 1918).

A Compromise Approach

It is difficult to propose a general model of environmental influences. Unlike with genetic influences, there is not a generally accepted comprehensive theoretical model. Any pattern of environmental effects is likely to be highly phenotype-specific. While any general model needs to include random variability in a measurement model, true environmental effects could consist of any combination of random effects, nonrandom quantitative effects, and/or major effects.

Latent Effects

As with genetic effects, the quantitative genetic model incorporates environmental influences as latent effects that can be either unique to the individual or shared by family members. As with latent genetic effects, there is limited power to consider models of complex phenomena beyond a simple additive model.

Measurable Effects

The incorporation of measurable environmental effects into quantitative genetic models is not particularly difficult. Collaboration between quantitative geneticists and environmentalists is key to developing such integrated models (Bronfenbrenner and Ceci, 1993; Horowitz, 1993; Wachs, 1993). Models that incorporate an index of multiple environmental influences were developed by Rao et al. (1982) to describe variability of risk factors for cardiovascular disease. When incorporating measures of the environment, it is important to select measures that are truly environmental and free of genetic influence and at the same time are of relevance to the phenotype of interest. In practice, identification of such environmental measures presents a challenge. Even factors that at first glance seem to be obvious environmental factors often, upon further examination, have complex relationships with genetically influenced factors. For example, smoking might be considered to be an obvious environmental influence on health, yet there is extensive evidence of a significant heritable component to smoking behavior (e.g., Heath et al., 1995; Pomerleau, 1995). Indicators of socioeconomic status are intertwined in a complex manner with genetic influences (Behrman et al., 1980; Vogler and Fulker,

1983). Even accidents may be related to genetically influenced personality attributes that contribute to variability in risk-taking behavior. Collaboration among geneticists, epidemiologists, demographers, and sociologists is essential to overcome this challenge.

Shared Environmental Effects

Study designs that incorporate groups of relatives will include environmental influences that are shared by relatives. Some study designs are more effective in distinguishing shared genetic effects from shared environmental effects. All study designs rely on a fairly strong set of assumptions regarding environmental influences. In contrast to quantitative genetics, there is no comprehensive theoretical model of environmental sources of familial resemblance that is generally applicable to any phenotype. Familial environmental effects can arise through a variety of mechanisms, including common within-family cultural effects, sibling shared environment, twin shared environment, parent-child cultural transmission, interaction effects among family members, environmental mechanisms of assortative mating, prenatal effects, etc. Some work has been done on developing models of cultural transmission (Karlin, 1979a-d; Cloninger et al., 1979a, 1979b; Rice et al., 1978; Vogler and Fulker, 1983), but the lack of a unified comprehensive model of environmental influence remains an issue.

SOURCES OF RESEMBLANCE AMONG FAMILY MEMBERS

The most practical extension to population-based survey methods in aging research is likely to involve the incorporation of siblings. However, it is important to briefly summarize alternative study designs to put sibling studies into the appropriate context.

Twin Studies

Classical twin studies remain a very useful design for decomposition of phenotypic variance into components (see Christensen in this volume). Twins provide the opportunity to differentiate between additive genetic influences, either shared environmental influences or genetic dominance, and unshared environmental influences. Twin studies are moderately easy to conduct, provide a regular data structure that has analytic advantages, and represent a relatively powerful design in terms of information content for statistical inference. A critical assumption that is difficult to test is that monozygotic and dizygotic twins share environmental influences to an equal extent. If this assumption is violated, then estimates of genetic influences will be biased. A second key assumption is that assortative mating is absent. The only option in traditional twin studies is to ignore assortative mating since there is no information in the data regarding this phenomenon. In the past, zygosity misclassification has been a source of bias in twin studies, but the opportunity to determine zygosity basically without error using molecular genetics has eliminated this as a problem. However, questions regarding the generalizability or representativeness of twin studies can be raised.

Nuclear Family Studies

Nuclear family studies consist of the traditional constellation of parents and their biological offspring. This is an effective design to demonstrate familial resemblance, but it is not possible to separate additive genetic effects from shared environmental effects based solely on phenotypic resemblance among family members (Rice et al., 1978). It assumes that the phenotypic measures in the parental generation are the same as the phenotypic measures in the offspring—a questionable assumption for any trait that shows either substantial developmental change or cohort effects. Data are relatively easy to obtain and there are few questions regarding generalizability or representativeness of samples of nuclear families, although the traditional nuclear family structure has become less representative of population family structure. The spouse correlation can be assessed and explicitly included in a model of familial resemblance, although it may be difficult or impossible to distinguish among competing models of assortative mating without further specialized data that specifically focus on spouse resemblance (e.g., Cloninger, 1980; Heath and Eaves, 1985; Carey, 1986). A model of cultural transmission may be incorporated, but it is a challenge to distinguish among competing models of cultural transmission in the absence of a well-developed theoretical expectation (Cloninger et al., 1979a). It is not possible to distinguish between shared genetic influences and shared family environmental influences in nuclear families without measuring at least one of these influences. The irregular data structure presents surmountable challenges for data analysis (Lange et al., 1976). Nonpaternity is a potential source of error.

Adoption Studies

Adoption studies feature a genetic relationship between biological parents and the adoptee and an environmental relationship between adoptive parents and the adoptee. The partial adoption design includes the adoptee and adoptive parents; the full adoption design includes the adoptee, adoptive parents, and biological parents. The assumption of no selective placement is critical and a potential problem (Hardy-Brown et al., 1980; Ho et al., 1979). The representativeness of adoptive relationships is also subject to question. The key advantage of adoption studies is that they provide a direct and powerful test of the distinction between genetic influences and shared environmental influences. Potentially powerful information about prenatal effects can also be obtained from the full adoption design. The key disadvantage of adoption designs is the increasing difficulty of obtaining a sample. Serious issues of sample representativeness are also a problem, since adoptive parents tend to be older and of higher socioeconomic status whereas biological parents tend to be younger and of lower socioeconomic status.

Other Designs

Twins reared apart combine features of twin studies and adoption studies. Twins and their parents combine features of nuclear family and twin studies (Jencks et al., 1972; Eaves et al., 1978; Fulker, 1982). Twins and their offspring combine features of nuclear families, twin studies, and extended pedigrees (Nance and Corey, 1976). Adoption studies that include biological offspring of the adoptive parents provide greater resolution of the information contained in both adoption and nuclear family studies (Plomin and DeFries, 1983).

Siblings

For quantitative genetic models of variance decomposition, sibling studies represent one of the weakest designs available. Sibs share both genetic and environmental influences that are completely confounded as latent variables. While there is little convincing evidence of strong sibling-shared environmental effects (Turkheimer and Waldron, 2000), particularly in the context of aging research, it remains unacceptable simply to assume that all sibling resemblance results from genetic effects.

Why, then, have sibling samples become one of the predominant designs in human genetics? The key is that there has been a fundamental shift in the question that is being addressed in human genetic studies. Convincing demonstration of genetically based variability is no longer the central issue. Instead, a primary issue is now the identification of specific genes. In this context, sibling covariation that is nongenetic in origin merely becomes irrelevant to the primary purpose of gene identification. Thus, a major role for sibling studies is in gene mapping investigations.

GENE MAPPING

The opportunity to merge advances in molecular genetic technology with advances in statistical techniques expanded in earnest with the development of DNA markers such as restriction fragment length polymorphisms (Lander and Botstein, 1989). Research exploded in the past decade with the continued refinement of molecular technology yielding a variety of DNA markers—e.g., short tandem repeats (STRs) or microsatellites; variable number of tandem repeats (VNTRs); single nucleotide polymorpohisms (SNPs), and gene expression microarrays or gene chips. A genetic marker is a measurable polymorphic sequence of DNA whose chromosomal location is known. Markers often have no known functional significance but are used as pointers to a particular chromosomal location. The logic of gene mapping technology is simple: Determine if there is a relationship between variability in a phenotype and variability in an anonymous DNA marker of known chromosomal location. If there is a relationship, it is taken as evidence that there is a gene that influences the trait at or near the marker.

Simply to look for an association between a marker and a phenotype in a sample drawn from the population requires that the marker and trait gene be in linkage disequilibrium, which is the preferential occurrence of a trait allele in association with a specific marker allele at the population level. Furthermore, association should not be the result of other phenomena, such as population stratification (discussed in detail under "Association Studies"), that are unrelated to genetic causality. A more general case is that a marker and trait locus are close together on a chromosome but are not necessarily in linkage disequilibrium at the population level. To detect linkage without assuming population linkage disequilibrium between marker and trait loci, family data are used. Since there is only a single meiosis between one generation and the next, linkage disequilibrium is expected within families for a linked marker and trait locus even if the population is in equilibrium.

Linkage Analysis of Pedigree Data

Classical LOD score linkage analysis of pedigree data (Ott, 1991) has been the method of choice for gene mapping of Mendelian major factors for disease loci. Linkage analysis is a parametric approach that generally requires specification of mode of inheritance for the major gene. Since a major gene model is not appropriate for many of the complex traits of relevance for aging, linkage analysis of pedigree data is not an appropriate strategy, even though this approach is highly sophisticated and has been extensively refined over the years. Furthermore, it is difficult to obtain appropriate multigenerational pedigree data and biological samples for DNA analysis in most aging studies when the index cases are elderly persons.

Affected Sib-Pair Linkage Analysis

A nonparametric alternative to classical LOD score linkage analysis of pedigree data is the affected sib-pair method (Fishman et al., 1978). Sib pairs in which both members are affected are likely to deviate from the expected genotypic frequencies at a marker locus if linkage to a disease locus occurs. Affected sib-pair methods are most appropriate for diseases that have a single major gene etiology. Since sampling to obtain pairs of affected sibs is best done through ascertainment of probands, it is not the design of choice for extensions to population-based survey research unless the disease occurs at a relatively high rate. A similar approach has been developed for other kinds of pairs of affected relatives (Weeks and Lange, 1988).

Sib-Pair Allele-Sharing Methods for QTL Mapping

The utility of using sib pairs for QTL gene-mapping studies is based on an approach developed by Haseman and Elston (1972). It capitalizes on the fact that siblings vary in the degree to which they share alleles at a locus identical-by-descent (IBD), which means the alleles in two siblings are identical because they have both been inherited from the same common ancestor. Sibs can share neither, one, or both alleles. Quite simply, linkage between a quantitative trait is inferred for members of sib pairs if there is a relationship between the degree of similarity at a marker locus, as assessed by IBD status, and the degree of similarity at a trait locus, usually inferred by phenotypic similarity. The Haseman-Elston approach has been the focus of a number of methodological refinements in recent years as the utility of sib pairs for gene mapping of complex traits has become widely recognized. These advances include maximum likelihood and variance component approaches, integration into more complex models of familial resemblance, multipoint mapping using more than one genetic marker, and integration of linkage and association methods (Amos, 1994; Xu and Atchley, 1995; Fulker and Cherny, 1996; Almasy and Blangero, 1998; Fulker et al., 1999).

The advantage of using sib-pair analysis from a genetic perspective is that it moves analysis one step closer to localization of specific genes that influence complex quantitative traits. For such traits, there are likely to be multiple genetic effects explaining modest proportions of the total phenotypic variance. A major issue in variance-component allele-sharing methods is that very large samples are required to localize genes of small effect in a population. Page et al. (1998) estimate that 2,000-20,000 sib pairs are required to map loci that explain 10 percent of the total phenotypic variance.

One method that has been advanced as an efficient strategy to boost the power to detect loci of small effect is selective sampling. Selection of sib pairs who are discordant from the extremes of the population phenotypic distribution is a highly effective way to boost power from the perspective of the number of subjects who need to be genotyped (Eaves and Meyer, 1994; Gu et al., 1996; Risch and Zhang, 1996). Other approaches that can be employed to boost power are the use of multivariate phenotypes (repeated measures or correlated phenotypes) and the use of sibships of greater than two (Schork, 1993). Each of these approaches can be readily implemented into a general model for the analysis of multiple phenotypes in an arbitrary sibship structure (Vogler et al., 1997).

Sib extensions of large-scale survey research projects can be highly effective for gene mapping studies of complex traits. Large samples of individuals with phenotypic information provide an ideal sample from which selected sib pairs can be drawn from the extremes of the distribution for further genetic investigations. This strategy works only for highly focused genetic studies. The ability to genotype selected subsamples will be lost for exploratory studies with multiple independent phenotypes under investigation, since a greater and greater portion of the population will be sampled as the number of phenotypes increases. Rich survey data sets can provide superb opportunities for analysis of multivariate phenotypes. Finally, if a subject is willing to provide contact information on siblings, he or she is likely to provide information on multiple sibs if they are available for study.

ASSOCIATION STUDIES

In theory, complete knowledge of the entire human genome generated by the Human Genome Project should make it possible simply to measure those genes that are predicted to affect a phenotype in a sample of unrelated individuals, making relative-pair-based methods of analysis obsolete. It is potentially possible simply to include all of the relevant genotypes (and environmental influences) in a large model, such as a regression analysis or a neural network model, using individuals from the population. This approach of demonstrating association between a particular genotype and a trait is likely to predominate in the near future. However, the most effective data structure will not be merely a sample of unrelated individuals.

Generic Association Using Candidate Genes
or Tightly Linked Markers

One strategy for association studies is to look for an association between a candidate gene, selected on the basis of an understanding of the mechanism of action of the candidate gene, and a reasonable hypothesis that a particular gene of known function is likely to affect the target phenotype. An association can occur if the gene is in fact directly affecting the phenotype or if the gene does not have a direct effect on the trait but is in linkage disequilibrium with another nearby gene. Linkage disequilibrium can arise from recent mutations, migrations, population bottlenecks, or other sources (Lander and Schork, 1994). Because recombination will break the linkage between a marker and trait, only those loci that are very close with limited opportunity for recombination will be cotransmitted from generation to generation over a period of time, retaining linkage at the level of the population. Consequently, in addition to functional candidate genes, it is possible to use anonymous DNA markers that are tightly linked to functional genes in the context of association studies.

An association can be detected in a population sample using a simple case-control design for qualitative traits or a test of mean differences as a function of genotype for a quantitative trait. While the association approach may be most appropriate for complex traits (Risch and Merikangas, 1996), it should be noted that statistical association can arise for reasons unrelated to physical linkage between a marker locus and a disease locus (Ewens and Spielman, 1995; Lander and Schork, 1994).

Founder effects (the high frequency of an allele in a population founded by a small ancestral group in which one or more founders carried the specific allele by chance) or genetic drift (random fluctuations in allele frequencies usually due to finite sample size) can cause variation in allele frequencies at marker loci among subdivisions of a population (Slatkin, 1991). If a trait locus is present at a higher frequency in a subgroup of the population that has a higher frequency of a particular allele at a marker locus, then a meaningless association will be present even if the marker and trait locus are completely unlinked. The potential for spurious associations to exist in population-based surveys with large samples is particularly acute. This is because different population subgroups (such as ethnic groups) that differ with regard to both disease frequency and marker allele frequency will be represented in a population-derived sample of individuals.

Recent admixture of two populations that differ in marker allele frequencies and trait locus allele frequencies will also exhibit spurious associations (Ewens and Spielman, 1995) until a sufficient number of generations of random mating and recombination move the population to a new equilibrium. Population-based survey research that involves the investigation of a population in which substantial migration has resulted in admixture within the past few generations is likely to have spurious associations arising from this phenomenon.

If a case-control study is conducted on a structured population in which stratification occurs and the focus is on selected candidate loci, it is possible to test for stratification by typing a panel of additional markers that are unlinked to the candidate loci (Pritchard and Rosenberg, 1999). However, this approach detects but does not control for stratification. It is applicable to the case where a small number of candidate loci are investigated but is difficult to apply for more exploratory approaches.

Transmission/Disequilibrium Tests

An approach that has received considerable attention and undergone considerable recent methodological development uses within-family tests of association in order to control for population stratification (Falk and Rubenstein, 1987; Knapp et al., 1993; Ott, 1989; Schaid, 1996; Spielman et al., 1993; Spielman and Ewens, 1996; Thomson, 1995). This transmission/ disequilibrium test (TDT), initially developed for application to traits such as insulin-dependent diabetes mellitus (Spielman et al., 1993), uses parents who provide genotypic data and who are heterozygous for marker alleles, and at least one affected child who provides genotypic and phenotypic data. The logic of the TDT test is that spurious associations due to population structure will not be present in transmission of marker alleles from one generation to the next within individual families. Genotypic data on marker alleles are obtained for parents and affected offspring, and a test is conducted to determine if the frequency of transmission of a marker allele to an affected child deviates significantly from the expected frequency of transmission in the absence of linkage.

While the TDT tests were originally developed and extended for application to qualitative disease traits, recent extensions have been made to accommodate continuously distributed quantitative traits (Allison, 1997; Rabinowitz, 1997). George et al. (1999) propose a regression-based test for transmission/disequilibrium that permits a more general arbitrary pedigree structure and nonindependence of observations by allowing for a residual correlational structure among the observations. This is an important step in the development of techniques that can be applied to complex traits.

Sibling Transmission/Disequilibrium Tests

Family-based control techniques that require data on parents and offspring are not well suited to investigate issues in aging since data on parents cannot generally be obtained. A number of procedures have been developed that employ the logic of the TDT for within-family control but that use sibling data and do not require genotypic information on parents. Curtis (1997) and Boehnke and Langefeld (1998) describe tests of association based on a discordant-sib-pair design in which marker alleles are counted in affected and unaffected members of discordant sib pairs and contrasted with the expectation, under no marker-disease association, of equal allele frequencies in affected and unaffected sibs. Spielman and Ewens (1998) describe a similar approach and present a method for combining data that can be analyzed only by the sib TDT test with data that have parental information that can be analyzed using the original TDT test.

As with the parent-offspring transmission-based TDT tests, the sibling-based tests have been extended to the analysis of quantitative traits. Allison et al. (1999) propose a method for the analysis of joint tests of linkage and association with quantitative traits using sibling data. Fulker et al. (1999) incorporate a sib-pair-based test of association into a variance-components procedure for mapping QTLs in sib pairs. This approach is generalized further by Abecasis et al. (2000) to the analysis of quantitative traits in nuclear families of arbitrary size that can optionally incorporate information on parental genotypes.

To summarize, methodological developments in the use of siblings to map the effects of specific loci using linkage-based or association-based models represent the cutting edge of quantitative analytical tools for the analysis of complex traits. These methods are extremely relevant for the analysis of complex traits in aging research. One of the great potential uses of these models is in incorporating environmental assessment into the models in a manner similar to how genetic marker information has been incorporated into the genetic aspects of the models.

ENVIRONMENT "MAPPING"

The analogy between mapping specific genetic effects and specific environmental effects is not perfect; we do not have an environmental analogy of the genetic map with markers pointing to positions of tightly linked factors for environmental influences, but we can specify candidate environmental agents analogous to specifying candidate genes. It might be possible to stretch the analogy of linked loci to shared family environmental influences that could be analyzed using some environmental analogy of linkage analysis, but its applicability would be limited to a very small number of special situations of marginal interest. However, certain features of genetic models of QTL influences could be developed more extensively for the environmental side of an integrated model of genetic and environmental effects.

The issue of spurious association due to population stratification or admixture is just as relevant for measured environmental influences as for genetic influences (e.g., Lilienfeld and Stolley, 1994). Stratified sampling (e.g., Thompson, 1992) is commonly applied in epidemiology to control for such confounding. Differences in irrelevant environmental risk factors among population strata that differ in frequency (or mean value) of a phenotype will result in spurious association. Within-family control can be effective in correcting for effects of stratification on environmental effects similar to how within-family control is used to correct for effects of stratification on genetic effects. The use of within-family data such as siblings basically redefines the subgroup unit to be the family. Consequently, it results in adjustment for between-family variability on any factor, observed or unobserved. In studies of aging, sib-based designs can control for factors that may have occurred decades earlier. For example, families may have differed in exposure to epidemics, exposure to environmental toxins, access to health care, childhood nutrition, and countless other factors early in life whose influence in late life might otherwise be uncontrolled for in samples of individuals. If some of these factors are measurable and show within-family variability as well as between-family variability, they can be analyzed for within-family effects that are independent of effects of stratification.

Clearly the use of sibling data is far more developed in the context of genetic influences than in the context of environmental influences. A systematic effort to enhance the environmental side using large-sample population-based sibling data would be valuable for enhancing the ability to understand the total constellation of multiple genetic and environmental influences on complex traits.

OPPORTUNITIES FOR INTEGRATED MODELS

Taking advantage of advances in molecular genetics, powerful methods have been developed recently to detect individual loci that contribute a relatively modest amount to the total phenotypic variance based on sibling TDT approaches. For example, Abecasis et al. (2000) present extensive power simulation results. A locus that accounts for 10 percent of the phenotypic variance can be detected with 80 percent power at the genome-screen alpha level of 5×10^{-8} using about 1,000 individuals in sib-pair configurations or 800 individuals in subtrios. A locus that accounts for 5 percent of the phenotypic variance requires about 2,000 individuals in sib-pairs or 1,600 individuals in trios. The prospect of having measurable genetic influences for complex multifactorial traits is particularly exciting because it provides new opportunities to explore influences at a vastly more complex level than afforded by the overly simple models that limit latent variable approaches. These new models are much more likely to be able to describe the true mechanism of action of multiple influences on a complex system than has previously been possible.

Equally exciting is the prospect of detecting and incorporating measurable effects of specific environmental influences into a comprehensive model. Geneticists, by and large, have focused on the exciting advances in genetics in recent years for gene mapping and identification. However, it is not reasonable to ignore nongenetic effects on complex traits. Genetic influences are likely to be complex and dynamic, with genes turning on and off in response to conditions of the system that are influenced by other genes and by the environment. As a result, true understanding of the influences that lead to a phenotype is likely to occur only in the context of a comprehensive model of interacting genetic and environmental influences. Gene expression technology is likely to provide further dramatic opportunities for model refinement by providing a means to quantify effects such as tissue specificity, developmental effects, genetic response to environmental agents, etc.

The success of this integrated approach will lie in effective cross-communication between researchers who are expert in exploiting genetic information and those who are expert in environmental assessment. Clearly it will not be adequate to simply take a moderate sample, measure everything, and conduct a huge multiple-regression analysis. Collaborative, large-scale data collection efforts will be essential to provide adequate power to detect small effects and especially to characterize interactions among small effects. Certain steps towards comprehensive integrated models can be taken rather rapidly with extensions of available technology. Some issues, however, will require innovative ideas from a multidisciplinary perspective.

REFERENCES

Abecasis, G.R., L.R. Cardon, and W.O.C. Cookson
    2000   A general test of association for quantitative traits in nuclear families. *American Journal of Human Genetics* 66:279-292.
Allison, D.B.
    1997   Transmission-disequilibrium tests for quantitative traits. *American Journal of Human Genetics* 60:676-690.
Allison, D.B., M. Heo, N. Kaplan, and E.R. Martin
    1999   Sibling-based tests of linkage and association for quantitative traits. *American Journal of Human Genetics* 64:1754-1764.
Almasy, L., and J. Blangero
    1998   Multipoint quantitative-trait linkage analysis in general pedigrees. *American Journal of Human Genetics* 62:1198-1211.
Amos, C.I.
    1994   Robust variance-components approach for assessing genetic linkage in pedigrees. *American Journal of Human Genetics* 54:535-543.

Behrman, J.R., Z. Hrubec, P. Taubman, and T.J. Wales
  1980   *Socioeconomic Success: A Study of the Effects of Genetic Endowments, Family Environ-
          ment, and Schooling.* Amsterdam: North-Holland.
Boehnke, M., and C.D. Langefeld
  1998   Genetic association mapping based on discordant sib pairs: The discordant-alle-
          les test. *American Journal of Human Genetics* 62:950-961.
Boerwinkle, E., R. Chakraborty, and C.F. Sing
  1986   The use of measured genotypic information in the analysis of quantitative pheno-
          types in man. *Annals of Human Genetics* 50:181-194.
Boerwinkle, E., S. Viscikis, D. Welsh, J. Steinmetz, S.M. Hamash, and C.F. Sing
  1987   The use of measured genotypic information in the analysis of quantitative pheno-
          types in man. II. The role of the apolipoprotein E polymorphisms in determining
          levels, variability, and covariability of cholesterol, betalipoprotein, and triglycer-
          ides in a sample of unrelated individuals. *American Journal of Medical Genetics*
          27:567-582.
Bronfenbrenner, U., and S.J. Ceci
  1993   Heredity, environment, and the question "How?": A first approximation. Pp.
          313-324 in *Nature, Nurture and Psychology*, R. Plomin and G.E. McClearn, eds.
          Washington, DC: American Psychological Association.
Carey, G.
  1986   A general multivariate approach to linear modeling in human genetics. *American
          Journal of Human Genetics* 39:775-786.
Cloninger, C.R.
  1980   Interpretation of intrinsic and extrinsic structural relations by path analysis:
          Theory and applications to assortative mating. *Genetical Research* 36:133-145.
Cloninger, C.R., J. Rice, and T. Reich
  1979a Multifactorial inheritance with cultural transmission and assortative mating. II.
          A general model of combined polygenic and cultural inheritance. *American Jour-
          nal of Human Genetics* 31:176-198.
  1979b Multifactorial inheritance with cultural transmission and assortative mating. III.
          Family structure and the analysis of separation experiments. *American Journal of
          Human Genetics* 31:366-388.
Cookson, W.
  1999   The alliance of genes and environment in asthma and allergy. *Nature* 402(6760
          Suppl):B5-11.
Curtis, D.
  1997   Use of siblings as controls in case-control association studies. *Annals of Human
          Genetics* 61:319-333.
Eaves, L.J., K.A. Last, P.A. Young, and N.G. Martin
  1978   Model-fitting approaches to the analysis of human behavior. *Heredity* 41:249-320.
Eaves, L.J., and J. Meyer
  1994   Locating human quantitative trait loci: Guidelines for the selection of sibling
          pairs for genotyping. *Behavior Genetics* 24:443-455.
Ewens, W.J., and R.S. Spielman
  1995   The transmission/disequilibrium test: History, subdivision, and admixture.
          American Journal of Human Genetics 57:455-464.
Falconer, D.C., and T.F.C. Mackay
  1996   *Introduction to Quantitative Genetics, 4th Edition.* Harlow, UK: Longman.
Falk, C.T., and P. Rubenstein
  1987   Haplotype relative risks: An easy reliable way to construct a proper control
          sample for risk calculations. *Annals of Human Genetics* 51:227-233.

Fisher, R.A.
    1918   The correlation between relatives on the supposition of Mendelian inheritance. *Transactions of the Royal Society of Edinburgh* 52:399-433.
Fishman, P.M., B. Suarez, S.E. Hodge, and T. Reich
    1978   A robust method for the detection of linkage in familial diseases. *American Journal of Human Genetics* 30:308-321.
Fulker, D.W.
    1982   Extensions of the classical twin method. Pp. 395-406 in *Human Genetics, Part A: The Unfolding Genome*, B. Bonne-Tamir, ed. New York: Alan R. Liss.
Fulker, D.W., and S.S. Cherny
    1996   An improved multipoint sib-pair analysis of quantitative traits. *Behavior Genetics* 26:527-532.
Fulker, D.W., S.S. Cherny, P.C. Sham, and J.K. Hewitt
    1999   Combined linkage and association sib-pair analysis for quantitative traits. *American Journal of Human Genetics* 64:259-267.
George, V., H.K. Tiwari, X. Zhu, and R.C. Elston
    1999   A test of transmission/disequilibrium for quantitative traits in pedigree data, by multiple regression. *American Journal of Human Genetics* 65:236-245.
Gu, C., A. Todorov, and D.C. Rao
    1996   Combining extremely concordant sibpairs with extremely discordant sibpairs provides a cost effective way to linkage analysis of quantitative trait loci. *Genetic Epidemiology* 13:513-533.
Hardy-Brown, K., R. Plomin, J. Greenhalgh, and K. Jax
    1980   Selective placement of adopted children: Prevalence and effects. *Journal of Child Psychology and Psychiatry* 21:143-152.
Haseman, J.K. and R.C. Elston
    1972   The investigation of linkage between a quantitative trait and a marker locus. *Behavior Genetics* 2:3-19.
Heath, A.C. and L.J. Eaves
    1985   Resolving the effects of phenotypic and social background on mate selection. *Behavior Genetics* 15:15-30.
Heath, A.C., P.A.F. Madden, W.S. Slutske, and N.G. Martin
    1995   Personality and the inheritance of smoking behavior: A genetic perspective. *Behavior Genetics* 25:103-117.
Ho, H., R. Plomin, and J.C. DeFries
    1979   Selective placement in adoption. *Social Biology* 26:1-6.
Horowitz, F.D.
    1993   The need for a comprehensive new environmentalism. Pp. 341-353 in *Nature, Nurture and Psychology*, R. Plomin and G.E. McClearn, eds. Washington, DC: American Psychological Association.
Jencks, C., M. Smith, H. Ackland, M.J. Bane, D. Cohen, H. Gintis, B. Heyns, and S. Michelson
    1972   *Inequality: A Reassessment of the Effect of Family and Schooling in America*. New York: Basic Books.
Kang, M.S. and H.G. Gauch, Jr., eds.
    1995   *Genotype-by-Environment Interaction*. Boca Raton, FL: CRC Press.
Karlin, S.
    1979a Models of multifactorial inheritance: I, Multivariate formulations and basic convergence results. *Theoretical and Population Biology* 15:308-355.
    1979b Models of multifactorial inheritance: II, The covariance structure for a scalar phenotype under selective assortative mating and sex-dependent symmetric parental-transmission. *Theoretical and Population Biology* 15:356-393.

1979c Models of multifactorial inheritance: III, Calculation of covariance of relatives under selective assortative mating. *Theoretical and Population Biology* 15:394-423.

1979d Models of multifactorial inheritance: IV, Asymmetric transmission for a scalar phenotype. *Theoretical and Population Biology* 15:424-438.

Khoury, M.J., T.H. Beaty, and B.H. Cohen

1993 *Fundamentals of Genetic Epidemiology.* New York: Oxford University Press.

Knapp, M., S.A. Seuchter, and M.P. Bauer

1993 The haplotype-relative-risk (HRR) method for analysis of association in nuclear families. *American Journal of Human Genetics* 52:1085-1093.

Lander, E.S., and D. Botstein

1989 Mapping Mendelian factors underlying quantitative traits using RFLP linkage maps. *Genetics* 121:185-199.

Lander, E.S., and N.J. Schork

1994 Genetic dissection of complex traits. *Science* 265:2037-2048.

Lange, K., J. Westlake, and M.A. Spence

1976 Extensions to pedigree analysis. III. Variance components by the scoring method. *Annals of Human Genetics* 4:171-189.

Le Marchand, L.

1999 Combined influence of genetic and dietary factors on colorectal cancer incidence in Japanese Americans. *Monographs: Journal of the National Cancer Institute* 26:101-105.

Lilienfeld, D.E., and P.D. Stolley

1994 *Foundations of Epidemiology (third edition).* New York: Oxford University Press.

Lovestone, S.

1999 Early diagnosis and the clinical genetics of Alzheimer's disease. *Journal of Neurology* 246:69-72.

Lynch, M., and B. Walsh

1998 *Genetics and Analysis of Quantitative Traits.* Sunderland, MA: Sinauer.

Nance, W.E., and L.A. Corey

1976 Genetic models for the analysis of data from the families of identical twins. *Genetics* 83:811-826.

Online Mendelian Inheritance in Man, OMIM (TM)

2000 McKusick-Nathans Institute for Genetic Medicine, Johns Hopkins University (Baltimore, MD) and National Center for Biotechnology Information, National Library of Medicine (Bethesda, MD). World Wide Web URL: http://www.ncbi.nlm.nih.gov/omim/

Ott, J.

1989 Statistical properties of the haplotype relative risk. *Genetic Epidemiology* 6:127-130.

1991 *Analysis of Human Genetic Linkage, Revised Edition.* Baltimore: Johns Hopkins University Press.

Page, G.P., C.I. Amos, and E. Boerwinkle

1998 The quantitative LOD score: Test statistic and sample size for exclusion and linkage of quantitative traits in human sibships. *American Journal of Human Genetics* 62:962-968.

Plomin, R. and J.C. DeFries

1983 The Colorado Adoption Project. *Child Development* 54:276-289.

Pomerleau, O.F.

1995 Individual differences in sensitivity to nicotine: Implications for genetic research on nicotine dependence. *Behavior Genetics* 25:161-177.

Pritchard, J.K., and N.A. Rosenberg
   1999   Use of unlinked genetic markers to detect population stratification in association studies. *American Journal of Human Genetics* 65:220-228.
Rabinowitz, D.
   1997   A transmission disequilibrium test for quantitative trait loci. *Human Heredity* 47:342-350.
Rao, D.C., P.M. Laskarzewski, J.A. Morrison, P. Khoury, K. Kelly, R. Wette, J. Rusell, and C.J. Glueck
   1982   The Cincinnati Lipid Research Clinic Family Study: Cultural and biological determinants of lipids and lipoprotein concentrations. *American Journal of Human Genetics* 34:888-903.
Rice, J., C.R. Cloninger, and T. Reich
   1978   Multifactorial inheritance with cultural transmission and assortative mating. I. Description and basic properties of the unitary models. *American Journal of Human Genetics* 30:618-643.
Risch, N.J., and K. Merikangas
   1996   The future of genetic studies of complex human diseases. *Science* 273:1516-1517.
Risch, N.J., and H. Zhang
   1996   Mapping quantitative trait loci with extreme discordant sib pairs: Sampling considerations. *American Journal of Human Genetics* 58:836-843.
Schaid, D.J.
   1996   General score tests for associations of genetic markers with disease using cases and their parents. *Genetic Epidemiology* 13:423-449.
Schork, N.J.
   1993   Extended multipoint identity-by-descent analysis of human quantitative traits: Efficiency, power, and modeling considerations. *American Journal of Human Genetics* 53:1306-1319.
Slatkin, M.
   1991   Inbreeding coefficients and coalescence times. *Genetical Research* 58:167-175.
Sörbom, D.
   1974   A general method for studying differences in factor means and factor structures between groups. *British Journal of Mathematical and Statistical Psychology* 27:229-239.
Spielman, R.S., and W.J. Ewens
   1996   The TDT and other family-based tests for linkage disequilibrium and association. *American Journal of Human Genetics* 59:983-989.
   1998   A sibship test for linkage in the presence of association: The Sib Transmission/ Disequilibrium Test. *American Journal of Human Genetics* 62:450-458.
Spielman, R.S., R.E. McGinnis, and W.J. Ewens
   1993   Transmission test for linkage disequilibrium: The insulin gene region and insulin-dependent diabetes mellitus (IDDM). *American Journal of Human Genetics* 52:506-516.
Thompson, S.K.
   1992   *Sampling*. New York: John Wiley and Sons.
Thomson, G.
   1995   Mapping disease genes: Family-based association studies. *American Journal of Human Genetics* 57:487-498.
Turkheimer, E. and M. Waldron
   2000   Nonshared environment: A theoretical, methodological, and quantitative review. *Psychological Bulletin* 126:78-108.

Vogler, G.P., and D.W. Fulker
    1983   Familial resemblance for educational attainment. *Behavior Genetics* 13:341-354.
Vogler, G.P., W. Tang, T.L. Nelson, S.M. Hofer, J.D. Grant, L.M. Tarantino, and J.R. Fernandez
    1997   A multivariate model for the analysis of sibship covariance using marker information and multiple quantitative traits. *Genetic Epidemiology* 14:921-926.
Wachs, T.D.
    1993   The nature-nurture gap: What we have here is a failure to collaborate. Pp. 375-391 in *Nature, Nurture and Psychology*, R. Plomin and G.E. McClearn, eds. Washington, DC: American Psychological Association.
Weeks, D.E., and K. Lange
    1988   The affected-pedigree-member method of linkage analysis. *American Journal of Human Genetics* 42:315-326.
Xu, S., and W.R. Atchley
    1995   A random model approach to interval mapping of quantitative trait loci. *Genetics* 141:1189-1197.

6

Opportunities for Population-Based Research on Aging Human Subjects: Pathology and Genetics

George M. Martin and Qubai Hu

Pathologists and geneticists have recently been empowered with new or greatly improved sets of instruments and methodologies that provide greatly enhanced sensitivity, specificity, and scope for the quantitation of biological parameters. These innovations should interest demographers and social scientists concerned with varying patterns of health and disease within human populations over the life course. The term "human populations" is used in various contexts in this essay. Most social scientists and demographers will have particular interest in population-based samples. Geneticists and pathologists can make important contributions to such investigations. But highly selected populations, such as large kindreds, and large populations used for genetic association studies, such as comparisons between patients with a late-life disease and age-matched controls, have often been used to enhance our understanding of the basis for varying susceptibilities to late-life disorders.

A cogent example of a new tool that is waiting to be exploited for studies of populations of human subjects is the analysis of gene expression using massive microarrays. This powerful methodology can provide a simultaneous description of how tens of thousands of human genes change their expression during development and aging (Brown and Botstein, 1999; Ferea and Brown, 1999; Friend, 1999; Thieffry, 1999). With the anticipated sequencing of virtually the entire human genome, essentially all human genes will eventually be subject to such evaluation. These and other exciting innovations will be described below in the section on

Genetics. The communication of these new research opportunities to the community of population scientists is the first goal of this chapter.

The second goal is to increase awareness by the greater community of scientists of neglected resources under the control of pathologists. Two major points will be made. The first is the astonishing neglect of the autopsy, which has never been employed for a population-based statistical sampling of any segment of the American population. Death certificates are notoriously unreliable instruments for documenting causes of death. Moreover, they can never provide the comprehensive analysis of the burden of preclinical and clinical disease that can be documented via a thorough autopsy. The second major point will be to describe the vast store of cells, tissues, and body fluids that are potentially available for research.

Our third and final goal will be to underscore the value of middle age as a stage of the life course that should receive greater attention by geneticists, physiologists, physicians, and population scientists concerned with the elucidation of varying patterns of aging in our species.

GENETICS

New Methods for the Comprehensive Assessment of Changes in Gene Expression During the Life Course

The expression of a large number of genes changes during the life course. These changes are thought to underlie the mechanism of tissue differentiation during development, the modulation of physiology during pubescence, the maintenance of physiological homeostasis in the adult, the reaction of tissues to disease states, and, perhaps, some fundamental processes of aging. Proteins, rather than the ribonucleic acid messages (messenger RNA or mRNA) that relay the information in the DNA genetic code to the protein synthesizing machinery of cells, are the proximal agents of these modulations. It is difficult, however, to comprehensively assess changes in proteins over the life course. Only a small proportion of the tens of thousands of proteins in a cell can be specifically identified by available antibodies. Many critically important proteins, such as transcription factors, which regulate the expression of many other genes, are present in only trace amounts. Methods such as two-dimensional electrophoresis lack sufficient sensitivity for their identification. Highly specific sensitive-quantitative methods have been developed, however, for the identification of the levels of a wide range of mRNA in cells and tissues. These offer the best hope for the development of a battery of molecular biomarkers of aging, although the protein approach, proteomics, is being vigorously pursued by a number of laboratories.

The physical vehicles for the large-scale screening of mRNAs are sometimes referred to as massive microarrays or gene chips because the thousands of stretches of the DNA sequences that represent specific genes that allow one to identify levels of expression of mRNAs are systematically arrayed as minute samples in rows and columns on various physical substrates, such as glass slides, membranes, or composite materials. The DNA sequences are of two types. The approach pioneered by the Affymetrix company (Table 6-1) uses short strings of the nucleotide coding units of a single strand of DNA (oligonucleotides) from several exons of interest. Exons are the multiple, physically separated segments of the DNA sequence of a gene that are spliced together to provide the mRNA; the intervening sequences, which may have regulatory information, are called introns. These oligonucleotides hybridize with mRNA that is purified from various cells or tissues (e.g., from cells or tissues from a young individual) and labeled with radioactive or fluorescent tags. For the latter, one can label the material from one specimen with a fluorescent chemical that, when optically excited by a laser, emits a signal in the green region of the spectrum of light. A different set of mRNAs (for example, from the homologous cell type or tissue from an older subject) can be labeled with another fluorescent compound, such as one that emits a red signal. These two sets of labeled mRNAs can be mixed and allowed to jointly hybridize to the oligonucleotide array of human cognate genes to determine the intensity of hybridization. If the expression of a given gene does not change with age, one would observe a yellow signal (an equal mixture of the red and green signals). A dominance of a red or green signal would indicate either an increase or decrease in the expression of that gene in the cells or tissues of the older individual.

A second approach uses cDNAs instead of DNA oligonucleotides to make the microarrays. The symbol "cDNA" refers to a DNA *copy* made from the cognate mRNA, using an enzyme called reverse transcriptase. These cDNAs are denatured so that single strands are available to hybridize with single-stranded molecules of mRNA, forming duplex molecules. The cDNAs are typically arrayed on glass slides or membranes. Directions for making such arrays can be found in the web site of the laboratory of Dr. Pat Brown of Stanford University (http://cmgm.stanford.edu/pbrown/). Commercially available sources of such microarrays can now be obtained, and can include access to software for the analysis of the results. Table 6-1 summarizes some current major sources of such materials. The reader will note, however, that these are very expensive reagents. The associated informatics software (e.g., Rosetta Inpharmatics, Inc., http://www.rii.com/about/overview.htm) required for the analysis of the vast amounts of data that emerge from such studies, including algorithms for cluster analysis, can also be very expensive. Moreover, there is

TABLE 6-1 Some Commercial Resources for Assay of Human Gene Expression Using cDNA Microarrays

Company Name	Products	Substrates[a]	mRNA-Labeling Methods	Number of Genes[b]	Cost
Affymetrix (www.affymetrix.com)	GeneChip[®]	Chips[c]	Biotin-labeled	12,000 full-length cDNA & 50,000 EST[d] clusters in 5 subsets	List: $10,000/subset Contract: $5,000/subset
				Custom arrays	Available
Clontech (www.clontech.com)	Atlas[™] Array	Glass slides	Radio-labeled or Fluorescence-labeled	1,081 cDNAs	$750
		Nylon Membranes	Radio-labeled	3,600 cDNAs in 3 subsets	$1,395/subset
				Cell function-specific (e.g., apoptosis, cell cycle, etc.) arrays	Available
Invitrogen (Research Genetics) (www.invitrogen.com)	GeneFilters[®]	Nylon Membranes	Radio-labeled	30,000 cDNAs on 6 membrans	$960/membrane
				Tissue-specific (prostate, ovary, breast, colon, DermArray skin) cDNA arrays	$1,440/membrane
Stratagene (www.stratagene.com)	GeneConnection[™] Discovery-3' Microarrays	Glass slides	Fluorescence-labeled	4,000 cDNAs	$995

[a]The materials on which oligonucleotides (short single strand DNA fragments) or cDNA fragments are immobilized.
[b]Each gene is represented by 16-20 pairs of specific 25-mer oligonucleotides (e.g., Affymetrix) or by a denatured double strand cDNA fragment, typically 300-1000 base pairs, from the 3' end of each of these cDNAs.
[c]The Affymetrix's substrate is proprietary. They contain oligonucleotides in high-density arrays immobilized on glass wafers by combinations of solid-phase chemical synthesis with photolithographic fabrication techniques employed in the semiconductor industry.
[d]EST: expressed sequence tags. These are short (~200 base pairs) sequences from the 3' end of a cDNA clone (i.e., an expressed gene).

still a lack of rigorous statistical analysis of many of the results. The need for replicate independent experiments for such statistical analysis will put such an approach out of the range of most laboratories and certainly could not reasonably be applied for the study of large populations.

This situation is likely to change, however, for several reasons. First, improvements in the technology are likely to decrease the variance. Second, the enormous interest and demand for such approaches will certainly lead to substantial decreases in costs. Third, more modest arrays designed for the investigations of genes of special interest to specific studies are likely to be developed by individual laboratories or by specialized centers within major institutions at reduced costs. Fourth, and most importantly, once a few particularly robust biomarkers of specific processes of aging have been discovered and replicated using microarrays, one can employ other, more rigorously quantitative and more rapid methods based upon the polymerase chain reaction (PCR).

PCR greatly amplifies small amounts of DNA, either directly from genomic DNA or from mRNA that has been converted to DNA using reverse transcriptase enzymes. The authors have successfully employed one such method in studies of groups of subjects with autopsy-documented dementias of the Alzheimer type (DAT) and compared the results with materials from other neurological degenerative disorders and neurologically normal age-matched controls. We found changes in the expression of a specific gene in relatively unaffected portions of the brain of DAT patients that we believe could represent a relatively early stage in the evolution of the disease process (Hu et al., 2000). The method is called quantitative reverse transcription-competitive PCR (RT-cPCR). The assay is extremely sensitive and very specific. For example, we could measure, in the same reaction, two alternatively spliced forms of the same gene (called isoforms) that differed in only six nucleotide base pairs. This should be considered in the context of the fact that each of the two sets of human genes in an individual cell has about 3.1 billion base pairs. The isoform with the extra base pairs, which results in a protein with an additional two amino acids, turned out to be an exclusive marker of neuronal cells (Hu et al., 1999). It would be feasible to perform approximately 1,000 such assays, which would score for both isoforms, in no more than 50 days. We estimate the cost per assay of both isoforms to be no more than $7, including the salary of a technician and the costs of all reagents. The application of robotic methods should greatly decrease the cost per specimen for very large-scale studies.

Once suitable conditions have been worked out, the methodology could be applied, in principle, to any species of mRNA from any source of mRNA, including cells from peripheral blood samples; from small biopsies of subcutaneous fat, skin, or skeletal muscle; or from cultured cells derived from such biopsies. There are already interesting clues as to what general classes of mRNA are deserving of further analysis in larger populations of aging animals and aging human subjects. A microarray analysis of the skeletal muscles of aging cohorts of mice revealed alterations of gene regulation involving loci included in several functionally related disease clusters (Lee et al., 1999). These included genes involved in energy metabolism, protein metabolism, DNA repair, and in the responses of cells to a variety of stress factors, such as oxidative and thermal stress. A large proportion of these changes could be reversed by partial caloric restriction, a well-established method in rodents for the enhancement of life span and the postponement of several late-life diseases. An interesting example of a specific gene whose expression was markedly diminished in aged muscles was one coding for a mitochondrial protease that is involved in the biogenesis of mitochondria, an organelle that is in abundance in skeletal muscles and that is the powerhouse of our cells. The use of expression arrays for the study of aging in human subjects has so far been confined to cultured skin fibroblast-like cells from only a few subjects (Shelton et al., 1999; Ly et al., 2000), but there is much more research in progress.

Other Uses of Microarray Technologies

These microarray technologies could also be adapted to determine the prevalence of a wide variety of inborn alterations in gene dosage, either deletions or DNA amplifications (Pinkel et al., 1998; Trent et al., 1997). To do this, one hybridizes fragments of genomic DNA, rather than messenger RNA, against an array of cognate DNA sequences. This approach has only just begun to be applied to human tissues and has so far been used only to demonstrate that one can get linear signals of gene dosage for genes on the X chromosome over the range of one to five copies of X chromosomes. Given a number of technical improvements, we may soon be in the position of being able to determine the contribution of inborn changes in gene dosage to late-life disorders. Malignant neoplasms are cogent examples. We know that individuals born with only one copy of a tumor suppressor gene are more likely to develop cancer or to progress towards cancer as a result of a lesion developing in the remaining good copy of that gene sometime during the individual's life span. There are likely to be hundreds of such genes. It would be of great interest to compare the relative prevalence of deletions in such genes in various populations and in different epochs. There is epidemiological evidence of secular trends towards the postponement of reproduction in many developed countries (Armitage and Babb, 1996; Guyer et al., 1998; Speroff, 1994; Ford and Nault, 1996; Kaufmann et al., 1998; Hoshi et al.,

1999). It is known that advanced paternal age is associated with increased risk of various mutations (Risch et al., 1987; Vogel and Ralhenberg, 1975). James Crow, a leading scholar in this field, has concluded that "the age of the father is the main factor determining the human spontaneous mutation rate, and probably the total mutation rate" (1993). An example of the importance of these issues to late-life diseases is the recent evidence that advanced paternal age is associated with increased risk of prostate cancer in offspring (Zhang et al., 1999). Could this be due, in part, to an increasing burden of deletions in tumor suppressor genes?

The use of massive oligonucleotide arrays can also be used for the detection of a wide range of polymorphisms (Halushka et al., 1999; Sapolsky et al., 1999; Chee et al., 1996). In contrast to mutations, which are rare events (~10^{-6}), polymorphisms represent common genetic variants (alleles). By definition, their allelic frequencies are at least 1-2 percent of all alleles at the particular genetic locus. Polymorphisms are being used for a very exciting emerging technology involving the use of ordered arrays of human genes cloned in what are called bacterial artificial chromosomes (BAC clones). These can be used for mapping disease genes via hybridization of genomic DNA using the principles of genomic mismatch repair and linkage disequilibrium (Cheung et al., 1998). (For further details, see the internet site of the laboratory of Vivian G. Cheung, http:// genomics.med.upenn.edu/vcheung/.) The method takes advantage of the fact that we humans have single nucleotide polymorphisms (SNPs) at an average of at least one for each one thousand of our base pairs. Chromosomal domains indicative of identity by descent for such SNPs permit one to map and clone disease genes of interest in the context of a vast amount of information on other regions of the genome. The term "identity by descent" refers to the sharing of an allelic form of a gene in two individuals because they have both been inherited from the same common ancestor. By contrast, the term "identity by state" refers to the situation in which such sharing is coincidental. This technology may well be the method of choice for the genomic characterization of large populations.

The polymerase chain reaction (PCR) has also been adapted to the analysis of tissue sections so that levels of gene expression (Barlati et al., 1999; Lee et al., 1996), the detection of genomic deletions (Chiang et al., 1999), and the detection of infectious agents (Fredericks and Relman, 1996; Montone and Litzky, 1995) can be related to specific cell types. The development of methods for the quantitative analysis of gene expression in single cells is of exceptional importance to gerontology because as people age, there is a shift in the population heterogeneity of complex tissues. Methods such as preparative cell sorting can provide one solution to this problem (Darzynkiewicz et al., 1994). It is often used, for example, to analyze specific subsets of peripheral blood lymphocytes.

Genetic Linkage Studies: The Identification of Pedigrees and Their Use for the Discovery of Major Genes that Modulate Life Span and Senescent Phenotypes

Although not systematic, large-scale screenings of populations with specific phenotypes of interest to gerontologists have led to the identification of unusual pedigrees with patterns of segregation consistent with the hypothesis that mutation at a single major genetic locus is responsible for the phenotype. These studies take advantage of the availability of a large number of genetic markers and the principle that a marker that is in close physical proximity to a disease gene is rarely separated from that disease gene during meiosis, thus "traveling" together from generation to generation. This is the basis of genetic linkage analysis, which permits the mapping of a disease gene to a specific segment of a specific chromosome. Given such mapping, it is possible to eventually clone the responsible mutant gene. The discoveries of autosomal dominant mutations at the beta amyloid precursor protein locus and at the two presenilin loci are good examples (Blacker and Tanzi, 1998). These mutations cause early-onset DAT. Mutation at the presenilin 1 locus is particularly virulent, leading to dementia as early as age 26 in a pedigree with the diagnosis confirmed by autopsy (Martin et al., 1991). These mutations affect virtually all carriers if they live long enough. The dementias are usually interpreted as resulting from dominant gain-of-function mutations, meaning that the mutation produced a protein having a new, deleterious function. The evidence is far from definitive on this point, however.

It is quite interesting that there is as yet no convincing evidence for autosomal recessive loci resulting in unusual susceptibility to DAT. Such mutations represent a loss of function, typically of an enzyme. One certainly has reason to suspect that such mutations might be found if one were to examine very large numbers of pedigrees in different parts of the world. One would especially want to search within populations having high degrees of consanguineous marriages, as two rare recessive mutations are more likely to show up in the offspring of such matings. Examples would include populations of Hindus in the Southern part of India, where first cousin and uncle-niece marriages are still prevalent. Muslims throughout India and other parts of the world, such as the Middle East, also sanction first cousin marriages. The advantage of a focus on India, of course, is that its population continues to grow at a rapid rate and is now approaching one billion.

The rationale for suspecting that an enzyme deficiency can cause a form of DAT comes from current views concerning its pathogenesis. These views center upon the processing of the beta amyloid precursor protein (Selkoe, 2000). This processing is carried out by enzymes that catalyze the cutting of the protein at various positions in the sequence of its amino acids. A "bad" way to process the protein is with enzymes known as beta and gamma secretases. The products of such processing are small peptides, called beta amyloids; these form insoluble aggregates that deposit in the brain, including its blood vessels. Beta amyloid is thought by many to be a major cause of the loss of synaptic connections between neurons and of the neurons themselves. There is evidence that a product of the presenilin 1 gene is in fact a gamma secretase or a protein closely associated with the relevant gamma secretase (Li et al., 2000). The "good" way to process the beta amyloid precursor protein is with an enzyme known as alpha secretase. It cuts roughly in the middle of the piece of protein destined to make the beta amyloid peptide, thus preventing the accumulation of this substance. It is therefore reasonable to believe that a deficiency of alpha secretase would accelerate the development of DAT.

Genetic diseases caused by single Mendelian genes, whether autosomal dominant, autosomal recessive, or X-linked recessive, although quite rare, are relatively easy to diagnose. Nowadays, once diagnosed, it is relatively straightforward to map and clone the responsible gene, especially if multiple pedigrees with the same phenotype or large affected kindreds can be identified. This is the reason why screening very large populations or focusing on screening a particular geographic area or ethnic group is important. An example of the importance of the latter strategy is the success in collecting a group of related pedigrees that permitted the mapping and cloning of the presenilin 2 gene mutation. It turned out that the original set of affected pedigrees were all ethnic Volga Germans (Bird et al., 1988). Their ancestors migrated from the Hesse area of Germany to one of two small villages on the west bank of the Volga River in about 1760. They did this at the behest of Catherine the Great, the Czarina of Russia, who was a fellow German. This "genetic founder effect" gave assurance that one was dealing with a common cause of familial DAT. One could therefore map the responsible mutations even with a relatively small number of pedigrees, since they were basically part of one large kindred.

All three autosomal dominant DAT mutations, those at the presenilin 1 and 2 loci and those at the beta amyloid precursor protein locus, result in relatively early-onset dementias. There is considerable variation in the age of onset for the case of the presenilin 2 mutations, however, including rare apparent "escapees" who may live into the ninth decade without becoming affected.

Pedigrees are now being collected by T.T. Perls and others for the purpose of using linkage analysis to identify genes that contribute to unusual longevities. One rationale for such a study was a finding consistent with the conclusion that siblings of centenarians tended to have relatively long life spans (Perls et al., 1998). It is too early to evaluate the success or failure of these studies, but there are reasons for pessimism. First of all, life span is subject to stochastic events (Finch and Kirkwood, 1999). Cancer, for example, can result in chance "hits" at particularly vulnerable parts of the genome (e.g., tumor suppressor genes). Two individuals might have the same basic rate of somatic mutations, but one may be lucky and never sustain "hits" in a tumor suppressor gene, thus escaping premature death from a cancer. Second, there is also concern that, at least for the case of human subjects, there are likely to be a very large number of genes impacting upon late-life disorders and, hence, upon life span (Martin, 1978). A proportion of such genes may be of exceptional importance, however. One such example may be the gene coding for a gene that helps to unwind double stranded DNA; when one inherits two doses of a severe mutation in that gene, it causes the Werner syndrome (Yu et al., 1996). People with that disorder display such features as premature arteriosclerosis, a variety of cancers, cataracts, osteoporosis, type 2 diabetes, gonadal atrophy, atrophy of skin and subcutaneous tissues, and premature graying and thinning of hair (Epstein et al., 1966). Twin studies indicate that perhaps a quarter of the variance of life span in humans has a genetic basis (Herskind et al., 1996). A search for these genes by large scale genomic screening of pedigrees with members exhibiting unusual longevities may therefore reveal several important genetic loci, perhaps including the Werner locus. The ascertainment of such families will require large-scale screening of populations and documentation of birth dates.

Genetic Association Studies and the Difficulties Inherent in Case-Control Designs

Most cases of DAT are not associated with single autosomal dominant genes and occur well after the age of 65 years, typically after the age of 85 years, when perhaps 50 percent of the population can be affected (Katzman and Kawas, 1998). Such a high "background" of affected individuals makes the search for genetic susceptibility factors very difficult. There is also the difficulty of matching cases and controls in genetic association studies. Typically, one sees the statement, in publications, that only Caucasian subjects were studied. But what is a Caucasian? That word obscures the enormous genetic heterogeneity in the U.S. population. Thus, differences in the prevalence of a particular polymorphism may be biased by an enrichment, in either controls or in diseased subjects, of a particular ethnic subtype having a different distribution frequency of the polymorphism of interest. This leads to both false positives and false negatives. These uncertainties have led to the development of various pedigree-based genetic association studies, including the use of various sib-pair strategies. The failure to replicate an apparently robust conclusion, however, may simply be due to the fact that the polymorphism of interest may not be relevant in a particular population in a particular environment. Despite these difficulties, however, there is evidence that polymorphic variations at a number of different genetic loci each contributes to differential susceptibility to DAT. Most of these are likely to make only small contributions to susceptibility. The best example of a *major* modulator of susceptibility to the common late-onset forms of DAT is the apolipoprotein E (APOE) polymorphism (Corder et al., 1993). There are likely to be other major modulators, however; one of these loci may even have a much greater impact than APOE, at least in some populations (Daw et al., 2000).

There have been several confirmations (Castro et al., 1999) of the report (Schachter et al., 1994) that long-lived individuals such as centenarians are statistically more likely to carry the APOE e2 allele and less likely to carry the e4 allele, but with interesting regional variations (Panza et al., 1999). This is consistent with a deleterious role of APOE e4 on cardiovascular disease (Lehtinen et al., 1995) and on DAT (Corder et al., 1993). The robustness of the Alzheimer effect, however, varies among different ethnic groups, the impact being less for American black and Hispanic populations (Tang et al., 1996). These association studies are also consistent with the reported protective effect of the e2 allele against DAT (Corder et al., 1993). Preliminary results have indicated enrichments of other polymorphic alleles in certain populations (e.g., De Benedictis et al., 1999).

The Paucity of Genetic Investigations of Differential Rates of Change of Specific Physiological Functions in Middle Age and the Many Advantages of Such an Approach

From the point of view of gerontology, it can be argued that medical scientists have been preoccupied with deleterious phenotypes. One would very much like to know the genetic contributions to *unusually robust* retention of specific physiological functions during aging. I have argued that one should begin such studies with middle-aged cohorts. First of all, population geneticists have determined that the force of natural selection has essentially disappeared for phenotypes that do not emerge until after around age 40 or 45 (reviewed by Martin et al., 1996). Thus, we are in a position to detect differential rates of change of relevant phenotypes beginning in middle age. Secondly, assays for specific physiological functions are less likely to be compromised by various co-morbidities that would be the case were one to investigate differential rates of decline of specific functions in much older individuals. Thirdly, a genetic analysis would benefit from the potential availability of DNA samples for at least three generations when the index cases are middle-aged subjects. Fourth, there are much larger populations of middle-aged subjects, most of whom would be fully cooperative and capable of undergoing various stress tests without undue danger to their health. Fifth, middle-aged sibs of such index cases should be readily available, thus permitting sib-pair genetic studies. One such approach would be to screen a very large population of such subjects for individuals who score in the upper one percentile for a specific physiological function. One could then identify sib pairs exhibiting extreme concordance or extreme concordance for the trait of interest; such methods can greatly increase the statistical power of the genetic analysis (Zhang and Risch, 1996; Risch and Zhang 1995, 1996). Such an experimental design could lead to the definition of alleles that underlie what one might call "elite" aging, as opposed to mere "successful" aging. These alleles could serve as entry points to mechanistic studies that could lead to interventions of benefit to much larger segments of our population.

What physiological functions could be so investigated? The answer is that virtually *all* physiological functions could be studied, given the availability of sufficiently sensitive assays. Ideally, such assays should also be relatively inexpensive, relatively noninvasive, and amenable to longitudinal study. A possible example would be the delayed paragraph recall test for hippocampal function (Golomb et al., 1994). The tests can be made more difficult in order to detect unusual degrees of preservation of short-term memory.

PATHOLOGY

Relevant Data from Anatomic Pathology

Surgical Pathology

In the United States, essentially all tissues removed at the time of surgery are examined by certified pathologists and their trainees. In the vast majority of cases, small samples are immersed in neutral formalin solutions within a few hours of their removal and fixed for periods of less than 24 hours, following which they are embedded in paraffin, sectioned to produce slices of around 6-8 microns in thickness, dehydrated in a series of ethanol solutions (with the unfortunate consequence of elimination of most lipids), stained with hematoxylin (for nucleic acids) and eosin (for proteins), and mounted on slides with coverslips for examination with the light microscope. Both the microscopic slides and the paraffin blocks are typically archived for many decades. This procedure is among the most venerable and informative in the entire field of medical practice and medical research. It is still the basis for diagnosis throughout the world. It provides a vast storehouse of definitive diagnostic historical information for large populations. It also provides the potential to uncover new definitive information with the use of an expanding toolkit of monoclonal antibodies to specific protein epitopes that have not been obscured by the formalin fixation. Nucleic acid probes, including those that provide amplification of genomic DNA, the DNA of infectious agents, and, to some extent, messenger RNA species, may also be applied to the archived materials. One can often carry out successful genotyping of loci of relevance to epidemiologists using such materials from long-deceased individuals. A good example is the tri-allelic polymorphism for the APOE gene, which greatly influences susceptibility to cardiovascular disease and dementias of the Alzheimer type, as noted above. It is in fact now standard practice to include APOE genotyping of all individuals involved in epidemiological studies of dementias.

At a few medical centers, segments of some surgically removed tissue are preserved cryobiologically. Cryopreserved surgical tissues can be utilized for a much greater variety of morphological, biochemical, and immunohistochemical studies. For optimal long-term preservation of tissues, preservation in liquid nitrogen is required. This expensive methodology, which requires careful monitoring and regular replenishments of nitrogen, might eventually be replaced, however, by long-term storage in improved mechanical freezers. A systematic program of cryopreservation of subsets of surgically removed tissues would provide vastly increased opportunities for population-based research on human health and disease. From such living tissues, a variety of cell types could be established in culture, providing unlimited amounts of materials for large-scale genotyping and investigations of variations of gene expression. The recently introduced massive microarray (chip) technologies, discussed above under the section on Genetics, could provide vast amounts of information given the availability of such tissues. Peripheral blood samples can of course provide suitable sources of DNA for genotyping, but they are much more limited as regards investigations of variations in gene expression, since one is dealing with only those cell types in circulating blood.

While seldom explored, cryopreserved surgically excised tissues can also be used for experimental investigations of organ or organoid cultures (Thesleff and Sahlberg, 1999; de Boer et al., 1996; Kruk and Auersperg, 1992; Kopf-Maier and Kolon, 1992). Unlike conventional cell cultures, these methods provide a more normal simulation of what obtains in the living organisms, including physiological cell densities and various interactions among cells and their matrix components. To the best of our knowledge, this powerful methodology has never been employed for any large-scale studies of materials from human populations.

Given the increasing economic constraints of medical services, preservation of even a subset of routinely obtained surgical tissues is very unlikely to be initiated without some form of subsidization by private and/or governmental agencies. This would of course require a prospective, peer-reviewed research proposal. Let us give a single possible example. Periodic flexible endoscopic examinations of the sigmoid colon and rectum have become standard medical procedures for subjects over the age of 50 years in order to detect and remove potentially pre-malignant hyperplastic and adenomatous polyps (Khullar and DiSario, 1997). A substantial fraction of older subjects are found to have such lesions, which are routinely fixed in formalin and examined microscopically. A small portion of such lesions and adjacent normal tissues, together with small biopsies from the normal tissues of subjects who are examined but who do not have polyps, could be routinely cryobiologically preserved or simply frozen as materials for a variety of research questions, given suitable informed consent. One such set of questions would relate to the recent surprising observations that many thousands of somatic mutations can be found in such lesions (Stoler et al., 1999) (Box 6-1). The methodology was the relatively simple yet informative inter-simple sequence repeat polymerase chain reaction, which can sample mutations over a very large portion of the genome. The use of frozen or cryopreserved mucosal/submucosal fragments for the detection of chemical and viral mutagenic agents and the response of these tissues to challenge by such agents would have the potential to elucidate underlying mechanisms. A viral agent known as the JC virus should be an interesting candidate as an environmental etiologic agent (Laghi et al., 1999; Neel, 1999).

Somatic mutations, by definition, are changes in the sequence of nucleotide base pairs of DNA. Epigenetic changes also occur during aging. In contrast to mutations, these involve chemical changes that are superimposed upon a normal sequence of DNA. These chemical changes are of two principal types: the addition or removal of methyl groups from cytosines; and the addition or removal of acetyl groups from histones, which are basic proteins closely associated with DNA that are thought to participate in the modulation of the expression of large blocks of genes. These epigenetic changes may be of basic importance to our understanding of the pathobiology of aging (Holliday, 1993; Sinclair et al., 1998; Young and Smith, 2000). In the context of the present discussion, a particularly interesting epigenetic change has been documented to occur in aging epithelial cells of the human colonic mucosa. It has been found that there is a steady increase, with aging, in the levels of methylation of a region of the promoter of a gene coding for an estrogen receptor (Issa et al., 1994). Promoters are DNA sequences that are essential for the transcription of genes into mRNA. The methylation of promoters is generally

BOX 6-1
Calculation of the Total Numbers of Large-Scale Mutations (insertions, deletions and translocations) in a Typical Colon Cancer Cell[1]

$N_{t\mu}$ = Total number "unique" inter-SSR PCR bands (insertions, deletions, and translocations) per typical colon cancer cell

N_{PCR} = Total number of alterations of all types, including changes in gene dosage, per set of PCRs

S_{PCR} = Total size of PCR fragments sampling the genome (basepairs)

H = Haploid genome size (basepairs)

N_{PCR-t} = Total number observed altered bands of all types

$N_{PCR-\mu}$ = Total number observed "unique" bands

P = Typical ploidy of a colon cancer cell

$$N_{t\mu} = \frac{N_{PCR}}{S_{PCR}} \times H \times \frac{N_{PCR-\mu}}{N_{PCR-t}} \times P$$

$$N_{t\mu} = \frac{3}{8.42 \times 10^4} \times 3 \times 10^9 \times \frac{18}{174} \times \sim 3$$

$$N_{t\mu} = 3.3 \times 10^4$$

---

[1] Such cancer cells typically have karyotypes that are near-triploid.

Source: From D.C. Stoler et al., 1999, with modifications by George M. Martin that give a greater number of mutations than that reported by the authors.

associated with gene silencing. Estrogen receptors participate in the regulation of the proliferation of colonic mucosal cells. When the receptor is active, the binding with estrogen (forms of which circulate in both males and females) inhibits proliferation. Methylation of the estrogen receptor thus leads to a dysregulation of the proliferative homeostasis of colonic epithelial cells. Not surprisingly, regions of the colon in which this occurs are exactly those that are highly susceptible to colonic cancer (Issa et al., 1994).

Population scientists should participate in such research, as the prevalence of colon cancer varies substantially in different regions of the country (Devesa et al., 1999; some of these data are available as county-specific maps on the National Cancer Institute website: www.nci.nih.gov/atlas/). Is this related to regional differences in diet or environmental mutagens such as the JC virus? Are there secular changes in the prevalence of the molecular alterations described above? Is the epigenetic component a robust marker of the aging colonic mucosa in all populations?

Cytology

Another vast storehouse of preserved cellular materials from subjects of various ages, particularly of females, can be found in the files of Divisions of Cytology in virtually all Departments of Pathology in the United States. Millions of females have been periodically examined with the famous "Pap" (Papanicolaou) smear for many decades. There has already been at least one important research application using such materials from various populations. Molecular techniques were used for the detection of specific strains of the human papillomavirus in the cells of archived Pap smears (Pillai et al., 1996; Wagner et al., 1985). Specific strains were found to be associated with cervical cancers (Evans and Mueller, 1990). Preserved cytological materials are also available from other sources, such as pleural and peritoneal fluids, amniotic fluids, and bronchoscopic lavages.

Autopsy Pathology

Numerous studies have documented the inadequacy of the death certificate as a source of information on causes of morbidity and mortality (Nielsen et al., 1991; Kircher et al., 1985; Engel et al., 1980; Lee, 1994). Nothing can take the place of a thorough autopsy for the full description of the burden of disease in an individual and in populations of individuals. Unfortunately, once hospital accreditation no longer required autopsies for a significant proportion of hospital deaths, the autopsy rates, especially in private hospitals, dropped precipitously. A recent survey by the American College of Pathology indicated a median rate of 8.5 percent (Nakhleh et al., 1999). These figures are often inflated by autopsies on stillborns and neonates. The rates for geriatric subjects are typically much below average (Campion et al., 1986; Nemetz et al., 1997). Moreover, there is great variation in the degree of thoroughness with which autopsies are performed. There are a number of reasons for this striking decline in the quality and quantity of the medical necropsy. First, there is the notion that laboratory tests such as X-rays and clinical chemistry will almost always suffice for the clarification of disease status. This has provided a false sense of security. Second, and most importantly, there is the fact that insurance companies, hospitals, medical schools, families, governmental agencies, and pathologists are reluctant to cover the substantial costs for a modern academic autopsy, or even simple focused autopsies to determine the major cause of death. At the University of Washington, a routine full autopsy currently costs about $3,000. This includes histological examination of all organs, a routine neuropathological examination, laboratory assays for HIV and hepatitis B, and the typical costs of transportation to and from funeral homes. Special studies, such as immunohistochemistry, electron microscopy, biochemical assays, postmortem imaging and photomicrography, cell culture, and molecular biological assays can double those costs. Third, there is the fear of lawsuits against attending physicians should the diagnosis prove erroneous or should additional treatable pathologies be discovered. Fourth, pathologists and residents avoid doing autopsies, or do them in a very cursory fashion, in part because of the pressures of time and because there is typically little or no financial incentive (the pathologist is not reimbursed for his autopsy services by Medicare). Surgical pathology is considered to be a more challenging occupation. Thus, we no longer have many highly experienced autopsy pathologists, as trainees have been getting minimal exposure to the autopsy as a tool in medical diagnosis and research. We urgently need solutions to these impediments to the maintenance and enhancement of a vital component of our system for the monitoring of the public health.

There are two major sources of autopsy materials in the United States, those resulting from the autopsy services of hospitals and those coming from medical examiner offices. By law, the latter are required to determine causes of accidental, suicidal, and homicidal deaths, and deaths that occur in hospitals and elsewhere under unusual circumstances. For purposes of population-based research in gerontology, by far the most valuable material is that which can be obtained from modern medical examiner facilities, given suitable informed consent. With a few exceptions, the research community has sadly neglected this material. Perhaps this is because medical examiners have only recently evolved in most urban areas of the country from the politically controlled system of county coroners. They are thus typically independent of or only loosely connected with academic medical centers. Their missions are clearly circumscribed by the need to determine a probable cause of death. Budgetary components for research are scarce and usually involve issues related to forensic pathology. Basic research could certainly be addressed, however, via the usual vehicle of research grants. Finland provides a very good model for how forensic pathologists can effectively interact with researchers (Kortelainen and Sarkioja, 1999; Viitanen et al., 1998; Lahti et al., 1998).

Fatal accidents, the most numerous being motor vehicle accidents, affect all age groups, all ethnic groups, and all regions of the country. They have been occurring over many decades and, unfortunately, are likely to continue to occur for the foreseeable future. Autopsies of such individuals can, in principle, provide samples of well-preserved normal tissues from essentially all organs of the body, as well as body fluids such as cerebrospinal fluid and fluid from the vitreous of the eye. They could thus be utilized, for example, to give information on the rates of deposition of soluble and insoluble moieties of the family of beta amyloid peptides (Lue et al., 1999) in the cerebral cortex and hippocampus from large numbers of individuals. The results could be related to age, ethnicity, and genotype (e.g., APOE polymorphisms). Secular changes in these patterns might suggest important environmental influences. This is just one of an almost unlimited range of research applications. Correlations with cognitive function could even be carried out retrospectively via standardized telephone interviews of informants (Gallo and Breitner, 1995). A second example would be an extension to human subjects of the recent exciting application of the microarray expression technology demonstrating altered gene expression, as previously discussed.

Hospital autopsies, of course, are never population-based samples of the spectrum of disease, as there are different kinds of selection biases, particularly in the academic centers, with respect to both the kinds of patients referred to those centers and the types of patients for whom autopsies are sought. To the best of our knowledge, there has never been a valid systematic population-based autopsy study of the geriatric population in the United States. One such study was reported for an Eastern German city (population 78,484) conducted in 1987 (Modelmog et al., 1992). Of the 1,060 subjects who died that year, 1,023 (96.5 percent) were autopsied. Despite the fact that thorough neuropathological evaluations appear not to have been pursued, the overall discrepancy between death certificate diagnoses and autopsy diagnoses was 47 percent, with higher proportions for the nursing home subset. It would be of great interest to see the results of follow-up studies over the next several decades, but this is unlikely to occur, given the dismantling of the system of socialized medicine that existed in East Germany at the time of the initial study.

Clinical Pathology (Laboratory Medicine)

Practicing pathologists are responsible for two major domains of activities. The first, anatomic pathology, has been discussed above. The second is known as clinical pathology, or, in some regions of the country, as laboratory medicine. This includes responsibility for the direction of a group of clinical hematology activities (blood counts, blood smears, bone marrow smears or sections, coagulation assays, transfusion services, etc.), clinical chemistry labs (charged with the assays of a very large number of biochemical determinations from body fluids), clinical immunology (assays for autoantibodies, cryoglobulins, antibodies to phospholipids, etc.), clinical microbiology (the isolation and characterization of infectious bacterial agents and fungi), clinical virology (the isolation and characterization of viral agents), clinical toxicology (assays for inorganic and organic substances, including drugs), and clinical genetics (tests for various heritable disorders). There is also increasing recognition of the importance of supporting associated divisions of informatics in order to expedite retrieval, analysis, and archiving of clinical laboratory data.

As one can imagine, an enormous repository of test results has emerged from these activities. Virtually all members of our population eventually undergo many of the assays listed above, particularly the geriatric subset. Many jurisdictions have implemented the screening of all newborn infants for certain genetic disorders, notably for phenylketonuria and congenital hypothyroidism. These programs have often provided for long-term storage of excess samples of capillary blood dried on filter papers. Imaginative uses of this material have been employed for population-based research. One example was its use for the determination of the prevalence of neonatal infection with *Toxoplasma gondii* by the detection of specific IgM antibodies (Petersen and Eaton, 1999; Paul et al., 2000). This protozoan is among the most prevalent causes of latent infection of the central nervous system throughout the world. Infection occurs primarily via the oral route, typically from eating undercooked meat or via contact with household cats. In a European study, cerebral toxoplasmosis was found in 34 percent of middle-aged subjects with AIDS (Martinez et al., 1995). It is probably the case that many patients thought to have dementia on the basis of their HIV infections are demented because of secondary infection with *Toxoplasma gondii*. No population-based study of the contribution of *T. gondii* to neuropathology in geriatric subjects has been carried out to the best of our knowledge.

Another example of an imaginative use of archival clinical pathology material for population-based research has been the application of the powerful method of tandem mass spectrometry for the screening of newborns, using the spare dried-filter paper samples of DNA mentioned above, for a great variety of inborn errors of metabolism about 700,000 newborns, 163 inborn errors of metabolism were detected, including 86 with amino acid metabolic errors, 32 with errors in the metabolism of organic acids, and 45 with errors in fatty acid oxidation (Naylor and Chace, 1999). These are largely recessive disorders, severe mutations having been inherited from both parents. It would be of great interest to discover the prevalence of heterozygous carriers for such mutations in middle-aged and older subjects. Such carriers are of course far more prevalent than are the homozygous deficient individuals. While there are often no obvious detectable phenotypic abnormalities in obligate heterozygous carriers (e.g., the parents of the homozygous deficient children), we have little or no information on the extent to which haploinsufficiency for at least a proportion of this substantial mutational load may increase the vulnerability of carriers to basic processes of aging and to late-life disease. Given the availability of population-based sampling of peripheral blood from such older subjects, one is in a position to apply a variety of methodologies to this question. Some of these methodologies have been reviewed under the section on Genetics.

SUMMARY

There is a vast repertoire of data being collected by anatomical and clinical pathologists. Their value has been greatly enhanced by the development of powerful new methodologies for chemical and genetic analysis. Despite these new opportunities, these materials are rarely used for population-based studies of interest to gerontologists. It is particularly disturbing that autopsy rates have declined precipitously in recent years, especially for the geriatric population. Remarkably, there has never been a valid, systematic population-based autopsy study of geriatric diseases in the United States. The result has been the over-reliance upon highly inaccurate death certificate data.

The screening of large populations for unusual pedigrees has already led to the identification of rare mutations of importance to our understanding of the pathogenesis of late-life disease. More attention, however, should be given to the discovery of genetic polymorphisms that modulate how we age. Of special interest would be programs of research designed to identify alleles that confer unusual resistance to age-related declines in specific functions. Large-scale screenings of populations of middle-aged subjects have the potential to identify such alleles.

REFERENCES

Arendt, G., H. Hefter, C. Figge, E. Neuen-Jakob, H.W. Nelles, C. Elsing, and H.J. Freund
    1991   Two cases of cerebral toxoplasmosis in AIDS patients mimicking HIV-related dementia. *Journal of Neurology* 238:439-442.
Armitage, B., and P. Babb
    1996   Population review: (4). Trends in fertility. *Population Trends* 7-13.
Barlati, S., N. Zoppi, A. Copeta, D. Tavian, G. De Petro, and M. Colombi
    1999   Quantitative in situ hybridization for the evaluation of gene expression in asynchronous and synchronized cell cultures and in tissue sections. *Histology and Histopathology* 14:1231-1240.

Bird, T.D., T.H. Lampe, E.J. Nemens, G.W. Miner, S.M. Sumi, and G.D. Schellenberg
  1988   Familial Alzheimer's disease in American descendants of the Volga Germans: Probable genetic founder effect. *Annals of Neurology* 23:25-31.
Blacker, D., and R.E. Tanzi
  1998   The genetics of Alzheimer disease: Current status and future prospects. *Archives of Neurology* 55:294-296.
Brown, P.O., and D. Botstein
  1999   Exploring the new world of the genome with DNA microarrays. *Nature Genetics* 21:33-37.
Campion, E.W., V.A. Reder, A.G. Mulley, and G.E. Thibault
  1986   Age and the declining rate of autopsy. *Journal of the American Geriatrics Society* 34:865-868.
Castro, E., C.E. Ogburn, K.E. Hunt, R. Tilvis, J. Louhija, R. Penttinen, R. Erkkola, A. Panduro, R. Riestra, C. Piussan, S.S. Deeb, L. Wang, S.D. Edland, G.M. Martin, and J. Oshima
  1999   Polymorphisms at the Werner locus: I. Newly identified polymorphisms, ethnic variability of 1367Cy/Arg, and its stability in a population of Finnish centenarians. *American Journal of Medical Genetics* 82:399-403.
Chee, M., R. Yang, E. Hubbell, A. Berno, X.C. Huang, D. Stern, J. Winkler, D.J. Lockhart, M.S. Morris, and S.P. Fodor
  1996   Accessing genetic information with high-density DNA arrays. *Science* 274:610-614.
Cheung, V.G., J.P. Gregg, K.J. Gogolin-Ewens, J. Bandong, C.A. Stanley, L. Baker, M.J. Higgins, N.J. Nowak, T.B. Shows, W.J. Ewens, S.F. Nelson, and R.S. Spielman
  1998   Linkage-disequilibrium mapping without genotyping. *Nature Genetics* 18:225-230.
Chiang, P.W., W.L. Wei, K. Gibson, R. Bodmer, and D.M. Kurnit
  1999   A fluorescent quantitative PCR approach to map gene deletions in the Drosophila genome. *Genetics* 153:1313-1316.
Corder, E.H., A.M. Saunders, W.J. Strittmatter, D.E. Schmechel, P.C. Gaskell, G.W. Small, A.D. Roses, J.L. Haines, and M.A. Pericak-Vance
  1993   Gene dose of apolipoprotein E type 4 allele and the risk of Alzheimer's disease in late onset families. *Science* 261:921-923.
Crow, J.F.
  1993   How much do we know about spontaneous human mutation rates? [published erratum appears in *Environmental and Molecular Mutagenesis* 1993;21(4):389]. *Environmental and Molecular Mutagenesis* 21:122-129.
Darzynkiewicz, Z., J.P. Robinson, and H.A. Crissman
  1994   *Flow Cytometry*. San Diego: Academic Press.
Daw, E.W., H. Payami, E.J. Nemens, D. Nochlin, T.D. Bird, G.D. Schellenberg, and E.M. Wijsman
  2000   The number of trait loci in late-onset Alzheimer disease. *American Journal of Human Genetics* 66:196-204.
De Benedictis, G., G. Rose, G. Carrieri, M. De Luca, E. Falcone, G. Passarino, M. Bonafe, D. Monti, G. Baggio, S. Bertolini, D. Mari, R. Mattace, and C. Franceschi
  1999   Mitochondrial DNA inherited variants are associated with successful aging and longevity in humans. *FASEB Journal* 13:1532-1536.
de Boer, W.I., M. Vermeij, S.G. Diez de Medina, E. Bindels, F. Radvanyi, K.T. van der, and D. Chopin
  1996   Functions of fibroblast and transforming growth factors in primary organoid-like cultures of normal human urothelium. *Laboratory Investigation* 75:147-156.
Devesa, S.S., D.J. Grauman, W.J. Blot, G.A. Pennello, R.N. Hoover, and J.F. Fraumeni
  1999   *Atlas of Cancer Mortality in the United States, 1950-1994*. Rockville: National Cancer Institute.

Engel, L.W., J.A. Strauchen, L. Chiazze, Jr., and M. Heid
    1980   Accuracy of death certification in an autopsied population with specific attention to malignant neoplasms and vascular diseases. *American Journal of Epidemiology* 111:99-112.
Epstein, C.J., G.M. Martin, A.L. Schultz, and A.G. Motulsky
    1966   Werner's syndrome: A review of its symptomatology, natural history, pathologic features, genetics and relationship to the natural aging process. *Medicine* (Baltimore) 45:177-221.
Evans, A.S., and N.E. Mueller
    1990   Viruses and cancer. Causal associations. *Annals of Epidemiology* 1:71-92.
Ferea, T.L., and P.O. Brown
    1999   Observing the living genome. *Current Opinion in Genetics and Development* 9:715-722.
Finch, C.E., and T.B.L. Kirkwood
    1999   *Chance, Development and Aging.* New York: Oxford University Press.
Ford, D., and F. Nault
    1996   Changing fertility patterns, 1974 to 1994. *Health Reports* 8:39-46.
Fredericks, D.N., and D.A. Relman
    1996   Sequence-based identification of microbial pathogens: A reconsideration of Koch's postulates. *Clinical Microbiology Reviews* 9:18-33.
Friend, S.H.
    1999   DNA microarrays and expression profiling in clinical practice. *British Medical Journal* 319(7220):1306-1307
Gallo, J.J., and J.C. Breitner
    1995   Alzheimer's disease in the NAS-NRC Registry of aging twin veterans, IV. Performance characteristics of a two-stage telephone screening procedure for Alzheimer's dementia. *Psychological Medicine* 25:1211-1219.
Golomb, J., A. Kluger, M.J. de Leon, S.H. Ferris, A. Convit, M.S. Mittelman, J. Cohen, H. Rusinek, S. De Santi, and A.E. George
    1994   Hippocampal formation size in normal human aging: A correlate of delayed secondary memory performance. *Learning and Memory* 1:45-54.
Guyer, B., M.F. MacDorman, J.A. Martin, K.D. Peters, and D.M. Strobino
    1998   Annual summary of vital statistics, 1997. *Pediatrics* 102:1333-1349.
Halushka, M.K., J.B. Fan, K. Bentley, L. Hsie, N. Shen, A. Weder, R. Cooper, R. Lipshutz, and A. Chakravarti
    1999   Patterns of single-nucleotide polymorphisms in candidate genes for blood-pressure homeostasis. *Nature Genetics* 22:239-247.
Herskind, A.M., M. McGue, N.V. Holm, T.I. Sorensen, B. Harvald, and J.W. Vaupel
    1996   The heritability of human longevity: A population-based study of 2872 Danish twin pairs born 1870-1900. *Human Genetics* 97:319-323.
Holliday, R.
    1993   Epigenetic inheritance based on DNA methylation. *Exegesis* 64:452-468.
Hoshi, N., R. Hattori, K. Hanatani, K. Okuyama, H. Yamada, T. Kishida, T. Yamada, T. Sagawa, Y. Sumiyoshi, and S. Fujimoto
    1999   Recent trends in the prevalence of Down syndrome in Japan, 1980-1997. *American Journal of Medical Genetics* 84:340-345.
Hu Q., M.G. Hearn, L.W. Jin, S.L. Bressler, and G.M. Martin
    1999   Alternatively spliced isoforms of FE65 serve as neuron-specific and non-neuronal markers. *Journal of Neuroscience Research* 58:632-640.

Hu Q, L.W. Jin, M.Y. Starbuck, and G.M. Martin
    2000   Broadly altered expression of the mRNA isoforms of FE65, a facilitator of beta amyloidogenesis, in Alzheimer cerebellum and other brain regions. *Journal of Neuroscience Research* 60:73-86.

Issa, J.P., Y.L. Ottaviano, P. Celano, S.R. Hamilton, N.E. Davidson, and S.B. Baylin
    1994   Methylation of the oestrogen receptor CpG island links ageing and neoplasia in human colon. *Nature Genetics* 7:536-540.

Katzman, R., and C. Kawas
    1998   Risk factors for Alzheimer's disease. *Neuroscience News* 1:27-34.

Kaufmann, R.B., A.M. Spitz, L.T. Strauss, L. Morris, J.S. Santelli, L.M. Koonin, and J.S. Marks
    1998   The decline in U.S. teen pregnancy rates, 1990-1995. *Pediatrics* 102:1141-1147.

Khullar, S.K., and J.A. DiSario
    1997   Colon cancer screening. Sigmoidoscopy or colonoscopy. *Gastrointestinal Endoscopy Clinics of North America* 7:365-386.

Kircher, T., J. Nelson, and H. Burdo
    1985   The autopsy as a measure of accuracy of the death certificate. *New England Journal of Medicine* 313:1263-1269.

Kopf-Maier, P., and B. Kolon
    1992   An organoid culture assay (OCA) for determining the drug sensitivity of human tumors. *International Journal of Cancer* 51:99-107.

Kortelainen, M.L., and T. Sarkioja
    1999   Coronary atherosclerosis associated with body structure and obesity in 599 women aged between 15 and 50 years. *International Journal of Obesity and Related Metabolic Disorders* 23:838-844.

Kruk, P.A., and N. Auersperg
    1992   Human ovarian surface epithelial cells are capable of physically restructuring extracellular matrix. *American Journal of Obstetrics and Gynecology* 167:1437-1443.

Laghi, L., A.E. Randolph, D.P. Chauhan, G. Marra, E.O. Major, J.V. Neel, and C.R. Boland
    1999   JC virus DNA is present in the mucosa of the human colon and in colorectal cancers. *Proceedings of the National Academy of Sciences of the United States of America* 96:7484-7489.

Lahti, R.A., S. Sarna, and A. Penttila
    1998   Exploitation of autopsy in determining natural cause of death: Trends in Finland with special reference to the diagnostics of ischemic heart diseases and cerebrovascular diseases in middle-aged males, 1974-1993. *Forensic Science International* 91:109-121.

Lee, C.K., R.G. Klopp, R. Weindruch, and T.A. Prolla
    1999   Gene expression profile of aging and its retardation by caloric restriction. *Science* 285:1390-1393.

Lee, M.K., H.H. Slunt, L.J. Martin, G. Thinakaran, G. Kim, S.E. Gandy, M. Seeger, E. Koo, D.L. Price, and S.S. Sisodia
    1996   Expression of presenilin 1 and 2 (PS1 and PS2) in human and murine tissues. *Journal of Neuroscience* 16:7513-7525.

Lee, P.N.
    1994   Comparison of autopsy, clinical and death certificate diagnosis with particular reference to lung cancer. A review of the published data. *APMIS Supplement* 45:1-42.

Lehtinen, S., T. Lehtimaki, T. Sisto, J.P. Salenius, M. Nikkila, H. Jokela, T. Koivula, F. Ebeling, and C. Ehnholm
    1995   Apolipoprotein E polymorphism, serum lipids, myocardial infarction and sever-
           ity of angiographically verified coronary artery disease in men and women. *Ath-
           erosclerosis* 114:83-91.
Li, Y.M., M. Xu, M.T. Lai, Q. Huang, J.L. Castro, J. DiMuzio-Mower, T. Harrison, C. Lellis,
A. Nadin, J.G. Neduvelil, R.B. Register, M.K. Sardana, M.S. Shearman, A.L. Smith, X.P. Shi,
K.C. Yin, J.A. Shafer, and S.J. Gardell
    2000   Photoactivated gamma-secretase inhibitors directed to the active site covalently
           label presenilin 1. *Nature* 405:689-694.
Lue, L.F., Y.M. Kuo, A.E. Roher, L. Brachova, Y. Shen, L. Sue, T. Beach, J.H. Kurth, R.E.
Rydel, and J. Rogers
    1999   Soluble amyloid beta peptide concentration as a predictor of synaptic change in
           Alzheimer's disease. *American Journal of Pathology* 155:853-862.
Ly, D.H., D.J. Lockhart, R.A. Lerner, and P.G. Schultz
    2000   Mitotic misregulation and human aging. *Science* 287:2486-2492.
Martin, G.M.
    1978   Genetic syndromes in man with potential relevance to the pathobiology of aging.
           Birth Defects Original Article Series 14:5-39.
Martin, G.M., S.N. Austad, and T.E. Johnson
    1996   Genetic analysis of ageing: Role of oxidative damage and environmental stresses.
           Nature Genetics 13:25-34.
Martin, J.J., J. Gheuens, M. Bruyland, P. Cras, A. Vandenberghe, C.L. Masters, K. Beyreuther,
R. Dom, C. Ceuterick, and U. Lubke
    1991   Early-onset Alzheimer's disease in two large Belgian families. *Neurology* 41:62-68.
Martinez, A.J., M. Sell, T. Mitrovics, G. Stoltenburg-Didinger, J.R. Iglesias-Rozas, M.A.
Giraldo-Velasquez, G. Gosztonyi, V. Schneider, and J. Cervos-Navarro
    1995   The neuropathology and epidemiology of AIDS. A Berlin experience. A review of
           200 cases. *Pathology, Research and Practice* 191:427-443.
Modelmog, D., S. Rahlenbeck, and D. Trichopoulos
    1992   Accuracy of death certificates: A population-based, complete-coverage, one-year
           autopsy study in East Germany. *Cancer Causes and Control* 3:541-546.
Montone, K.T., and L.A. Litzky
    1995   Rapid method for detection of Aspergillus 5S ribosomal RNA using a genus-
           specific oligonucleotide probe. *American Journal of Clinical Pathology* 103:48-51.
Nakhleh, R.E., P.B. Baker, and R.J. Zarbo
    1999   Autopsy result utilization: A College of American Pathologists Q-probes study of
           256 laboratories. *Archives of Pathology and Laboratory Medicine* 123:290-295.
Naylor, E.W., and D.H. Chace
    1999   Automated tandem mass spectrometry for mass newborn screening for disorders
           in fatty acid, organic acid, and amino acid metabolism. *Journal of Child Neurology*
           14 Suppl 1:S4-S8.
Neel, J.V.
    1999   The Colonel Harlan D. Sanders Award Address for 1998: JC virus and its possible
           role in oncogenesis. *American Journal of Medical Genetics* 83:152-156.
Nemetz, P.N., C. Leibson, J.M. Naessens, M. Beard, E. Tangalos, and L.T. Kurland
    1997   Determinants of the autopsy decision: A statistical analysis. *American Journal of
           Clinical Pathology* 108:175-183.
Nielsen, G.P., J. Bjornsson, and J.G. Jonasson
    1991   The accuracy of death certificates. Implications for health statistics. *Virchows
           Archiv. A. Pathological Anatomy and Histopathology* 419:143-146.

Panza, F., V. Solfrizzi, F. Torres, F. Mastroianni, A. Del Parigi, A.M. Colacicco, A.M. Basile, C. Capurso, R. Noya, and A. Capurso
  1999 Decreased frequency of apolipoprotein E epsilon4 allele from Northern to Southern Europe in Alzheimer's disease patients and centenarians. *Neuroscience Letters* 277:53-56.
Paul, M., E. Petersen, Z.S. Pawlowski, and J. Szczapa
  2000 Neonatal screening for congenital toxoplasmosis in the Poznan region of Poland by analysis of *Toxoplasma gondii*-specific IgM antibodies eluted from filter paper blood spots. *Pediatric Infectious Disease Journal* 19:30-36.
Perls, T.T., E. Bubrick, C.G. Wager, J. Vijg, and L. Kruglyak
  1998 Siblings of centenarians live longer. *Lancet* 351:1560.
Petersen, E., and R.B. Eaton
  1999 Control of congenital infection with *Toxoplasma gondii* by neonatal screening based on detection of specific immunoglobulin M antibodies eluted from phenylketonuria filter-paper blood-spot samples. *Acta Paediatrica Supplement* 88:36-39.
Pillai, M.R., S. Halabi, A. McKalip, P.G. Jayaprakash, T.N. Rajalekshmi, M.K. Nair, and B. Herman
  1996 The presence of human papillomavirus-16/-18 E6, p53, and Bcl-2 protein in cervicovaginal smears from patients with invasive cervical cancer. *Cancer Epidemiology, Biomarkers, and Prevention* 5:329-335.
Pinkel, D., R. Segraves, D. Sudar, S. Clark, I. Poole, D. Kowbel, C. Collins, W.L. Kuo, C. Chen, Y. Zhai, S.H. Dairkee, B.M. Ljung, J.W. Gray, and D.G. Albertson
  1998 High resolution analysis of DNA copy number variation using comparative genomic hybridization to microarrays. *Nature Genetics* 20:207-211.
Risch, N., E.W. Reich, M.M. Wishnick, and J.G. McCarthy
  1987 Spontaneous mutation and parental age in humans. *American Journal of Human Genetics* 41:218-248.
Risch, N., and H. Zhang
  1995 Extreme discordant sib pairs for mapping quantitative trait loci in humans. *Science* 268:1584-1589.
Risch, N.J., and H. Zhang
  1996 Mapping quantitative trait loci with extreme discordant sib pairs: Sampling considerations. *American Journal of Human Genetics* 58:836-843.
Sapolsky, R.J., L. Hsie, A. Berno, G. Ghandour, M. Mittmann, and J.B. Fan
  1999 High-throughput polymorphism screening and genotyping with high-density oligonucleotide arrays. *Genetic Analysis* 14:187-192.
Schachter, F., L. Faure-Delanef, F. Guenot, H. Rouger, P. Froguel, L. Lesueur-Ginot, and D. Cohen
  1994 Genetic associations with human longevity at the APOE and ACE loci. *Nature Genetics* 6:29-32.
Selkoe, D.J.
  2000 The origins of Alzheimer disease: A is for amyloid. *Journal of the American Medical Association* 283:1615-1617.
Shelton, D.N., E. Chang, P.S. Whittier, D. Choi, and W.D. Funk
  1999 Microarray analysis of replicative senescence. *Current Biology* 9:939-945.
Sinclair, D., K. Mills, and L. Guarente
  1998 Aging in *Saccharomyces cerevisiae*. *Annual Review of Microbiology* 52:533-560.
Speroff, L.
  1994 The effect of aging on fertility. *Current Opinion in Obstetrics and Gynecology* 6:115-120.

Stoler, D.L., N. Chen, M. Basik, M.S. Kahlenberg, M.A. Rodriguez-Bigas, N.J. Petrelli, and G.R. Anderson
   1999   The onset and extent of genomic instability in sporadic colorectal tumor progression. *Proceedings of the National Academy of Sciences of the United States of America* 96:15121-15126.

Tang, M.X., G. Maestre, W.Y. Tsai, X.H. Liu, L. Feng, W.Y. Chung, M. Chun, P. Schofield, Y. Stern, B. Tycko, and R. Mayeux
   1996   Relative risk of Alzheimer disease and age-at-onset distributions, based on APOE genotypes among elderly African Americans, Caucasians, and Hispanics in New York City. *American Journal of Human Genetics* 58:574-584.

Thesleff, I., and C. Sahlberg
   1999   Organ culture in the analysis of tissue interactions. *Methods in Molecular Biology* 97:23-31.

Thieffry, D.
   1999   From global expression data to gene networks. *Bioessays* 21:895-899.

Trent, J.M., M. Bittner, J. Zhang, R. Wiltshire, M. Ray, Y. Su, E. Gracia, P. Meltzer, J. De Risi, L. Penland, and P. Brown
   1997   Use of microgenomic technology for analysis of alterations in DNA copy number and gene expression in malignant melanoma. *Clinical and Experimental Immunology* 107 Suppl 1:33-40.

Viitanen, M., K. Johansson, N. Bogdanovic, A. Berkowicz, H. Druid, A. Eriksson, P. Krantz, H. Laaksonen, H. Sandler, P. Saukko, I. Thiblin, B. Winblad, and H. Kalimo
   1998   Alzheimer changes are common in aged drivers killed in single car crashes and at intersections. *Forensic Science International* 96:115-127.

Vogel, F., and R. Rathenberg
   1975   Spontaneous mutation in man. *Advances in Human Genetics* 5:223-318.

Wagner, D., E.M. de Villiers, and L. Gissmann
   1985   Detection of various papilloma virus types in cytologic smears of precancerous conditions and cancers of the uterine cervix. *Geburtshilfe und Frauenheilkunde* 45:226-231.

Young, J., and J.R. Smith
   2000   Epigenetic aspects of cellular senescence. *Experimental Gerontology* 35:23-32.

Yu, C.E., J. Oshima, Y.H. Fu, E.M. Wijsman, F. Hisama, R. Alisch, S. Matthews, J. Nakura, T. Miki, S. Ouais, G.M. Martin, J. Mulligan, and G.D. Schellenberg
   1996   Positional cloning of the Werner's syndrome gene. *Science* 272:258-262.

Zhang, H., and N. Risch
   1996   Mapping quantitative-trait loci in humans by use of extreme concordant sib pairs: Selected sampling by parental phenotypes [published erratum appears in *American Journal of Human Genetics* 1997 Mar;60(3):748-9]. *American Journal of Human Genetics* 59:951-957.

Zhang, Y., B.E. Kreger, J.F. Dorgan, L.A. Cupples, R.H. Myers, G.L. Splansky, A. Schatzkin, and R.C. Ellison
   1999   Parental age at child's birth and son's risk of prostate cancer. The Framingham Study. *American Journal of Epidemiology* 150:1208-1212.

7

Indicators of Function in the Geriatric Population

Jeffrey B. Halter and David B. Reuben

Assessment of function of an elderly person can be conducted at a number of different levels and using methods which span a wide range of sophistication. On a clinical level, assessment of overall functional capability is a central theme of the field of geriatric medicine. However, with rapid advances in technology, assessment of function of individual organs or organ systems, of individual cells, and even of specific molecules will become increasingly feasible, even in the context of a household survey or evaluation. This chapter will review aspects of function at each of these levels in humans, the various types of total organism functions that are usually assessed clinically and can predict outcomes, and issues related to choice of measures of function for this population.

Measurement of function at any of these levels may define the presence of a disease state. For example, a diagnosis of congestive heart failure or renal failure is based on a certain level of functional impairment of the heart or kidneys. However, most diseases are characterized either by overt pathology like tissue damage (e.g., myocardial infarction), inflammation (e.g., infection), or invasion (e.g., cancer); the presence of defined clinical characteristics in a patient (e.g., depression or malnutrition); or a laboratory measurement which predicts subsequent pathology (e.g., high blood pressure or high cholesterol level).

LEVELS OF FUNCTION

Molecular

Samples of tissue or body fluid provide a wide range of molecules for possible identification and characterization. Assessment of activity of certain key enzymes can provide insight into the metabolic state of a tissue sample. Molecules on the surface of circulating blood lymphocytes can provide insight about activity of the individual's immune system and predict immune system responses to certain challenges including transplantation.

Analysis of the hemoglobin molecule can provide insight about the functional characteristics of this molecule, which is critical for delivering oxygen to tissues. Abnormalities of hemoglobin can impair the appropriate function of the hemoglobin molecule and result in a serious illness such as sickle cell anemia. Exposure of the hemoglobin molecule over time to glucose, the main sugar in the blood, leads to molecular attachment of glucose, creating glycosylated hemoglobin. Thus the amount of glycosylated hemoglobin provides a quantitative index of overall body exposure to glucose over a period of time. Glycosylated hemoglobin is now a readily available clinical test for degree of elevation of blood sugar in people with diabetes (Halter, 1999). Glycosylated hemoglobin can be quantitated from a drop of blood with a rapid test that can be administered in a doctor's office or done in the home setting. It turns out that this structural change of the hemoglobin molecule also affects an important functional characteristic, its oxygen carrying capacity. The amount of glucose attached to other important body proteins can be assessed in tissue samples, as from a skin biopsy. Again, not only does such a measurement provide an estimate of exposure to increased blood sugar, but functional characteristics of the glucose-modified molecules are affected and may contribute directly to diabetes-related complications.

Advances in technology will likely make it possible to carry out molecular screening of a large number of molecules in body fluids or tissue samples that may identify genetic variation or be markers of disease processes (Burns et al., 1998). Similarly, future technology will allow rapid quantitation in such samples of the amount of messenger RNA, the template for synthesis of cell proteins. The amount and structure of specific messenger RNAs provide measures of functional capability of individual genes. Furthermore, the pattern of messenger RNA in a given cell may provide a biological fingerprint of the cell's functional response to a given set of biological circumstances.

Cellular

Specific cells can be isolated from blood or tissue samples for testing of functional capability. In particular, white blood cells, some of which are responsible for initiating inflammation (polymorphonuclear leukocytes) and others for immunologic responses (lymphocytes), can be isolated from blood and tested in vitro with a variety of molecules called cytokines which can stimulate specific responses. Such measures can provide insight about an individual's risk for infection or impaired inflammatory response to injury. More generally, alterations in intercellular signaling systems may play an important role in aging processes (Roth and Yen, 1999). Function of the blood coagulation system can be assessed by measures of clotting proteins in blood and functional characteristics of platelets, which are important constituents of the blood clotting response. Tissue samples can provide access to a wider variety of cells, such as those of the skin, muscle, and fat, all of which could provide insight about functional characteristics of these cell types. A more readily available cell type is epithelial cells. However, there is currently no direct link between the functional status of these cells and disease states.

Organ

The most traditional clinical laboratory measurements of body fluids provide direct or indirect assessment of one or more organ systems. For example, blood levels of thyroid hormones provide measures of over- or under-function of the thyroid gland. Similarly, blood samples can be analyzed to provide estimates of kidney, liver, and bone marrow function. Function of other endocrine glands such as the adrenals, gonads, pituitary, and parathyroids can also be assessed. Overall function of metabolic systems controlling glucose and lipid metabolism are also available from analysis of blood samples.

Another dimension for assessment of organ system function is change over time. Current technology allows noninvasive continuous monitoring of heart rate and blood pressure for up to several days in the home setting for clinical purposes to document cardiac arrhythmias and diurnal fluctuations of blood pressure. Such testing provides substantially more information about rapidly changing variables than a single measure. Small motion detectors can be worn to quantitate the degree of physical activity over time. Sleep monitoring equipment can be used in the home setting to document nocturnal activity and sleep patterns. Noninvasive continuous monitoring of the blood glucose level will be available in the near future.

Simple mechanical devices are available to estimate pulmonary function, which can be carried out in a household survey situation. Simple measures of cardiovascular system function such as blood pressure and heart rate can also be measured readily in a home situation. However, these measures provide only indirect assessment of function of the heart or other aspects of the cardiovascular system. Advances in technology may greatly enhance the capability of quantitating organ system function. Already, portable ultrasound equipment can be used to obtain quantitative measures of cardiac function and evaluate whether there is evidence of significant atherosclerosis in major blood vessels such as the carotid artery or leg arteries. Portable equipment can also be used to quantitate body composition and to carry out sophisticated pulmonary function testing. The National Institute on Aging's Baltimore Longitudinal Study of Aging is about to send into the field a mobile research laboratory that has such capabilities. With such experience and some further refinement of technology, it is not hard to imagine a suitably trained technician in the home setting using portable equipment to carry out such measures and transmitting data via internet connection to a central site for quantitative analysis. There is little doubt that the capability for making quantitative, noninvasive measurements will increase in the future, thereby refining our ability to quantitate function of organ systems only estimated crudely with current measurements of blood products.

Total Organism

The contributions of the many organ systems are integrated to permit functioning of the total organism. Such functions may include the completion of specific tasks (e.g., movement of a limb) or be integrated to achieve a goal (e.g., preparing a meal). Integrated functioning may be directed at accomplishing personal survival tasks or towards fulfilling societal roles. Function at the level of the total organism is described in greater detail below.

Society

Function in society is the highest level of integration of function and represents the individual's role with respect to other humans in achieving communal goals. Societal functioning includes work, family, community service, social, and recreational roles. These roles typically change with aging. As people retire they relinquish parenting and assume grandparenting responsibilities, and their physical (and sometimes cognitive) capacity declines as the result of age-associated physiological or disease processes. Superimposed upon these changes are stereotypic expectations of aging by society and older persons themselves that influence societal roles among capable older persons. Finally, there may be a wide range of degree of personal choice in fulfilling societal roles. Some older persons have accumulated wealth in the form of savings and pensions to allow them to choose to cease certain societal roles (e.g., paid employment), whereas others have much more limited financial and social supports and so may have limited choices of function in society.

TYPES OF FUNCTION—TOTAL ORGANISM

Physical

Physical functional status is an essential component of the health of older persons, and its measurement has been widely incorporated into research and clinical settings. In the strictest sense, physical function refers to voluntary motor function; however, adequate cognitive function is also required for higher-level activities. For example, severely demented persons may have the capacity for physical function but may be too cognitively impaired to successfully perform even the most basic physical task. More commonly, impaired cognition limits new learning which may be required to overcome a disability. For example, cognitive function may be a limiting factor in determining whether a stroke patient regains the ability to walk or transfer independently. A diagnosis of dementia is an important predictor of subsequent decline of functional capability of older adults (Agüero-Torres et al., 1998).

When cognition is adequate, limitations of physical function are the result of impairments of strength, coordination, flexibility, balance, and endurance, or the result of being unable to integrate these into purposeful activities. Measurement of physical functional status has been used for several purposes, including: to gauge the functional status of individuals and populations, to provide prognostic information, to determine the need for assistive services, to assess the effectiveness of specific interventions in individual persons, and to monitor the course of illness.

Physical function can be conceptualized as a series of increasingly integrated steps beginning with basic components and progressing through three levels of increasingly more integrated function (Figure 7-1). This framework can be overlaid on existing models of pathways from disease or injury to disability, and provides an expanded approach to measurement of the functional component of these models. Moreover it fits well with existing self-report and performance-based instruments (see below). The basic components (coordination/fine motor, balance, strength, flexibility, and endurance) are not functional tasks per se, but are the necessary elements that permit performance of more integrated functional tasks. At each subsequent level of integration, more than one

164

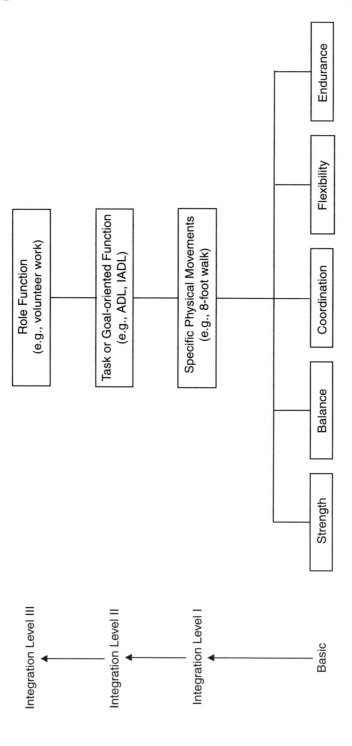

FIGURE 7-1 A framework for the hierarchy of physical functional status.

basic component is usually necessary, and additional components unrelated to physical capability (e.g., cognitive, sensory, and affective) influence performance. Motivation, perceived self-efficacy, and physical environment also modify how the basic components are integrated into levels of higher function.

Examples of the basic components and integration levels are provided in Table 7-1. The first level of integration is performance of specific movements. These tasks are the most basic level at which impairments of range, strength, endurance, balance, and coordination begin to have an impact on function. At the second level, these physical movements are conjoined to complete specific goal-oriented functional tasks (e.g., instrumental activities of daily living). At the third (highest) level, goal-oriented functional tasks are integrated into behaviors aimed at fulfilling societal roles and recreational activities, the so-called advanced activities of daily living (Reuben and Solomon, 1989). At this level, function is often determined by personal choice rather than by physical capacity. For example, a person may have the physical capacity to play golf and tennis but may choose only one because of personal preference. With progressively higher level integration, the many dimensions that contribute to functional status become inextricably entwined. Consider a concert violinist whose ability to perform a concert recital depends upon each of the basic

TABLE 7-1 Examples of Physical Activities and Their Level of Integration

Basic Components	Integration Level I Specific Physical Movements	Integration Level II Goal-Directed Activities	Integration Level III Personal Choices of Roles
Strength	Roll over in bed	Transfer from bed	Employment/
Balance	Move up in bed	to chair	unpaid work
Coordination	Supine to sit	Rise from chair and	Recreation
Flexibility	Sit	walk	Family relationships
Endurance	Rise from chair	Climb stairs	Social interaction and
	Stand	Eat	activities
	Walk	Dress	Community participation
	Reach	Groom	Caregiving
	Turn	Toilet	
	Bend	Cook	
	Grip	Shop	
	Lift	Clean house	
		Take medication	
		Write	

and integrated components of physical functioning, as well as vision, hearing, memory, and affect. Attempting to isolate the physical component from the remainder is a meaningless exercise.

Neuropsychological

There are several major dimensions of neuropsychological function, including cognition, affect (mood), anxiety, spirituality, and personality, including self-efficacy (empowerment). Some of these have been long established as aspects of health (e.g., cognition and affect), whereas others (e.g., spirituality and self-efficacy) are becoming increasingly recognized as contributors to health.

Within cognitive function, there are also several subdimensions including attention, memory, language, visual spatial performance, and executive function. Attention is a measure of alertness and ability to interact with one's environment. It is primarily impaired in settings of acute illness (e.g., delirium) or affective disorders (e.g., depression). Nevertheless, attention is a key element of neuropsychological function, as some preservation of attention is necessary for all further neuropsychological testing (and objective testing of other dimensions) to be conducted. Inattention can dramatically affect performance and may preclude testing entirely. Although formal tests of inattention have been developed, they are not commonly performed. Rather, implicit decisions or assumptions about the level of attentiveness are made. In community-based settings, major attention deficits are uncommon and such assumptions may be appropriate.

Memory has been divided into immediate (recall), short-term (recent), and long-term (remote) (Cummings and Benson, 1992). Immediate refers to the ability to retain small amounts of material with high accuracy for very short periods of time (e.g., digit span). Short-term memory requires learning of new material (e.g., delayed recall or orientation). Long-term memory is usually tested by evaluating common historical items (e.g., recalling the last several presidents). Language refers to the content and vehicle for communication in contrast to speech, which represents the mechanical aspects of verbal communication. Commonly evaluated language functions include spontaneous verbal output, comprehension of spoken language, repetition of spoken language, naming, reading, and writing (Cummings and Benson, 1992). Although some unusual neurological diseases can cause isolated language impairment, usually these deficits are in the context of cerebrovascular disease (e.g., stroke) or dementia. Visual spatial impairments may be the result of primary visual impairment (see below) or the result of cognitive processing of vision, which in older persons is usually due to cerebrovascular disease or dementia.

Commonly used tests of visual spatial function are copying objects and clock drawing. Executive function represents integrative cognitive function that requires sequencing and manipulation of information to perform tasks such as problem solving, abstract reasoning, and planning ahead. Some common tests of executive function include calculations, interpreting proverbs, and identifying similarities and differences.

A variety of objective short screens that incorporate each of these dimensions are available, many of which can be performed by nonprofessional evaluators. However, patients and their families sometimes resent these questions and tasks, even when assessed by physicians. The most commonly used screen is the Mini-Mental State Examination, a 30-item interview-administered assessment of several dimensions of cognitive function (Tombough and McIntyre, 1992). Shorter screens also have been validated (e.g., recall of 3 items at one minute, the clock drawing test, the serial sevens test, and the Time and Change test (Siu, 1991; Froehlich et al., 1998)). People with normal results on these tests are very unlikely to have clinical dementia, while abnormal results increase the odds that dementia is present. It must be recognized, however, that most of these tests rely on tasks that are not routine aspects of everyday life. Moreover, often they do not account for educational level, languages other than English, and cultural differences.

Affective status is a measure of mood and depressive symptoms. The assessment of affective status among older persons is complicated by the common presence of somatic symptoms (e.g., fatigue, loss of appetite) accompanying medical illness. These symptoms can mimic symptoms of depression and are therefore less specific for affective disorders in older persons. Affective symptoms can be assessed using a single question, "Do you often feel sad or depressed?" (Lachs et al., 1990), though this one-item evaluation is not as accurate as longer instruments. A number of other brief self-administered screens are available, including the Mental Health Index from the Medical Outcomes Study SF-36 (Ware and Sherbourne, 1992) and the Geriatric Depression Scale, which has 5-, 15- and 30-item versions (Sheikh and Yesavage, 1986; Hoyl et al., 1999).

Sensory

Although aging and diseases associated with aging may affect all senses, the most commonly assessed senses are vision and hearing. Impairments of these two sensory systems are among the most prevalent disorders affecting older persons (AARP/AOA, 1998). Visual function encompasses several components including acuity (near and far), visual fields, contrast sensitivity, depth perception, and resistance to glare. Dimensions of hearing impairment include acuity, speech discrimination, and central auditory processing. In addition, the impact of these sensory impairments on integrated function can be measured. The standard method of screening for problems with visual acuity is the Snellen Eye Chart, which requires the patient to stand 20 feet from the chart and read letters, using corrective lenses. Several interviewer and self-administered instruments to detect functional problems due to visual impairment have been developed, including the "Activities of Daily Vision Scale" (Mangione et al., 1992), the VF-14 (Steinberg et al., 1994), and the National Eye Institute Visual Functioning Questionnaire (Mangione et al., 1998).

Pure-tone audiometry is the standard basic evaluation of hearing but alternative methods that are more feasible in survey settings are available. The Welch Allyn Audioscope™ (Welch Allyn, Inc., Skaneateles Falls, NY) is a hand-held otoscope with a built-in audiometer. When administered under comparable conditions, Audioscope findings are highly correlated with those of pure-tone audiometry. Alternatives are the whispered voice test (Mulrow and Lichtenstein, 1991) and a 6-item screen for hearing impairment based on questions from the National Health and Nutrition Examination Survey (Reuben et al., 1998). Similar to vision assessment, a self-administered test of emotional and social problems associated with impaired hearing, the Hearing Handicap Inventory for the Elderly-Screening Version (HHIE-S), has been developed (Ventry and Weinstein, 1982).

Integrated

A number of conceptual models describe functional status and the pathways from disease or injury to impairment to disability (Nagi, 1976; Verbrugge and Jette, 1994; WHO 1980; Fried and Guralnik, 1997). Functional status is usually assessed at three levels: basic activities of daily living (BADLs), instrumental or intermediate activities of daily living (IADLs), and advanced activities of daily living (AADLs) (Reuben and Solomon, 1989). BADLs assess the ability of the patient to complete basic self-care tasks (e.g., bathing, dressing, toileting, continence, feeding, and transferring). The loss of BADL function implies the need for direct personal assistance either by family or paid help in the home or at an institution. IADLs measure the patient's ability to maintain an independent household (e.g., shopping for groceries, driving or using public transportation, using the telephone, meal preparation, housework, handyman work, laundry, taking medications, and handling finances). Many of the community-based services (e.g., homemaker, meals-on-wheels) are aimed at providing IADL services and thereby permitting disabled older persons to remain in their homes. AADLs measure the patient's ability to fulfill societal, community, and family roles as well as participate in recreational or occupational tasks. These advanced activities vary considerably from individual to individual but may be exceptionally valuable in monitoring functional status prior to the development of disability. A commonly employed measure of more difficult functional tasks is the Rosow-Breslau scale, which measures the ability to perform heavy housework; walk half a mile; work full-time; climb stairs; and participate in activities such as going to a movie, to church or a meeting, or to visit friends (Rosow and Breslau, 1966).

MEASURES OF FUNCTION

Qualitative vs. Quantitative

At the most fundamental level, a qualitative measure may be sufficient. For example, if a specific gene product is completely absent it is clear that the gene in question is not present or functioning. Such qualitative assessment of genetic risk usually identifies only rare individuals with specific single gene disorders. However, in the future it is likely that qualitative evaluation of specific patterns of gene expression may be utilized to assess risk for illness or injury. At the level of the whole organism, qualitative measures are somewhat more commonly in use. Handedness or ethnic background is usually presented in qualitative terms, as is assessment of key functional characteristics such as individual activities of daily living.

However, most measurements in current use are quantitative. Thus, while clinical diagnoses are qualitative in nature (i.e., the subject either does or does not have hypertension, diabetes, congestive heart failure, coronary artery disease), the measures used to establish such diagnoses are almost always quantitative. We measure the blood pressure, blood sugar, or blood lipid levels quantitatively and use established criteria to assign a diagnostic category. Quantitative measures of overall functional capability are increasingly in use as well. For example, rather than simply determining whether or not an individual can get out of a chair without assistance, the speed and stability with which an individual gets out of a chair can be measured quantitatively (Alexander et al., 1996).

For quantitative measures which may require substantial time, effort, and cost, investigators must consider the marginal value in relation to simpler qualitative measures. The tradeoff in a household survey is to determine the relative cost versus accuracy, for example, of simply asking whether someone has diabetes versus quantitative measurement of the blood sugar; simply asking whether someone can get out of a chair without assistance versus carrying out an objective, quantitative measure of chair rise capability; or simply asking whether an individual has a memory impairment versus quantitative measurement of multiple domains of cognitive function. Particularly for asymptomatic disorders such as diabetes, hyperlipidemia, and hypertension, simply asking an individual for knowledge of presence of these conditions will lead to substantial underestimation of their true prevalence. For example, epidemiologic studies have demonstrated that 30-50 percent of people who meet criteria for diabetes mellitus are not aware that they have this condition (Harris et al, 1998). Quantitative testing of blood sugar is required to narrow this gap.

Resting vs. Challenge

A key issue in the assessment of functional capability is the relationship between function at rest versus function during a challenge. For purposes of standardization across a population, the resting state has many advantages. However, key characteristics of disease or aging processes are often not present in the resting state and are elicited only during a challenge. The term functional reserve is sometimes used to describe the difference between a functional impairment of a tissue or organ and the degree of impairment needed to cross the threshold at which clinical detection will occur. For example, only a small proportion of people with congestive heart failure or significant coronary artery disease have symptoms at rest. Clinical features become apparent with exercise or cardiac stress. We also know that there can be substantial organ system damage without perturbation of the resting state. For example, humans can lose 50 percent of kidney function without clinical findings or even abnormalities on common quantitative laboratory measures. As technology improves, it is likely that we will be able to detect organ damage using noninvasive functional imaging with increasing success prior to evidence of clinical disease. Such advances will challenge some of our concepts of disease, but may reduce the need for physiologic stress testing to elicit clinical signs.

One characteristic of aging is a loss of homeostasis, leading to a decline in adaptive capability. From this perspective aging may have little impact on the resting state, but age-related declines in functional capability become apparent during a challenge to homeostatic control mechanisms, thereby unmasking a loss of functional reserve. One example of this issue of resting versus challenge is in the area of glucose regulation. Abnormal glucose metabolism meeting criteria for diabetes mellitus can be detected in many individuals by simple measurement of the blood glucose level after an overnight fast. However, in some individuals, the fasting glucose level may not exceed diagnostic limits, but glucose values after ingesting a challenge dose of glucose (called a glucose tolerance test) may demonstrate a marked abnormality. Though not obvious clinically, such abnormality indicates a substantial loss of functional reserve of the endocrine cells of the pancreas, which produce the metabolic hormone insulin (Halter, 1999). The finding of post-challenge hyperglycemia, which is particularly common in older adults (Barrett-Conner and Ferrara, 1998), is associated with the same risk for diabetes-related vascular disease as in individuals who have fasting hyperglycemia (Barzilay et al., 1999). Thus a research project interested in risk factors and outcomes related to cardiovascular disease will underestimate the impact of diabetes if subjects do not receive an oral glucose tolerance test.

Type of Measure

Tissue or Body Fluid Sample

The type, site, and timing of a sample that is obtained from an individual can have a profound effect on interpretation of the measurement. We are just beginning to understand the complexity of some of the issues. Blood is readily accessible and the standard diagnostic material for noninvasive evaluation for many disease states or risk factors. A summary of some of the measures commonly made from blood samples is provided in Table 7-2. However, a blood sample provides only certain

TABLE 7-2 Some Indicators of Function in Blood

Measure	Organ System
Cellular elements	
PMNs	Bone marrow
Lymphocytes	Immune system
Platelets	Bone marrow
Red blood cells/hemoglobin	Bone marrow
Plasma	
Hormones	Endocrine
Metabolic products	
Glucose	Endocrine, liver, digestive system
Lipids	Liver, digestive system, endocrine
Protein	Liver, digestive system
Enzymes	Organ specific: liver, heart
Coagulation factors	Liver, digestive system
Creatinine, urea nitrogen	Kidney
Vitamins	Liver, digestive system, kidney
Minerals	Digestive system, bone, endocrine, kidney
Inflammatory markers (e.g., cytokines, C-reactive protein)	Liver, immune system

information about function of body systems, and results must be interpreted with caution. Just as there are sampling issues in survey research regarding how well a given study population represents the population at large, so are there also issues regarding blood sampling. The content of blood in a vein coming from heart tissue may differ from that of a vein in the arm or a vein draining a kidney. There are also sampling issues regarding the cells in a given blood sample. The population of white blood cells in the circulation may not accurately reflect the much larger population at extravascular sites in terms of subtype distribution or functional characteristics.

The concentration of a substance in blood reflects the kinetics of the turnover of that substance, that is, the balance between the rate of entry of the substance into the blood and the rate of its removal. The kinetics of such turnover may be very complex, reflecting multiple sources for input (e.g., for cholesterol: GI absorption and liver production) as well as multiple tissue sites for removal (e.g., for cholesterol: skeletal muscle, smooth muscle, vascular endothelium), each with different kinetic characteristics. Furthermore, we now recognize that the concentration of many molecules in the blood is not constant, but changes over time, sometimes frequently and dramatically. Such fluctuations occur in response to exogenous physiological stimuli (e.g., environmental change, movement, food ingestion). They also occur as part of internal physiologic control systems. For example, blood levels of most hormones (i.e., molecules in the blood that carry signals from one part of the body to another, such as insulin or cortisol) fluctuate substantially over 24 hours with cycles that are circadian as well as superimposed bursts of secretion (Van Coevorden et al., 1991). Clearly, measurement of a single blood sample cannot account for this variation and may be difficult to interpret in isolation.

Analysis of urine can provide useful information regarding kidney function, salt and water metabolism, presence of infection, or body production rates of some hormones or metabolites that are excreted via the kidney. However the kinetics of kidney excretion and reabsorption are also complex. For example, glucose is normally fully reabsorbed from the kidney and does not appear in the urine. But if the glucose level is sufficiently elevated and/or there is some degree of renal tubular damage, glucose can begin to appear in the urine and provide a marker for abnormal glucose metabolism or kidney damage. However, the relationship between hyperglycemia and appearance of glucose in the urine can vary substantially within a given individual and between individuals, so glucosuria has not been a very useful marker for diagnosis or clinical management of diabetes.

Since all cells from an individual carry the same genome, any cellular source could provide suitable material for genetic analysis. Thus analysis of white cells from blood or epithelial cells scraped from the mucosa of the mouth should provide equivalent information, depending on the amount and quality of genetic material needed for a given analysis. Some analysis can be done on a sample as small as a drop of blood (obtained by pinprick), but a larger blood sample would provide many more cells to work with. White cells in blood can be kept viable for a period of time after collection and can be kept alive in culture in the laboratory, providing an opportunity to study dynamics of gene expression as well as simply documenting gene content.

While less applicable for household surveys, minor office-type procedures such as skin biopsy or needle biopsy can provide specific tissues for analysis. Such samples can complement information available from blood and address site-specific research questions. Study of fat cells can provide added information about metabolic disorders, and study of muscle cells insight about problems with mobility and neuromuscular control. There are sampling issues, since different muscles have different types of fiber distribution and contractile properties, and the metabolic characteristics of fat cells vary somewhat by location.

Overview of Testing at the Levels of Total Organism and Society

There are two general methods of measuring function at the levels of total organism and society, subjective and objective. Each of these methods can be further subdivided. Subjective measures rely on the perception of the subject (or a proxy) and may be obtained by questionnaires completed by the subject or by interview. In contrast, objective (also called performance-based) measures rely on observation by a trained observer. This evaluation may be qualitative or include instrumentation (e.g., audiometry testing). When functional status information is provided by a proxy, the distinction between subjective and objective may be less clear depending upon the nature of the measurement and the rigor of the observer.

Although many aspects of functional status can be assessed by either subjective or objective methods, some of the domains described above (e.g., neuropsychological function) must be assessed by objective testing. Subjective and objective measures may be combined to provide additional information regarding function. For example, a subject may be observed performing a task and then be asked to rate how difficult or tiring the task was.

In addition, the measurement of function in older persons in surveys must consider unique aspects of this population. Many diseases, including those that impair cognition and compromise participation and validity of responses, are more common with advancing age. Respondent burden (e.g., the length of time that a subject can be evaluated before becoming fatigued) may also be an important factor. Accordingly, the selection of measurement instruments must balance scientific accuracy with efficiency and practicality.

Subjective (Self-Report) Testing

Subjective assessment of the ability to function is the most commonly used method of evaluating physical and integrated function. This method may also be used to measure sensory function. It has the advantages of being inexpensive and portable. Moreover, subjective assessment generally focuses on items that have direct clinical relevance. When collecting population data on self-reported physical and integrated functional status, the results are quite sensitive to the wording of both the stems and response items. Among the sources of variation are differences related to duration of disability, whether human assistance is needed, whether assistive devices are used, level of difficulty, and degree of limitation. When comparing essentially equivalent ADL measures across surveys, such minor inconsistencies in wording can result in large differences. For example, the National Medical Expenditure Survey estimated that there are 60 percent more elderly people with ADL problems than did the Supplement on Aging (Wiener et al., 1990). Some items may not be relevant because of traditional gender-specific roles (e.g., some men have never cooked). When administered in written form, language and educational barriers may also preclude accurate assessment.

Finally, when assessing integrated function, subjective measures may be inaccurate because subjects may overestimate or underestimate their capabilities. Such discrepancies between capacity and actual performance are a source of concern when measuring self-reported function (Glass, 1998). Using the hypothetical tense "could do" and the enacted tense "does do," subjects can be categorized into four groups: (1) "cannot do, doesn't do" (low functioning), (2) "cannot do, does do" (overachievers), (3) "can do, doesn't do" (underachievers), and (4) "can do, does do" (high functioning). Recently, an intermediate step between independence and dependence, "independence *with* difficulty," has been identified that may help reconcile some of the discrepancies between capacity and performance (Gill et al., 1998).

Objective Testing

Over the past decade, there has been increasing interest in using performance-based measures to assess physical function. In this context, a performance-based measure can be defined as a test in which a subject (or a patient) performs a movement, behavior, or task according to a standardized protocol, which is scored by an observer. Performance-based tests rate the ability to do a behavior or task. These measures differ from tests that measure physiologic capacity or impairment within a specific dimension, such as pulmonary function or treadmill stress tests. Observations may be qualitative (e.g., rating the steadiness of balance) or quantitative (e.g., timed performance). The approach to objective measures ranges from sophisticated technology that can precisely characterize movements (e.g., joint movements) to coarse but reliable judgments of the quality of tasks (e.g., steadiness when turning 360 degrees). Much of the appeal and promise of performance instruments is the ability to provide standardized and objectively scored data that are suitable for robust statistical analysis. Performance-based data may be predictive of subsequent health events and may be useful in monitoring disease progression and response to therapy (Reuben et al., 1992; Guralnik et al., 1994). Although objective measurements have theoretical advantages (Guralnik et al., 1989), they are not necessarily superior to subjective measures (Myers et al., 1993). Rather they may be measuring different, though related, constructs (Reuben et al., 1995) and may provide complementary information.

Selecting a Measurement Method

For physical functioning, the most appropriate method of measurement depends, in part, upon the level of function that is being assessed. The basic components are best measured directly by performance testing. The remaining levels of integration may be measured by multiple methods: performance-based testing, observer rating, self or proxy report. Currently available performance-based instruments measure physical function at the basic component, specific physical movement, and task- or goal-oriented levels of integration. Many instruments measure physical functioning at more than one level. No performance-based instrument measures societal role function (except, perhaps, if competitive athletics is considered a societal role function). This level of function, highly idiosyncratic to the individual, is probably best assessed by self- or proxy-report methods.

Role of the Individual

Regardless of the functional task assessed or the method employed, the subject's motivation and immediate state (e.g., fatigue, acute illness) must be considered. The abovementioned discrepancies between self-reported "can do" and "does do" may relate to such factors or be due to misperceptions of capacity. Similarly, discrepancies between performance-based measured function and actual performance in everyday life may reflect such factors. For example, motivation to climb a flight of stairs may be higher if meals are served on the second floor. Conversely, subjects may want to impress the examiner and perform better than in the home environment.

Testing Conditions

When considering performance-based measures, several test administration factors must be considered. Among these are standardization of both the test administrator/rater (through training) and the task being performed. The same amount of encouragement and scoring rules must be enforced and subjects need to be told whether the effort is to reflect "usual" or "maximal" effort. Another important issue is that of accommodating to the test and fatiguing. The number of attempts at performing a task and how data from multiple attempts are interpreted need to be determined to account for both the "learning effect" and impaired performance due to fatigue. Finally, the testing site and equipment used can make large differences in performance-based measures. For example, chairs vary in height and flights of stairs vary in number of steps.

Conditions within a subject's home are likely to vary considerably from those in clinics or laboratories. Yet, documenting an impairment of function in the laboratory setting may have little real meaning if the subject can perform the same function at home. Patients with cognitive problems or visual loss may function surprisingly well in a familiar environment but be extremely limited in an unfamiliar clinic or laboratory setting.

REFERENCES

Agüero-Torres, H, L. Fratiglioni, Z. Guo, M. Viitanen, E. von Strauss, and B. Winblad
    1998   Dementia is the major cause of functional dependence in the elderly: 3-year follow-up data from a population-based study. *American Journal of Public Health* 88:1452-1456.
Alexander, N.B., D.J. Koester, and J.A. Grunawalt
    1996   Chair design affects how older adults rise from a chair. *Journal of the American Geriatrics Society* 44:356-362.
American Association of Retired Persons/Administration on Aging
    1998   *A Profile of Older Americans: 1998.* Washington DC: U.S. Department of Health and Human Services. PF3049 (1298) D996.
Barrett-Connor, E., and A. Ferrara
    1998   Isolated postchallenge hyperglycemia and the risk of fatal cardiovascular disease in older women and men. *Diabetes Care* 21:1236-1239.

Barzilay, J., C.F. Speikerman, P.W. Wahl , L.H. Kuller, M. Cushman, C.D. Furberg, A. Dobs, J.F. Polak, and P.J. Savage
  1999   Cardiovascular disease in older adults with glucose disorders: Comparison of American Diabetes Association criteria for diabetes mellitus with WHO criteria. *Lancet* 354:622-625.
Burns, M.A., B.N. Johnson, S.N. Brahmasandra, K. Handique, J.R. Webster, M. Krishnan, T.S. Sammarco, P.M. Man, D. Jones, D. Heldsinger, C.H. Mastangelo, and D.T. Burke
  1998   An integrated nanoliter DNA analysis device. *Science* 282:484-487.
Cummings, J.L., and D.F. Benson
  1992   *Dementia: A Clinical Approach*, 2nd Edition. Boston: Butterworth-Heinemann.
Fried, L.P., and J.M. Guralnik
  1997 · Disability in older adults: Evidence regarding significance, etiology, and risk. *Journal of the American Geriatrics Society* 45:92-100.
Froehlich, T.E., J.T. Robison, and S.K. Inouye
  1998   Screening for dementia in the outpatient setting: The Time and Change test. *Journal of the American Geriatrics Society* 46:1506-1511.
Gill, T.M., J.T. Robison, and M.E. Tinetti
  1998   Difficulty and dependence: Two components of the disability continuum among community-living older persons. *Annals of Internal Medicine* 128:96-101.
Glass, T.A.
  1998   Conjugating the "tenses" of function: Discordance among hypothetical, experimental, and enacted function in older adults. *The Gerontologist* 38:101-112.
Guralnik, J.M., L.G. Branch, S.R. Cummings, and J.D. Curb
  1989   Physical performance measures in aging research. *The Journals of Gerontology: Medical Sciences* 44:M141-146.
Guralnik, J.M., E.M. Simonsick, L. Ferrucci, et al.
  1994   A short physical performance battery assessing lower extremity function: Association with self-reported disability and prediction of mortality and nursing home admission. *The Journals of Gerontology: Medical Sciences* 49:M85-M94.
Halter, J.B.
  1999   Diabetes mellitus. Pp. 991-1011 in *Principles of Geriatric Medicine and Gerontology*, 4th edition, W.R. Hazzard, J.P. Blass, W.H. Ettinger, J.B. Halter, and J.G. Ouslander, eds. New York: McGraw-Hill.
Harris, M.I., K.M. Flegal, C.C. Cowie, et al.
  1998   Prevalence of diabetes, impaired fasting glucose, and impaired glucose tolerance in U.S. adults. The Third National Health and Nutrition Examination Survey, 1988-1994. *Diabetes Care* 21:518-524.
Hoyl, M.T., C.A. Alessi, J.O. Harker, et al.
  1999   Development and testing of a five-item version of the Geriatric Depression Scale. *Journal of the American Geriatrics Society* 47:873-878.
Lachs, M.S., A.R. Feinstein, L.M. Cooney, et al.
  1990   A simple procedure for general screening for functional disability in elderly patients. *Annals of Internal Medicine* 112:699-706.
Mangione, C.M., S. Berry, K. Spritzer, K.N. Janz, R. Klein, C. Owsley, and P.P. Lee
  1998   Identifying the content area for the 51-item National Eye Institute Visual Function Questionnaire: Results from focus groups with visually impaired persons. *Archives of Ophthalmology* 116:227-233.
Mangione, C.M., R.S. Phillips, J.M. Seddon, et al.
  1992   Development of the "Activities of Daily Vision Scale:" A measure of visual functional status. *Medical Care* 30:1111-1126.

Mulrow, C.D., and M.J. Lichtenstein
  1991 Screening for hearing impairment in the elderly: Rationale and strategy. *Journal of General Internal Medicine* 6:249-258.
Myers, A.M., P.J. Holliday, K.A. Harvey, and K.S. Hutchinson
  1993 Functional performance measures: Are they superior to self-assessments? *The Journals of Gerontology: Medical Sciences* 48:M196-206.
Nagi, S.Z.
  1976 An epidemiology of disability among adults in the United States. *Milbank Memorial Fund Quarterly. Health and Society* 54:439-467
Reuben, D.B., A.L. Siu, and S. Kimpau
  1992 The predictive validity of self-report and performance-based measures of function and health. *The Journals of Gerontology: Medical Sciences* 47:M106-110.
Reuben, D.B., and D.H. Solomon
  1989 Assessment in geriatrics: Of caveats and names. *Journal of the American Geriatrics Society* 37:570-572.
Reuben, D.B., L.A. Valle, R.D. Hays, and A.L. Siu
  1995 Measuring physical function in community-dwelling older persons: A comparison of self-administered, interviewer-administered, and performance-based measures. *Journal of the American Geriatrics Society* 43:17-23.
Reuben, D.B., K. Walsh, A.A. Moore, M. Damesyn, and G.A. Greendale
  1998 Hearing loss in community-dwelling older persons: National prevalence data and identification using simple questions. *Journal of the American Geriatrics Society* 46:1008.
Rosow, I., and N. Breslau
  1966 A Guttman Health Scale for the aged. *The Journal of Gerontology* 21:556-559.
Roth, J., and C.J. Yen
  1999 The role of intercellular communication in diseases of old age. Pp. 45-59 in *Principles of Geriatric Medicine and Gerontology*, 4th edition, W.R. Hazzard, J.P. Blass, W.H. Ettinger, J.B. Halter and J.G. Ouslander, eds. New York: McGraw-Hill.
Sheikh, J.I., and J.A. Yesavage
  1986 Geriatric Depression Scale: Recent evidence and development of a shorter version. *Clinical Gerontology* 5:165
Siu, A.L.
  1991 Screening for dementia and investigating its causes. *Annals of Internal Medicine* 115:122-132.
Steinberg, E.P., J.M. Tielsich, O.D. Schein, et al.
  1994 The VF-14: An index of functional impairment in patients with cataract. *Archives of Opthalmology* 112:630.
Tombaugh, T.N., and N.J. McIntyre
  1992 The Mini-Mental State Examination: A comprehensive review. *Journal of the American Geriatrics Society* 40:922-935.
Van Coevorden, A.V., J. Mockel, E. Laurent, M. Kerkhofs, M. l'Hermite-Balériaux, C. Decoster, P. Nève, and E.V. Cauter
  1991 Neuroendocrine rhythms and sleep in aging men. *American Journal of Physiology* 260 (Endocrinol. Metab. 23):E651-E661.
Ventry, I.M., and B.E. Weinstein
  1982 The hearing handicap inventory for the elderly: A new tool. *Ear and Hearing* 3:128-134.
Verbrugge, L.M., and A.M. Jette
  1994 The disablement process. *Social Science and Medicine* 38:1-14.

Ware, J.E., and C.D. Sherbourne
  1992   The MOS 36-item short-form health survey (SF-36). *Medical Care* 30:473-483.
Wiener, J.M., R.J. Hanley, R. Clark, and J.F. Van Nostrand
  1990   Measuring the activities of daily living: Comparisons across national surveys. *The Journals of Gerontology: Social Sciences* 45:S229-237.
World Health Organization
  1980   *The International Classification of Impairments, Disabilities and Handicaps.* Geneva: World Health Organization.

8

Biomarkers and the Genetics of Aging in Mice

Richard A. Miller

L aboratory mice, compared to people, present important advantages for investigations of the biological underpinnings of aging, late-life illness, and age-dependent physiological changes. Although they are far from ideal respondents in household surveys, they are relatively easy to persuade to donate samples of biological tissues, can be followed from birth to natural death in a few years, and can be coaxed to mate with spouses or consume most diets of the investigator's choosing. They are more like people than worms and flies—those favorite invertebrate models for gerontogenetics—are like people, providing some basis for hope that aging of mice will resemble aging of people in helpful ways. The goal of this essay is to present, for the nonbiologist, a summary of how studies of age-sensitive biological traits can contribute to our knowledge of aging, its measurement, and its genetics. We will begin with a discussion about the nature of aging and whether its rate can be measured, present a set of proposed criteria for deciding if an age-sensitive trait provides a useful biomarker of aging, illustrate these validation criteria with examples drawn from T-cell subset testing, and show how genetic data can help to sort out the relation of age-related physiological changes to disease risk and life span. After digressions to consider the idea that genes affecting growth rates in early life have pleiotropic effects on longevity and late-life illnesses, and to introduce new, high-tech approaches that produce catalogs of gene expression data for biomarker and genetic analysis, we will conclude with three suggestions as to how biological data might best be integrated into population survey programs.

BASIC DEFINITIONS AND PREMISES

What Is Aging?

Does aging start at conception, at birth, at the age of lowest mortality risk (around puberty), or only when the effects of aging become obvious to clinicians and pathologists? Is it a single process or a group of processes that occur in parallel throughout life? Does it occur in tissue culture, in individual cells, or only in whole organisms? Is the "senescence" that causes oak leaves to turn red and die a form of aging? When a person gives up smoking and chocolate nut sundaes and takes up broccoli and jogging, thereby adding 10 years of healthy life to middle age, has "aging" been reversed? Terms in colloquial use bring with them dangerous baggage when they sneak into scientific discussions, and gerontologists quickly discover that most of their honorable and respected colleagues use the term "aging" in different, idiosyncratic, misleading, tricky, indefensible ways. To simplify my presentation, I will start with a formal definition, one defended in more detail elsewhere (Miller, 1997a, 1999). When I talk about aging, I mean the process that progressively converts healthy young adults (whole mice or whole people, for example) into frailer adults with increased risks of death and disability. It is important to note that this process does not occur only in old age: although 90-year olds are more aged than 20-year olds, there is no reason to think that 90-year olds are aging any more rapidly than they did when they were themselves young adults. Studies of senior citizens are needed to tell us what aging does, but studies of young and middle-aged adults may be at least as informative about how aging creates old people from young ones. Indeed, contrary to some versions of intuition, studies of young adults are likely to tell us more about aging than studies of old individuals, because the former are less affected by two important confounders: (a) the effects of specific serious diseases that often afflict the elderly, and (b) differential survival, which removes individuals from their age cohort and does so nonrandomly with respect to age-dependent physiological effects.

Is There An "Aging Process" Per Se?

Or does the conversion of young adults to noticeably different, more vulnerable, old adults reflect the simultaneous, more-or-less well-synchronized progression of multiple processes, some of which alter muscles and others bone marrow, some of which operate within cells and others on extra-cellular material, some of which alter DNA and others membranes or proteins or cell numbers or circuitry? The latter theory, conveniently termed the "multiple-clocks" model, is by far the most popular among theoretically inclined gerontologists, from John Maynard Smith (1962) through Edward Masoro (1995) and many others. It is difficult to imagine how a single cellular or biochemical mechanism might lead to alterations in so many apparently disparate manifestations of aging. In my view, however, the notion that aging is indeed regulated by a single clock—or a very small collection of clocks—is supported by strong circumstantial evidence. The argument includes four elements:

• Caloric restriction, i.e., the imposition of diets containing about 40 percent fewer calories than a rodent would voluntarily consume, seems to retard nearly all aspects of aging, including changes in protein cross-linking, patterns of gene expression, loss of function in many organ systems, and risks of multiple forms of death (Weindruch and Walford, 1988). Restricted mice and rats stay active and vigorous at ages at which nearly all control animals have died (McCarter et al.,1997). This mass of evidence is very difficult to reconcile with models in which these aspects of aging are independently timed.

• Mutations at single genes can extend life span by about 50 percent in df/df and dw/dw dwarf mice (Brown-Borg et al., 1996; Miller, 1999), and by 200 percent or more in nematode worms (Kenyon et al., 1993). The dw/dw mice, at least, retain youthful levels of immune function into old age (Flurkey et al., unpublished results). Single gene changes that produce dramatic increases in longevity are again tough to reconcile with multiple-clock models of aging.

• Natural selection can rapidly generate subpopulations of mammals that live much longer than the founding population. The clearest example of this comes from Austad's study of an opossum population, stranded for a few thousand years on a relatively risk-free island. Selective pressures in this new ecological niche favored slow-aging genotypes, and the resulting population survives much longer than their mainland cousins. Initial mortality rates do not differ greatly between the two populations, suggesting that differences in predation pressure per se contribute relatively little to these survival statistics, but changes in the slope of the mortality risk curve support the idea that the island opossums age more slowly than their mainland cousins by a factor of nearly two. Furthermore, island opossums not only exhibit life-span extension, but also show decelerated changes in collagen cross-linking and reproductive performance (Austad, 1993). Under a multiple-clock system, production of a new, longer-lived species or subspecies would require multiple adjustments in genes that time each of the multiple systems affected by aging, and would have to do so in a population of animals whose other protective systems continue to decay at the original, rapid rate. The single-clock model, in contrast, does not depend upon a rare concatenation of low-impact mutations, but hypothesizes a fairly small number of genes in which mutation can alter multiple downstream processes in parallel. Natural selection has produced long-lived species and subspecies from shorter-lived ones dozens of times (e.g., turtles, tuna, elephants, bats, parrots, and chimps do not share a recent common ancestor!). Evolution of extended longevity seems to emerge over and over again from selective conditions that promote large body size, slowed development, and relatively small litter sizes.

• The single-clock model predicts that those individuals within a species who appear particularly "youthful" in one respect (e.g., immune function) are likely to appear relatively youthful in others (e.g., muscle function, collagen biochemistry, or mortality risk). Compelling evidence on this point is not yet available, but some recent data from our own laboratory, presented below, have begun to address this issue.

These two viewpoints—aging as a single process or as a collection of processes—are not difficult to combine into a unified perspective. The electrical network in a residence can be viewed as a set of circuits, one running the toaster, another running the radio, a third running the light bulbs, each of which is subject to its own regulatory pathways (switches, rheostats), each engineered and fixable by specialists who need know little about the other appliances beyond their likely demands on the current. Each of these parallel processes, however, can be influenced by a reduction in the available voltage in a summer heatwave. The obvious fact that many systems break down, in different ways, in old people and old rodents does not by itself disprove the hypothesis that these multiple endpoints of aging might be timed, in part, by a shared mechanism. The question is an empirical one, with the evidence not yet fully assembled.

Can Aging Be Measured?

Alas, not yet. Researchers who wish to test whether a particular diet, exercise program, drug, or gene alters aging often use age at death as an indirect measure of the effects of aging itself. In these situations—for example, in studies of caloric restriction (Yu et al.,1985)—they determine if the experimental condition extends the mean life span of a test population, with particular attention to the longevity of longest-lived individuals (the "maximum life span," conveniently estimated as the mean life span of the longest-lived 5 or 10 percent of the group), and conclude that aging has been slowed if the proportion achieving very old age increases. A related measure, the time over which mortality rate doubles, provides an index of actuarial aging useful when population size is high enough (Finch et al., 1990). These approaches have some face validity; because the risk of many forms of lethal injury or illness increases so dramatically at advanced ages, interventions that influence only one cause of death have relatively small influence on overall mortality rates (Olshansky et al., 1990), and dramatic reduction in overall mortality at very old ages implies effects on many types of diseases—good grounds for concluding that aging itself has been retarded.

The actuarial approach to quantification of aging presents several problems, however. For one thing, age at death is influenced by multiple factors, among which biological aging will in some cases play an insignificant role. An individual unlucky enough to inherit the genes for cystic fibrosis, be infected by HIV, or hit by a bus may die at an age at which aging has yet to cause much increase in vulnerability. Although changes in the mean longevity of a test population may be altered by interventions with little effect on aging, the slope of the mortality curve (or the mortality rate doubling time) and the age at death of the final few percent of the population seem more likely to be useful indicators of interpopulation differences in aging rate. These indices may be less valuable for invertebrate species, in which large population studies have documented a small subset of extremely long-lived individuals among which the mortality rate may stabilize in very old age (Carey et al., 1992; Curtsinger et al., 1992). It is worth noting, however, that longevity rate deceleration in mammals, if it exists at all, is much less dramatic than in the insect populations in which it was first noted. In Mediterranean fruit flies, for example, one fly per million lives to an age that is fivefold higher than the age at which 90 percent of the cohort has died (Carey et al., 1992). A similar life table in humans would create approximately 300 U.S. citizens aged 400 years or older; this discrepancy is thus good news for the Social Security Administration, but bad news for those who seek to develop and test general principles about mammalian aging from demographic studies of invertebrates.

BIOMARKERS OF AGING

Assessment of Interindividual Differences in Aging Rate

Developing measures of aging that can assess interindividual differences is a tougher nut to crack, but in my view deserves a high priority among the issues facing research gerontologists. The concept of biomarkers has earned a useful niche in toxicology: measuring some effect of the toxin may be more convenient than trying to measure the integrated levels of the agent itself. Thus, for example, measures of glycated hemoglobin provide a valuable surrogate marker for exposure of cells to ill-regulated glucose levels, and measures of DNA damage may provide a useful way to judge exposure to specific mutagens (e.g., after Chernobyl) or to whole classes of mutagenic agents (e.g., in those living close to oil refineries).

Attempts to derive analogous indices of "biological age" have been cogently criticized on methodological grounds (Costa and McCrae, 1988, 1995), and indeed those who are convinced philosophically that there is no such thing as the biological age of an individual would argue that biomarker measurement has no likelihood of success and correspondingly little importance. But in my view—from the perspective that multiple aspects of aging are indeed likely to be coordinated in their timing by a single factor—developing a reliable way to measure interindividual differences in aging would have great importance in two respects: it would help to settle the debate as to whether aging can be treated as a unitary process, and it would provide a yardstick with which to measure the effects of genetic or environmental factors thought to have an effect on aging. Development of a replicable, validated set of tests that could discriminate between individuals aging at different rates would have the same effect in biogerontology as the effect of the sphygmomanometer on studies of hypertension or the invention of the clock on studies of celestial motion.

How Would We Know if We Had Successfully Validated One or More Biomarkers of Aging?

It is regrettably safe to agree that "it is too early to constitute a definitive panel of biomarkers for either animal models or humans" (Sprott, 1999:464). Proposed validation rules for candidate biomarkers vary widely among different experts, and sometimes between different formulations from the same experts. Some definitions (Lipman et al., 1999) propose that a biomarker of aging must be able to distinguish physiologically young from old, but such a formulation merely rewords the problem without offering an operational solution. I would propose an alternate definition, specifically, that a biomarker of aging should meet both of the following criteria simultaneously:

(a) It should correlate well, among middle-aged adults, with a wide range of other age-sensitive traits in multiple domains, *after* statistical adjustment for the effects of calendar age per se; and

(b) It should be a good predictor of life expectancy for individuals whose death is due to any of a wide range of lethal illnesses.

Each of these criteria deserves some amplification. A biomarker validation program would start with a list of candidate biomarkers, each known to be age-sensitive (by cross-sectional and/or longitudinal analyses) in adults. By hypothesis, some of these traits would reflect interindividual differences in the aging process, but each would also be sensitive to genetic and nongenetic factors that also vary among individuals, statistical "noise" that would interfere with the extraction of the "signal" attributable to aging itself. A correlation between age-sensitive immune parameters—for example, T-cell proliferation and T-cell cytokine production—would be relatively unhelpful in evaluating each of these parameters as potential biomarkers of aging, because the two assays are closely related and likely to be influenced by many factors unrelated to aging (e.g., recent infection, vaccination history, polymorphisms in immune system genes). However, a correlation between T-cell proliferation and, for example, muscle strength, or reflex speed, or lens protein cross-linking, or age at menopause, would be difficult to attribute to any obvious metabolic or pathophysiological mechanism other than linkage to some fundamental aging rate that might by hypothesis retard or accelerate changes in a wide range of age-sensitive traits.

Because each such candidate biomarker is already known to be age-sensitive, merely showing that pairs of these traits are mutually correlated would be unsurprising and uninteresting. However, correlations that remain strong after adjustment for the effects of calendar age would not be as easy to explain away and could provide good prima facie evidence that the components of the test battery measure, even if indirectly and imprecisely, some common factor that contributes to impairment of function in multiple cells and organ systems.

The second proposed criterion—correlation of the candidate biomarker with life expectancy regardless of the specific cause of death—is designed to link the assays to physiological decline. Loss of physiological reserve is not the only outcome of aging, but it is the outcome that causes most concern, and has furthermore been extensively studied in previous intervention studies. Loss of physiological reserve therefore serves, imperfectly, as the "gold standard" for most demonstrations of decelerated aging. An ability to predict subsequent longevity is not by itself sufficient to evaluate biomarker candidates, because risk factors (genetic or nongenetic) for specific forms of death would otherwise qualify: unstable angina, high titers of serum HIV, or a consistent history of cigarette or drug use are all predictors of subsequent longevity because of their association with specific causes of death, but these traits do not provide information about the kind of underlying aging processes that would, by hypothesis, increase risk factors for the wide range of late-life causes of death.

Secondary Criteria for Biomarker Evaluation

A test that is strongly correlated with other age-dependent traits and also predicts life span would merit further evaluation as an indirect index of aging per se. To be practical, such a test would have to meet a number of secondary criteria relevant to its incorporation into research protocols. The test should be relatively inexpensive to perform and show good agreement between closely spaced replicate assays of the same individual. Tests that meet the two primary criteria in multiple subpopulations (e.g., different human population groups, different rodent stocks, preferably different mammalian species) would also have practical advantages and meet our theoretical expectations that aging should be similar in many ways among mammals. The test should also be innocuous, neither harming the subject nor influencing the outcome of later tests of the same property at more advanced ages.

CD4 Memory T-Cells: A Candidate Biomarker in Aging Mice

In our own work we have attempted to test whether age-sensitive T-cell subsets might be useful biomarkers of aging in mice. There are several varieties of T-lymphocyte in the blood, spleen, and lymph nodes of mice (most of them with human counterparts), and their relative proportions change dramatically with age in adult animals and people. The CD4 lymphocytes—so called because they express the CD4 protein on their surface—act as "helper" cells in immune responses, assisting other cells in making antibodies and protective cytokines. The CD8 T-cells specialize in killing tumor cells and virus-infected cells. These are mutually exclusive classes: to a first approximation, all peripheral T-cells are either CD4+ or CD8+ but not both. The CD4 pool can be further subdivided into two mutually exclusive subsets: the naive CD4 cell (sometimes called the "virgin" CD4 cell, CD4V), and the memory CD4 cell (CD4M). Newborn CD4 cells, fresh from the thymus, are considered naive and can be identified by a specific pattern of surface proteins. Once stimulated by a virus or a bacterial antigen, they can produce clones of CD4M cells that are specific for the antigen in question and can help to protect against later encounters with the same or closely related pathogens. CD8 cells, too, can be divided into naive CD8 cells and the CD8M memory cells to which they give rise. Aging of both rodents and humans leads to a progressive increase in the proportion of CD4 cells in the CD4M subset, with a corresponding fall in the proportion of CD4 cells with the CD4V phenotype. The shift from CD4V to CD4M can be seen in blood and internal lymphoid tissues such as lymph nodes and spleen (Lerner et al.,1989), and is decelerated by calorically restricted diets that postpone aging and death (Miller, 1997b). The ability to measure CD4M levels in blood cells allows for repeated assessment of each individual mouse and could facilitate comparisons with human populations.

For these reasons, we assessed in several ways the possibility that CD4M levels could serve as a biomarker of aging. A group of genetically heterogeneous mice was used for these analyses, to diminish the possibility that our findings would later prove to be applicable only to a single genotype of inbred or F_1 hybrid mouse (Miller et al., 1999). Each mouse in a group of 46 males and 83 females was tested at 8 months of age, and the survivors (93 percent) tested again at 18 months of age. Each animal was then observed until it died or became severely ill (and was euthanized on humane grounds). Regression analysis was then used to examine the dependence of longevity on CD4M values, with gender as a covariate. The results (Figure 8-1) showed a strong association between high CD4M values at 18 months of age and lower longevity; after adjustment for

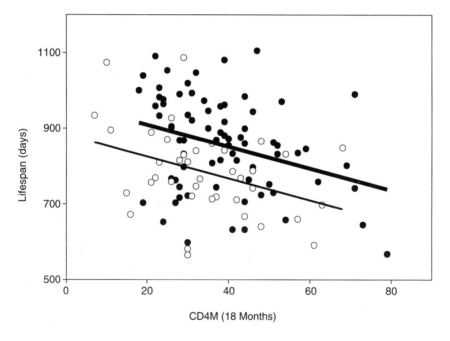

FIGURE 8-1 Correlation of mouse longevity with the percentage of CD4M cells measured at 18 months of age. The filled circles and darker line represent female mice, and the open circles and lighter line represent males. There is a significant correlation between CD4M levels and longevity; $R^2 = 0.18$, $p = 0.0003$ after adjustment for gender effects. SOURCE: Miller et al. (1997).

gender, the CD4M effect had $p(t) = 0.0003$, and 18 percent of the variance in longevity could be accounted for by gender and CD4M alone ($R^2 = 0.18$). The direction of the association was consistent with theoretical expectations, in that high levels of CD4M cells are characteristic (in cross-sectional and longitudinal studies) of older mice, and in the biomarker analysis were seen to be associated with diminished longevity. Seven other age-sensitive T-cell subsets were also tested in this initial set of mice (Miller et al., 1997), and four of these were found in univariate analyses to be associated with differences in longevity, but only at marginal significance levels that could have resulted from chance in a series of multiple comparisons.

If CD4M levels are indeed useful as biomarkers of an underlying aging process, then their association with longevity should be equally apparent for a wide range of terminal diseases. Indeed, the strength of this association was found to be similar in subgroups of the mice dying of different causes, including fibrosarcoma, lymphoma, mammary carcinoma, and a miscellaneous group of other neoplasms (Miller et al., 1997); the association reached statistical significance in the two subgroups with the largest numbers of cases. The number of deaths attributable to non-neoplastic causes was too low ($N = 13$) to provide adequate statistical power, although in these mice, too, high CD4M levels were associated with poor survival.

A stronger test of the potential status of CD4M as a biomarker would be to determine whether mice with high levels of CD4M cells also displayed relatively extreme levels of age-dependent traits outside the immune system. A group of 59 genetically heterogeneous mice was tested for CD4M levels and also on several age-sensitive measures of muscle strength between 9 and 12 months of age, and then the surviving 42 mice were tested again at ages 20-22 months. Because muscle force generation declines with age, the hypothesis was that within each age group, force generation would be inversely proportional to CD4M levels. Figure 8-2 presents the results: mice with high CD4M levels did indeed, as predicted, tend to have significantly lower muscle strength at each of these ages (Faulkner et al., unpublished results). Similar tests conducted on these mice at intermediate ages (14-16 months), however, did not show this relationship ($R = -0.06$), contrary to hypothesis. Additional work is now in progress to see whether CD4M levels correlate, in these heterogeneous mouse populations, with age-sensitive measures of bone density, cataract formation, protein oxidation, and spontaneous activity, as well as tests of functional immunity.

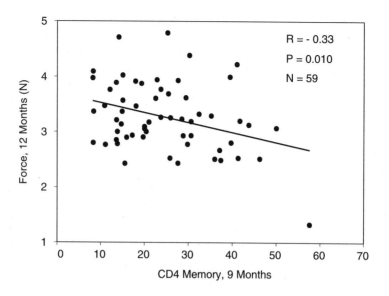

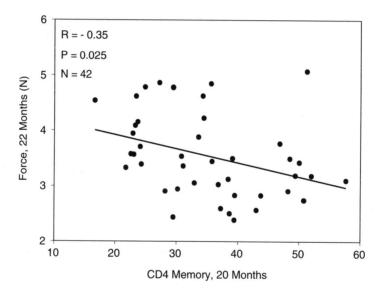

FIGURE 8-2 Correlation of CD4M cell percentage with muscle force generation in mice. CD4M levels were measured in each mouse at 9 and (in survivors) at 20 months of age, and muscle force measured at 12 and 22 months. There is a significant inverse correlation at each age: mice with high levels of CD4M cells tend to have low levels of muscle force. SOURCES: Faulkner et al. (unpublished results); Miller et al. (1996).

Effects of Gender and Hormonal History

To see if associations between T-cell subsets and longevity might differ between males and females, we reanalyzed the data separately for animals of both sexes, and found one example of a sex-specific association. A subset of T-cells distinguished by high level expression of the surface membrane pump P-glycoprotein (P-gp) had previously been shown to increase with age in mice in both the CD4M and CD8M populations (Witkowski and Miller 1993), and interestingly the P-gp^{hi} subset of CD4M had been shown to be refractory to stimulation (Bining and Miller, 1997). The regression analysis showed (Figure 8-3) that high levels of CD4P cells—the subset characteristic of older mice—were indeed associated with shorter life expectancy, but only in male mice (Miller et al., 1997).

The strongest associations in these initial studies had involved T-cell subsets measured on 18-month-old mice, i.e., mice that had already completed 70 percent of the median life span (approximately 26 months) of the population, but correlations of longevity and T-cells subsets tested in

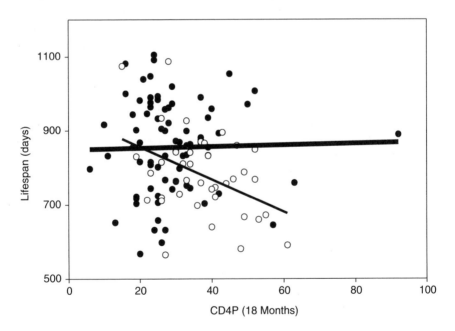

FIGURE 8-3 Correlation of mouse longevity with percentage of CD4P cells (i.e., proportion of CD4 cells with high levels of P-glycoprotein) measured at 18 months of age. Female mice (dark line, filled circles) show no association between CD4P levels and life expectancy, but male mice (lighter line, open circles) show a strong correlation ($t = -2.72$, $p = 0.01$). SOURCE: Miller et al. (1997).

8-month-old mice were of only marginal significance ($p = 0.06$). A second study, however, has produced promising results with mice tested at 8 months of age and provides another example of sex-specific associations. The test population included 121 virgin males, 135 virgin females, and 292 mated females, i.e., females that had been housed together with a stud male until 6 months of age. (The two virgin populations included the mice analyzed in our previous publication—see Figures 8-2 and 8-3—plus additional animals.) Of the 121 males, 33 died of a peculiar mouse urinary syndrome (MUS) involving bite wounds on the genitals, urethral obstruction, and rupture of the bladder (Tuffery, 1966), which is seen only in nondominant males housed with more aggressive males. This lesion, thought to be secondary to adjustments in dominance hierarchy, typically causes death at relatively early ages, and therefore mice dying of MUS are treated as a separate subgroup. None of the T-cell subsets tested at 8 months of age was able to predict subsequent longevity in the virgin males or virgin females, but there was a significant inverse correlation between CD8M cells and longevity in the mated females. Figure 8-4 shows the scatterplots for all four sets of mice. The correlation for mated females ($R = -0.22$, $p < 0.001$) is in the predicted direction, that is, with high levels of memory cells associated with lower life expectancy. There is no correlation in virgin females or in the virgin males dying of causes other than MUS. Males dying of MUS, similar to mated females, show an inverse correlation ($R = -0.27$, $p = 0.13$), which, however, is not statistically significant.

These data thus support the idea that tests of age-sensitive traits, measured at ages as early as the first third of the life span, may be able to predict subsequent longevity, but raise the concern that the associations may vary with gender and either hormonal exposure or reproductive history. Levels of CD4M and CD8M cells are strongly and positively correlated at all ages ($R = 0.70$, 0.65, and 0.40 at 8, 14, and 20 months, respectively, all $p < 0.005$) (Miller, 1997b), and there is no a priori reason to expect that the former subset would be associated with longevity only in virgin animals and the latter only in mated females. We have now initiated a number of collaborations to see if these subsets correlate in expected directions with indices of age-sensitive change in cells and tissues outside the immune system, as well as with life span and protective immune function in these heterogeneous mice.

GENETIC ANALYSIS OF LONGEVITY, OF AGING, AND OF AGE-SENSITIVE TRAITS IN MICE

Biogerontology has just begun to benefit from the attention and skills of professional geneticists. Geneticists can attack problems of aging from

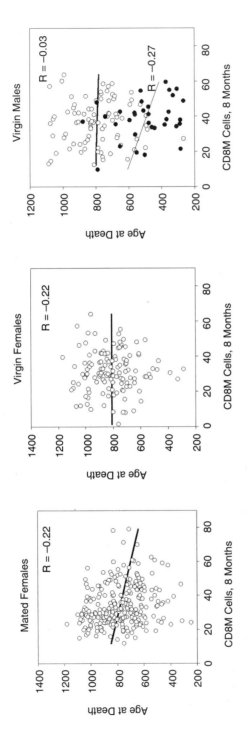

FIGURE 8-4 Correlations between CD8M cells at 8 months of age and life span in four groups of genetically heterogeneous mice. High levels of CD8M cells are associated with diminished longevity in mated females (left panel; $p < 0.001$), but not in virgin females (center panel). Among virgin males, those dying of diseases other than the urinary syndrome MUS show no association between CD8M and longevity (open circles, upper line), but those dying because of MUS show a nonsignificant trend (filled circles, lower line, $R = -0.27$, $p = 0.13$) similar to the relationship observed in mated females. SOURCE: Miller et al. (unpublished results).

several related but fundamentally distinct directions. Studies of rare mutations at individual loci, such as the Werner's syndrome locus WRN, whose mutant form produces, in middle-aged people, several of the diseases typically not seen until old age, can give attractive points of entry into the pathophysiology of age-related diseases. In mice there are now four reports of mutations—two naturally occurring and two artificially produced—that lead to impressive increases in mean and maximal longevity (Miskin and Masos, 1997; Brown-Borg et al., 1996; Miller, 1999; Migliaccio et al., 1999), and thus provide extremely valuable models for testing mechanistic ideas and the control of aging. Some of these, such as the dw/dw and df/df dwarfing mutations that affect levels of growth hormone and thyroid hormone, provide clues to endocrine-dependent pathways that could regulate age effects in multiple cells and tissues. The recent report (Migliaccio et al., 1999) that mouse life span can be extended by an induced mutation that diminishes cell susceptibility to apoptotic death after injury should stimulate new inquiries into the effects of altered cell turnover on age-dependent changes. Each of these mutations, however, is exceptionally rare in natural populations; despite their effect on longevity, perhaps mediated by a direct effect on aging, each of the mutations is likely to have, overall, a negative effect on reproductive success and thus fail to become fixed in natural mouse populations.

Our own work has taken a different tack: we have attempted to determine whether mutations with differential effects on aging may be present within the many available populations of laboratory-adopted inbred mice. The goal is not so much to clone these genes—if indeed they exist— because positional cloning strategies of this kind require many thousands of animals and would be extremely expensive using an assay, age at death, that is itself so costly. Instead, the goal has been to use gene mapping methods to test hypotheses about aging and to develop new animal models that will be useful for testing well-specified hypotheses about the molecular basis for age-dependent changes. In the absence of a validated battery of biomarkers of aging, we (like most others) have reluctantly decided to use mouse life span as a crude surrogate for aging itself, reasoning that genetic alleles that extend life span well beyond the median for the tested population may be operating via an influence on aging itself. Work conducted using recombinant inbred mouse stocks (Gelman et al., 1988; de Haan and Van Zant, 1999) has suggested that life-span differences between pairs of inbred mouse lines might reflect the influence of as few as 4-7 polymorphic loci, providing some basis for hope that some of these would have an effect large enough to be detected by a genome scan experiment involving 300-1,200 mice.

The strategy for mapping such quantitative trait loci (QTL) involves looking for preferential segregation of specific alleles or allele combinations in mice that differ in life span (or, more generally, any age-sensitive trait of interest). Our test population, called UM-HET3, consisted of a group of mice bred as the progeny of females of the (BALB/c × C57BL/6)F1 genotype and males of the (C3H/HeJ × DBA/2)F1 genotype. Mice bred in this way are, from a genetic perspective, all siblings; each shares a random half of its alleles with every other animal in the UM-HET3 population. The current set of analyses was conducted when genotype and longevity data were available from a group of 110 virgin males and 143 virgin females. The analytical method adjusted, by permutation testing, for Type I errors attributable to the simultaneous evaluation of multiple linkage hypotheses, and also included gender as a covariate to look for instances of sex-specific genetic effects. Because we had particular interest in regulation of late-life diseases rather than in causes of premature death, and because of evidence that genetic influences on mouse longevity were particularly strong when early deaths were not considered (Covelli et al., 1989), we repeated each analysis after exclusion of those animals dying before 657 days of age, i.e., the age at which 20 percent of the animals had already died.

This strategy revealed strong evidence (adjusted, experiment-wise $p < 0.01$) for two segregating loci with effects on longevity, and suggestive evidence (experiment-wise $p < 0.18$) for three others (Jackson et al., unpublished results). The QTL approach does not provide the sequence of the genes in question and does not reveal what proteins they encode, but only provides an approximate map position within the genome. Four of these five effects were sex-specific, with three influencing life span only in males, one only in females, and only one with equivalent effects in both sexes. The two strongest effects were a locus on chromosome 9 (D9Mit110) for which the C3H allele was associated with an increase in male longevity of 88 days (considering only those males living >657 days), and a locus on chromosome 12 (D12Mit167), for which the combination of the C57BL/6 and C3H alleles was associated with an increase of 93 days for both males and females living longer than 657 days. A further analysis (Jackson et al., unpublished results) was then conducted to see if pairs of loci might interact to influence longevity, and revealed that one combination—the C3H allele at D2Mit58 together with the BALB allele at D16Mit182—was associated in females with a 173-day increase in longevity (adjusted $p < 0.05$). These data suggest that common laboratory inbred mouse lines differ at loci that can have impressively large effects on life span in a segregating population. They argue against models in which the genetic influence on longevity is attributed to polymorphisms at very large numbers of loci, each with only a very small total effect on life span.

Coordinated Genetic Influences on Life Span
Regardless of Cause of Death

The QTL data also provide analytical tools for addressing hypotheses about the relationship of longevity to aging, disease, and age-sensitive changes in cell and organ function. In particular, we have looked to see whether genetic alleles associated with differences in longevity have equivalent effects in subgroups of mice dying of different lethal illnesses. We reasoned that if a specific allele or allele combination had an influence on aging itself, then it might have detectable effects on many different consequences of aging, including both cancer and non-neoplastic diseases. Figure 8-5 shows the results of such an analysis (Miller et al.,

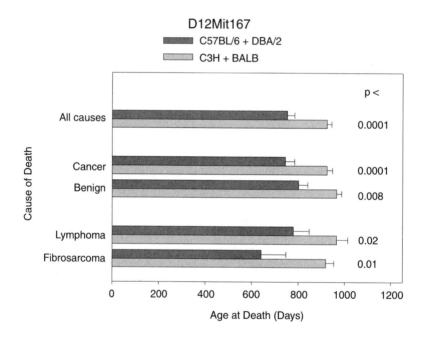

FIGURE 8-5 Genetic regulation of longevity in mice stratified by cause of death. Female mice that inherit the C3H allele at D2Mit58 plus the BALB allele at D16Mit182 (light gray bars) have significantly higher longevity than their sisters (dark gray bars) with the C57BL/6 plus DBA/2 allele combination ("all causes" of death combined). Subsets of mice that died either of cancer or of a non-neoplastic ("benign") illness both show the association between genotype and longevity. Among the mice dying of neoplasia, subsets dying of lymphoma or of fibrosarcoma show equivalent, and significant, genotypic effects. Bars indicate means plus standard error of the mean. SOURCE: Miller et al. (unpublished results).

unpublished results). Female mice that inherit the C3H allele at D2Mit58 plus the BALB allele at D16Mit182 live, on average, 173 days longer than their sisters with the DBA/2 plus C57BL/6 combination (pointwise $p <$ 0.0001, adjusted $p = 0.05$). Of the 132 females for which both genotype and necropsy data were available, 97 died of one or another form of cancer, and among these the favorable allele combination was associated with a 180-day increment in mean life span ($p < 0.0001$) compared to the least favorable combination. Twenty-two of the mice died of congestive heart failure, inanition, amyloidosis, endometritis, or another non-neo-plastic illness, and among these the favorable allele combination was as-sociated with 165 days of additional life span. The bottom two bars in the figure document the effects of the C3H-plus-BALB alleles on the 39 mice dying of lymphoma (effect size 186 days, $p = 0.02$) or in the 24 mice dying of fibrosarcoma (effect size 277 days, $p = 0.01$).

The data in Figure 8-5 thus show that genetic combinations that post-pone death in mice dying of cancer also improve longevity, to a similar extent, in mice dying of non-neoplastic illnesses. In three other cases—D4Mit171 in males, D9Mit110 in males over 657 days of age, and D12Mit167 in males and females over 657 days—the favorable alleles had significant effects in mice dying of neoplastic causes and in those dying of non-neoplastic disease. We interpret these data as evidence that multiple forms of lethal illness can be regulated, in their age of incidence or rate of progression, by shared elements that are themselves under genetic con-trol. If it can be shown that these loci, individually or in combination, also influence differences among mice in other age-sensitive traits—T-cell sub-sets, muscle strength, cataract progression, etc.—we will take this as evi-dence that they may affect longevity through an effect on the aging process per se.

The available dataset also provides examples in which genetic vari-ants seem to influence the risk of specific late-life diseases. Figure 8-6, for example, shows longevity results for mice stratified by their inheritance at the 12th chromosome locus D12Mit167. This is a locus associated with differential longevity in both male and female mice, with the strongest effect (adjusted $p < 0.01$) seen in those mice living more than 657 days (Jackson et al., unpublished results). The longest-lived mice are those that inherit both the C57BL/6 allele from their mother and the C3H allele from their father; on average, they survive 93 days longer than siblings with the BALB plus C3H combination. Figure 8-6 shows that the D12Mit167, like the pair of loci illustrated in Figure 8-5, has significant and similar effects in mice dying of cancer (85 days) and in mice dying of non-neoplastic diseases (126 days). A more detailed analysis of the cancers, however, suggests that while lymphoma and hepatoma victims are equally pro-tected by the favorable alleles (effect sizes of 93 and 167 days, respec-

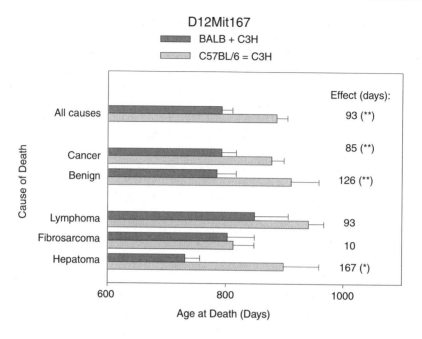

FIGURE 8-6 Genetic regulation of longevity in mice stratified by cause of death. Male or female mice that inherit the C57BL/6 (maternal) and C3H (paternal) alleles at D12Mit167 (light gray bars) are longer lived than their siblings that inherit the BALB plus C3H combination. The "effect size" shown at the right represents that difference in mean longevity between mice in the two genetically different groups, with (**) = $p < 0.01$ and (*) = $p < 0.05$ by t-test. Similar effect sizes are seen for mice dying of cancer or of non-neoplastic illnesses ("benign"), and among the cancer deaths the genetic effect is similar for deaths due to lymphoma and hepatoma. The genetic effect on longevity seems to be minimal, however, for mice dying of fibrosarcoma. Bars show means plus standard errors. SOURCE: Miller et al. (unpublished results).

tively), the effect on mice dying of fibrosarcoma is negligible (10 days). A similar analysis (not shown) revealed that the D4Mit171 allele was associated with exceptional longevity in male mice dying of non-neoplastic diseases (177 days, $p = 0.03$) and of pulmonary adenocarcinoma (155 days, $p = 0.03$), but not in males dying of other forms of neoplasia (26 days).

A last example illustrates two additional principles: (a) that genes that delay death for certain lethal illnesses can accelerate it for others; and (b) that risk of a condition and timing of a condition can be regulated by different loci. The top panel of Figure 8-7 depicts age at death in male

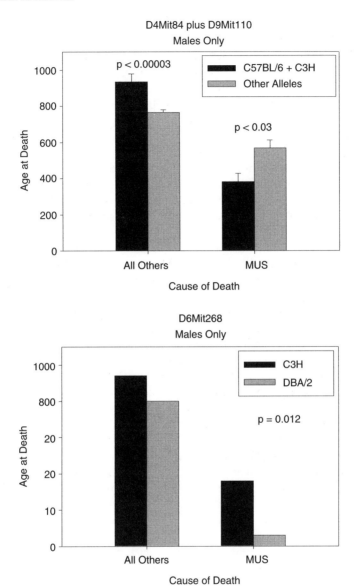

FIGURE 8-7 Separate genetic regulation of incidence and timing of a lethal urinary syndrome. The top panel shows that the C57BL/6 allele of D4Mit84 plus the C3H allele of D9Mit110 (black bars) are associated with a dramatic (170-day) postponement of death in male mice dying of diseases other than MUS, but are associated with a significant acceleration of death in those mice that do die of MUS. The bottom panel shows that the risk among males of dying of MUS is associated with the C3H allele at D6Mit268. SOURCE: Miller et al. (unpublished results).

mice of two subgroups: those dying of the urinary syndrome MUS, and those dying of all other causes. The genetic analysis contrasts mice with both the C57BL/6 allele at D4Mit84 and the C3H allele at D9Mit110 to mice with any of the three other allele combinations. In the males dying of causes other than MUS, this allele pair is associated with a 170-day increment in longevity (post-hoc $p < 0.00003$). But for males that do die of MUS, the same allele combination is associated with a 187-day *decline* in mean life span (post-hoc $p < 0.03$). This effect is thus pleiotropic, in that these alleles accelerate death in mice susceptible to MUS, while postponing death for all other males in the population. Although these loci are associated with differential longevity in mice that do develop MUS, they do not have a significant effect on the chances that MUS will indeed occur (not shown). The risk of developing MUS seems to be under control of a separate locus on chromosome 6. As shown in the bottom panel of Figure 8-7, males that inherit the C3H allele at D6Mit268 are far more likely to develop MUS (28 percent risk) than are their brothers who receive the DBA/2 allele at this locus (7 percent risk; $p = 0.012$ by two-tailed Fisher's exact test).

It will be worthwhile, once larger numbers of mice have been examined, to determine whether these increases in longevity reflect changes in the rate at which mortality risks increase over the life span, differences in the age at which these risks begin to increase, or age-independent declines in risk without alteration in the slope of the risk/age curve. Large differences in longevity across species are sometimes due to alterations in mortality rate doubling time, but in other cases reflect alterations in initial mortality risks; Finch (1990), for example, notes that the threefold difference in longevity between rhesus monkeys and humans reflects a 100-fold difference in initial mortality rate without any detectable difference in mortality rate doubling time. It will be interesting to determine whether or not the set of genes segregating in crosses among laboratory-adapted inbred stocks includes loci with an influence on the initial mortality rate, the pace of increase in mortality risks, or both. Nonetheless, evidence of genetic loci that retard death regardless of the specific cause of death should provide useful tools for analysis of how aging coordinates multiple late-life processes, including illnesses.

Genetic Control of Age-Sensitive Traits

The preceding discussion has concentrated on age of death and cause of death, but the same strategies (and indeed the same animals) can be applied to questions about genetic regulation of other age-sensitive traits, including those that seem likely to serve as biomarkers of aging rate. Our own analyses of the genetic control of age-sensitive T-cell subsets provide an example. Blood samples taken from genotyped UM-HET3 mice at two ages (8 and 18 months) were tested for eight different T-cell subsets, including five that were known to be age-sensitive from cross-sectional and longitudinal data. Figure 8-8 illustrates two of the findings, adapted from the original paper (Jackson et al., 1999). The top panel shows an example of a QTL, linked to D12Mit34 on the 12th chromosome, that influences the proportion of CD4 cells that have the CD4M memory cell phenotype. Mice inheriting the BALB allele of D12Mit34 have higher proportions of CD4M cells; this differential is clear at 8 months of age (about 30 percent of the median longevity), and is equally apparent by age 18 months, an age at which the proportion of CD4M cells clearly shows the typical age-dependent increase. The effect is statistically significant with an experiment-wise $p = 0.03$. The D12Mit34-associated locus affects this age-sensitive trait, but exerts its influence in the first third of the life span. The bottom panel of Figure 8-8 shows an association between the DBA/2 allele at D9Mit110 and differences in expression of P-glycoprotein on CD4 cells; cells with high levels of P-glycoprotein expression ("CD4P"), shown in other work to be age-sensitive (Witkowski and Miller, 1993) and nonfunctional (Bining and Miller, 1997), accumulate to higher levels in mice inheriting the C3H allele at D9Mit110 (experiment-wise $p = 0.02$). In contrast to the D12Mit34 effect on CD4M cells just discussed, the D9Mit110 effect is not apparent in mice tested at 8 months of age, but is instead associated with a relatively rapid accumulation of CD4P cells between 8 and 18 months of age. Of the eight significant gene/T-cell phenotype associations documented in the original pilot study (Jackson et al., 1999), three (including D9Mit110) were detectable only in 18-month-old mice; two affected 8-month-old mice but had no influence on the subsets at 18 months of age; two (including D12Mit34) had effects seen in mice of both ages, and one other had a more complex, crossover effect. It is clear that longitudinal datasets, in which phenotypes are assessed periodically over the entire life span of individual genotyped subjects, have great potential for sorting out the ways in which genetic variations might influence health through continuous, delayed, or transient effects.

It is worth stressing that this initial study involved analysis of only 145 mice, and thus had very low statistical power for detecting genetic effects that controlled less than 25 percent or so of the phenotypic variance. Similar analyses are now underway in larger samples of the same genetic constitution and should reveal additional examples of gene/subset associations. The study in progress includes tests of a much wider range of age-sensitive traits, and one outcome should be a preliminary list of QTLs that affect traits that are of interest in their own right: QTLs for collagen modifications, for cross-linking of eye lens proteins, QTLs with an effect on bone density, antibody production, spontaneous activity, glucocorti-

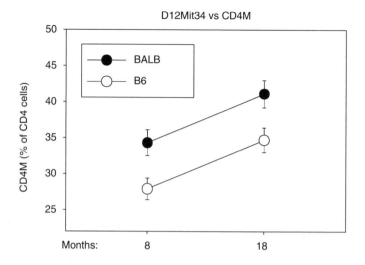

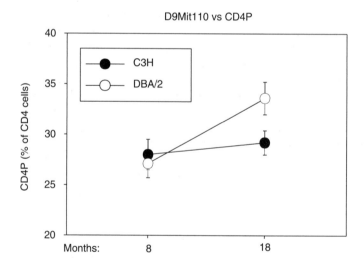

FIGURE 8-8 Genetic influences on age-sensitive T-cell subsets in mice: two representative examples. The top panel shows the association between the BALB allele at D12Mit34 and relatively high levels of CD4M cells; the association is apparent in mice as young as 8 months, and is equally significant in mice at age 18 months. The bottom panel shows the relationship between genotype at D9Mit110 and the CD4P subset: mice inheriting the C3H allele have higher levels of CD4P cells at 18 months of age, but there is no genotypic effect at 8 months. SOURCE: Jackson et al. (1999).

coid levels, etc. The mapping project should thus help to guide the search for human genes that regulate these interesting phenotypes and at the same time spark new investigations, in animal models, for the biochemical differences that mediate the genetic effects we detect.

At the same time, the dataset that emerges should also allow us to test more general questions about the nature of aging and its genetic control. We may, for example, be able to identify QTLs that not only retard the development of one or more age-sensitive T-cell subsets, but also retard age-dependent changes in protein conformation, bone matrix turnover, and brain GFAP levels. Such a finding would imply that these changes are influenced, together, by a common biochemical pathway, and the corresponding QTLs would be excellent candidates for genes that regulate aging per se, rather than merely one among the many more age-sensitive traits. In the same way, it will be of particular interest to determine if QTLs that regulate age-sensitive traits also are associated with differences in life span, and conversely if QTLs identified on the basis of longevity effects modify one (or nearly all?) of the age-sensitive traits in our test battery.

Mice selected on the basis of longevity QTLs may be of particular value for testing hypotheses about the role of specific biochemical and cellular mechanisms in aging and disease. It should be possible to identify mice that inherit combinations of genetic alleles associated with optimal longevity, and to do so within a few weeks of birth. Mice with this particular combination of alleles, together with randomly chosen sibling controls, could then be tested, at any age, for factors—telomere length, fibroblast growth patterns, levels of protein oxidation, immunological vigor—hypothesized to play a role in controlling age-sensitive physiological changes or disease risks. By providing a way to identify siblings destined for longer or shorter lives, the gene-selected mouse populations could provide an approach to sorting the long list of potential aging mechanisms into those that do or do not show the expected association with longevity.

The Wrong Lamppost—A Brief Technical Digression

It is worth mentioning here a technical, but potentially fatal, objection to the entire QTL-plus-biomarker enterprise just outlined. The objection is based upon the concern that the laboratory-adapted inbred mouse lines used for these (and most other) biomarker and mouse QTL studies of aging, may have lost, over their many generations of inadvertent selection for laboratory lifestyles, exactly those genetic variations that are most informative for biogerontological work. The argument, set forth in more detail elsewhere (Miller et al., 1999, 2000b), notes that the mouse stocks typically used for laboratory work have gone through two very strong sets of selective pressures. First, the development of laboratory mouse stocks from wild-caught animals tends to favor genetic alleles and allele combinations that promote rapid breeding, i.e., the production of large litters as early in life as possible. Selection for large body size—the better to bear large litters with—typically accompanies this selection process (Roberts, 1961). These selection pressures are thus the opposite of those thought to lead to development of races or new species with slower development and longer life span. Genetic variants that decelerate aging and development, if they exist at all in natural mouse populations, may well be lost during the first few dozen laboratory generations. Second, nearly all rodent gerontology is conducted with inbred animals or their progeny, despite the risks that the inbreeding process may select for rare combinations of alleles that preserve viability and reproductive performance in fully homozygous individuals. We have elsewhere described the case (Miller et al., 1999) for seeking the keys to mammalian aging under a different lamppost, one infested with mice freshly derived from wild populations, and preferably from populations (Miller et al., 2000b) that exhibit the characteristics (small body size, small litter size, and modestly elevated glucocorticoid levels) one expects to see in slow-aging races. Genetic and biomarker analysis of mice whose great-grandparents include both wild-derived and laboratory-derived stocks could help to determine which early life traits—growth rate, reproductive scheduling, early or sustained immune function—are best associated with differences in life span and disease risk, and set the stage for mapping the corresponding QTL that distinguish wild-derived from laboratory-derived mice in these respects.

The Height-Life Span Nexus

Several observations and lines of experimentation have raised the issue of whether interindividual differences in aging rate are influenced by genes that modulate body size and early-life growth patterns. These include (a) the association between small stature and exceptional longevity in calorically restricted rodents (Yu et al., 1985), methionine-restricted rats (Orentreich et al., 1993), and mutant dwarf mice (Brown-Borg et al., 1996; Miller, 1999); and (b) the association between small body size and longer life span in natural populations of mice (Falconer et al., 1978), flies (Hillesheim and Stearns, 1992), dogs (Li et al., 1996), and, possibly, people (Samaras and Storms, 1992). The correlation in dogs is particularly striking: selective breeding for dogs of different body size has produced breeds varying in size from Chihuahua to Irish wolfhound. These breeds also vary greatly in mean longevity, from approximately 7 to 10.5 years, and the correlation between breed longevity and breed body weight (Miller, 1999) is a remarkable $R^2 = 0.56$. These differences are genetic and affect stature rather than obesity: no amount of overeating will convert a West Highland white terrier to a St. Bernard. The selective pressures applied were designed to create dogs of specific sizes and temperaments and were not intended to influence aging rate or life span. The clear implication is that the effects on longevity are pleiotropic, i.e., that genes selected for their effect on body size and conformation influenced life span as a side effect. It is of interest to note that the few analyses (Eigenmann et al., 1984, 1988) of the hormonal basis for interbreed differences in body size have shown that the genes in question influence levels of IGF-1, the most likely mediator of the life-span effects in the long-lived df/df and dw/dw mouse mutants. Could it be mere coincidence that long-lived mutant nematode worms (Kimura et al., 1997) also show mutations in genes related to insulin and IGF-1 receptors?

To carry out a more general test of the hypothesis that early-life differences in growth rate might influence life span, we have conducted a study of mouse lines selectively bred for differences in weight gain between 0-10 days of age or between 28-56 days. Starting from a group of genetically heterogeneous mice, Atchley and his colleagues (Atchley et al., 1997) created six lines of large-sized mice by picking breeding pairs that had shown rapid early-life weight gain, and six other stocks of smaller mice whose ancestors were chosen based on slow rates of growth early in life. Three unselected stocks served as controls. These mouse stocks proved to be remarkably different in mean longevity (Miller et al., 2000a): the longest-lived stock, with mean life span of 941 days, lived 36 percent longer than the median for the 15 tested stocks and 1.7-fold longer than the shortest-lived stock. Among the 15 stocks, weight was strongly correlated with stock longevity measured at six months of age ($R = 0.69$, $p = 0.004$). The differences reflected stature rather than obesity, in that the correlation was strong when weight was measured at early ages (3 months), and became smaller, though still significant, when peak weight was considered. Differences among these stocks in longevity did not reflect major differences in the cause of death, except for one large, short-lived stock in which most animals died of pituitary adenoma, potentially a source of growth hormone overproduction. These results are thus consistent with the idea that genetic effects on life span may, to an important degree, be the side effects of genes selected (naturally by ecological forces or artificially by selective breeding schemes) because they alter rates of early-life growth and maturation. The findings offer many opportunities for follow-up studies. Where are the relevant genes, and how many are there? In crosses between long-lived and short-lived stocks, is there a good correlation between individual longevity and various measures of growth, size, and body proportions? Do the long- and short-lived stocks differ system-atically in production of or response to growth regulatory hormones in early life, and do these differences persist throughout adult life? Would temporary growth retardation at specific periods of the developmental process produce increases in longevity similar to those seen in mice whose short stature reflects inherited genes? Would studies of humans, care-fully controlled for the many potential confounding variables, also reveal a connection between early-life growth trajectory and later susceptibility to the perils of old age?

GENE EXPRESSION SCREENING

Gene mapping methods deal with questions of inherited characteris-tics—the variations in DNA sequences that influence differences between people in body size, eye color, life span, and personality characteristics. Gene expression studies, in contrast, generate lists of which genes are expressed in specific cell types. The liver cells, brain cells, and T-cells of any one person all possess the same inherited DNA sequences, but express different subsets of these genes. Among the 40,000 genes expressed in a neuron, for example, perhaps 20,000 will also be expressed by a liver cell, and a different subset of 20,000 or so will be expressed by a CD4 memory T-cell. Until about five years ago, producing a catalog of genes expressed by any one kind of cell—a T-lymphocyte, for example—was a tedious process, proceeding one gene at a time, and the list of genes known to be expressed by even well-studied cell types was only a few hundred genes long. The recent development of methods for screening large numbers of genes simultaneously has placed the production of gene catalogs well within the grasp of even modest sized laboratories. The technology is undergoing rapid evolution, and the amount of information produced for a given investment of time and money is growing quickly, with today's advanced techniques sure to be obsolete within a year or two. Even today's immature methods, however, permit research laboratories to ask and answer many important questions that would have been hopelessly ambitious a few years ago. A few examples—concocted for relevance to biogerontology and geriatrics—may be of use to those unfamiliar with this "high-throughput" approach:

• A list of genes expressed by T-cells of young adults but not of old adults, and the complementary list of genes expressed only by T-cells from older people, is likely to provide insights into the molecular basis for immune senescence.
• A list of gene expression differences between calorically restricted mice and those on a normal caloric intake would include important clues

about the ways in which the restricted diet retards aging rate. A similar comparison between long-lived dw/dw mice and their nonmutant siblings would be equally informative. Genes that found their way onto both lists—i.e., overexpressed or underexpressed both by restricted mice and by dw/dw animals—would merit special attention. Would some of these genes also prove to be differentially expressed by mice inheriting the genetic alleles associated with longer life span in the QTL analyses? Would a subset also prove to distinguish longer-lived mouse stocks in the Atchley set or to discriminate wild mice from those born into laboratory stocks?

• Gene expression data could also, in principle, help in the selection of bioindicators of specific clinical states of interest. If, for example, a group of investigators wished to develop a method to evaluate the level of chronic psychological stress to which individual subjects had been exposed, they might begin with a validation study in which control subjects and those known to have experienced highly stressful circumstances were asked to donate blood samples for analysis. Screening these samples for expression of 1,000-5,000 genes might identify genes whose expression was dramatically different between the two subject groups. A list of such genes—perhaps 5-15 among the set of thousands examined—would be valuable in two respects: as inexpensive quantifiable measures of a biological state of clinical interest, and as pointers to the underlying biology of psychological stress and its putative connections to health. Although the cost of screening thousands of genes simultaneously is too high to make the method appropriate for population surveys—a situation not likely to change for a decade—the cost is now sufficiently low to be useful for picking and validating smaller subsets of genes whose expression levels *are* informative and affordable to employ in population surveys. Moreover, these gene products are not mere anonymous markers of the underlying clinical state, but are embedded in a network of biologically interpretable relationships. Thus, for example, a list of genes associated with psychological stress might be found to contain several genes known to respond, in other tissues, to endorphins or catecholamines or sex steroids, providing links to new areas for investigation and, perhaps, intervention.

BIOLOGICAL MATERIALS SUITABLE FOR LARGE-SCALE HUMAN STUDIES

Other chapters in this volume have given a great deal of thought to the question of how best to exploit biological data for population surveys, and how best to exploit the elaborate and expensive infrastructure developed for population studies to address biological questions. My own contribution to this aspect of the discussion would be to urge colleagues to consider three points:

• Tests of specific research questions. In some cases, biological information should be included in population surveys on the grounds that the data are necessary to answer specific well-formulated hypotheses. Sociologists who become familiar with the current, but rapidly changing, toolkit of biological analyses will be best positioned to formulate and then answer questions linking clinical and psychological issues to their biological substrates. The specific kind of materials needed will depend on the specific questions to be answered. Some questions about genetic influences on traits of interest will require genotyping at a very small number of loci and thus require no more DNA than that available from a small blood sample; other genetic questions may require a stable, larger supply of DNA and thus justify the expense of setting up long-term cultures from blood cells or cheek scrapings. Questions that require information about transient hormonal levels, chronic exposure to blood chemicals, patterns of gene expression, or responsiveness of specific cell types will each imply very different sample collection (and in some cases sample preparation and archiving) requirements.

• Archives for future exploitation. In other cases, managers of large-scale population surveys may be tempted to collect and archive biological materials from their study subjects "on spec," that is, in the hope that future technical developments will someday allow them to make good use of these materials, associated as they are with highly valuable datasets of clinical, psychological, and economic information. I hope that leaders of such projects give in to such temptations, but then give careful attention to the key specifics—which samples, from which population subsets, stored in what circumstances—that are likely to preserve or undermine the future utility of the resulting archives. If the samples are to be used, for example, for analyses of genetic variation and its effects on traits of interest, future users of the materials will be particularly grateful for archives that include sets of siblings or parent/offspring pairs. As gene mapping strategies come, in the next decade, to rely less on large pedigrees and more on large-sample analysis of sequence polymorphisms linked to effector loci, samples that provide sufficient DNA for extensive study (or live cells that can be grown in culture for DNA extraction) will be of particular value. If the samples are to be used for analyses of bioindicators that provide transient markers of clinical or psychological status, archives that include live cells may be more valuable than those that bank only serum samples or tissue extracts.

• Animal studies as stalking horses for human biogerontology. For the most part, studies on the biology of aging are as difficult and impractical in humans as are studies of health insurance in rodents. It is fairly easy, of course, to study *aged* humans, but much harder to study the 50-80 year process that creates aged people from teenagers. Analytical strategies that depend upon correlations between variables measured in middle age and those tested in old age are reasonably straightforward in rodent colonies, but exceptionally difficult in human populations. The hypothesis that T-cell subsets predict future health status, or that diets high in a specific antioxidant might help to postpone neoplasia or cataracts, or that the rate of skeletal growth in the first 10th of the life span influences cancer risk at late ages, or that mildly elevated serum glucocorticoid levels in young adulthood are associated with higher mean longevity, can be tested first in mouse or rat populations; those hypotheses that still appear promising after such a screening process will thus earn consideration for incorporation into studies of human populations. Mapping human genes that influence the aging process can be guided by mouse studies in a similar way, because nearly all segments of the human genome correspond to known sections of mouse chromosomes. Thus a demonstration that a given section of mouse chromosome 12 carries genes that confer resistance to age-dependent neoplastic and non-neoplastic illnesses could justify analyses of the corresponding human chromosome segment in family-based or polymorphism-dependent mapping projects.

ACKNOWLEDGMENTS

The original work presented here represents a collaboration with Drs. David Burke, Andrzej Galecki, Clarence Chrisp, Jack van der Meulen, Kevin Flurkey, and John Faulkner and Ms. Anne Jackson, with technical assistance from Luann Linsalata and Gretchen Buehner. This research was supported by NIA grant AG11687, AG16699, AG08808, and AG13283, and by the Ann Arbor DVA Medical Center.

REFERENCES

Atchley, W.R., S. Xu, and D.E. Cowley
    1997   Altering developmental trajectories in mice by restricted index selection. *Genetics* 146:629-640.
Austad, S.N.
    1993   Retarded senescence in an insular population of Virginia opossums (*Didelphis virginiana*). *Journal of Zoology* 229:695-708.
Bining, N., and R.A. Miller
    1997   Cytokine production by subsets of CD4 memory T-cells differing in P-glycoprotein expression: Effects of aging. *Journals of Gerontology, Series A, Biological Sciences and Medical Sciences* 52A:B137-B145.
Brown-Borg, H.M., K.E. Borg, C.J. Meliska, and A. Bartke
    1996   Dwarf mice and the ageing process. *Nature* 384:33.

Carey, J.R., P. Liedo, D. Orozco, and J.W. Vaupel
    1992   Slowing of mortality rates at older ages in large medfly cohorts. *Science* 258:457-461.
Costa, P.T., and R.R. McCrae
    1988   Measures and markers of biological aging: "A great clamoring . . . of fleeting significance." *Archives of Gerontology and Geriatrics* 7:211-214.
    1995   Design and analysis of aging studies. Pp. 25-36 in *Handbook of Physiology. Section 11: Aging*, E.J. Masoro, ed. New York: Oxford University Press.
Covelli, V., D. Mouton, V. Di Majo, Y. Bouthillier, C. Bangrazi, J.C. Mevel, S. Rebessi, G. Doria, and G. Biozzi
    1989   Inheritance of immune responsiveness, life span, and disease incidence in inter-line crosses of mice selected for high or low multispecific antibody production. *Journal of Immunology* 142:1224-1234.
Curtsinger, J.W., H.H. Fukui, D.R. Townsend, and J.W. Vaupel
    1992   Demography of genotypes: Failure of the limited life-span paradigm in Drosophila melanogaster. *Science* 258:461-463.
de Haan, G., and G. Van Zant
    1999   Genetic analysis of hemopoietic cell cycling in mice suggests its involvement in organismal life span. *FASEB Journal* 13:707-713.
Eigenmann, J.E., A. Amador, and D.F. Patterson
    1988   Insulin-like growth factor I levels in proportionate dogs, chondrodystrophic dogs and in giant dogs. *Acta Endocrinologica* 118:105-108.
Eigenmann, J.E., D.F. Patterson, and E.R. Froesch
    1984   Body size parallels insulin-like growth factor I levels but not growth hormone secretory capacity. *Acta Endocrinologica* 106:448-453.
Falconer, D.S., I.K. Gauld, and R.C. Roberts
    1978   Cell numbers and cell sizes in organs of mice selected for large and small body size. *Genetical Research* 31:287-301.
Finch, C.E.
    1990   *Longevity, Senescence, and the Genome*. Chicago: University of Chicago Press.
Finch, C.E., M.C. Pike, and M. Witten
    1990   Slow mortality rate accelerations during aging in some animals approximate that of humans. *Science* 249:902-905.
Gelman, R., A. Watson, R. Bronson, and E. Yunis
    1988   Murine chromosomal regions correlated with longevity. *Genetics* 118:693-704.
Hillesheim, E., and S.C. Stearns
    1992   Correlated responses in life-history traits to artificial selection for body weight in (Drosophila melanogaster). *Evolution* 46:745-752.
Jackson, A.U., A. Fornes, A. Galecki, R.A. Miller, and D.T. Burke
    1999   Longitudinal QTL analysis of T-cell phenotypes in a population of four-way cross mice. *Genetics* 151:785-795.
Kenyon, C., J. Chang, E. Gensch, A. Rudner, and R. Tabtiang
    1993   A C. elegans mutant that lives twice as long as wild type. *Nature* 366:461-464.
Kimura, K.D., H.A. Tissenbaum, Y. Liu, and G. Ruvkun
    1997   daf-2, an insulin receptor-like gene that regulates longevity and diapause in Caenorhabditis elegans. *Science* 277:942-946.
Lerner, A., T. Yamada, and R.A. Miller
    1989   PGP-1[hi] T lymphocytes accumulate with age in mice and respond poorly to Con-canavalin A. *European Journal of Immunology* 19:977-982.

Li, Y., B. Deeb, W. Pendergrass, and N. Wolf
    1996   Cellular proliferative capacity and life span in small and large dogs. *Journals of Gerontology, Series A, Biological Sciences and Medical Sciences* 51:B403-B408.

Lipman, R.D., G.E. Dallel, and R.T. Bronson
    1999   Lesion biomarkers of aging in B6C3F1 hybrid mice. *Journal of Gerontology: Biological Sciences* 54A:B466-B477.

Masoro, E.J.
    1995   Aging: Current concepts. Pp. 3-21 in *Handbook of Physiology. Section 11: Aging*, E.J. Masoro, ed. New York: Oxford University Press.

McCarter, R.J.M., I. Shimokawa, Y. Ikeno, Y. Higami, G.B. Hubbard, B.P. Yu, and C.A. McMahan
    1997   Physical activity as a factor in the action of dietary restriction on aging: Effects in Fischer 344 rats. *Aging: Clinical and Experimental Research* 9:73-79.

Migliaccio, E., M. Giorgio, S. Mele, G. Pelicci, P. Reboldi, P.P. Pandolfi, L. Lanfrancone, and P.G. Pelicci
    1999   The p66shc adaptor protein controls oxidative stress response and life span in mammals. *Nature* 402:309-313.

Miller, R.A.
    1997a When will the biology of aging become useful? Future landmarks in biomedical gerontology. *Journal of the American Geriatrics Society* 45:1258-1267.
    1997b Age-related changes in T-cell surface markers: A longitudinal analysis in genetically heterogeneous mice. *Mechanisms of Ageing and Development* 96:181-196.
    1999   Kleemeier Award Lecture: Are there genes for aging? *Journal of Gerontology: Biological Sciences* 54A:B297-B307.

Miller, R.A., S. Austad, D. Burke, C. Chrisp, R. Dysko, A. Galecki, and V. Monnier
    1999   Exotic mice as models for aging research: Polemic and prospectus. *Neurobiology of Aging* 20:217-231.

Miller, R.A., F. Bookstein, J.H. van der Meulen, S. Engle, J. Kim, L. Mullins, and J. Faulkner
    1996   Candidate biomarkers of aging: Age-sensitive indices of immune and muscle function co-vary in genetically heterogeneous mice. *Journal of Gerontology: Biological Sciences* 52A:B39-B47.

Miller, R.A., C. Chrisp, and A. Galecki
    1997   CD4 memory T-cell levels predict lifespan in genetically heterogeneous mice. *FASEB Journal* 11:775-783.

Miller, R.A., C. Chrisp, and W. Atchley
    2000a Differential longevity in mouse stocks selected for early life growth trajectory. *Journals of Gerontology, Series A: Biological Sciences and Medical Sciences* 55A:B455-B461.

Miller, R.A., R. Dysko, C. Chrisp, R. Seguin, L. Linsalata, G. Buehner, J.M. Harper, and S. Austad
    2000b Mouse (Mus musculus) stocks derived from tropical islands: New models for genetic analysis of life history traits. *Journal of Zoology* 250:95-104.

Miskin, R., and T. Masos
    1997   Transgenic mice overexpressing urokinase-type plasminogen activator in the brain exhibit reduced food consumption, body weight and size, and increased longevity. *Journals of Gerontology, Series A, Biological Sciences and Medical Sciences* 52:B118-B124.

Olshansky, S.J., B.A. Carnes, and C. Cassel
    1990   In search of Methuselah: Estimating the upper limits to human longevity. *Science* 250:634-640.

Orentreich, N., J.R. Matias, A. DeFelice, and J.A. Zimmerman
    1993   Low methionine ingestion by rats extends life span. *Journal of Nutrition* 123:269-274.
Roberts, R.C.
    1961   The lifetime growth and reproduction of selected strains of mice. *Heredity* 16:369-381.
Samaras, T.T., and L.H. Storms
    1992   Impact of height and weight on life span. *Bulletin of the World Health Organization* 70:259-267.
Smith, J.M.
    1962   The causes of ageing. *Proceedings of the Royal Society of London. Series B-Biological Sciences* 157:115-127.
Sprott, R.L.
    1999   Biomarkers of aging. *Journal of Gerontology: Biological Sciences* 54A:B464-B465.
Tuffery, A.A.
    1966   Urogenital lesions in laboratory mice. *Journal of Pathology and Bacteriology* 91:301-309.
Weindruch, R., and R.L. Walford
    1988   *The Retardation of Aging and Disease by Dietary Restriction.* Springfield, IL: Charles C Thomas.
Witkowski, J.M., and R.A. Miller
    1993   Increased function of P-glycoprotein in T lymphocytes of aging mice. *Journal of Immunology* 150:1296-1306.
Yu, B.P., E.J. Masoro, and C.A. McMahan
    1985   Nutritional influences on aging of Fischer 344 rats: I. Physical, metabolic, and longevity characteristics. *Journal of Gerontology* 40:657-670.

9

The Relevance of Animal Models for Human Populations

Gerald E. McClearn

To set the stage for considering the relevance of animal models to the ventures that are the focus of this volume, it may be useful to contemplate briefly the various meanings that have become attached to the term "model." In general discourse, among many definitions, a model can be regarded to be "a tentative ideational structure used as a testing device" (*The American Heritage Dictionary of the English Language*), or "a description, a collection of statistical data, or an analogy used to help visualize often in a simplified way something that cannot be directly observed" (*Webster's Third New International Dictionary*).

Philosophers of science have provided more technical definitions, of which the following examples are illustrative. Kaplan (1964:263) observes that "any system A is a model of a system B if the study of A is useful for the understanding of B without regard to any direct or indirect causal connection between A and B." Rapaport (1954:206) identifies models as "scientific metaphors" and comments thusly on their usage: "Like every other aspect of scientific procedure, the scientific metaphor is a pragmatic device, to be used freely as long as it serves its purpose to be discarded without regrets when it fails to do so." In the philosophical literature a distinction between conceptual models and physical models is often encountered, and further taxonomic distinctions can be found among analogical, descriptive, explanatory, formal, heuristic, iconic, inferential, interpretive, measuring, predictive, semantical, statistical, symbolic, and syntatical models. Many of these categories are nonexclusive, so any particular model system can be a blend of several types. Indeed, Sattler

(1986) observes that the term is increasingly used to denote biological generalizations across the entire range from traditionally labeled theories to laws, rules, and hypotheses.

So, models can be of various kinds for various purposes, ranging from an abstract mathematical expression to a practical experimental or observational system. It is the latter general type of model with which this note will be concerned.

MODEL SYSTEMS

Common to all these definitions of models is the understanding that the essence of models is a simplification or abstraction of the phenomenon being modeled. The establishment of an experimental model is an attempt to isolate a part of a more complex system in order to study a particular element or subset of elements of that system. This process can be characterized in the familiar terms of the prototypic experimental design: one or a few elements are selected to be the manipulated, independent variables; other variables are subjected to control by fixation or randomization; and one or more others are identified as the outcome or dependent variable(s) to be measured. Similarly, in terms of associational research, elements can be predictor or predicted variables. In the broad sense used here, model systems are ubiquitous in the scientific enterprise: every questionnaire item, every score on a cognitive task, every demographic category, invokes a model of some sort.

Among this abundance of model systems is a subset that utilizes other living beings to address questions about some aspect of human life. Although plants can also be informative in this type of research (see Finch, 1990), it has mostly involved other animals, so the generic title is usually given as "animal model research."

Species Choice

The fundamental rationale for the use of animal models derives from the phyletic relatedness of living things. These phyletic relationships constitute general themes and variations on these themes. When we study some species other than our own, there is a hope that we share with that species enough of the pertinent theme that information from the model system will illuminate something about ourselves. As the molecular exploration of the human genome and genomes of a select group of other species has proceeded, there has been an increasing realization of the extent of syntenic relationhips between these models and humankind. This realization has strengthened enormously the logical base for expectations of successful application of these animal models to complex human phenotypes. A striking example of this potential is provided by Rubin et al. (2000), who describe orthologs in *Drosophila* for 177 of 289 human disease genes examined.

There is a general presumption that the closer the phyletic relationship, the more informative will be the model. Other things being equal, then, a species from the same family as *H. sapiens* might be preferred to another species from a different family but from the same order, and so on. However, some themes might be so pervasive and fundamental that almost any species from the same phylum (or even kingdom) will be informative. Species closely related to us are rare and expensive, however, so species choice is usually a matter of trade-off between family resemblance and cost-efficiency. The optimal choice for a particular human phenomenon may be quite different from the best selection for some other phenomenon. So we can't expect that there will be a single gold-standard reference species, suitable for all purposes.

For myriad reasons, including both availability and demonstrated utility, but also with an element of historical accident, certain species have become traditional or standard model systems in different research domains. As literature has accumulated about these animals, as matters of husbandry and testing procedures have become incorporated into the scientific lore as appropriate and state-of-the-art, and as review groups and editorial boards have developed expectations, the motivation to continue the employment of the familiar animals has become very powerful. Thus, the animal-model-derived knowledge that has been accumulated in each substantive domain has been filtered through these standard animal groups and perhaps constrained by the sparse sampling we have made from the enormous phyletic array that is available to us.

It might be argued that the particular choices have served us well. Genetic science, for example, is certainly thriving from data generated from fruit flies, round worms, yeast, and mice, and it is clearly wise to invest more effort where there has been so handsome a payoff. What we don't know, of course, is what we could have learned from wallabies, octopi, kinkajous, or dragonflies. Austad (1993) has commented pungently on this issue with special reference to gerontological research and has urged a broadening of our horizons. It is to be expected that the model systems for the immediate future will be constructed with the traditional species, but it would be desirable to develop a strategy that encourages exploration of new species while continuing to exploit the old.

Environmental Variables in the Total Model System

As central as the species issue is, there's more to a model system than the species that is chosen to serve as a surrogate for humanity. The "animal model" consists not only of the species employed, but also the totality of the assessment situation, with all of its manipulated, controlled, and measured variables (McClearn and Vandenbergh, 2000). With respect to most complex phenotypes, the investigator has numerous choices concerning all of these types of variables. Consider, as an example, the decisions to be made in the construction of a mouse model of human cognition. The critically important issue is whether the performance of the animal in whatever test situation we devise will be homologous, or at least usefully analogous, to some human cognitive process. But, leaving aside this issue of trans-specific generality or validity for the moment, there is the nitty-gritty issue of the specific test situation from which the measurement will be obtained. Should it be a maze, an operant conditioning apparatus, or classical Pavlovian conditioning? How should the animals be motivated to perform: hunger, thirst, escape from shock, escape from water, or curiosity? If hunger, should they be maintained at a standard percentage of initial body weight or subjected to 20-hour food deprivation? What sensory cues should be provided: visual, auditory, or spatial? If visual, what light intensity and what pattern? If auditory, what frequency and intensity? What time of day should be used for testing? Should it be at night, given the nocturnal proclivities of the animals? What response should be required? What interval should be allowed to elapse between successive trials? Should performance be measured in speed of response or in number of errors? It is well understood that the performance of an animal in any situation is a function of all of these variables as well as its cognitive functioning. Is the performance of an animal swimming for its life (as far as it knows, presumably) in a deep water maze displaying its best cognition, its relative ability to detect pertinent extra-maze cues, or its state of panic? In what proportion do these sources contribute to the observed performance?

General husbandry conditions are pertinent as well: temperature, humidity, light/dark cycle. Other possibly influential variables may not be susceptible to control by deciding on some fixed level. All animals cannot be the first tested, so order of testing may need to be randomized. The position of a home cage on the cage rack may expose the animal to different illumination levels, sound levels, or air flow, so it might be desirable to distribute animals of different experimental groups randomly on the racks, and so on for many similar variables.

It is obvious that the particular assemblage of controlled and randomized environmental features may yield idiosyncratic results relative to another assemblage differing in some respect, and it follows that no single constellation of factors constituting the model can be regarded as definitive with respect to the target phenomenon. There is not, and cannot be, a "gold standard"—an utterly valid single model that reflects all of the pertinent attributes of a complex system. Each model system constitutes an operational definition of the target phenomenon, and humility is called for in assumptions about the extent of "coverage" of that target provided by that model. Indeed, in complex systems (and most everything of interest in the present context certainly qualifies as complex), the very definition of the target phenomenon usually emerges pragmatically from converging evidence from numerous models. Again, practical considerations clearly militate against the indefinite proliferation of models in any given area of research, but an area is probably best served if there are several operational definitions in deployment on its research scene.

These considerations pertain to the setting of the model. An essential ingredient is the animal to be placed in the setting, and genotype is a major defining feature of the animal.

Genetic Variables in the Total Model System

The basic selection of the surrogate species for an animal model study is, of course, a selection based on genotype—the differences among species in their gene pools. The genome of a species is fundamental in establishing the "theme" mentioned earlier, but among animals within the same species there exists enormous genetic variation that provides the variation on the theme. Our present focus is on the exploitation and control of this intraspecific genetic variation in the construction of animal model systems. Just as in the case of the situational and measurement variables in the model, the genotype can usefully be considered in terms of the role it plays as a variable (or conglomerate of variables) that can be controlled by fixation or by randomization, and that can be manipulated.

Genotypic Constraint

The primary method of fixing a genotype is inbreeding—the mating of relatives. After about 20 consecutive generations of mating of siblings, for example, the animals in a family lineage asymptotically approach the condition of being homozygous in like allelic state for all genetic loci. That is to say, they are nearly genetically uniform. The reservation refers to the fact that the process is asymptotic, that strong selective advantage to heterozygotes might maintain segregation at a very few loci within a strain (Falconer and Mackay, 1996), and that mutation might occur and be propogated in the strain. But, for most purposes, these considerations are quibbles; inbred strains closely approach genetic uniformity. They approximate an indefinitely large number of clones or of monozygotic twins, with an additional uniformity conferred by their homozygosity at all or nearly all loci, and the logic of their use is similar to that which can be used with these latter groups. Inbred strains constitute a major, robust animal model strategy in biomedical research.

Each inbred strain is derived from a single sibling pair. The genes of a pair of animals obviously can be only a partial sample of the gene pool of the population from which they are taken. Because they are siblings, the mates will be alike in homozygous state at some genetic loci, but they will be in unlike state at others and will be heterozygous at still others. The inbreeding process will eliminate the allelic differences at the polymorphic loci in a more-or-less stochastic way. Thus, the resulting inbred strain is only one configuration of homozygous loci derivable from the mini-gene pool represented by the initial mating pair (which, as noted, is only a tiny sample of the species gene pool).

The methodological virtue of an inbred strain is its relative genetic uniformity and stability. These attributes confer on inbred strains a replicability so that the basic biological properties of the animal in the animal model can be assured in different laboratories and at different times (Festing, 1971; McClearn and Hofer, 1999a). In terms of opportunity to conduct cumulative researches on the same basic animal material, not only by one laboratory but by anyone in the world, this is an enormous advantage over animals of unknown origin and unsystematic maintenance. Many different inbred strains exist (Festing, 1971), differing widely in almost every phenotype that has been explored, so a screening is likely to identify one that displays a desired level of a phenotype, and this strain can serve thereafter as a reliable, repeatable element in the model system.

The price that is paid for the stable replicability of inbred strains is that they represent such a sparse genetic sampling from the species and their phenotypic variance is due solely to environmental agencies. The first feature raises questions of representativeness of the chosen strain for the species in general. Remembering that construction of a model involves simplification and abstraction from the totality of the "real" phenomenon, this constraint may be acceptable for many purposes. A particular strain may provide a very nonrepresentative, exaggerated phenotype that makes it particularly valuable. An example is that of the C57BL/6 strain, which is atypical of mouse strains in general in displaying a high preference for a 10 percent alcohol solution when offered a choice between that beverage and plain water. These animals have played a useful role in a variety of research programs which require animals that will voluntarily ingest ethanol. If broader representation is required, the use of multiple strains offers an approach: if a particular finding can be shown in several strains, confidence is increased that the relationship being explored is at least not idiosyncratic to a single genotype. It remains the case that each of the inbred strain genotypes is an "abnormal" one, in the sense that homozygosity at all loci will not be found in a randomly mating population.

The second feature—displaying only environmentally caused variance—constitutes a limitation on the exploration of covariation of variables. It is certainly conceivable that a research program has interest only in the pattern of interrelationships of variables that can be attributed to variation in the environmental circumstances experienced by the individual animals. Most purposes, however, will likely be served better by a variance/covariance structure in which there have also been contributions from genotypic differences among the individuals. Again, one partial solution is to employ a number of inbred strains. The limitation in this case is that the interesting genetic covariance is the covariance among strain means, and statistical power is related to the number of strains rather than individuals (McClearn and Hofer, 1999a).

Obviously, the study of a single inbred strain is uninformative about genetics. All one knows is that the genotype is uniform. Comparisons among strains begin to provide some genetic information, however. The logic of inbred strain comparisons is as follows: the animals of each strain are replicas of the same genotype; variability within strains is attributable to environmental sources; animals of different inbred strains have different genotypes; mean phenotypic differences between strains (reared and tested in the same environment) are attributable to these genetic differences between strains. This logic applies to all loci that affect the phenotype for which the compared strains possess different alleles. Obviously, such a comparison cannot assess the influence of loci for which the strains happen to possess the same alleles.

The level of genetic information yielded by strain mean differences is a modest one, in and of itself. Data of this sort, however, set the stage for further analyses by other mating schemes (McClearn, 1991).

Genetically Heterogeneous Stocks

There are research questions that are best answered by samples of animals from genetically heterogeneous populations. Such samples are a counterpoint to the genotypic fixation of inbreeding and can be attained by several routes. Some colonies are maintained with no particular mating plan. These are almost certain to contain genetically variable animals. Live trapping from the wild will certainly provide genetic heterogeneity. Intercrossing of two or more inbred strains will produce animals of differing genotypes.

The first situation, the unsystematic colony, suffers from the replicability difficulties mentioned earlier. Such stocks are often of unknown origin and of unknown degree of inbreeding or heterogeneity. Clearly, results obtained from these groups are not uninformative—they show that representatives of the species can provide the outcome described. With respect to replicability, an investigator with such a colony can obviously return for further samples, but with unsystematic mating protocols, the stability of the gene pool over time is problematic, and the prospects of investigators from other laboratories making use of the material is usually limited. The shortcomings of unspecified groups are increasingly appreciated by the scientific community, and, in some research areas, results from genetically unspecified or unspecifiable animals are simply unpublishable.

Live trapping from the wild is sometimes recommended to overcome a perceived shortcoming of the typically used laboratory stocks (Miller et al., 1991). It is contended that generations of existence in the laboratory have made them nonrepresentative of the species in the wild state. Wild-trapped animals can be of particular value to research with a strong evolutionary or comparative orientation. They will also provide the basis for the desirable broadening of the phyletic sampling used in gerontological research (Austad, 1993). There are, however, some associated problems. For example, with respect to representativeness of the sampled species, selective trapability can introduce a substantial bias in the sample actually obtained, and quickly acting selective survival and reproduction once the wild-caught specimens have entered into laboratory existence will rapidly reduce the genetic variability represented in the original trapped sample (McClearn, 1998). With regard to specifiability in this type of research, some degree of replicability of sampling can be obtained by careful repeating of the trapping procedures in the same ecological area. For some purposes this may suffice, but problems of availability to other investigators may be significant. Until a sufficient body of data concerning live-trapped groups has accumulated and become a standard research resource, it is likely that genetically heterogeneous stocks will be obtained by mating of stocks and strains already abundantly available in laboratory colonies.

Assembling heterogeneous stocks from the existing inbred strains has the problems of derivation from the clearly "abnormal" starting points but has the substantial advantage of a high degree of replicability. That is, although the genotypes of individual animals in a genetically heterogeneous stock are not repeated, the operations for constructing the stock are clearly specifiable and repeatable. Although the ways in which matings can generate heterogeneity from inbred beginnings are many, there are several more-or-less standard outcomes: F_2s, backcrosses, four-way crosses, and advanced intercrosses.

The initial step in most of the "recipes" is to produce an F_1 generation. Mating of individuals of two different strains will generate offspring which are heterozygous for all loci for which their parental strains differed in allelic configuration. This heterozygosity is a dramatic difference from their homozygous parents, and F_1s figure prominently in basic genetic studies of the phenomena of dominance, hybrid vigor, fitness, developmental canalization, and so on (see Lerner, 1954, for an early review; Mitton, 1997, for a recent one). But it is important to note that all of the animals within an F_1 generation are genetically alike. They are each heterozygous at the same loci and homozygous at all the loci for which their parents did not differ.

It has long been observed that F_1 hybrids between two strains may be less variable phenotypically than their parent strains. One interpretation is that the heterozygosity of the F_1 animals confers a higher degree of developmental homeostasis (see Phelan and Austad, 1994; McClearn and Hofer, 1999a, 1999b; Miller et al., 1999). As a consequence, F_1 animals are sometimes recommended instead of inbred strains in studies requiring genetic uniformity of the subjects.

F_1s can thus be used with advantage in many circumstances, but it should be noted that they cannot be maintained in the genetically uniform state simply by mating inter se. Instead, each F_1 sample must be generated anew by strain crossing.

In the generation of gametes, crossing over regularly occurs, and genetic information is swapped between members of a chromosome pair. That doesn't matter within inbred animals, because the swapped parts are identical. In an F_1 animal, however, the chromosomes of a particular pair are genetically different, one each having come from each parent. Each gamete produced will be unique, as will be each F_2 zygote formed by uniting of the gametes from two F_1 parents. An F_2 group thus provides for expression of some genetic variability. This variability is limited to the allelic differences existing between the parent strains of the F_1s, so that another F_2, derived from different inbred strains, will express different genetic differences.

Even greater genetic heterogeneity can be achieved by mating of F_1s that were derived from different parent strains. The progeny of such a cross are "four-way cross" animals, which, relative to F_2s, offer scope for more loci at which allelic differences can exist and for more than two allelic alternatives at these segregating loci. Four-way crosses are clearly specifiable, and can be constituted in relatively short order as required. The general principle can be extended, of course, but eight-way crosses appear to be something of a limit as a useful compromise between genetic diversity and manageability (McClearn et al., 1970).

From a statistical point of view, heterogeneous stocks offer a more substantial model system for the evaluation of associations between and among variables than that provided by inbred strains. The opinion expressed earlier—that the characterization of complex systems will require multiple measurements—carries with it an implicit need for multivariate descriptive and analytical procedures. The heterogeneous stocks will provide a favorable vehicle for generating the variance/covariance matrices and other statistical bases for these purposes.

From a genetic point of view, the segregating of multiple loci makes possible the manifestation of various forms of epistasis, or interactions among genes, which are hidden within inbred strains. Although not yet well explored for the phenotypic domains of particular interest in this volume, the general evidence for epistasis in complex systems is substantial and growing. Two early examples from mouse research will make the point. Coleman and Hummel (1975) showed that the pathophysiological expression of a diabetes gene differed dramatically depending upon the genetic background. Fowler and Edwards (1961) found that a gene severely affecting growth behaved as a model Mendelian gene in the population in which it initially was found but yielded non-Mendelian ratios in matings in another population. Molecular analyses of epistasis are proliferating, adding reductionist underpinning to observations at the whole-organism level. Theoretical perspectives (e.g., Bonner, 1988; Kauffman, 1993) also make the case for the importance of epistatic relationships in complex genetic systems.

As the avalanche of genome-mapping information continues, heterogeneous stocks of mice are proving of great value in the quest for quantitative trait loci (QTL). Until recently, the genes of a polygenic set affecting a complex phenotype were anonymous, and their influence was explored by statistical description. Very recently, it has become possible because of the mapping information now available for human beings, as well as the model organisms of mice, yeast, fruit flies, and nematodes, to individuate many of these loci by identifying a chromosomal region in which they reside. Such identifications open the way to subsequent molecular analysis, and the result will undoubtedly be an enormous enrichment of understanding of the dynamics of polygenic systems.

In the first generation of the heterogeneous stocks, linkage relationships persist, so that some observed associations among phenotypes may be spurious. This possibility can be evaluated by observations in an "advanced intercross"—groups derived by subsequent generations of mating within the heterogeneous stock. The linkage relationships will break down systematically as a function of number of generations, and obtained correlations among phenotypes will more assuredly be due to shared mechanisms causally downstream from the same gene or genes rather than fortuitous location of independent genes on the same chromosomes. In the QTL and mapping endeavors, different purposes are served by heterogeneous stocks in different stages of linkage disequilibrium. Initial detection of a QTL, for example, is more readily accomplished in a group with extensive linkage; finer localization is facilitated by a more advanced intercross.

Genetic variability can be explored usefully by yet another classical procedure—the production of backcross groups. F_1 animals are mated with one of the parental types, yielding offspring that are intermediate in allelic frequencies to those of the F_1 and the parent. Thus, while genetically heterogeneous, that heterogeneity is reduced relative to the F_2. Backcrosses can be obtained in either direction, and their means and variances are interpretable in the context of quantitative genetic theory in estimating parameters of the polygenic system. Continued successive backcrossing will result in increasing genetic uniformity, and, coupled with selection for possession of a particular allele, generates useful test-beds for examining the effect of allelic differences at that locus.

The combination of genetic fixation and variability provided by recombinant inbred strains is proving itself of particular value in the current search for quantitative trait loci. Recombinant inbred (RI) strains are derived by consecutive sib mating from a common F_2 group. Thus, the genetic differences between the original strains that produced the F_1 that produced the F_2 are reshuffled (by virtue of genetic recombination) into different lines and rehomogenized by inbreeding. In the use of this type of population, the advantages of genetic uniformity are possessed by the individual RI strains, each of which is a different combination of the allelic differences between the progenitor strains, thus providing genetic heterogeneity. Genetic influence is represented by differences among the RI means, and environmental influence is revealed by the within-RI strain variance. The power for correlational analysis is, of course, limited to the number of strains. Because many of the panels of RI strains have been characterized with respect to chromosomal markers, they are highly cost-efficient material for initial nomination of QTL (though they require confirmation because of inevitable false positive indications due to the large number of statistical tests required).

In view of the general advantages and the special applicability of heterogeneous stocks, their relatively modest record of employment in animal epidemiological models is regrettable. Given the genetic heterogeneity of human populations, cogent arguments can be advanced for the particular appropriateness of such stocks for this type of research, and there have been several recent reviews encouraging their more widespread deployment in future research (McClearn, 1999; McClearn and Hofer, 1999b; Miller et al., 1991, 1999).

MANIPULATION OF THE GENOTYPE

The manipulation of genes—through mating procedures—has been stock in trade of the science of heredity since Mendel. In the case of major genes, the genotypes of individual animals can be deduced from their phenotype or from the phenotypes of their offspring or other relatives. Appropriate matings can generate offspring groups of known or strongly inferred genotypes. This procedure can test hypotheses about mode of inheritance of a particular phenotype, or, in the case of a well-established genetic condition, can be useful for providing different genotypes for the study of mechanism of gene action, and so on.

It is also possible to manipulate genes even when nothing is known about their number, effect size on the phenotype in question, chromosomal location, or mode of action. This general procedure, phenotypic selective breeding, also relies on inferring something about the genotype from the phenotype. Thus, if any of the variance of a phenotype is due to genetic differences among the individuals in the population (i.e., the heritability is nonzero), then individuals from the low and high extremes of the distribution will possess, on average, fewer and more "increasing" alleles, respectively, than the population in general. If members of the like extremes are mated, their offspring will thus have reduced and increased allelic frequencies, respectively, relative to those of their parents' generation. Further selection of mates from the appropriate extremes will lead, ultimately, to two groups of animals: one containing all, or most, of the increasing alleles; and another with all, or most, of the decreasing alleles at all of the unknown, and possibly multitudinous, loci in the gene pool provided by the foundation stock that can influence the phenotype in question. From the rigor of the selection and the rate of divergence of phenotypes of the two lines of animals, deductions can be made about certain parameters of the genetic "architecture" of the phenotype. Perhaps more importantly, once generated, these selectively bred animals can serve as prime research material for the investigation of the mechanisms through which the genetic influences are mediated.

Phenotypic selective breeding is an extremely effective method for manipulating entire blocks of anonymous genes, operating on all loci affecting the phenotype that are segregating in the foundation (necessarily heterogeneous) population, and sorting those alleles associated with increased expression into one group and those for decreased expression into another group. These groups then constitute prime research material for the exploration of mechanisms underlying the phenotypic differences. In short, phenotypic selective breeding is a method for the systematic generation of animal models. Research fields differ widely in their utilization of this tool-making procedure. Examples of areas in which selected lines have contributed fundamentally include body growth (see Falconer and Mackay, 1996, for review) and alcohol-related processes (see Crabbe et al., 1994; McClearn et al., 1981). In gerontological science, selection studies in *Drosophila* (reviewed by Shmookler Reis and Ebert, 1996) have provided extremely valuable model systems, and similar projects in mice are contemplated (Harrison and Roderick, 1997).

Advances in molecular genetics have made it possible to manipulate the genotype in more specific ways. In contrast to the genetic collectivity involved in phenotypic selective breeding, these methods permit the manipulation of specified individual genes. By various techniques, it is possible to introduce new genes into an organism or to negate expression of a particular gene. Use of these transgenic and knock-out preparations is expanding at a spectacular rate, and they will undoubtedly be major components of animal model systems of the future.

These methods will be particularly valuable in identifying mechanisms of expression of single genes identified by other methods. They are likely to provide valuable opportunities to explore gene-gene interactions, given the frequent observations of dependence of outcome on the genetic background of the host animal. A noteworthy example of the prospects for this type of research is the work of Sullivan et al. (1997). These authors replaced the mouse apolipoprotein E (APOE) gene with the human APOE e3 allele, providing a model system for the study of diseases associated with the human APOE isoforms.

Another manipulation that becomes possible with identification of specific loci is that of genotypic selective breeding. Such a procedure, with mate assignments based on measured genotype rather than measured phenotype, will be particularly useful for exploration of the complexities of gene-gene interaction, because the genetic systems can be assembled in any desirable combination. Whereas genotypic selection will be particularly illuminating when conducted with actual genes, the principle can be extended to QTL selection. Thus, genetic complexes of yet-anonymous genes can be built in various configurations based on mate assignment according to QTL genotypes, capable of generating, as in the case of phenotypic selection, animal models purpose-built to investigator specification.

SUMMARY AND CONCLUSION

In epidemiological and demographic research arenas, where genes and biological markers can be sought directly in human populations as well as animal models, the utility of research on animals lies in, among other attributes, their shorter lifetimes, shorter generation intervals, and accessibility for study of putative mechanisms. The major concern with the animal model in this context is its validity, which by informal definition is the extent to which it measures what it purports to measure. There are two subissues here: does the particular model represent the target phenomenon adequately in the animal, and does the animal phenomenon have points of similarity with the target phenomenon in humankind? For some phenotypes, there is a reasonableness about inferring from animal data to human traits. The human-validity of genetic observations from various invertebrate and vertebrate species is resounding. Similarly, it appears likely that blood pressure; hematocrit; glucose tolerance; collagen cross-linkage; proliferative response; white cell count; growth hormone; and similar neurological, physiological, endocrinological, and immunological variables in mammalian systems will be informative about the human condition. These face-validity assumptions are not so easily made in connection with behavioral and sociological variables. An earlier example explored the issues in establishing an animal model for human cognition. What does black-white discrimination under hunger motivation and food reward have to do with human general intelligence? It is not obvious on the face of the matter. But it is very unlikely that the functioning of the central nervous system in changing behavioral responses in what we call learning situations is totally unrelated in mouse and man. We lack, unfortunately, criteria that permit confident a priori predictions about the utility of any particular model for any particular complex human attribute. So, the proof of the model is in its application. The matter calls for caution (perhaps cautious optimism) in making the interspecific connection, and, given the nonexistence of gold standard model situations, for seeking converging evidence from different model systems. Our understanding, indeed, our definition of these phenomena, will evolve as information from the different avenues is collated and integrated.

For many demographic or epidemiological purposes, the target phenomenon of the model will have a complex genetic architecture with a large number of genes affecting the phenotype. For these circumstances, the quantitative genetic model is the apposite one. The pertinent analytical procedures yield bottom-line assessments of the relative influence of the genetic system and of various environmental domains. Molecular genetics has made enormous strides in the identification and molecular characterization of single genes that, by themselves, exert detectable influence on a wide array of medical and other phenotypes. Furthermore, the generation of marker genotypes permits the localization of some of the genes (QTL) in polygenic systems to general chromosomal regions. Thus both identified genes and implicated anonymous genes can be investigated.

The genetic tools that are available to the animal researcher are many and varied, and they are differentially useful and powerful for different purposes. The important phenomena addressed in this volume deserve optimal utilization of these tools. To this end, it should be remembered that the logic of animal model research requires efficient communication between the worlds of the animal modelers and the human population researchers. In the real world, of course, these research communities develop their own traditions, literatures, and networks; communication is less than optimal between communities. The situation is reminiscent of the current concern over "translational" research from the bench to the bedside. It is reasonable to expect that a systematic program to improve this two-way communication could enhance the relevance of studies on our phyletic relatives to the understanding of ourselves.

REFERENCES

Austad, S.N.
　　1993　The comparative perspective and choice of animal models in aging research. *Aging and Clinical Experimental Research* 5:259-267.
Bonner, J.T.
　　1988　*The Evolution of Complexity*. Princeton, NJ: Princeton University Press.
Coleman, D.L., and K.P. Hummel
　　1975　Influence of genetic background on the expression of mutations at the diabetes locus in the mouse. II. Studies on background modifiers. *Israeli Journal of Medical Science* 11:708-713.
Crabbe, J.C., J.K. Belknap, and K.J. Buck
　　1994　Genetic animal models of alcohol and drug abuse. *Science* 264:1715-1723.
Falconer, D.S., and T.R.C. Mackay
　　1996　*Introduction to Quantitative Genetics*, 4th ed. Essex, England: Longman.
Festing, M.F.W.
　　1971　*Inbred Strains in Biomedical Research*. London: The Macmillan Press Ltd.
Finch, C.E.
　　1990　*Longevity, Senescence and the Genome*. Chicago: The University of Chicago Press.
Fowler, R.E., and R.G. Edwards
　　1961　'Midget,' a new dwarfing gene in the house mouse dependent on a genetic background of small body size for its expression. *Genetical Research* 2:272-282.
Harrison, D.E., and T.H. Roderick
　　1997　Selection for maximum longevity in mice. *Experimental Gerontology* 32:65-78.
Kaplan, A.
　　1964　*The Conduct of Inquiry: Methodology for Behavioral Science*. New York: Chandler, Harper & Row.
Kauffman, S.A.
　　1993　*The Origins of Order*. New York: Oxford University Press.
Lerner, I.M.
　　1954　*Genetic Homeostasis*. New York: John Wiley & Sons.
McClearn, G.E.
　　1991　The tools of pharmacogenetics. In *The Genetic Basis of Alcohol and Drug Actions*. New York: Plenum Press.
　　1998　Heterogeneous reference populations in animal model research in aging. *ILAR Journal* 38:119-123.
　　1999　Commentary. Exotic mice as models for aging research: Polemic and prospectus by R. Miller et al. *Neurobiology of Aging* 20:233-236.
McClearn, G.E., R.A. Deitrich, and V.G. Erwin, eds.
　　1981　Development of animal models as pharmacogenetic tools (DHEW Publication No. [ADM] 81-113). Washington, DC: U.S. Government Printing Office.

McClearn, G.E., and S.M. Hofer

1999a Genes as gerontological variables: Uniform genotypes. *Neurobiology of Aging* 20:95-104.

1999b Genes as gerontological variables: Uses of genetically heterogeneous stocks. *Neurobiology of Aging* 20:147-156.

McClearn, G.E., and D.J. Vandenbergh

2000 The structure and limits of animal models: Examples from alcohol research. *ILAR Journal* 41(3):144-152.

McClearn, G.E., J.R. Wilson, and W. Meredith

1970 The use of isogenic and heterogenic mouse stocks in behavioral research. In *Contributions to Behavior-Genetic Analysis: The Mouse as a Prototype*. New York: Appleton-Century-Crofts.

Miller, R.A., S. Austad, D. Burke, C. Chrisp, R. Dysko, A. Galecki, A. Jackson, and V. Monnier

1991 Exotic mice as models for aging research: Polemic and prospectus. *Neurobiology of Aging* (Mar-Apr) 20:217-231.

Miller, R.A., D. Burke, and N. Nadon

1999 Announcement: Four-way cross mouse stocks: A new, genetically heterogeneous resource for aging research. *Biological Sciences* 54A:B358-B360.

Mitton, J.B.

1997 *Selection in Natural Populations*. New York: Oxford University Press.

Phelan, J.P., and S.N. Austad

1994 Selecting animal models of human aging: Inbred strains often exhibit less biological uniformity than F1 hybrids. *Journal of Gerontology* 49(1):B1-11.

Rapaport, A.

1954 *Operational Philosophy: Integrating Knowledge and Action*. New York: Harper and Brothers Publishers.

Rubin, G.M, M.D. Yandell, J.R. Wortman, and others.

2000 Comparative genomics of the eukaryotes. *Science* 287:2204-2215.

Sattler, R.

1986 *Biophilosophy: Analytic and Holistic Perspectives*. Berlin: Springer-Verlag.

Shmookler Reis, R.J., and R.H. Ebert, II

1996 Genetics of aging: Current models. *Experimental Gerontology* 31:69-81.

Sullivan, P.M., H. Mezdour, Y. Aratani, C. Knouff, J. Najib, R.L. Reddick, S.H. Quarfordt, and N. Maeda

1997 Targeted replacement of the mouse apolipoprotein E gene with the common human APOE3 allele enhances diet-induced hypercholesterolemia and atherosclerosis. *The Journal of Biological Chemistry* 272(29):17972-17980.

10

Applying Genetic Study Designs to Social and Behavioral Population Surveys

Robert B. Wallace

It is clear that population surveys comprising social and behavioral issues and hypotheses can be extended to include and explore epidemiological, public health, genetic, and other biologically oriented scientific themes, in part through the collection of genetic and other bioindicators that will inform these questions (Wallace, 1997). Well-defined, geographically representative cohorts are an important opportunity for many types of population research because they are expensive and uncommon, particularly those that are national in scope. They often contain a wealth of personal and family information that is important to understanding the causes and management of health problems. With the rapid advance of genetic knowledge and measurement technology, behaviorally oriented surveys may become important "laboratories" to seek genetic and other biological explanations for personal and social behaviors as well as to answer a broad range of scientific questions.

It is also clear that such surveys will not lend themselves well to all possible scientific questions equally. As much forethought and planning as possible should be undertaken before such surveys go into the field, so that there will be a maximum ability to shape design and data-collection methods. Surveys that are already in place will present special design challenges for enhancement with genetic marker or other bioindicator-collection activities, for both scientific and logistical reasons. For these same reasons, one must not assume that routine collection of particular specimen types, such as blood or urine, will automatically address a wide range of yet-to-be-defined general scientific questions, since type of specimen and preliminary handling and processing may not be appropriate for many cogent hypotheses that may be identified later. Also, no matter what the primary purposes of an existing survey and investigator expertise, there should be wide interdisciplinary consultation in order to assure that genetic or other bioindicator-related hypotheses are precise and feasibly assessed, and that the effort has a reasonable chance of providing useful scientific outcomes.

The purpose of this chapter is to introduce design and other methodological considerations on how to optimally extend geographically referent health and social survey cohorts to enhance their application to additional biological questions, focusing on genetic issues and collection of genetic bioindicators. While genetic studies may address any human trait or characteristic, the emphasis will be on health problems. It begins with a consideration of identifying and defining the basic age-related diseases, conditions, and other traits that are potential objects of genetic study. Next is a discussion on how to assess family structures within household surveys and the value of determining the familiality of diseases, conditions, and other traits of interest. This is followed by a review of genetic study designs and methods that could be applied to representative household surveys in order to address the contribution of genes and inheritance to disease etiology or progression and to age-related physiological and functional change. Finally, there is an overview of logistical considerations in approaching community-dwelling survey participants for specimen collection. It should be noted that here are many ethical issues related to the acquisition, processing, and interpreting of genetic and other bioindicators; these are addressed elsewhere in this volume by Botkin and by Durfy.

It is axiomatic that most human illnesses are due to both genetic and environmental causes. Thus, while this chapter emphasizes genetic bioindicators and their relation to health outcomes among older persons, it should be emphasized that many community-based surveys offer the opportunity to make environmental observations and collect environmental specimens that may be potentially important to defining health outcomes. For example, even before an interviewer approaches and enters a household, it is possible to collect outdoor air and soil samples for pollutants and to make observations on the quality and maintenance of the residence as well as impediments to outdoor mobility and the general challenges of the geographic terrain. Once inside the household, with appropriate consent it may be possible to collect (a) air samples within or near specific households for general air pollutants or specific contaminants such as radon or carbon monoxide; (b) peeling paint samples for lead or other heavy metal content; (c) household dust samples for toxic agents or pollutants; (d) temperature measurements in times of extreme weather conditions; (e) industrial hygiene monitors worn by inhabitants to assess physio-chemical exposures over an extended period; or (f) biological specimens from household pets, which may reflect a wide variety of physiochemical exposures in common with the occupants, including diet. Environmental observations are critical in their own right, but are often important cofactors for genetically related diseases and other outcomes.

DEFINING THE PHENOTYPIC OUTCOMES
IN POPULATION STUDIES

All rigorously observed living things undergo age-related changes in physiology, metabolism, structure, and behavior. The measures of these changes are the bioindicators of aging. Pursuing the biological mechanisms of age-related change is extremely important, and in less complex species (e.g., bacteria, yeast, roundworms), where a substantial amount of basic research is conducted, a variety of predictable age-related changes in physiology and metabolism have been observed. On the other hand, the concept of "disease" is an extremely complex notion, generally reserved for more complex organisms higher up on the evolutionary tree, since diseases often involve dimensions such as anatomic change, altered function, and suffering. Species in which diseases have received attention and study experience age-related increases in the rates of an important series of chronic conditions, many of which may lead to death directly or to a cascade of secondary events that are ultimately fatal. Of great interest, it appears that the rates of age-related changes and of diseases can vary widely within a species, and there is a large body of experimental evidence demonstrating that these changes are modifiable by both environmental and genetic manipulation.

However, one of several important dilemmas when studying aging mechanisms in simpler organisms is the problem of understanding how the biology of aging relates, if at all, to the occurrence of diseases and conditions in humans and other more complex organisms. An important question, as one explores the association of genetics and bioindicators with health outcomes, is whether the distinction between aging processes and formally conceived and designated diseases can be made. In genetic explorations, the question may be whether there are aging measures (in genetic parlance—phenotypes) that are conceptually, statistically, and pathogenetically independent of disease processes. Much useful study has been devoted to the processes of aging, but biological aging remains an extremely difficult commodity to define. The thesis here is that for purposes of studying empirical associations between genetic bioindicators and health outcomes, whether the genetic exposures and phenotypic outcomes are part of some underlying, unique biological process called aging or are abnormal clinical conditions such as atherosclerotic heart disease, and cancer is largely immaterial and possibly distracting.

There are several reasons for the contention that distinguishing between biological aging and disease processes may be problematic. There is little agreement on a precise definition of aging, although many have offered general characteristics; this is usefully discussed by Arking (1998). Most scientific papers on the study of aging, basic or applied, do not offer definitions of aging as an explicit biological process separate from disease and dysfunction. Survivorship and longevity, among the most widely studied attributes of aging across species, are insufficient outcomes for the study of complex animal processes, particularly in humans or other mammals; nearly all humans die of one or more discrete, identifiable medical conditions. Further, most if not all hypothesized biological mechanisms of aging encompass concepts that have also been applied to disease causation and progression. For example, age-related shortening of chromosomal telomeres has been related both to aging processes and to carcinogenesis (Shay, 1997), as have cumulative somatic mutations (Vijg, 2000; Hernandez-Boussard et al., 1999) and age-related, progressively inefficient DNA repair processes (de Boer and Hoeijmakers, 2000). Even an environmental factor that experimentally has been shown to dramatically prolong mammalian survivorship as well as decrease the occurrence of age-related physiological change and disease, caloric restriction, has been shown to alter the rate of change in age-related gene function (Lee et al., 1999).

In summary, until further understanding of the biology of aging emerges, it seems best to consider that organisms have a set of complex, interactive, biologically malleable cell and tissue/organ machinery that is responsible for both diseases and age-related change. This malleability suggests that all age-related phenomena are not obligate, whether physiological or pathogenetic, and that interventions targeted to these phenomena may become very important for the enhancement of successful aging. Genetically related bioindicators of age-related change should be equally suited for their associations with endpoints that include disease and dysfunction as well as other age-related changes. Because the number of cell mechanisms that might be related to genetic bioindicators is so large, some way to conceptualize them may be helpful. Holliday (1998) has suggested one approach. He divides the energy flow that allows cells to survive into three categories: normal cell functions, reproduction, and organism maintenance. Examples of each are shown in Table 10-1, which provides a working taxonomy for considering categories of bioindicators for future study.

As a caution when applying genetic bioindicators in the search for the

TABLE 10-1 Energy Resource Allocation in Mammals

Normal Functions	Reproduction	Maintenance
Biochemical synthesis	Gonads, gametes, and sex	Wound healing
Metabolism	Development	Immunity
Respiration	Gestation	Protein turnover
Cell turnover	Suckling	Defense against free radicals
Movement	Care of offspring	Synthesis of macromolecules
Excretion	Growth to adulthood	DNA repair
		Detoxification
		Epigenetic controls
		Apoptosis
		Fat storage
		Homeostasis

SOURCE: Reprinted with permission from Holliday, R. 1998. Causes of aging. *Annals of the New York Academy of Sciences* 854:61-71.

causes of disease outcomes in populations, it should be noted that almost all phenotypes of interest are biologically complex and related to multiple body systems and processes, including human and animal behaviors. Broad survival traits in aging studies, such as longevity, active life expectancy, or rates of change in important age-related functional activities, are emblematic of this issue. Age-related disease outcomes, including most of the major chronic illnesses, are also extremely complex and difficult to define as homogeneous phenotypes. Ellsworth and Manolio (1999) explain why this is the case:

• Complex diseases have a high level of genetic complexity, where multiple genes, each with a relatively small effect, act independently *or* interact in important ways. For example, essential hypertension, proximal to many cardiovascular conditions, starts with 4 to 10 genes interacting with several environmental factors, leading to several intermediate phenotypes and finally to diseases in association with other genetically related factors such as obesity and alcohol use (Carretero and Oparil, 2000).

• A single disease may have multiple manifestations with varying relationships to genetic influences.

• Apparently homogeneous diseases may have multiple causes and pathogenetic mechanisms. For example, atherosclerosis may be due to combinations of lipid accumulation, endothelial injury, inflammation, and clotting abnormalities.

- Individuals with preclinical illnesses may be indistinguishable from otherwise healthy persons because early detection methods may be inadequate. Most chronic illnesses in western societies have variable ages-at-onset of clinical symptoms.
- Environmental factors may alter incidence rates and interact with important genes so that the severity of the condition may range from almost imperceptible to debilitating.
- At times, the failure to find an association between a bioindicator and a condition with genetic causes may be due to the misclassification and aggregation of heterogeneous conditions that appear phenotypically similar.

ASSESSING THE FAMILIALITY AND HERITABILITY OF DISEASES, CONDITIONS, AND AGE-RELATED CHANGE

One of the most important preliminary ways to determine the likelihood that genetic factors play an important role in the genesis of disease, dysfunction, and age-related change is to assess the extent to which these phenotypes (diseases and other traits) occur more frequently within families than in the general population. Once this is determined, more detailed studies may be justified. While the clustering or unusual occurrence of age-related conditions or functional alterations within certain families does not per se distinguish between environmental and genetic explanations, their absence makes genetic factors less likely.

Other common approaches to preliminarily assessing whether a trait has a genetic component are twin studies and adoption studies. In twin studies, some degree of genetic inheritance is inferred if a trait has a higher rate of concordance among monozygotic (i.e., identical) than among dizygotic (i.e., fraternal) twins. Despite some discussion on the meaning and interpretation of twin studies, evidence from these studies has served to suggest a role for genetic factors in conditions important to elders, such as macular degeneration (Gorin et al., 1999) and cognitive disability (Plomin and DeFries, 1998), but they have not fully resolved the role of inheritance in Parkinson's disease (Langston, 1998). In general, most representative population surveys, even those of substantial size, do not contain sufficient numbers of twin pairs to conduct twin studies per se. Rather, surveys may identify some twins that can be reported to regional twin registries for later studies, with appropriate permission of the participants.

Similarly, adoption studies can shed light on genetic contributions to disease. Here, siblings raised in different households are contrasted for disease concordance and rates of familiality with those raised in the same household. This method, although used less than twin studies, has been fruitful in several disease domains, including mental illnesses such as schizophrenia (Heston, 1966). A recently suggested variation is to explore familiality among unrelated children of the same age raised in the same household (Anonymous, 2000).

These study models are not efficiently addressed using population methods, but knowing the population-referent character of study twins and adoptive families adds to their credibility. Other population applications, such as migration studies, have been used to explore the role of environmental exposures. Once there is reasonable evidence that genetic factors are important for a given health problem or other trait, examining family members of known relation to each other (i.e., a pedigree) using a variety of complex genetic study designs and models helps determine whether genetic markers are statistically linked to each other and are environmentally interactive as well.

Most pedigrees containing an unusual occurrence of a particular disease or trait are not discovered in population surveys, but rather in the clinical setting. This is mostly a matter of efficiency, because if population cohorts or registers were large enough and sufficiently well documented, informative pedigrees could be obtained from them. However, population surveys that emphasize demographic, family, and social hypotheses and collect family structure data and associated histories of diseases or other age-related phenomena can serve genetic study designs in other ways. They allow determination of the distribution of pedigree sizes available for more detailed genetic study. They provide detailed ethnic and other demographic characterization of the population, which can help avoid confounding in genetic studies (see below). They can also provide methods for locating participants and ascertaining vital status with improved accuracy. Finally, for certain studies, they can provide substantial samples of geographically referent sib pairs and other core family groups that form the basis for some genetic inquiries and models. Other uses of assembled population cohorts are described below.

If collection of pedigree information is undertaken, there are computer programs that can assist with this activity, available at regional genetics clinics or population genetics research programs. A typical pedigree contains the full names (including maiden names) of individuals, as well as their date and location of birth, vital status, residential location, gender, nature of relation to the index household individual or couple, and the presence of the particular disease, condition, or trait of interest. Useful pedigree data can be obtained from postal surveys (McKinley et al., 1996) as well as from personal interviews. It may be of value within population surveys to collect pedigree information in stages, taking more detailed information from subsampled families that meet certain eligibility criteria, such as having a member with a given condition or comprising a certain size or composition.

There are potential problems in collecting family structure and concomitant disease occurrence information, most of which are common to general survey data collection. Putative blood relatives may in fact not be, and issues of paternity may be present. Survey respondents or other informants may not have accurate information on the age or disease status of even close family members. This has been observed in the study of Alzheimer's disease and dementia, where responses on familial presence of dementia were found to be sensitive but nonspecific (Kukull and Larson, 1989). A similar problem was observed in the reporting of familial orofacial birth defects (Romitti et al., 1997). In addition, many potentially informative family members are deceased or living remote from the site of the informant interview, making contact or specimen collection logistically more difficult. Some family members may choose not to participate in genetic studies. Thus, there are many reasons to be cautious in interpreting pedigree information.

However, there are ways to confirm and expand pedigree health information. One important method is to link pedigree members, when ethically feasible, to other data sources such as medical records, church or administrative records, or regional disease registries. In the United States, linkage to Health Care Financing Administration (HCFA) records, at least for persons 65 years of age and older, may confirm or refute the presence of many medical conditions. Similarly, linkage to regional vital record sources, the National Death Index, or the mortality file of the Social Security Administration (Hussey and Elo, 1997) may confirm deaths of relatives as well as help establish family relationships. Some family information may be contained within extended genealogy record systems that are available and suitable for analytic use (Thomas et al., 1999) or other more specialized registers, such as geographic disease or twin registers.

STUDY DESIGNS AND GENETIC BIOINDICATOR APPLICATIONS IN POPULATION STUDIES

There are a substantial number of genetic study designs used to find associations between gene markers or gene function and health outcomes. If one includes all bioindicators that might be collected using simple techniques, such as from venipuncture or urine collection, there would be nearly limitless opportunities for associational studies between these indicators and health, functional, or other aging outcomes. These could span a large number of social science, health, biological, ecological, and environmental disciplines and could be quite fruitful with the appropriate collaboration. The discussion below begins with some methodological cautions and continues with the population intersection with genetic studies.

General Methodological Issues

Sample Size Considerations

Approaching genetic applications in population surveys often begins with sample size considerations. In general, specific genes, alleles, or gene markers must be common enough to make a study informative, even if there are thousands of participants. This issue becomes more problematic when there is substantially heterogeneity (i.e., allelic variation) at a given genetic locus or when multiple genes may be involved. Even robust, geographically representative (generally household) survey populations may or may not be suitable for many hypotheses; this needs to be evaluated on an individual basis. This issue arises also when exploring gene-environment interactions, where occurrence rates for both the environmental exposures and the genetic markers of interest may be uncommon. Thus, some exposures cannot be adequately addressed, even in large survey cohorts.

The same issues apply to various health and functional outcomes. They must be common enough to avoid Type I errors in models of exposure/ outcome associations. For example, among older western cohorts of substantial size, some conditions such as clinical coronary artery disease; breast, colon and prostate cancer; and Alzheimer's disease, are likely to be quite common if the observation period is long enough. However, other conditions such as ovarian cancer, Parkinson's disease, or even hip fracture, may not be suitably assessed in prospective population studies unless the sample size and the follow-up interval are large. One way to enhance the number of outcomes for genetic studies of diseases is to consider intermediate outcomes. For example, very low bone density may serve as a surrogate for hip fracture, and adenomatous colon polyps may serve the same role for colon cancer. The use of intermediate outcomes requires consensus on their biological appropriateness. If the outcomes are age-related physiological or functional characteristics or traits that can be assessed in all or most survey participants over time, such as decreased renal or cognitive function, then smaller sample sizes may be feasible. Methods for addressing these sample size considerations are available and improving, and are very dependent on the particular genetic analytical models employed.

Incident Versus Prevalent Outcomes in Populations

When exploring genetic markers for associations with diseases or other aging outcomes, the distinction between prevalent and incident outcomes needs to be considered, or biases and spurious findings may occur as in epidemiological and social studies that explore environment-disease associations (Goldman et al., 1983). For example, cross-sectional analyses can be difficult to interpret because a gene or allele may be associated with surviving a disease rather than in its etiology. Further, the influence of a particular gene on a disease may cause clinical emergence at an earlier age, making the age structure and competing causes of death important determinants of the associations found. Even in prospective cohort studies, temporal associations between specific alleles present for a lifetime and disease occurrence can be complex to interpret because many clinical conditions develop in a preclinical state over many years, and many participants may be misclassified as normal when in fact nascent illnesses will emerge given enough time.

The Intersection of Defined Survey Populations with Genetic Studies

The following are some approaches to utilizing population-based cohorts for answering scientific questions related to genetics and health outcomes among older persons. Social science surveys are taking place in many countries, industrialized and developing, and the opportunities may be different according to the geographical locale and the prevalent environmental exposures and clinical conditions at hand. These approaches are not exhaustive, but highlight existing and emerging applications.

The Distribution of Gene Markers in Demographically Defined Populations—General Research Applications

Assessing the fundamental distributions of various gene markers in a population according to basic demographic characteristics can be extremely important for genetic research applications. Population surveys may supplement ongoing population registers in constructing genealogies by reconstructing biological kinship relationships among inhabitants (Gaimard et al., 1998). The study of populations with an increased occurrence of a known genetic disease may lead to identification of the ancestors and related demographic and geographic factors that were responsible for the increased population disease rates, such as has been done for cystic fibrosis (deBraekeleer et al., 1996). Repeated genetic sampling of spatially diverse populations may also provide substantial information on patterns of geographic migration (Epperson, 1998) and the population age of rare, nonrecurrent mutants (Rannala, 1997).

As noted above, gene-marker distributions characterized according to age, gender, ethnicity, or geographic locale can provide important information about population genetic heterogeneity and support sample-size calculations for more detailed genetic inquiries. Determining accurate population allele frequencies is important in the application of various genetic analytical models and for meeting their assumptions. In some of these models, selecting population controls for persons with a particular trait or condition for gene marker-disease association studies can lead to a kind of confounding bias called "population stratification," where gene frequencies and penetrances at a locus vary between subpopulations and are not adequately controlled for by usual methods (Caporaso et al., 1999). Demographically well-characterized populations may help avoid some of this confounding by providing information on factors associated with these various gene frequencies.

One ancillary research application of gene frequencies derived from population surveys is to assess the quality and completeness of disease registries for conditions that are known to be caused by major genes. Such population gene frequencies can supplement population-based disease registers by providing corroborating evidence on the changing occurrence of these conditions, such as the eye tumor retinoblastoma (Moll et al., 1997).

Founder Populations

Some populations are chosen for special genetic study, particularly for complex genetic traits, because they are more genetically homogeneous than other populations, often because of social or geographic isolation over many generations. At least in theory, this may allow easier detection of gene-phenotype associations because there is less genetic "noise." Such approaches have several applications, such as in determining mutant mitochondrial DNA associated with dementia in a French-Canadian founder population (Chagnon et al., 1999) or in searching for genetic linkages to susceptibility genes for asthma (Ober et al., 1998). The founder population within Iceland has also received much attention, and the combined genetic and clinical information available is being used for many purposes (Enserink, 2000), despite ethical and political concerns. Founder populations that are well characterized according to demographic, social, and environmental factors can be extremely helpful in addressing genetic issues.

Gene Frequencies and Disease Occurrence—Association Studies

It is possible to utilize defined population cohorts to identify specific genes that may cause chronic conditions and disability among older persons. Standard population methods for exploring associations between gene markers and phenotypes, particularly disease outcomes, can be applied here as in other situations, including standard case-control and cohort analytic approaches that have been used for studies of environment-disease associations. Case-control studies may be less subject to bias when cases (i.e., persons with particular diseases or traits) and controls are obtained from geographically referent populations. Nesting case-control studies from within well-defined cohorts is an important way to better understand a study population.

Cohort studies addressing genetically defined "exposures" have an advantage over case-control studies in that many hypothesized outcomes can be evaluated simultaneously. Participants' genetic markers may be defined in different ways. They may be particular "candidate" (i.e., hypothesized) markers followed to determine whether they predict a particular outcome, or markers known to cause a condition followed to determine the general population impact. For example, a particular homozygous mutation has been detected in 85-90 percent of northern Europeans with the iron storage disease hemochromotosis. However, when this mutation was determined in a general Australian cohort (Olynyk et al., 1999), only half of the homozygous persons had clinical or serological features of the disease over a four-year period. This emphasizes one potential contribution of population-based studies relative to other designs.

In the past most population genetic studies were designed, for reasons of efficiency, to evaluate candidate genes or gene markers selected for study based on prior linkage or associational methods, molecular or other studies, or on a priori reasoning. With 50,000-100,000 genes and wide allelic variation in the human genome and a much larger number of gene markers, including the potential to exploit the exact nucleotide sequence of the entire genome, it would seem difficult under the best of circumstances to determine and test all potential markers. Moreover, most chronic conditions of older persons are thought to be due to multiple, interactive genes as well as important environmental exposures (Collins, 1999), making the study of one or a few candidate genes increasingly likely to be unproductive. Due to rapidly advancing gene measurement technology, alternative approaches are emerging. One suggested approach, in essence, is to screen the entire genome using closely spaced genetic markers for associations to disease outcomes. This is still a resource-intensive activity that has not yet borne fruit, but it holds future promise.

Other approaches to defining genetic roles in disease and identifying the chromosomal location of these genes are based more on pedigrees and families. Linkage studies are performed in large pedigrees, where genetic heterogeneity is limited and the condition occurs with a high frequency. There are variations of pedigree studies performed to determine if particular gene markers are related to phenotypes when large pedigrees are not available, using related individuals in nuclear families, such as sibpairs (Goring and Terwilliger, 2000), trios (i.e., two parents and an off-spring), and co-twin, half-sib or other models that employ various combinations of family members (Nance, 1993). Participants for many of these study models can be recruited from population surveys if appropriate disease or phenotype information is available. It is not the intent of this paper to review these methods; each must be performed with care and has incumbent problems in conduct, analysis, and interpretation.

Thus, there are many potential applications for population studies in the discovery and characterization of genes related to diseases and age-related change. In the past, population studies were more effectively employed to verify if gene-disease associations found in pedigrees through the study of nuclear families were relevant to representative population groups, and to examine the clinical and public health implications of the associations. Important recent examples include studies where particular genes have been shown to have direct relevance to the risk of common disabling conditions of older persons in the community, such as the relation of apolipoprotein E alleles to Alzheimer's dementia (Saunders et al., 1993) and HPC alleles to the occurrence of prostate cancer (Xu et al., 1998). However, technological and analytical advances have given new importance to gene discovery studies in defined populations. It has been the history of gene-disease searches that many valid associations found within individual, high-occurrence families often are not relevant to many other families or to the large number of persons with that condition in the community. This does not diminish the importance of the findings, particularly for addressing the clinical and genetic concerns of certain high-risk pedigrees or for understanding the pathogenesis of the disease, but the further application to population studies may be limited.

Gene-Environment Interaction

Since many population surveys have collected a variety of environmental data on individuals or environments, there are opportunities to use this information in association with genetic bioindicators. Some examples include the search for genetic susceptibility to conditions such as lung cancer associated with cigarette smoking (Shields, 1999), the demonstration of genetically based interindividual differences in the metabolism of environmental toxicants (Guengerich et al., 1999), and the demonstration of the genetic role in the regulation and clinical presentation of environmentally acquired infections (Garcia et al., 1999). Case-control methodology has been used to address the genetic susceptibility to conditions where environmental exposures play a major role (Brennan, 1999). Community-based behavioral and psychiatric studies have profitably evaluated genetic and environmental effects on various mental illnesses (McGuffin and Martin, 1999).

Public Health and Clinical Applications of Genetically Characterized Populations

Determining the genetic characteristics of defined populations can have immediate and important clinical or public health implications. Such information is critical for planning and locating genetic screening and counseling programs, such as for neonatal metabolic disorders or conditions common among older persons. Characterization of gene frequencies by age, gender, ethnicity, or other factors will allow more efficiently targeted screening. As genes for disease or dysfunction susceptibility within individuals are identified, clinical prevention programs (Coughlin, 1999) can be invoked with greater intensity, or various environmental exposures can be more rigorously avoided. Knowing the distribution of relevant gene markers in populations can improve disease diagnosis and prognosis. In the future it may be possible to use the information obtained for targeting various local populations or individual families for disease prevention or treatment through gene therapy itself (Collins, 1999).

THE LOGISTICS OF SPECIMEN COLLECTION IN POPULATION SURVEYS

There are many issues involved in specimen collection in population surveys, from respondents' willingness and ability to participate to the handling and biological determinations of materials collected. All of these have to be considered when approaching populations; each potential specimen and bioindicator will have its own set of logistical challenges and methodological difficulties. The following are some of the major considerations.

The Impact of Specimen Collection on Survey Participation

There is very little formally published information or synthesis on how specimen collection affects participation rates. In general, there is some decrement in specimen acquisition rates among respondents to interview surveys, even when specimens are collected at a separate session. Some interviewees may be less willing to participate, even if prior detailed study explanations and informed consent procedures suggest minimum risk and high potential scientific payoff. This reticence may be based on unlikely fears (e.g., revealing fatal illnesses, surreptitious testing for the Human Immunodeficiency Virus) or on prior untoward experiences in survey or clinical settings (e.g., fainting after venipuncture). Such situations should be anticipated as much as possible and avoided by appropriate staff training and pretesting of presentation techniques to potential respondents. The overriding issue is whether specimen collection imperils long-term participation rates in panel (cohort) studies, where further waves of data collection are planned and long-term participation is paramount. More documentation and field experiments need to be performed in order to acquire and document more experience with this issue, particularly among older persons.

Sites of Specimen Collection

An important early logistical consideration is to determine where biological specimens should be collected. Experience dictates that blood and urine specimens can reliably be obtained in the home, although in the latter case explicit participant instruction and monitoring is necessary. Hair clippings, skin scrapings, cheek swabs, and washes/rinses for genetic analysis can usually be obtained without difficulty in the home. Successful self-collection of DNA from oral epithelial cells has been reported (Harty et al., 2000). However, there are other types of specimens that require more equipment or a medical setting to acquire, such as semen specimens, skin or adipose tissue biopsies, multiple blood specimens over many hours, or specimens collected in association with complex physiological testing. Here, transporting participants to facilities structured to deal with complex specimen issues may be necessary. In certain circumstances, an additional option for venipuncture is to send a voucher, instructions, and a mailing container to participants and request that blood be drawn by their local physician, clinic, or laboratory.

Irrespective of where the specimens are collected, close attention to rigorous protocols are needed to maximize the scientific yield. Table 10-2 highlights the problems that may occur at almost any stage of the acquisition and determination process. Specimen acquisition from older populations may pose special problems. Older persons may be living in institutional or other long-term care settings or in guarded residential environments, and may not be easily available for study. Even among community-dwelling elders, cognitive impairment or the absence of assistance and supervision may lead to failures in specimen collection protocols at home. Older persons may not tolerate extracting the amounts of blood that would be tolerated in younger participants, or venipuncture may be more complex due to poor vein anatomy or access, perhaps partly due to prior intensive medical care. Frequent incontinence may make urine collection procedures more difficult. The extent of these and related problems may be anticipated by appropriate pretesting procedures.

TABLE 10-2 Sources of Problems in the Acquisition of Bioindicator
Specimens in Field Studies

Potential Problem Sources	Examples
Survey respondent	Failure/inability to attend study site Failure to follow instructions (e.g., fasting) Concerns about disposition of specimens
Failure of the collection apparatus	Equipment failure or damage in transportation Loss of electrical power Technician absence
Errors in specimen collection	Failure to follow specific protocols Mislabeling of containers Breakage, loss, or mishandling of specimens
Mishandling in specimen transport	Failure to get specimen to laboratory in a timely manner Loss or breakage of containers Microbial contamination or failure to store at correct temperature
Long-term specimen storage	Loss, breakage, or contamination of specimens Inadequate labeling/transcription
Laboratory determinations	Lack of appropriate procedures Inadequate quality control

Specimen Transport and Storage

As more sophisticated bioindicators have been applied to population surveys, the logistics of specimen acquisition has similarly become more challenging. Various bioindicators have different levels of chemical stability after removal from the body and require different processing techniques; this must be known in advance. Some specimens require immediate icing or freezing for transport to the laboratory (a type of "cold chain") for long-term storage or processing; others are relatively stable and can be handled with less rigor. Cells that will be kept alive in culture will require immediate special-handling techniques.

These same issues pertain to long-term storage of specimens as well. Some molecules, such as serum immunoglobulins (e.g., antibodies to infectious agents), steroid hormones (e.g., estrogen or testosterone), and DNA, are relatively stable and can be profitably processed and stored (frozen) with relatively little loss or degradation. The same is true for

DNA adducts, DNA to which environmental chemicals are bound, and for other environmental, elemental chemicals, such as heavy metals. Other molecules, however, such as certain enzymes, lipids, or fatty acids or small peptides (proteins) may require precise and rapid processing; long-term storage may not be feasible. If the bioindicators are to include complex cell functions, such as for the study of gene function, living cells such as lymphocytes must be rapidly isolated and placed in cell cultures. Cells obtained for cytogenetic studies will also require rapid processing. It is also possible to "immortalize" and store, for future study, living cells that are necessary for assessment of gene function, but fastidious procedures and protocol adherence are necessary. Specimen processing and storage issues are paramount and must be planned well in advance of fieldwork.

Investigators should also be alert to the challenges of long-term specimen storage. One issue is that the long-term preservation of many chemicals is not always known and must be determined by trial and error. This is particularly a problem with analyses that are not anticipated at the time of specimen collection. Additional problems may include lack of storage space or its requisite long-term funding to maintain the specimens, enhanced degradation of specimens from repeated freezing and thawing (usually avoidable by aliquoting a given specimen into multiple, small containers), and contamination of specimens due to chemicals in the storage containers. Ethical issues also exist with respect to long-term specimen ownership and competing scientific themes for specimen disposition, particularly after the main activities of the study have been completed.

Alternative Sources for Genetic Bioindicators

In some circumstances, such as when a potentially informative individual is deceased or otherwise not available for genetic study, it may be possible to acquire genetic or other bioindicator specimens from alternative sources. As noted by Martin and Hu in this volume, stored tissue specimens on which genetic or other determinations can be performed may be archived in hospitals or pathology laboratories. Such sources may include surgical and autopsy specimens, cytology specimens (e.g., Pap smears), and other blood specimens obtained for hematological or chemical determinations. Unfortunately, these specimens are not being retained as long as might be desired for investigational purposes. In some cases, there may be additional genetic specimen sources other than from routine clinical care, if the scientific needs are compelling. For example, blood may have been archived in certain occupational settings, such as where employees may be exposed to infectious agents, and it is routinely collected from those serving in military careers. It is also possible to extract analyzable DNA from some serum specimens (Goessl, 2000), even if no cellular material is available. Some research institutions maintain long-term tissue archives for specific organs or conditions, often related to brain disease or cancer. An individual may have stored ova or semen that could be retrieved and analyzed. However, one must be alert to selection bias in the acquisition of specimens from tissue banks (Winn and Gunter, 1993), possibly leading to spurious analytical results. In summary, there may be special opportunities to enhance specimen acquisition if appropriate investigational and ethical hurdles can be overcome.

What Is the Optimal Age for Genetic Specimen Acquisition?

This is not always clear, but there is a reasonable argument for collecting genetic information on pedigree members before the senium. Often in human aging studies the phenotype is longevity, and the shorter-lived members (i.e., the control group) are by definition not available when the oldest-lived persons are studied. This is one justification for routine collection of DNA at the start of panel studies at an age when most participants are still available for study.

CONCLUSION

Substantial opportunities exist for important scientific contributions when specimen collection for genetic and environmental bioindicators is applied to existing or planned representative population surveys originally intended for behavioral, social, or economic purposes. In some instances, questions of import can be answered only by this approach. Attention to study design and specimen collection, as well as the ethical dimensions of human participation, are critical areas. Partnering with geneticists, environmental scientists, epidemiologists, and molecular biologists should be highly productive.

REFERENCES

Anonymous
    2000   Offbeat twins. *Science* 288:1735.
Arking, R.
    1998   *Biology of Aging*. Second Edition. Sinauer Associates, Inc.
Brennan, P.
    1999   Design and analysis issues in case-control studies addressing genetic susceptibility. *IARC Scientific Publications* (Lyon) 148:123-132.
Caporaso, N., N. Rothman, and S. Wacholder
    1999   Case-control studies of common alleles and environmental factors. *Monographs of the National Cancer Institute* 26:25-30.
Carretero, O.A., and S. Oparil
    2000   Essential hypertension. Part I: Definition and etiology. *Circulation* 101:329-335.

Chagnon, P., M. Gee, M. Filion, Y. Robitaille, M. Belouchi, and D. Gauvreau
    1999   Phylogenetic analysis of the mitochondrial genome indicates significant differences between patients with Alzheimer's disease and controls in a French-Canadian founder population. *American Journal of Human Genetics* 85:20-30.
Collins, F.S.
    1999   Shattuck Lecture: Medical and societal consequences of the Human Genome Project. *New England Journal of Medicine* 341:28-37.
Coughlin, S.S.
    1999   The intersection of genetics, public health, and preventive medicine. *American Journal of Preventive Medicine* 16(2):89-90.
de Boer, J., and J.H. Hoeijmakers
    2000   Nucleotide excision repair and human syndromes. *Carcinogenesis* 21(3):453-460.
deBraekeleer, M., J. Daigneault, C. Allard, F. Simard, and G. Aubin
    1996   Genealogy and geographical distribution of CFTR mutations in Saguenay Lac-Saint-Jean (Quebec, Canada). *Annals of Human Biology* 23:345-352.
Ellsworth, D.L., and T. Manolio
    1999   The emerging importance of genetics in epidemiological research II. Issues in study design and gene mapping. *Annals of Epidemiology* 9:75-90.
Enserink, M.
    2000   Start-up claims piece of Iceland's gene pie. *Science* 287:951.
Epperson, B.K.
    1998   Gene genealogies in geographically structured populations. *Genetics* 86:156-161.
Gaimard, M., I. Dilumbu, P. Louame, G. Bellis, A. Assouan, and A. Chaventre
    1998   Registers and follow-up methods of populations in a public health survey: The example of the village Glanle in Ivory Coast. *Collegium Anthropologicum* 22:63-75.
Garcia, A., L. Abel, M. Cot, P. Richard, S. Ranque, J. Feingold, F. Demenais, M. Boussinesq, and J.P. Chippaux
    1999   Genetic epidemiology of host predisposition to microfilaraemia in human loiasis. *Tropical Medicine and International Health* 4:565-574.
Goessl, C.
    2000   Laser-fluorescence microsatellite analysis and new results in microsatellite analysis of plasma/serum DNA of cancer patients. *Annals of the New York Academy of Sciences* 906:63-66.
Goldman, L., G.H. Mudge Jr., and E.F. Cook
    1983   The changing "natural history" of symptomatic coronary artery disease: Basis versus bias. *American Journal of Cardiology* 51(3):449-454.
Gorin, M.B., J.C. Breitner, P.T. De Jong, G.S. Hageman, C.C. Klaver, M.H. Kuehn, and J.M. Seddon
    1999   The genetics of age-related macular degeneration. *Molecular Vision* 5:29.
Goring, H.H., and J.D. Terwilliger
    2000   Linkage analysis in the presence of errors IV: Joint pseudomarker analysis of linkage and/or linkage disequilibrium on a mixture of pedigrees and singletons when the mode of inheritance cannot be accurately specified. *American Journal of Human Genetics* 66:1310-1327.
Guengerich, F.P., A. Parikh, R.J. Turesky, and P.D. Josephy
    1999   Inter-individual differences in the metabolism of environmental toxicants: Cytochrome P450 1A2 as a prototype. *Mutation Research* 428:115-124.
Harty, L.C., P.G. Shields, D.M. Winn, N.E. Caporaso, and R.B. Hayes
    2000   Self-collection of oral epithelial cells under instruction from epidemiological interviewers. *American Journal of Epidemiology* 151:199-205.

Hernandez-Boussard, T., R. Montesano, and P. Hainaut
    1999   Analysis of somatic mutations of the p53 gene in human cancers: A tool to gener-
            ate hypotheses about the natural history of cancer. *IARC Scientific Publications*
            (Lyon) 146:43-53.
Heston, L.L.
    1966   Psychiatric disorders in foster home reared children of schizophrenic mothers.
            British Journal of Psychiatry 112:819-825.
Holliday, R.
    1998   Causes of aging. *Annals of the New York Academy of Sciences* 854:61-71.
Hussey, J.M., and I.T. Elo
    1997   Cause-specific mortality among older African-Americans: Correlates and conse-
            quences of age misreporting. *Social Biology* 44(3-4):227-246.
Kukull, W.A., and E.B. Larson
    1989   Distinguishing Alzheimer's disease from other dementias. Questionnaire re-
            sponses of close relatives and autopsy results. *Journal of the American Geriatrics
            Society* 37:521-527.
Langston, J.W.
    1998   Epidemiology versus genetics in Parkinson's disease: Progress is solving the age-
            old debate. *Annals of Neurology* 44(Suppl 1):S45-52.
Lee, C.K., R.G. Klopp, R. Weindruch, and T.A. Prolla
    1999   Gene expression profile of aging and its retardation by caloric restriction. *Science*
            285(5432):1390-1393.
McGuffin, P., and N. Martin
    1999   Science, medicine and the future: Behavior and genes. *British Medical Journal*
            319:37-40.
McKinley, A.G., S.E. Russell, R.A. Spence, W. Odling-Smee, and N.C. Nevin
    1996   Hereditary breast cancer in Northern Ireland. *Ulster Medical Journal* 65(2):113-117.
Moll, A.C., D.J. Kuik, L.M. Bouter, W. Den Otter, P.D. Bezemer, J.W. Koten, S.M. Imhof, B.P.
Kuyt, and K.E. Tan
    1997   Incidence and survival of retinoblastoma in The Netherlands: A register-based
            study 1962-1995. *British Journal of Ophthalmology* 81:559-562.
Nance, W.E.
    1993   1992 American Society of Human Genetics presidential address: Back to the fu-
            ture. *American Journal of Human Genetics* 53:6-15.
Ober, C., N.J. Cox, M. Abney, A. Di Rienzo, E.S. Lander, B. Changyaleket, H. Gidley, B. Kurtz,
J. Lee, M. Nance, A. Pettersson, J. Prescott, A. Richardson, E. Schlenker, E. Summerhill, and
S. Willadsen
    1998   Genome-wide search for asthma susceptability loci in a founder population. *Hu-
            man Molecular Genetics* 7:1393-1398.
Olynyk, J.K., D.J. Cullen, S. Aquilia, E. Rossi, L. Summerville, and L.W. Powell
    1999   A population-based study of the clinical expression of the hemochromatosis gene.
            New England Journal of Medicine 341:718-724.
Plomin, R., and J.C. DeFries
    1998   The genetics of cognitive abilities and disabilities. *Scientific American* 278:62-69.
Rannala, B.
    1997   On the genealogy of a rare allele. *Theoretical Population Biology* 52:216-223.
Romitti, P.A., T.L. Burns, and J.C. Murray
    1997   Maternal interview reports of family history of birth defects: Evaluation from a
            population-based case-control study of orofacial clefts. *Americal Journal of Medical
            Genetics* 72:422-429.

Saunders, A.M., W.H. Strittmatter, D. Schmechel, et al.
  1993 Association of the apolipoprotein E allele E4 with late-onset familial and sporadic Alzheimer's disease. *Neurology* 43:1467-1472.
Shay, J.W.
  1997 Telomerase in human development and cancer. *Journal of Cellular Physiology* 173(2):266-270.
Shields, P.G.
  1999 Molecular epidemiology of lung cancer. *Annals of Oncology* 10 (Suppl 5):S7-S11.
Thomas, A., L. Cannon-Albright, A. Bansal, and M.H. Skolnick
  1999 Familial associations between cancer sites. *Computers & Biomedical Research* 32(6):517-529.
Vijg, J.
  2000 Somatic mutations and aging: A re-evaluation. *Mutation Research* 447(1):117-135.
Wallace, R.B.
  1997 The potential of population surveys for genetic studies. Pp. 234-244 in *Between Zeus and the Salmon: The Biodemography of Longevity*, K.W. Wachter and C.E. Finch, eds. Washington, DC: National Academy Press.
Winn, D.M., E.W. Gunter
  1993 Biological specimen banks: A resource for molecular epidemiologic studies. Pp. 217-234 in *Molecular Epidemiology: Principles and Practices*, P.A. Schulte and F.P. Perera, eds. New York: Academic Press.
Xu, J., D. Meyers, D. Freije, et al.
  1998 Evidence for a prostate cancer susceptibility locus on the X chromosome. *Nature Genetics* 20(2):175-179.

11

Stretching Social Surveys to Include Bioindicators: Possibilities for the Health and Retirement Study, Experience from the Taiwan Study of the Elderly

Maxine Weinstein and Robert J. Willis

L arge-scale surveys have become an integral part of the landscape of social science research. They have evolved into highly complex, multidimensional instruments that have been used to document and explore virtually every aspect of an individual's life and, more recently, how an individual's life is embedded in the networks and structures that constitute our larger social environment. The study of aging, although a relative latecomer to survey research, is no exception to this trend. A recent summary (Wallace, 1997) of large-scale population studies showed ten such surveys in the United States sponsored by the National Institute on Aging (NIA) alone.

An important advantage of these surveys is that we are able to examine, with adequate statistical power, questions and hypotheses about potential pathways that tie a wide variety of outcomes with life experiences. The surveys allow us to target representative populations; to generalize findings based on insights from qualitative, local, or small, indepth investigations; and to replicate the results across time and across cultural settings. In all, large-scale surveys have been a powerful tool for social scientists.

In particular, the data collected in these surveys have enabled social scientists to contribute importantly to identifying, documenting, and understanding the reciprocal links between health and the social and economic environment. Of course, the very success of these surveys in investigating a wide spectrum of health-related issues makes them a tempting vehicle for bearing information that would supplement the customary self-reported data. One way that the surveys have been expanded is by linking them to administrative data such as Social Security earnings and benefits, Medicare claims records, and the National Death Index. The potential for further expanding survey machinery to collect additional health-related information from examinations and biological specimens (i.e., "bioindicators" or "biomarkers") is large, but it needs to be evaluated carefully.

This paper is motivated by the need for that evaluation. We ground our discussion in two studies that share important characteristics: The Health and Retirement Study (HRS) and the Taiwan Study of the Elderly. Both are longitudinal, large-scale, nationally representative surveys of the elderly that comprise extensive questionnaires. The HRS was developed specifically in order to study the economics and demography of aging. Recent growth in knowledge about the biology of aging and the development of mechanisms that allow biological markers to be collected as part of large-scale surveys have stimulated discussion about whether the HRS should be expanded to include the collection of biological data. The Taiwan Study offers a concrete example of the scientific purposes and the practical costs and benefits associated with collecting biomarkers within such a social survey context.

The costs—financial and other—of collecting biological data within the context of the HRS are potentially high. These costs may include: compromising cooperation of participants by imposing excessive burdens; reducing sample size and representativeness; uncertain or unforeseen implications of data collected from biological materials; problematic ethical considerations; and long-term effects on the design of the HRS, which proposes to follow its participants until death. Balanced against these potential costs is a wide range of benefits. This chapter begins with a brief description of the two studies that anchor our discussion, and then discusses some of the benefits and costs. We end by proposing some considerations regarding future directions for these kinds of activities.

SURVEY OVERVIEWS

The HRS is conducted under a cooperative agreement between the NIA and the Institute for Social Research at the University of Michigan. The longitudinal study began in 1992 with a survey of 12,600 persons born between 1931 and 1941 who were 51-61 years of age, plus their spouses (Juster and Suzman, 1995). It was joined in 1993 by a companion study, Assets and Health Dynamics Among the Oldest Old (AHEAD), consisting of 8,200 persons born before 1924 who were aged 70 and over and their spouses (see Soldo et al., 1997). Baseline response for the two surveys was 81.7 percent and 80.4 percent, respectively; reinterview percentages have been in the mid-90s. In 1998, the HRS added cohorts of individuals born in 1942-1947 and 1924-1930 who were entering their 50s and their 70s, respectively, creating a sample of over 22,000 persons who are representative of the entire U.S. population over age 50 (see Willis, 1999). Continued funding has been approved to survey three more waves of these cohorts in 2000, 2002, and 2004, and in 2004, to add a cohort of "Early Baby Boomers," born in 1947-1953, who will be entering their 50s. Given the importance of the baby boom cohorts to public policy issues in an aging society, it is likely that the study will be continued for at least another three waves in 2006, 2008 and 2010. Thus, beginning in 1998, the HRS has become a "steady state" sample which, in cross section, is representative of the entire U.S. population over age 50 and which follows respondents longitudinally until they die. While it represents the noninstitutionalized population at baseline, the HRS follows respondents longitudinally into nursing homes or other institutional settings.

From its inception, the HRS was designed to provide rich longitudinal data for the community of scientific and policy researchers who study the health, economics, and demography of aging. The design and execution of the survey has involved the active participation of a large number of scientists from a broad array of disciplines including economics, sociology, demography, psychology, and medicine from institutions in all parts of the United States. An important motivation for the HRS is the concern about the implications of the aging American population in terms of the health and economic well-being of its citizens during the latter part of life. A second motivation is a growing concern about the economic well-being of those supporting older family members through family transfers or through public programs such as Social Security, Medicare, and Medicaid. Increasingly, scientific research on aging, health, and retirement has turned to dynamic and life cycle models to address these policy concerns.

To support these goals, the HRS collects detailed information in several domains including economic status, physical and mental health, utilization of health services, health insurance coverage, and family structure and transfer behavior. Following the death of a respondent, a proxy interview is obtained to collect information about health, the utilization of medical care and decision-making at the end of life, and about the disposition of the decedent's assets. In addition to survey data, the HRS is linked to several bodies of administrative data including Social Security earnings and benefit histories, Medicare cost and diagnoses, employer pension plan characteristics, and the National Death Index. Altogether, these longitudinal data provide a resource for researchers to understand the trajectories of the economic, health, and family status of Americans over age 50, and to test theories and estimate the parameters of dynamic behavioral models. By providing data in several domains typically studied by separate disciplines, the HRS facilitates interdisciplinary research and encourages the creation of cross-cutting conceptual frameworks.

Our second reference is the Study of Health and Living Status of the Elderly in Taiwan. This study was initiated by the Taiwan Provincial Institute of Family Planning (now the National Institute of Family Planning, Department of Health) in collaboration with the University of Michigan. The first survey in 1989 comprised about 4,000 individuals age 60 and above (Chang and Hermalin, 1989). An important facet of the survey is that, with the exception of a small indigenous population, it represents the entire elderly population of the country. In contrast, most other surveys of the elderly draw their samples from the noninstitutionalized population, a practice that is likely to bias estimates of illness as well as of the association between social factors and health.[1] A combination of persistent callbacks and traces of those who moved resulted in a response rate of nearly 92 percent (Chang and Hermalin, 1989). The survey contained eight modules that solicited a wide range of information about the respondents. They comprised data on: (1) marital history and other demographic characteristics; (2) household roster, social and economic networks and exchanges; (3) health, health care utilization and behaviors; (4) occupational/employment history; (5) activities and general attitudes; (6) residential history; (7) economic and financial well-being; and (8) emotional and instrumental support.

Since 1989, follow-up interviews have been conducted in 1991, 1993, 1995, 1996, and 1999. The 1993 survey also included interviews with both resident and nonresident children, and the coresident daughter-in-law (if present). Like the HRS, in 1996 the study "refreshed" the sample from younger ages, adding a sample of "near-elderly" persons between ages 50 and 66, so as to provide a sample of persons age 50 and above. Also, like the HRS, proxy interviews are carried out for decedents, and information about the death is obtained from the household and death registration systems. In early 1998, biological markers (and self-reported information based on a questionnaire) were collected from a pilot study of just over 100 of the original 1989 respondents. Fieldwork is slated to begin in March 2000 for the collection of biological markers, and face-to-face interviews for demographic and health updates from 1,000 respondents drawn from the refreshed sample.

A wide variety of bioindicators are potentially available for an expansion of social surveys. In the Taiwan study, the protocol for the 1998 collection of biological markers comprised several segments including:

---

[1]Persons in institutionalized settings are likely to be less healthy than the noninstitutionalized population. Their omission is therefore likely to result in an underestimate of the burden of disease.

(1) blood specimens in hospital; (2) a 12-hour urine specimen at the respondent's home; and (3) a spot urine in hospital. In addition, (4) a physical exam (the approximate equivalent of the National Heath Insurance exam); and (5) anthropometric measurements were conducted in hospital. The blood specimens were used to provide routine biochemistry and blood tests, measures of cholesterol, DHEAS, glycosylated hemoglobin, and material for APOE genotyping. The 12-hour urine specimen provided estimates of cortisol, epinephrine, and norepinephrine.

The costs—social, logistical, and financial—of collecting bioindicators can be high. The need, therefore, to consider carefully the underlying motivating hypotheses and questions is particularly pronounced in deciding whether to include bioindicators, and if so, which ones are most crucial. What, then, can we learn from adding bioindicators to social surveys and how does that affect our choice?

WHAT CAN WE LEARN FROM BIOINDICATORS IN SOCIAL SURVEYS?

The addition of biological markers to self-reported data expands the range and depth of research questions that can be addressed. In this paper we discuss the following: obtaining population-representative data from nonclinical samples; calibrating self-reports with other measures of health and disease; and explicating pathways and elaborating the causal linkages between social environment and health. Finally, although our focus is on mid-level biological indicators, we will suggest some considerations related to linking genetic markers with survey materials.

Obtaining Population-Representative Data from Nonclinical Samples

An important contribution of the combination of bioindicators with data from social surveys is the documentation of function in nonclinical populations. Estimates of prevalence based on clinical populations—and even on some of the more customary epidemiological field studies—depend on highly selected samples, difficult to control and difficult to generalize to the entire population. Diagnosis of an illness depends upon numerous factors. It is affected by the probability that a person recognizes and acknowledges an "aberrant" status; by the likelihood that he will seek treatment; and by the location at which treatment is sought, the resources available for treatment, and compliance to the treatment protocol. We know that there is heterogeneity in all of these factors. Women, for example, are more likely to seek medical attention than men, especially for certain kinds of illness (Kroenke and Mangelsdorf, 1989; Cohen and Rodriguez, 1995; Walling et al., 1994; Russell et al., 1992). Examination procedures, test protocols, and guidelines for the administration of protocols may depend on where the patient presents (Aaron et al., 1996). And access to care and the quality of care are tied to social and financial resources. Estimates of the prevalence of a disorder and of the experience and attributes that characterize those whom a disease affects are therefore intertwined with differential rates of care-seeking behaviors and modes of therapy. Heterogeneity in these behaviors across sex, ethnicity, and position in social orderings can bias assessment of risk and of the burden of disease. The advantage of the social survey machinery is clear: a large, well-drawn sample allows us to draw inferences about population parameters; it allows comparisons within population subgroups and across time and place.

While data from both the HRS and the Taiwan Study can be examined cross-sectionally, the advantages of their longitudinal design are especially compelling. In particular, a longitudinal design can provide information on population-representative disease trajectories. A longitudinal design allows one to track the emergence of disease, to identify the important correlates of differences in disease trajectories, and to explore how differences in outcomes are related to differences in earlier experiences and behaviors. For example, longitudinal data would allow one to focus on people who make a transition between rounds. Such persons could be screened for characteristics that might have identified them earlier as being at elevated risk for illness. Longitudinal data would also make it possible to follow outcomes relative to behavioral responses.

Another important contribution of the longitudinal design is the documentation of patterns of biological markers across both an individual's life span and across the population. How, for example, do biological markers themselves change as a function of change in the environment? In the context of the HRS, one could also ask questions about the degree to which individual and family choices about medical care, purchase of insurance, or asset accumulation or "decumulation" interact with biological indicators. As scientific knowledge about the relationships among biological, health, and socioeconomic spheres expands, it may also become possible to gauge the potential for behavioral responses in these and other domains by households, insurance companies, health providers, and government policymakers. Of course, troublesome ethical and confidentiality issues concerning HRS respondents arise precisely because of these potential interactions and behavioral responses.

Even in the cross-section, however, the data can be valuable. For example, increasingly, we have come to understand that there is remarkable diversity across populations in biological parameters (Weiss,1998a; Campbell and Wood, 1994). Systematic cross-cultural studies may reveal differentials that are of substantive interest. Results from the Taiwan data, for example, can be compared with analogous U.S. data from the MacArthur Study of Successful Aging. The MacArthur sample was drawn from participants in three Established Populations for the Epidemiologic Study of the Elderly. The three communities were in the Eastern United States. The participants responded to a 90-minute interview in which health status was assessed, and they provided blood specimens and 12-hour overnight urine specimens (Berkman et al., 1993; Seeman et al., 1997). The participants ranged in age from 70 to 79 years old (the Taiwan participants were 67 to 94). Results for a number of parameters differ between the U.S. and Taiwanese elderly. Blood pressure readings were higher among the Taiwanese than the U.S. sample. Unlike in the United States, women in Taiwan had slightly higher readings than men. The waist/hip ratio among Taiwanese men was lower than their U.S. counterparts, but higher among Taiwanese women than among U.S. women. The ratio of total to HDL cholesterol for both Taiwanese men and women was lower than in the United States, but the sex differential was reversed: in Taiwan, the ratio was higher for women than for men. Glycosylated hemoglobin was lower in Taiwan than in the United States among both men and women. Average levels of DHEAS were higher for both men and women in Taiwan than in the United States, and HDL cholesterol—at least among men—was also higher. On average, using an invariant scale, these differences put the Taiwanese elderly at higher risk than the Americans of health disorders related to hypertension, and at lower risk (despite the slightly higher average age of the Taiwan sample) of illness related to indicators of cholesterol (ratio of total to HDL), the waist/hip ratio, glycosylated hemoglobin, and DHEAS (Goldman et al., 1999). But how these differentials change over time, what their environmental and behavioral correlates are, and how they are connected to differentials in health outcomes are questions that can be addressed only by the use of longitudinal data.

Calibrating Self-Reports with Other Measures of Health and Disease

The use of self-reported health-related information from surveys has the advantage—relative to clinical or field studies—of data from a representative sample of the population, but self-reported data (like other sources) are subject to a variety of errors. Evaluations of the quality of health-related data that have been collected through self-reported (or proxy) responses to survey questions have been performed in various ways, including comparisons with medical records and with physical exams (Beckett et al., 2000; Haapanen et al., 1997; Edwards et al., 1996; Strauss and Thomas, 1996; Turner et al., 1997). The addition of biological indicators to survey machinery provides another powerful, direct way to assess and calibrate self-reported data for certain kinds of information.

Reliability over time of self-reported information from health interview surveys may be inadequate for many purposes. A recent study by Beckett and her colleagues (2000), for example, shows that the consistency of reports of diabetes across surveys taken between 1989 and 1996 as part of the Taiwan Study of the Elderly averaged just over 80 percent. In the United States, the analogous figure from the National Health and Nutrition Examination Survey (NHANES) (1971/1975-1982/1984) was 78 percent. Reports of hypertension in Taiwan were even less consistent (averaging 73 percent), although the corresponding figure for the United States was higher—86 percent.

Estimates of validity, which are even bleaker than the estimates of reliability, serve to underscore the need for calibration. For example, fewer than half of the respondents who were identified as hypertensive based on (objective) blood pressure readings in the NHANES-I reported the condition in the interview (Beckett et al., 2000). In Taiwan, the figures for high blood pressure are equally troubling. Only two-thirds of the participants in the 1998 biological marker study who were identified as having at least moderately high blood pressure (>160 mgHg) based on the in-hospital measurement reported having the condition in the concurrent health interview; only 60 percent reported it at the time of the 1996 interview. These estimates from Taiwan are are not inconsistent with results from other studies. In Pakistan, for example, based on clinical evaluations that were conducted as part of the National Health Survey of Pakistan, 80 percent of men who were clinically diagnosed as hypertensive were *unaware* of the condition; the corresponding figure for women was 60 percent (Pappas, 2000).

Whether these discrepancies arise from the respondents' lack of awareness of the condition, failure to recall information provided by their physicians, or an unwillingness to report the condition, they can have an important impact on health, on estimates of the burden of disease, and on health policy.

Diabetes is a particularly important example because so many aspects of the condition are amenable to behavioral management. The earlier the diagnosis, the better the opportunities for behavioral modifications that can ameliorate the disease. The ability to screen for the condition in a representative and longitudinal study provides an important vehicle for its identification and remediation. The results from Taiwan illustrate this point. In 1998, only 56 percent of the participants with elevated glucose levels reported having diabetes to the examining physician as part of the disease history that was collected at the same time as the biomarkers. Only 48 percent reported the condition at the time of the 1996 interview.

A second important example, particularly among the elderly, relates to cognitive function. Currently, the HRS is considering a proposal to conduct a clinical assessment of dementia on a subset of respondents. A syndrome with several underlying causes and rapidly increasing incidence rates at older ages, dementia is projected to become an increasingly important burden to families and the public as rates of competing causes of death fall and more people survive to advanced ages. The HRS has the potential to become a valuable source of information on the economic and social burden of dementia for a nationally representative population. It provides detailed longitudinal information from the respondent or a proxy on their assets, income and health care utilization and costs, income and asset transfers between respondents and their children, assessments of informal and formal care, measures of cognitive functioning, and measures of basic and instrumental activities of daily living (ADLs/IADLs).

At the present time, however, the HRS is limited by the lack of a clinical diagnosis of dementia. Such a diagnosis would allow more precise cost estimates as well as additional epidemiological analyses. In response to this need, and with the advice of experts on the diagnosis and economic impact of dementia, the HRS is developing a supplementary proposal to conduct in-home clinical assessments of the dementia status and severity of a stratified random sample of 500-700 respondents, possibly with longitudinal follow-up to clarify the diagnosis of those with ambiguous status. This supplementary project would provide a highly valuable body of data on the prevalence of dementia in a nationally representative sample, together with a rich array of information with which to study the dynamics over time of the burden of this disease on families and the public. If the clinical diagnosis proves to be sufficiently well correlated with survey measures of cognitive decline and disability or Medicare diagnoses, it may be possible for researchers to impute the dementia status of HRS respondents who are not assessed in the supplementary clinical protocol.

An additional benefit related to "calibration" is made possible by combining survey data with biological specimens. The combination would provide significant material relative to documenting and understanding characteristics of individuals who provide self-reports that differ from the objective measures. The data could offer insight into how those characteristics are related to differentials in reporting. For example, based on analyses of the consistency over time of self-reports alone, Beckett and her colleagues (2000) found that in the United States differentials were related to sex and to cognitive status (women and persons with better cognitive scores were likely to be more consistent reporters). In Taiwan, where information on the severity of the condition was also available, it proved to be an important predictor of consistency. Objective measures of function would provide data that would permit us to assess validity as well as consistency.

Explicating Pathways and Elaborating Causal Linkages Between Social Environment and Health

Health at any age, but especially among the elderly, embodies and reflects the accumulation of complex interactions among genetic endowment, developmental influences that affect gene expression, and life experience including environmental exposures. A large literature in sociology, economics, and epidemiology has been devoted to documenting and exploring the associations between the social environment and health outcomes; another area of intensive research has been the relation between challenge (i.e., stress-provoking experience) and health. Figure 11-1 provides a diagram of a highly simplified model of the theory that underlies

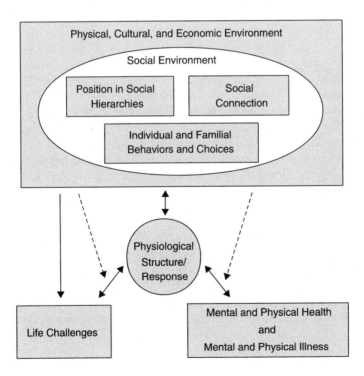

FIGURE 11-1 Linkages among the social environment, health, life challenge, and physiological response

much of this research. It illustrates two important points. First, it makes explicit the physiological interactions with health, challenge, and the social and economic environment that are so often treated as implicit or "unobservable" by most social research. Second, it shows individual biological response linked to collectives via membership in networks and social aggregates and to choices about lifestyle, work, consumption, medical care, and insurance that influence and are influenced by health at the individual and familial levels. The importance of group membership—its power to parsimoniously explain individual behaviors—has long been recognized by social scientists; indeed, acknowledgement of such emergent properties of groups and their effects is, arguably, a hallmark of sociological research. Likewise, the role of prices and incomes working through markets and public policies are emphasized in economic models of health. The inclusion in Figure 11-1 of physiological function makes explicit the linkage between (aggregate) social and economic processes and the biological processes of an individual.

Over many years, social scientists have examined—and they continue to explore—the relationships among health, position in social hierarchy, and social connection that are shown in Figure 11-1. It is now well established that there is a simple, direct, monotonic relation between socioeconomic status—measured across the multiple dimensions of income, education, and occupation—and both morbidity and mortality. These differentials have been found across the full range of these hierarchies (Adler et al., 1994; House et al., 1994; Marmot et al., 1996) and have been replicated across the life span, across sex, and across time and place. Similarly, a large literature dating back as far as the 1800's (Goldman et al.,1995; Hu and Goldman, 1990) has established large differences in mortality associated with marital status; married people live longer than those who are not. This result—that better social connection is conducive to reduced mortality—also holds for nonmarital ties: higher levels of social integration and having close relationships lead to better survival and health outcomes (Thoits, 1983, 1995).

The bottom portion of Figure 11-1 links exposure to challenge with health. Again, a large and growing literature has established an association between stressful experience and health. Exposure to challenge is associated with (both) heightened and depressed function of the autonomic nervous system, with cardiovascular health, with gastrointestinal stability, and to immune response. Specifically, stressful experience has been shown to be associated with asthma, diabetes, gastrointestinal disorders, myocardial infarction, cancer, viral infection, autoimmune diseases, depression, anxiety and other psychiatric disorders, task management, and memory (Lupien et al., 1994, 1995; Weiner, 1992; McEwen and Stellar, 1993).

The social environment affects exposure to challenge and it mediates the effects of challenge on health. Stressful experience is more frequent among those who are lower on SES ladders, and access to the resources that can potentially cushion its effects is more limited. A strong social network can reduce the physiological burden of challenge by affecting both the perception and interpretation of experience as stressful and by providing a safety net to lessen its effects.

Research from the HRS both confirms the well-known strong correlation between health and economic status and extends our understanding of it in several important ways. For example, the correlation between health and wealth, which can be measured for the first time in the HRS, is even stronger than the correlation between health and income. While many researchers have shown that socioeconomic status has a strong effect on health during earlier portions of the life cycle, studies using the HRS have shown that health has a powerful impact on the income and wealth of individuals over the age of 50. Although some of this influence operates through medical expenses, especially for the uninsured, a large portion of the effect operates through the impact of health on labor supply and earnings (see Smith, 1999).

Analogous work on the Taiwan survey data has established that, as expected, multiple dimensions of health are influenced by position in social hierarchies, by social networks, and by exposure to challenge. The probability, for example, of being unhealthy in 1996 (or having died by 1996) is significantly related to paternal socioeconomic status and to the respondent's education; to contact with friends, neighbors, and children; to participation in social activities; to exposure to chronic financial difficulties; and to having a spouse in poor health or a spouse who died in the recent past (Beckett et al., 1999). Based on the self-reported data, Yamazaki (2000) has shown that depression (measured using the CES-D, i.e., the Center for Epidemiological Studies Depression Scale) is significantly increased by exposure to challenges in the preceding three years and by recent daily strains, and significantly reduced by affectional exchanges (see also Ofstedal et al., 1999).

Apart from the HRS and the Taiwan Study, these associations have all been well documented by repeated, large-scale surveys. Still, little is known about how the social environment is linked to the physiological factors that influence well-being and mortality, so the biological pathways through which the social factors influence health remain largely unspecified. Similarly, while we are increasingly able to document the scale and dimensions of the (physiological) stress response, we have only a limited understanding of how that physiological response is affected by social factors. Without joint biological and social data, the linkages among challenge, social environment, and mental and physical health are certain to remain "in the black box."

Social/psychological studies are beginning to be used to unpack this black box in a number of ways. The Taiwan Study, for example, has been designed specifically to allow us to specify more completely the effects of challenge on biological markers; to relate self-reported physical decline and measures of cognitive function to those biological markers; to explore the consequences for health of cumulative challenge, social advantage, and adversity; and to explore sex-based differences in these factors.

We found that the biological markers collected in the Taiwan pilot study were consistent with results based on the self-reported data and that they offered some help toward progress in elaborating the pathways. Using an index developed by the MacArthur Study of Successful Aging (Seeman et al., 1994, 1995) to summarize biological function, Goldman and her colleagues (1999) found that the index was related in expected directions to self-reported measures of both physical and mental well-being and function, to education and sex, to economic and financial status and strains, and to important life events including the death of a spouse or of a child.

To date, the HRS has relied completely on self-reports of an individual's subjective health status, health conditions, and functional status, and on their self-reports of medical utilization, health insurance, and out-of-pocket costs. Only in the case of cognitive status and depression does the HRS provide measures that are similar in part to those that would be obtained in a medical setting. Sometime this year, the HRS will complete a linkage with the Medicare records of respondents age 65 and over which will give researchers access to physician's diagnoses and administrative records of care received.

Just as biological markers can be used to elaborate links among health and social, demographic, and economic factors, the addition of the markers, and more generally, of health-related information to social surveys can provide important, much-needed assistance in confirming and disclosing medical hypotheses. Insights into the relationship between health and disease might also emerge from examining the combination of self-reported data on health and biological markers associated with particular diseases. As Weiner (1992:91-92) persuasively argues, health and disease are not the same: "A patient may have a disease and either be in good health or be ill. Conversely, a patient may be in ill health without having a disease . . . . Most patients seeking medical care do not have diseases but are in ill health . . . Persons in ill health express their distress in bodily symptoms . . . yet the relationship of one to another manifestation of ill health . . . is largely unsolved."

The utility of large-scale surveys in identifying constellations of illnesses and their diagnostic markers and correlates, particularly in relation to health conditions linked to dysregulation of the central nervous system, is great. These conditions include fibromyalgia, chronic fatigue, irritable bowel syndrome, and migraine headaches, hypothesized to be caused by the interaction of both genetic and environmental factors resulting in changes in immune function (Clauw and Chrousos, 1997). The environmental factors include physical trauma (automobile accidents, for example), but also emotional stressors, particularly experiences which are perceived as inescapable, which are unpredictable, or which occur without emotional supports. The medical community has increasingly become sensitized to, and aware of, the importance of behavioral and social pathways affecting disease onset and severity. The collection of psychosocial data as part of a medical history has become more widespread. But most medical data are collected from nonrepresentative populations.

Although we are not advocating the transformation of social or demographic surveys into medical investigations, they clearly have the potential for informing such work. The extent of the contribution will almost certainly depend on disease prevalence and heterogeneity in its distribution across the population.

Linking Genetic Markers with Survey Materials

The rapid advance of knowledge in genetics and the relationship of genetics to health and behavior have led to suggestions that we collect biological specimens for genetic typing from respondents of population-representative surveys. In particular, the discovery of the link between late onset Alzheimer's disease and the APOE e4 genotype (Corder et al., 1993) provides an example of the potential predictive value of genetic information in the context of studies of older persons. Recently, the National Long Term Care Survey (NLTCS) used cheek swabs to obtain DNA samples from which information about a respondent's APOE genotype could be determined.

Wallace (1997) discusses the value of collecting genetic information in population surveys, including both pedigree data and specimens from which DNA may be obtained and coded, with an emphasis on the determination of genotype frequencies in well-defined populations. What has to date received less attention is the potential value of genetic information to population surveys, such as the HRS, whose major goals involve understanding determinants and consequences of behaviors related to work, earnings, saving, retirement; to heath status, health care expenses, and utilization; and to formal and informal caregiving and intergenerational transfers of time and money. The authors of the present chapter, who themselves have no special expertise on genetic issues, hope that broader discussion will begin to clarify this potential. Meanwhile, in this section we offer some speculation about some possible uses of genetic information in social surveys, particularly in the HRS, and some discussions of limitations and dangers in the use of the HRS for this purpose.

As described by Hermalin (1999), if genetic markers are modeled as part of an individual's physiological structure, they can provide controls for predisposing factors that affect more proximate mid-level markers of function as well as downstream health outcomes. This potential benefit of genetic information—i.e., its power in explicating the black box of Figure 11-1—may outweigh, or at least precede, its near-term potential for discovering genetic links to chronic disease. As discussed by Weiss (1998b), the situation with chronic disease differs from single locus disorders that are inherited following well-identified Mendelian rules. In general, we cannot expect to find relationships that are even as straightforward as the APOE links to cardiovascular and Alzheimer's disease. Variation across populations, difficulty in identifying a small enough area on the chromosome to search for disease-associated genes, and the problems inherent in identifying continuous outcomes with particular genes may limit finding the connections.

Our experience with APOE genotyping in Taiwan underscores some of these points. In our pilot study, of the 110 blood specimens which were typed, only 18 cases (16 percent) were e3/e4 and no one was identified as e4/e4. This distribution is consistent with other estimates of prevalence of the e4 allele in Chinese populations (see, for example, Ewbank in this volume), but with such a small sample and such a low prevalence we found no links between APOE type and an individual's health outcomes. Whether the upcoming larger sample of 1,000 will provide enough power to discriminate signal from noise remains to be seen.

Consideration of the HRS suggests additional concerns. As knowledge about the relationship between genetics and health increases, it is quite likely that private and public institutions and individual behavior will be affected in profound ways. One example concerns the availability, pricing, and demand for health insurance. If genetic information at birth is predictive of health conditions that occur later in life, will there emerge a market for "genetic insurance"? Providing insurance to populations with heterogeneous risks is already an important and difficult issue both at the theoretical level and for practical policy, in part because differences in information between those supplying and demanding health insurance lead to possibilities of adverse selection and instability of insurance markets (see Phelps, 1992, for a discussion). Moreover, the inequalities in access to or pricing of health insurance that may arise because of advances in genetic understanding are similar to those already confronted by individuals with differing pre-existing conditions. Collection of genetic information on HRS respondents might enable future researchers to study how individuals and families respond to new sources of perceived risk and attempt to deal with these risks through existing or newly created institutions. Other examples of potential research interest might be the role of genetics in the intergenerational transmission of health status or studies of the interaction between gene expression and measures of the economic and social environment over the life cycle.

These examples of research possibilities from the collection of genetic information in the HRS also serve to warn us about the limitations and dangers of the HRS as a vehicle for such data collections. The most obvious limitations of the HRS are (a) that data collection begins at a relatively late age, thus potentially obscuring and confounding important gene-environment-behavioral interactions that begin earlier in life,[2] and (b) that HRS respondents consist of genetically unrelated individuals (i.e., spouses), thus reducing a researcher's capacity to distinguish genetic from behavioral and environmental effects.

The collection of genetic information could also pose a serious threat to the value of the HRS. First, it is possible that HRS respondents would be frightened or alienated by requests for biological specimens. In this regard, the experience with the Taiwan survey effort reported in this paper provides some reassurance as does the experience in collecting cheek swabs in the NLTCS. Second, depending on the nature of the informed consent that would be used to collect specimens, there is considerable scope for contamination of the behavior of HRS respondents. For example, if we were to report back to a respondent that he had the APOE e4 genotype and explain what that implies for the probability of being stricken with Alzheimer's disease, the respondent might try to purchase long-term care insurance, increase asset accumulation to pay for care, or "spend down" assets to qualify for Medicaid, experience divorce, and so on. This scenario suggests that it is important to craft informed consent agreements in ways that consider the inevitable tension between the possibility of affecting the behavior of respondents with our overarching obligations to the participants. We do not see a simple solution to this problem.

POTENTIAL LIABILITIES OF ADDING BIOMARKERS

Admittedly, the costs of collecting biological markers are high. Some of the costs are simply financial: given current technology, many—

---

[2]Problems related to missing information from earlier life histories are not limited to genetic issues. We believe that many health conditions would be better understood with data on early exposure.

although not all—biological specimens and measurements are expensive to collect; they are expensive to assay. Other costs may be subtle and more difficult to assess.

Respondent Burden

For studies that have been driven primarily by questions related to the social sciences—whether demographic, economic, or sociological in nature—the additional burdens imposed on the participants by the collection of bioindicators may constitute an important potential concern. We see two particularly relevant aspects: first, whether agreement to participate in the bioindicator study itself is adequate; and second, whether participation in subsequent rounds of interviews is compromised.

For the HRS, it will be important to consider the impact on respondent cooperation before deciding to engage in the collection of clinical data or biological specimens. Indeed, if the HRS proceeds with the clinical dementia assessments described above, a careful study would be carried out to determine the effect of this additional effort on respondent cooperation in future waves of the survey. Similarly, any effort to collect biological specimens would first be piloted on a subset of respondents to determine effects on survey participation rates.

To date, the experience in Taiwan and elsewhere has been encouraging. In Taiwan, participation in the biomarker project was high. Most refusals to participate were unrelated to the collection procedures. Just under 72 percent of the targeted respondents completed the full protocol: they replied to a short survey that was administered by a public health nurse; they collected an overnight 12-hour urine specimen; they underwent a physical examination and provided a brief medical history in hospital; and they had blood drawn and provided a spot urine specimen in hospital. Another 23 percent of the targeted respondents could not be located or refused to participate. Of these nonparticipants, about a quarter were out of the country or out of reach of the hospital (temporarily located in another city, for example). More than a quarter had just recently completed a physical exam (either privately, or under the sponsorship of the National Health Insurance Program, which has made specific provisions for free examinations for the elderly). Only a small percentage (about ten percent) of the refusals were related to concerns about the procedures, the results, or the time commitment required for the protocol (Goldman et al., 1999). We also found that there was no negative effect of participation in the biomarker protocol on participation in the subsequent 1999 interview. Ninety-six percent of the (surviving) participants in the biomarker study responded to the 1999 interview, compared with a follow-up value of 92 percent for the entire population of survivors. That said, however, the

1998 collection of biomarkers was based on a subsample of the older respondents, that is, those who were age 69 and above. Our current fieldwork (due to begin in April 2000) will target people ages 53 and above. We recognize that recruitment of members of this younger cohort into a protocol that requires approximately two to three hours away from work may be more difficult than our experience with the older sample. The results from the elderly sample also lead one to suspect that another type of self-selection is operating: that the more highly motivated respondents agreed to participate in the bioindicator study. Whether this pattern is sustained when we examine a larger subsample of respondents or whether the motivation is related to health status are questions that we will examine carefully as the current fieldwork goes forward.

Beyond Taiwan, experience with the collection of biomarkers relative to participation and nonresponse has also been encouraging. The DHS, which has extensive experience with anthropometric and anemia measurement, reports that nonresponse (i.e., nonparticipation) has not been an important issue; to the contrary, they found that the biomeasures were an important motivation for participation in the studies (Vaessen, 2000). Even with a more extensive health examination in Pakistan, a similar experience was reported (Pappas, 2000).

Financial and Logistical Constraints

Financial and logistical constraints are considerable and are related to the choice of biomarkers and to location. Logistical problems for the potential collection of biomarkers in the HRS are exacerbated by the fact that it is a nationally representative survey of the United States with primary sampling units (PSUs) scattered across the country. For instance, in the proposed dementia assessment, two-person teams consisting of a nurse and a psychometric technician would conduct assessments in the homes of HRS respondents. Transportation of "flying squad" teams is a major component of the cost of such an endeavor.

For the Taiwan study, as for the HRS, PSUs are located geographically throughout the country but, of course, the total area is much smaller. The collection of the 12-hour urine specimen also adds substantially to both the expense and the complexity because it involves an additional visit to the respondent's home for the delivery of the collection supplies, and because the equipment and assay costs for cortisol and the catecholamines are high. Also, in Taiwan, phlebotomy must be performed by, or under the supervision of, a physician, so the cost of drawing blood is higher than it might be in locations where a technician could be employed. However, that cost is offset in Taiwan by the substantially lower charges for the blood and urine assays and the lower interviewing costs. In all, we estimate that the cost per respondent is about U.S. $400 for the interview, in-hospital physician's examination, and the blood and urine collection and tests. The logistics are not trivial. For the Taiwan study, the logistical constraints were significantly eased—and the response rate maintained at a high level—because of the experience of the Taiwan National Institute of Family Planning under the direction of Dr. Chang Ming-Cheng; the Director of Research and Planning, Mr. Chuang Yi-Li; and the project liaison, Ms. Lin Yu-Hsuan. The Institute has over 40 years of experience in fielding large-scale surveys and has well-established ties with public health nurses and other members of the medical community.

In general, it is difficult to imagine trying to accomplish these tests without adequate access to good communications and transport systems and to reliable refrigeration. In particular, challenges arising from inadequate cold chain equipment have been experienced by a number of studies (Vaessen, 2000; Makubalo, 2000).

The Taiwan protocol also involves extensive cooperation with the local public health nursing staff and with hospitals throughout the country. Drivers and interviewers who are knowledgeable about the local geographic areas are needed to find respondents; deliver and explain the urine collection equipment; and pick up, drop off, and return participants for the hospital visit.

Finally, other logistical considerations are significant as well. These include disposal of biohazardous waste materials, access to and training for a cadre of professional and technical assistants, quality control, and ensuring consistency of laboratory assays.

The Potential to Compromise Research Objectives

The collection of biomarkers also has the potential to exacerbate problems that affect all surveys. One concern common to virtually all research, for example, is the well-documented possibility that the research process itself affects behaviors that we wish to study. In the case of studies that include bioindicators as measures of health status, this concern is salient. Our earlier discussion of APOE testing suggested this possibility. More generally, this concern extends beyond genetic testing. Our clear obligation to provide participants with information related to their own health that is identified in the course of the study, indeed our obligation to encourage them to take action to address risk, may directly affect the course of the trajectories that we originally proposed to study. The data may become less representative of the population as a whole and reflect the effects of the intervention of the study itself.

While the possibility of such "contamination effects" should be considered seriously, it is also important not to exaggerate the problem. The information provided to a respondent by participating in a survey is typically only a small part of the information that is used in making important decisions. The contamination effects themselves may also be of independent scientific interest to researchers interested in the effects of interventions such as screening tests. Overall, it is important to ask whether there are mechanisms that meet acceptable ethical standards and allow for the collection of biological material without creating unacceptable risks of distorting the data either through the data collection process itself or by altering the behavior of respondents.

OBLIGATIONS TO THE PARTICIPANTS

Providing a Benefit to the Participants— Diagnosis, Treatment, and Counsel

A primary consideration in the design of the Taiwan biomarker study has been ensuring that our participants benefit from their involvement in the study. We have taken a number of concrete steps to secure this result. The protocol simplifies access to a free health examination that is more comprehensive than the nationally funded exam for the elderly. The Institute arranges and confirms the appointment at the hospital, and arranges transportation for the participant to and from his home. Throughout the entire hospital visit the participant is attended by a member of the Institute staff; this staff member is there to answer questions and ensure the comfort of the participant. After the hospital routine, the participants are offered a light breakfast and a given a token gift. The results of the tests are reported promptly and with follow-up directions, information, and resources. In all, the Taiwan protocol cuts through hospital red tape, eases the hospital procedures, provides more extensive testing than the free national exam, and promotes follow-up.

Not all the decisions have been easy. For example, we have had persistent concerns about balancing obligations to report test results to the participants against the uncertainties of interpretation for some of the tests—the ones which are not routinely used in medical examinations or which are at the experimental stage. This concern has been particularly thorny in regard to the 12-hour urine protocol from which we obtain data that are important only for our research. We have also struggled to find the right balance between informing our participants about unusual test results and encouraging them to seek follow-up care while trying to avoid alarming them unnecessarily.

Informed Consent

Ensuring informed consent has been a serious concern throughout our work. Several factors related to the collection of biomarkers make informed consent an unusually complex task; among an aging sample, issues of cognitive function add to the complexity. Among the Taiwanese elderly, the inability of many of our respondents to read compounds the difficulties.

We have addressed these concerns in part by using a multistage process. Project goals and the protocol are described in a letter that is sent to each participant prior to the first visit by the public health nurse. During the nurse's visit, a second statement is read to each potential participant. Consent is obtained separately for the nurse's interview and for participation in the biomarker protocol. Following the visit by the public health nurse, those who have agreed to participate in the biomarker protocol are sent a letter confirming the date and time of their hospital visit and explaining the urine collection and hospital protocols. Another explanation is provided at the time the urine collection equipment is distributed to the participants. A final consent statement is given *and* read to the participant on the date of the hospital visit. At each stage, the respondents are reminded that their participation is voluntary and that they can choose to stop at any time.

If we look at data from our initial survey in 1989, they show that most of our elderly respondents—about 71 percent of the men and 83 percent of the women—reside with their adult children. Our experience to date has been that these children have played an active role in the informed consent decision process. In our 1997/1998 biomarker study, only seven of the participants had cognitive impairments that created concerns regarding comprehension of the study protocol. In these instances, the guardian (generally the child) provided permission for the physical examination. This small number, however, may in part be related to the residual refusal rate discussed earlier. Some of the targeted respondents who refused were too ill, possibly reflecting an effect of selection on our sample that may create analytical concerns. Although the longitudinal social surveys do use proxy reports for respondents who are unable to participate for various reasons, including cognitive disability, we know that study attrition is related to proxy status (Beckett et al., 2000).

Confidentiality

The need to protect the identity of survey participants and the confidentiality of the data that they provide is a paramount consideration for any study. Its importance relative to the collection of biological and health indicators cannot be overemphasized. The sensitivity of the data, the (currently) unknown implications of biological materials that may be established in the future, and the extensive linkage across both private and government-run data archives raise the potential consequences of violations to new levels that require strict oversight.

FUTURE DIRECTIONS

Given the high monetary and nonmonetary costs of adding biomarker data to household surveys, we believe that some consideration should also be given to the turnabout alternative of adding social, psychological, and economic information to health studies in which biological specimens and other detailed biomedical data are already being collected. The marginal cost of adding survey information to biomedical studies may be quite low compared with the marginal cost of adding biological data to household surveys. A number of possibilities spring to mind. One would be to add socioeconomic information to ongoing large-scale representative surveys such as NHANES. Another would be to add such information to clinical trials which, as a matter of course, collect detailed biological and medical information.

If the turnabout option were to be pursued, it would be important to provide crosswalks between the supplemented biomedical data sets and the major household surveys in order to maximize the research value of the combined data sets. Thus, for example, one could administer relevant portions of the HRS questionnaire to individuals over age 50 who volunteered for a clinical trial. These additional data might be of direct value to the investigators running the trial because they would be able to learn the degree to which their self-selected subjects represent the population for all variables that are collected by both the HRS and the trial. In addition, it would have value for researchers outside the clinical trial who are seeking to understand linkages between socioeconomic and biological variables.

Already, to varying degrees, we see that the collection of biological specimens and clinical data in conjunction with more traditional social survey information is happening. The DHS has incorporated anthropometric measures and has recently initiated tests for anemia based on blood from finger pricks (Holt, 2000). Studies in Bangladesh, Indonesia, Egypt, China, and other countries include, or have included, biological markers. In the United States, biomarkers have been incorporated into the MacArthur Study of Successful Aging, the survey of Midlife in the United States (MIDUS), in research on the perimenopause in the Tremin Trust Study and the Study of Women's Health Across the Nation (SWAN), and are being considered for the Wisconsin Longitudinal Study and the National Survey of Family Growth. These data have increased, and will continue to increase dramatically, the opportunities to document and explicate differentials in health and biological parameters across ethnicities, across cultures, and across life circumstances.

Informally, of course, information about both our successes and failures has been exchanged among the researchers involved in these protocols. However, it is increasingly apparent that more formal, or at least more standardized protocols would facilitate better comparative work. At the current juncture, given the rapidly developing technology and base of information, it may well be the case that such standardization would be premature. At a minimum, however, we can surely assemble and pool documentation of the protocols and experiences that have recently been applied.

Research in the social sciences is often used as a basis for informing and directing policy initiatives. Much of the research that emerges from large-scale social surveys falls at the intersection of description and prescription. The collection of health-related indicators based on biological markers forges new ties to medical and epidemiological research, research that has strong, explicit, and normative traditions of advocacy. These new opportunities for collaboration across disciplines open exciting possibilities for developing and testing new theoretical paradigms and for bringing the results of research to bear in improving quality of life across all ages.

ACKNOWLEDGMENTS

We gratefully acknowledge comments and suggestions from Noreen Goldman, Jane Menken, and two anonymous reviewers. This paper was supported in part by the Behavioral and Social Research Program of the National Institute on Aging under grant number R01-AG16661-01 and by the Graduate School of Arts and Sciences, Georgetown University.

REFERENCES

Aaron, L.A., L.A. Bradley, G.S. Alarcon, R.W. Alexander, M. Triana-Alexander, M.Y. Martin, and K.R. Alberts
    1996   Psychiatric diagnoses in patients with fibromyalgia are related to health care-seeking behavior rather than to illness. *Arthritis and Rheumatism* 39:436-445.
Adler, N.E., T. Boyce, M.A. Chesney, S. Cohen, S. Folkman, R.L. Kahn, and S.L. Syme
    1994   Socioeconomic status and health: The challenge of the gradient. *American Psychologist* 49(1):15-24
Beckett, M., N. Goldman, M. Weinstein, I-F Lin, and Y-L Chuang
    1999   Social environment, life challenge, and health among the elderly in Taiwan. Manuscript.
Beckett, M., M. Weinstein, N. Goldman, and Y-H Lin
    2000   Do health interview surveys yield reliable data on chronic illness among older respondents? *American Journal of Epidemiology* 151(2):315-323.

Berkman, L.F., T.E. Seeman, M. Albert, D. Blazer, R. Kahn, R. Mohs, C. Finch, E. Schneider, C. Cotman, G. McClearn, J. Nesselroade, D. Featherman, N. Garmezy, G. McKhann, G. Brim, D. Prager, and J. Rowe
   1993   High, usual and impaired functioning in community-dwelling older men and women: Findings from the MacArthur Foundation Research Newtwork on Successful Aging. *Clinical Epidemiology* 46:1129-1140.
Campbell, K.L., and J.W. Wood
   1994   Human reproductive ecology: Interactions of environment, fertility and behavior. *Annals of the New York Academy of Sciences* 709:1-8.
Chang, M-C, and A. Hermalin
   1989   The 1989 survey of health and living status of the elderly in Taiwan: questionnaire and survey design. *Comparative Study of the Elderly in Four Asian Countries.* Research report 1. Ann Arbor, MI: Population Studies Center, University of Michigan.
Clauw, D.J. and G.P. Chrousos
   1997   Chronic pain and fatigue syndromes: Overlapping clinical and neuroendocrine features and potential pathogenic mechanisms. *Neuroimmunomodulation* 4(3):134-153.
Cohen, S., and M.S. Rodriguez
   1995   Pathways linking affective disturbances and physical disorders. *Health Psychology* 14:374-380.
Corder, E.H., A.M. Saunders, W.J. Strittmatter, D.E. Schmechel, P.C. Gaskell, G.W. Samll, A.D. Roses, J.L. Haines, and M.A. Pericak-Vance
   1993   Gene dose of apolipoprotein E type 4 allele and the risk of Alzheimer's disease in late onset families. *Science* 261(5123):921-923.
Edwards, W.S., D.M. Winn, and J.G. Collins
   1996   Evaluation of 2-week doctor visit reporting in the National Health Interview Survey. *Vital and Health Statistics, Series 2: Data Evaluation and Methods Research, 122.* DHHS publication (PHS) 96-1396. Hyattsville, MD: National Center for Health Statistics.
Goldman, N., A. Hedley, Y-H Lin, T. Seeman, and M. Weinstein
   1999   Social and biodemographic linkages to health among the elderly: A project update. Paper presented at the annual meeting of the Population Association of America, New York, April.
Goldman, N., S. Korenman, and R. Weinstein
   1995   Marital status and health among the elderly. *Social Science and Medicine* 40:1717-1730.
Haapanen N., S. Miilunpalo, M. Pasanen, P. Oja, and I. Vuori
   1997   Agreement between questionnaire data and medical records of chronic diseases in middle-aged and elderly Finnish men and women. *American Journal of Epidemiology* 145:762-769.
Hermalin, A.
   1999   Notes on the methodological and philosophical implications of increased collection of bio-indicator data in aging research. Workshop on Bio-Indicators of Aging, Carolina Population Center, Chapel Hill, NC, April 27-28.
Holt, E.
   2000   The challenges of biological and clinical data collection in large-scale population-based surveys in less developed countries. Paper presented at the Conference on Biological and Clinical Data Collection in National Surveys—Potential and Issues, National Academies, Washington, DC, January 24-25.
House, H.S., J.M. Kepkowski, A.M. Kinney, R.P. Mero, R.C. Kessler, and A.R. Herzog
   1994   The social stratification of aging and health. *Journal of Health and Social Behavior* 35:213-234.

Hu, Y., and N. Goldman
    1990   Mortality differences by marital status: An international comparison. *Demography* 27:233-250.
Juster, F.T., and R. Suzman
    1995   An overview of the health and retirement study. *The Journal of Human Resources* 30(Supplement 1995):S7-S56.
Kroenke, K., and A.D. Mangelsdorf
    1989   Common symptoms in primary care: Incidence, evaluation, therapy, and outcome. *American Journal of Medicine* 86:262-266.
Lupien, S., A.R. Lecours, I. Lussier, et al.
    1994   Basal cortisol levels and cognitive deficits in human aging. *Journal of Neuroscience* 14:2893-2903.
Lupien, S., S. Gaudreau, S. Sharma, N.P.V. Nair, R.L. Hauger, and M.J. Meaney
    1995   The effects of a psychological stress on memory performance in healthy elderly subjects: Relationships with actual and past cortisol history. In *International Society of Psychoneuroendocrinology Abstracts*.
Makubalo, L.
    2000   Country perspective on the need for better measurement of health status. Paper presented at the Conference on Biological and Clinical Data Collection in National Surveys—Potential and Issues, National Academies, Washington, DC, January 24-25.
Marmot, M., M. Shipley, and B. Singer
    1996   Mapping SES onto psycho-social hierarchies: Toward explanation of SES/health gradients. Manuscript, Princeton University.
McEwen, B.S., and E. Stellar
    1993   Stress and the individual: Mechanisms leading to disease. *Archives of Internal Medicine* 153:2093-2101.
Ofstedal, M., Zimmer, Z., and H-S Lin
    1999   A comparison of correlates of cognitive functioning in older persons in Taiwan and the United States. *Journal of Gerontology* 54B:S1-11.
Pappas, G.
    2000   Experience with health examination surveys in developing countries. Paper presented at the Conference on Biological and Clinical Data Collection in National Surveys—Potential and Issues, National Academies, Washington, DC, January 24-25.
Phelps, C.E.
    1992   *Health Economics*. New York: Harper-Collins.
Russell, I.J., G.A. Vipraio, J.E. Michalek, and Y.G. Lopez
    1992   Insulin-like growth factor in fibromyalgia, rheumatoid arthritis, osteoarthritis, and healthy normal controls: Roles of diagnosis, age, sex, and ethnic origin. *Arthritis and Rheumatism* 35(9S):B263.
Seeman, T.E., L.F. Berkman, D. Blazer, and J.W. Rowe
    1994   Social ties and support and neuroendocrine function: The MacArthur Studies of Successful Aging. *Annals of Behavioral Medicine* 16(2):95-106.
Seeman, T., B. Singer, and P. Charpentier
    1995   Gender differences in patterns of HPA axis response to challenge: The MacArthur Studies of Successful Aging. *Psychoneuroendocrinology* 20(7):711-725.
Seeman, T.E., B.H. Singer, J.W. Rowe, R.I. Horwitz, and B.S. McEwen
    1997   Price of adaptation—allostatic load and its health consequences. *Archives of Internal Medicine* 157:2259-2268.

Smith, J.P.
  1999   Healthy bodies and thick wallets: The dual relation between health and economic status. *Journal of Economic Perspectives* 13(2):145-166.
Soldo, B.J., M.D. Hurd, W.L. Rodgers, and R.B. Wallace
  1997   Asset and health dynamics among the oldest old: An overview of the AHEAD study. *The Journals of Gerontology: Social Sciences* 52B(Special Issue):1-20.
Strauss, J., and D. Thomas
  1996   Measurement and mismeasurement of social indicators. *American Economic Review* 86:30-34.
Thoits, P.
  1983   Dimensions of life events as influences upon the genesis of psychological distress and associated conditions: An evaluation and synthesis of the literature. Pp. 33-104 in *Psychosocial Stress: Trends in Theory and Research*. New York: Academic Press.
Thoits, P.A.
  1995   Stress, coping, and social support processes: Where are we? What next? *Journal of Health Social Behavior* (extra issue):53-79.
Turner, C.F., T.K. Smith, L.K. Fitterman, T. Reilly, K. Pate, M.B. Witt, A.M. McBean, J.T. Lessler, and B.H. Forsyth
  1997   The quality of health data obtained in a new survey of elderly Americans: A validation study of the proposed Medicare beneficiary health status registry (MBHSR). *Journal of Gerontology* 52B:S49-58.
Vaessen, M.
  2000   Issues in collecting biological and clinical data in population-based surveys in developing countries. Paper presented at the Conference on Biological and Clinical Data Collection in National Surveys—Potential and Issues, National Academies, Washington, DC, January 24-25.
Wallace, R.B.
  1997   The potential of population surveys for genetic studies. Pp. 234-244 in *Between Zeus and the Salmon: The Biodemography of Longevity*, K.W. Wachter and C.E. Finch, eds. Committee on Population, Commission on Behavioral and Social Sciences and Education. Washington, DC: National Academy Press.
Walling, M.K., M.W. O'Hara, R.C. Reiter, A.K. Milburn, G. Lilly, and S.D. Vincent
  1994   Abuse history and chronic pain in women. II. A multivariate analysis of abuse and psychological morbidity. *Obstetrics and Gynecology* 84:200-206.
Weiner, H.
  1992   *Perturbing the Organism: The Biology of Stressful Experience*. Chicago: The University of Chicago Press.
Weiss, K.
  1998a Coming to terms with human variation. *Annual Review of Anthropology* 27:273-300.
  1998b In search of human variation. *Genome Research* 691-697.
Willis, R.J.
  1999   Theory confronts data: How the HRS is shaped by the economics of aging and how the economics of aging will be shaped by the HRS. *Labour Economics* 6:119-145.
Yamazaki, A.
  2000   The role of intergenerational relations in the association between life stressors and psychological distress among the Taiwanese elderly population. Paper presented in partial fulfillment of the MA degree, Georgetown University, Department of Demography.

12

Informed Consent for the Collection of Biological Samples in Household Surveys

Jeffrey R. Botkin

T he National Bioethics Advisory Commission (NBAC) estimates that there are over 282 million human biologic specimens being stored in the United States, and that this number is growing by 20 million samples per year (NBAC, 1999). These tissue samples have been collected by hospitals in the course of routine clinical care, investigators, public health agencies, health care companies, and nonprofit organizations. While many of these collections have existed for generations, controversy has arisen in the past decade over the appropriate use of these resources for research. This debate has its roots in several developments: (1) contemporary genetic technology permits a detailed analysis of small tissue samples; (2) a wide variety of mutations have been identified that are associated with serious health problems; (3) there is substantial concern in medicine and the general public over genetic discrimination in insurance and employment; and (4) many samples have been collected without informed consent for their use in research.

To a large extent, the most heated controversy has focused on the use of existing samples collected over years or decades for new genetic research projects. Large repositories that are linked with demographic and health information about the tissue sources can be a valuable tool for research (Wallace, 1997). However, if the analysis of stored tissues poses some risk to the tissue source, and adequate informed consent has not been obtained, then use of the specimens may not be appropriate. Recontacting tissue sources for consent may be prohibitive in terms of time, effort, and expense, thereby rendering the repository useless for research purposes. This is the situation in which the Centers for Disease Control (CDC) found itself following the National Health and Nutrition Examination Survey (NHANES) III study (Steinberg et al., 1998). Through this extensive national project, the CDC collected information on approximately 40,000 individuals, blood and urine samples on 19,500, and developed 8,500 permanent cell lines. Unfortunately, the detailed consent from participants did not explicitly cover genetic research on the specimens. Thus a crisis arose over whether the samples could be used for genetic research without recontacting participants for their specific approval.

To address these concerns, a conference and working group were convened in 1994. The CDC and the National Human Genome Research Institute sponsored the effort that resulted in a statement of guidelines published in 1995 (Clayton et al., 1995). This statement proved to be somewhat controversial in its own right, fostering broad discussion from a variety of perspectives (American Society of Human Genetics, 1996; American College of Medical Genetics, 1995; Grizzle et al., 1999; National Heart, Lung, and Blood Institute, 1997; Office for Protection from Research Risks, 1997). The use of stored tissues in research became one of the first issues to be addressed by the NBAC in its 1999 report titled "Research Involving Human Biologic Materials: Ethical Issues and Policy Guidance." Similar debates have arisen in recent years over the use of DNA databanks in criminal law (McEwen, 1998) and in the military (Kipnis, 1998).

This brief sketch of the recent controversies over stored tissue samples illustrates two points. First, the current discussion of the collection of biologic samples in household surveys occurs within a charged atmosphere. Given the appropriate, renewed scrutiny being applied to human subject protections in research, a cursory approach to consent issues may impair or destroy the value of specimens obtained in household surveys. Second, the debate over informed consent for tissue storage and research use is sufficiently mature to enable the development of prudent consent procedures that can maximize the utility of specimens while respecting the prerogative of subjects to control their contributions to research and the risks associated with research participation. For the purposes of this chapter, we need not address the controversy over the use of existing specimens. The following discussion will focus on consent for the prospective collection of specimens in household surveys.

INFORMED CONSENT

The purpose of informed consent is severalfold. In the clinical environment, the primary purpose is to permit patients to make informed choices about appropriate options for care. To a significant extent, the concept of informed consent did not arise within medicine, but rather was promulgated through the courts in response to cases in which patients had adverse consequences following procedures that had not been fully discussed. The emergence of informed consent parallels the consumer rights movement in society more broadly and the rejection of paternalism in medicine more specifically. The corollary to the protection of a patient's prerogative to make informed decisions about his or her own care is the legal protection that informed consent confers on care providers. While malpractice suits involving inadequate informed consent are relatively rare, a full discussion of medical options and clear documentation of these discussions protects providers from successful suits (based on inadequate consent) if a choice leads to a poor outcome.

Unfortunately, the legal dimensions of informed consent tend to overshadow the fundamental importance of this doctrine in medicine. The basic principle is that patients should be active participants in deciding their course of care. The central dialogue in medicine, that is, discussing what is wrong with the patient, what options are available, and what course should be followed, constitutes the process of informed consent. The signing of the consent form, when appropriate or necessary, documents what was discussed but should not be misconstrued as informed consent itself.

In therapeutic research, informed consent serves a similar role as that in clinical care, with the obvious difference that the experimental option remains to be fully evaluated. Offering a potentially ineffective or harmful option requires more thorough consent procedures than those in clinical medicine, including more detailed disclosures, consent forms, and prior review of protocols and forms by an institutional review board (IRB).

Nontherapeutic research is the most complex from an ethical perspective. The most egregious examples of abuse in U.S. biomedical research have involved nontherapeutic research projects, including the Tuskegee syphilis experiments, the Jewish Chronic Disease Hospital, Willowbrook, and the human radiation experiments (Advisory Committee on Human Radiation Experiments, 1995). It is notable that several of the most notorious of these experiments (Tuskegee and the radiation experiments) involved active participation by federal agencies. Public concern following the revelation of some of these projects led to the federal regulations currently in place to govern the conduct of research (Caplan, 1992).

By definition, nontherapeutic research offers no prospect of direct benefit to the subject. The benefit, if any, may accrue to the subject in the future, through a better understanding of the treatment or prevention of disease, or the benefit may accrue to others in society. When properly conducted, nontherapeutic research appeals to the altruism of individuals to place themselves at some risk, largely for the uncertain benefit of others. When not properly conducted, nontherapeutic research simply uses poorly informed or unwitting subjects as tools for research ends. Detailed consent for participation in research is at the core of the ethical justification for involving subjects in nonbeneficial research. The other essential pillar on which the ethical justification of research rests is peer review.

THE COMMON RULE

A household survey with the collection of biologic specimens constitutes nontherapeutic research and, if conducted under the auspices of the federal government, is subject to federal regulations under Title 45, Part 46 of the Code of Federal Regulations (Department of Health and Human Services, 1991). The regulations exempt research on existing databases, records, or specimens if these resources are publicly available or if the resource has been stripped of all individual identifiers. Any prospective collection of individual information and tissue samples would not be exempt from federal regulations. However, the regulations permit research without informed consent in specific circumstances, subject to IRB approval:

(1) the research involves no more than minimal risk to the subjects;
(2) the waiver or alteration will not adversely affect the rights and welfare of the subjects;
(3) the research could not practically be carried out without the waiver or alteration; and
(4) whenever appropriate, the subjects will be provided with additional pertinent information after participation.

These criteria are unlikely to be met by a household survey involving biologic specimens.

The definition of minimal risk provided by the regulations is relatively vague and is intended to be interpreted by IRBs in the context of specific proposals. The definition states:

> *Minimal risk* means that the probability and magnitude of harm or discomfort anticipated in the research are not greater in and of themselves than those ordinarily encountered in daily life or during the performance of routine physical or psychological examinations or tests.

We can imagine a household survey with specimen collection that would meet several of the requirements for waiver of informed consent. A survey to include limited demographic data and a cheek swab for ABO/Rh blood type would meet the standard of minimal risk and waiver of consent would not adversely affect the rights or welfare of the subject. However, it would be difficult to argue that consent was not practical in the context of a household survey. At a minimum, subjects have the right to know the purpose of the research and what was going to be done with the data and the biologic specimen. Of course, most useful household surveys will involve extensive data collection, including sensitive information such as health status, and collection of specimens for a variety of analyses. Therefore, it is unlikely that household surveys with specimen collection would qualify for waiver of consent under any circumstances.

The federal regulations require the following elements to be included in the consent process:

(1) a statement that the study involves research, and explanation of the purposes of the research and the expected duration of the subject's participation;

(2) a description of any reasonably foreseeable risks or discomforts to the subject;

(3) a description of any benefits to the subject or to others which may reasonably be expected from the research;

(4) a disclosure of the appropriate alternative procedures or courses of treatment, if any, that might be advantageous to the subject;

(5) a statement describing the extent, if any, to which confidentiality of records identifying the subject will be maintained;

(6) for research involving more than minimal risk, an explanation as to whether any compensation and an explanation as to whether any medical treatments are available if injury occurs;

(7) an explanation of whom to contact for answers to pertinent questions; and

(8) a statement that participation is voluntary, refusal to participate will involve no penalty or loss of benefits, and the subject may discontinue participation at any time without penalty or loss of benefits to which the subject is otherwise entitled.

Some of these elements, such as point 4, have limited relevance to household surveys with the collection of samples. Further, there are additional considerations relevant to the collection of specimens for a repository, that is, when specimens are collected for use in future, unspecified research projects. These issues will be discussed in detail below.

The extent of the information provided in the consent process is determined largely by the magnitude of the risks, discomforts, and inconveniences involved in the research. This is not to say that these burdens are the only consideration. Individuals have prerogatives to control information about themselves even when there is no risk involved. More specifically, privacy rights are not contingent solely on the presence of risk (Allen, 1997). Conversely, privacy is not absolute, and a variety of public health and public policy activities involve the collection and sharing of personal information. Personal financial information and data on our purchasing behaviors are often widely shared in the private sector. In addition, as noted above, research projects need not always obtain subject consent to be included if certain criteria are met. But public sensitivity toward privacy issues is growing and, at least in the public sector, there must be clear justification for any threats to individual privacy. The point here is that in this context detailed consent is appropriate, not necessarily because there are profound risks involved in this research, but because potential subjects have the right to exert substantial control over information about themselves and their families.

RISKS OF RESEARCH ON TISSUE SAMPLES

The nature of the informed consent will be strongly influenced both by the magnitude of the risks involved and by the *perceived* magnitude of the risks by potential subjects. In recent years, there has been extensive discussion of genetic privacy issues, including numerous newspaper and magazine articles directed to the general public. This discussion has raised widespread concern in the United States over breaches in privacy or confidentiality leading to discrimination in insurance and employment secondary to genetic testing (Fuller et al., 1999). Some of these risks may have been overstated; nevertheless, they are an important part of discussions and disclosures to potential research subjects.

Of course, not all testing of tissue samples involves genetic testing. Genetics has received the lion's share of attention due to the perception that our DNA constitutes a "future diary," readable by those with new technical capabilities (Annas, 1993; Annas et al., 1995). The primary fear is that genetic testing may reveal a high risk of a specific future illness. Learning this predictive information, particularly if there are no effective interventions to prevent or treat the disease, might cause personal distress, social stigma, and discrimination. In addition, genetic testing may reveal family information, including the mutation status of a parent, or revelations like misattributed paternity. Third, the concern over genetic information is heightened by the history of abuse of genetic information during the eugenics era and under German National Socialism, but also more recently with the sickle cell screening program in the United States during the 1970s. This claim that genetic tests deserve special scrutiny has been termed "genetic exceptionalism" (Murray, 1997).

Several authors have taken the position that genetic testing is not unique or fundamentally different from other testing modalities (see, e.g., Murray, 1997). It can be argued that the problematic nature of tests is not governed by whether they are genetic or not, but by whether the test is strongly predictive of future illness and whether the information has implications for others such as family members. HIV testing is not genetic in nature, for example, but shares many of the problematic aspects of genetic testing. Conversely, most genetic tests should not raise particular concerns because most tests are not highly predictive of future illness, nor do they have serious implications for other individuals. Genetic tests may have these problematic characteristics more often than nongenetic tests, but it is the attributes of the specific tests that are important to informed consent, not the fact that the tests are genetic.[1]

Further, one aspect that nongenetic tests have that many genetic tests do not is the ability to detect current disease. Genetic tests (other than perhaps tumor markers) are not generally useful for detecting silent or presymptomatic disease. For example, inclusion of nongenetic tests such as liver or renal function tests on a household survey would confer the ability to detect current liver or kidney dysfunction—problems about which the subject may not be aware. Learning this unanticipated information may constitute a benefit in otherwise nontherapeutic survey research, assuming the results are returned to subjects and there are effective interventions to improve health. However, this diagnostic information also could produce distress, stigma, and discrimination. These potential risks and benefits would need to be addressed in developing the research protocol and in the consent process. Therefore, in this context, the attributes of the specific tests to be included on a household survey must be individually evaluated, and considerations about consent should not be overly influenced by the technology used to run the tests.

One unique aspect of genetic tests that does deserve additional scrutiny is the potential of genetic information to stigmatize entire communities. Perceived genetic differences between racial and ethnic groups have been a powerful source of discrimination and even genocide in the past. The use of genetic information to characterize (or mischaracterize) whole communities is a rational fear. Genetic research to evaluate genes associated with alcoholism in the Native American population, or for criminality in the African-American population would be viewed with great suspicion and hostility in these communities (Coombs, 1999). Clearly any finding that purported to demonstrate a genetic basis for a stereotype of a racial or ethnic group could be harmful to all those who share the racial or ethnic identity, whether or not they were involved in the research. In addition, different cultures place different values on tissue samples, decision-making, and health research that have significant implications for how specimens might be obtained and handled (Freedman 1998; Foster et

---

[1]I am indebted to Michael Green, M.D., for his insights on these issues.

al., 1998). For these reasons, there is legitimate concern over some kinds of genetic research in specific ethnic and racial groups, even when individual specimens have been rendered anonymous (Clayton, 1995). This concern has led to suggestions that subjects be afforded choice over the use of their tissues even when the tissues are unlinked to individual identities but retain demographic links, and that protocols be subject to review and approval by communities in addition to individual subjects (Freedman, 1998). This issue is discussed in greater detail by Durfy (2000) in this volume.

TYPES OF REPOSITORIES AND SAMPLES

A key strategy to reduce the risk of research with medical data and tissues is to remove individual identifiers from the data and/or samples. A useful framework and terminology has been provided by the NBAC (1999) in their discussion of this strategy. First, there is a distinction between how the specimens are handled in a repository and how individual samples might be used or distributed from the repository. Using the NBAC terminology, *specimens* are retained in repositories, while *samples* from the specimens are distributed to investigators from the repository.

An initial decision with any proposal to conduct a household survey with tissue acquisition will be about the storage and management of the specimens. A repository refers to a tissue bank that is established as a source of samples for future, currently unspecified research. If the purpose of the project is to run only a predetermined battery of tests on the tissue, then a repository would not be necessary. Presumably, residual tissues would be destroyed after the completion of the test battery. From the perspective of subject consent, this approach has the advantage of enabling a full discussion of the scope of the research and its risks and benefits. However, the obvious disadvantage is that a potentially large specimen collection is not available for future research using new ideas and technologies as they develop. For this reason, a large household survey would maximize the utility of the specimens by creating a repository that could be utilized by future investigators. From the perspective of subject consent, this approach becomes considerably more complex since the ultimate use of the samples is presently unknown.

Specimens in a repository can be either identified or unidentified. In the terminology being used in this domain, unidentified samples are those that *cannot* be traced back to the specimen source by anyone. Therefore the word unidentified is equivalent to anonymous. Identifying information obviously includes personal information such as names, addresses, social security numbers, but it also may include a pattern of information that is sufficiently unusual to identify an individual. For example, to label a specimen with information that the source is an elderly African-American man with scleroderma in North Dakota might make it traceable to a single individual in the survey database. Therefore, labeling in a repository with unidentified specimens must be sufficiently complete to make the specimens useful, but not so detailed that some sources can be identified.

An advantage to developing a repository with unidentified specimens is that the specimens are no longer considered human subjects under federal regulations (Department of Health and Human Services, 1991). Human subject means "a living individual about whom an investigator (whether professional or student) conducting research obtains (1) data through intervention or interaction with the individual, or (2) identifiable private information." Subsequent use of unidentified specimens would not require informed consent from the subjects or IRB review. The disadvantage of a repository with unidentified specimens is the limited data on the tissue sources that can be used in the analysis of the samples.

NBAC has defined several different types of research *samples*, depending on the degree to which they are linked with the tissue source. *Unidentified samples* are those from unidentified specimens in a repository. *Unlinked samples* are those that have been "anonymized," meaning that the samples came from identifiable specimens but have been stripped of all identifying information. Again, this means that no one can trace the sample back to the source. *Coded samples*, or *linked samples*, are labeled with a code that permits identification of the tissue source. In many circumstances, only the repository or a designated third party will have access to the database containing the link between the code and the individual identifiers. In this situation, investigators using linked samples cannot identify the source of the tissue, although the repository (or a third party) would retain this ability. Because the tissues remain linked to their sources under this option, use of the samples remains under federal regulation and must be approved by an IRB.

The National Institute of Health's Office for Protection from Research Risks (OPRR, which is now called the Office for Human Research Protections) has explicitly recommended that repositories not release identifiable samples. In its 1997 guidelines on stored tissues, the OPRR (1997) stated: "[An] IRB should set the conditions under which data and specimens may be accepted and shared. OPRR strongly recommends that one such condition stipulate that recipient-investigators not be provided access to the identities of donor-subjects or to information through which the identities of donor-subjects may readily be ascertained." The advantage of this approach is that it permits use of samples for a variety of projects in the indefinite future without the need to return to tissue sources for consent for each project—as long as the projects are consistent with the original consent provided by the subjects.

A complexity of using linked samples is that information that is clinically relevant to the tissue source may be generated in research projects. As long as the tissue source is identifiable, this creates the dilemma over whether to notify the subject or his or her family members about the results. These issues will be discussed in more detail below. Finally, *identified samples* are those that retain individual identifiers such as names or medical record numbers.

In summary, specimens can be stored in an identifiable or unidentifiable state. Identifiable specimens in a repository can be distributed to investigators in an unlinked, coded, or identifiable state. There is an inherent tension between the amount of subject information linked with the sample and the stringency of the consent requirements and security measures necessary. The scientific value of the samples is enhanced with more information about the subjects available, but the threats to subject privacy and confidentiality are increased as well. Depending on the nature of the project, a common balance between these competing interests is struck by maintaining a repository with identified specimens and by establishing procedures for distributing unlinked or coded samples to qualified investigators subject to IRB review. Figures 12-1, 12-2, and 12-3 illustrate these options.

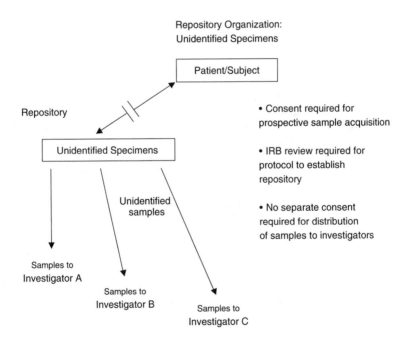

FIGURE 12-1 Repository organization: Unidentified specimens.

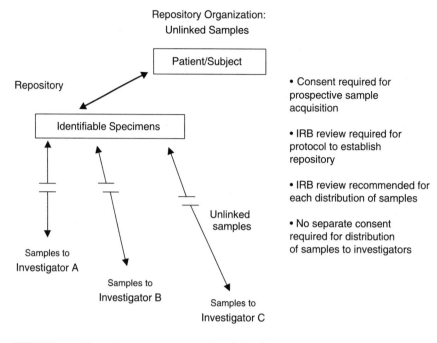

FIGURE 12-2 Repository organization: Unlinked samples.

ELEMENTS OF INFORMED CONSENT

Investigators and an IRB have final authority over the content of informed consent discussions and documents. The following issues will be presented as points to consider in developing a consent process for a household survey involving biological samples. An assumption in developing these points is that specimens will be identifiable in a repository. As discussed above, creation of a repository with unidentified specimens reduces the complexity of creating the repository and accessing the specimens, but also reduces the scientific value of the resource. Further, many of the points will be developed here with the assumption that samples will be distributed from the repository for research projects that will be conceived in the future. Consistent with the guidelines developed by the NBAC (1999), the OPRR (1997), the NIH/CDC Working Group (Clayton et al., 1995), and the College of American Pathologists Ad Hoc Committee on Stored Tissue (Grizzle et al., 1999), each application to use identifiable specimens in a repository requires separate IRB review.

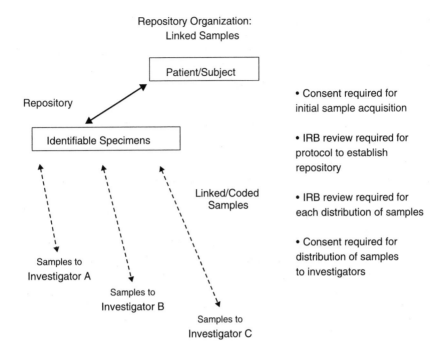

FIGURE 12-3 Repository organization: Linked samples.

Purpose of the Survey and the Biological Samples

This section is largely self-explanatory, although it is remarkable how often a simple description of the purpose of the project is overlooked. Many people will have a very limited understanding of the potential value of this work, so it may be helpful to illustrate the goals of the project with a brief example. It also will be important to explain to potential subjects why they have been asked to participate. Particularly in the context of a household survey (that is, outside a health care environment), it may be important to describe how individuals were selected, perhaps with reassurances that invitations are based on chance or some broad demographic factor, rather than on any knowledge of an individual's health status by the sponsoring agency.

What Is Expected of Participants?

A brief description of the expectations and responsibilities of the subjects is important. Questions to be addressed might include: What kinds of questions will be asked? How much time will the survey take? Will subjects need to collect information on other family members? Will subjects be recontacted in the future for additional information or tissue specimens? In addition, a brief description of the method used to collect the biological sample will be important.

The Nature of the Database and Repository

This discussion would include the key information on how individual data will be stored and accessed. Consistent with the recommendations of the OPRR (1997), the following issues should be considered for discussion:

- What will happen to the information and specimens provided by the subject?
- Will the data and specimens be used for research only by investigators currently affiliated with the survey, or will investigators from other institutions be afforded access to samples in the future?
- What kinds of research will be done with the data and samples?
- Will data and specimens be coded or individually identifiable, or will individual identifiers be permanently removed from data and/or specimens?
- If specimens are identifiable, will investigators from other institutions have access to personally identifiable information or samples?
- How long will specimens be retained? If specimens are to be retained and used indefinitely, this should be communicated to potential subjects. More specifically, subjects should be informed if their specimens will continue to be used after their death.

A clear and concise discussion on these points, when relevant, will be essential for potential subjects to understand the following information and their choices as part of the project.

Communicating Results of the Research

When and how to return research results to subjects remains somewhat controversial. In some circumstances, research protocols use validated tests, the results of which may be clinically valuable for the subject (such as cholesterol measurements or renal function tests). Unless specimens are unidentifiable, it usually is appropriate to return these kinds of results to subjects. Conveying test results is a complex task and is best conducted in a therapeutic relationship where additional evaluation and follow-up can be pursued. Investigators as part of a large household survey may not be able to fill this role appropriately, so investigators should consider managing this information in collaboration with the subject's physician. The release of information to the subject's physician would require the consent of the subject. Some subjects will not have a physician or may decline consent to have the information sent to their physician. In anticipation of these possibilities, the protocol could either provide for clinically experienced individuals to provide results and counsel to subjects through the project, or could decline to enroll these subjects. Providing clinical results can be labor intensive and expensive, so funding agencies should be prepared to support these efforts in well-designed projects.

The NHANES III project returned clinically valid results to subjects directly through letters to the subjects. Subjects who had results that were medically concerning were advised to make an appointment with their physician. Whether subjects who were so advised utilized the information in an effective manner to improve their health status is unclear.

In other circumstances, analyses will be used that have no established clinical utility. There are no meaningful results to be returned to subjects in this situation and therefore returning research results typically has not been required by IRBs. It also is important to note that current federal regulations do not permit the return of results to patients or subjects if the tests were not conducted in a CLIA-approved[2] laboratory (Holtzman and Watson, 1997). Since many research laboratories are not CLIA approved, results from these labs should not be returned to subjects. In some circumstances, repeating the test in a CLIA-approved lab may be feasible and appropriate. In any case, subjects should be clearly informed in the initial consent process whether or not they will receive individual results from the project.

There are two gray areas in this domain. The first arises when test results have not been fully validated by peer review, publication, and replication by other investigators, but for which there is solid reason to believe that the results have some validity. Whether it is appropriate to return the results will depend on several factors and should be subject to IRB review. First, how strong is the evidence of test validity? Second, what are the clinical implications of the test results? If the results could be used to treat or prevent serious disease, the impetus to return the results will be stronger. However, a corollary is that the impact of *misinformation* must also be weighed. Subjects may make burdensome, irreversible decisions based on information that ultimately may be proven false.

The second gray area is the appropriate response to results that gain

---

[2]CLIA is the acronym for the Clinical Laboratory Improvement Amendments of 1988, which resulted from Congressional examination of deficiencies in the quality of services provided by some of the nation's clinical laboratories.

clinical utility with time. A test result may be impossible to interpret today but be meaningful to clinicians in 5 to 10 years. What is the responsibility of investigators to subjects who participated years ago in their protocols? Is there a "look back" responsibility to contact former subjects to alert them to health risks? In clinical medicine, a look back responsibility has been found in some situations. Physicians who inserted certain IUD's in women were found to have a responsibility to contact those women years later when problems with the devices were identified (Andrews, 1997). In the research context, the relationship between investigator and subject is different than the relationship between doctor and patient, so it is unclear whether such a responsibility exists. A duty to recontact former subjects may be strongest when clinically relevant information was provided to subjects in the past, but that information is now considered incorrect or substantially incomplete. As noted by Clarke and Ray (1997), the limited guidance provided to clinicians on this issue tends to *permit* recontacting of patients with new genetic information but stops short of *requiring* recontact. It is possible in the future that courts will find investigators responsible for warning former research subjects when investigators have unique information that would be highly useful in reducing morbidity and mortality in former subjects and recontact is considered feasible.

A potential compromise solution in these gray areas is to send a follow-up newsletter to research subjects at the completion of the project, or even later if the situation warrants. A newsletter could contain general research results from the project, news on related developments, and recommendations on health care options. This approach can alert subjects to important changes in the field and encourage them to seek additional evaluation or advice from their own health care provider. This step may fulfill the responsibility of investigators to subjects without incurring the complexities and cost of providing individual results or follow-up.

Benefits of Participation

The benefits to subjects of household surveys with biologic sampling are likely to be minimal or nonexistent. When clinically valid tests are part of the protocol, such as cholesterol or blood pressure measurement, subjects may benefit from individual results provided conveniently without financial cost. However, assuming subjects are not being selected based on disease status and provided therapeutic interventions, survey projects are nontherapeutic research. The consent discussion and documents should state clearly that benefits cannot be expected by subjects. Of course, the pride and self-satisfaction that comes from contributing to a worthwhile research effort can be an intangible but substantial benefit.

Risks of Participation

The risks to participation are discussed in more detail by Durfy (2000) in this volume. In general, the risks of the physical intervention necessary to acquire a biologic sample are trivial. The primary risks to participation are psychosocial, meaning stigma and discrimination if sensitive information is generated in the project and there is a breach of privacy or confidentiality involving sensitive information. This may be the most significant consideration by potential subjects. As noted above, the degree of public concern over this issue may be greater than currently is justified by the data on discrimination. Whether this will become a serious problem in the future remains to be seen. Many reported instances of genetic discrimination are due to insurance or employment discrimination against people who are currently affected with genetic conditions (Lapham et al., 1996). Unfortunately this is a feature of our health care system in general, which does not guarantee health insurance coverage at affordable rates to those who are ill. People can lose their insurance or pay increased rates when they get sick from genetic and nongenetic conditions alike. The new feature of *genetic* discrimination is potential discrimination against those who are currently healthy, but who are highly susceptible to future illness based on genetic test results. Of course, this kind of discrimination need not be due to genetic testing alone. A survey that newly diagnosed subjects with hyperglycemia or significant hypertension would confer the same risks on subjects.

A further complexity of this issue arises from the different levels of risk of insurance or employment discrimination that different individuals will run. A retired woman on Medicare is at limited risk for employment or health insurance discrimination, and life or disability insurance discrimination is unlikely to be a problem. However, a self-insured young executive at a small company might be at substantially greater risk for discrimination for employment, as well as for all forms of insurance, if she were found to be at high risk for future illness. In addition, federal law and legislation in approximately 35 states provides some measure of protection against genetic insurance and/or employment discrimination (National Human Genome Research Institute). Therefore, unless comprehensive federal legislation is passed, a multistate household survey would approach potential subjects who have a complex mix of baseline risks for discrimination based on the results of testing.

The complexity of this issue is too great to be adequately covered in an informed consent document. Investigators who are enrolling subjects should be familiar with this issue in some detail so that the discussion can be tailored to the concerns and the life situation of the potential subject. It is simply not accurate to state or imply that all subjects are at risk for insurance or employment discrimination. Indeed, it may be reasonable not to include any information about employment or insurance discrimination if the survey will not be collecting potentially sensitive information. If sensitive information is being collected, or might be generated in the tissue analysis, then the issues of stigma and discrimination should be included and recruiters should be prepared to discuss these topics. If insurance discrimination is an issue, it may be important to make subjects aware that the subjects themselves may be asked to disclose clinical or research results in the process of applying for an insurance policy.

An occasional risk in genetic research projects is the detection of misattributed paternity, that is, the finding that the subject's social father is not his or her genetic father. A history of adoption also might be discovered through genetic testing, although this is a less common problem. These potential issues will arise only when samples are being obtained from one or both parents and their children. In the context of prenatal diagnosis or the diagnostic testing of children, knowledge of misattributed paternity is important in assessing the genetic risk to the couple's future offspring. Therefore the information is often relayed to the mother and subsequently to the social father with the consent of the mother. In the context of household surveys, a finding of "nonpaternity" is likely to be incidental to the research effort and of no clear benefit to the research subjects (indeed, it may be quite harmful). Therefore it is probably inappropriate to communicate this incidental finding to family members. If misattributed paternity destroys the scientific value of the specimens, then an option is to remove the survey data and specimens from the project without retaining this sensitive information in a linked fashion. If the protocol calls for this information to be communicated to family members, then this risk must be part of the consent process. If misattributed paternity could be detected in a project, but the information will not be communicated or retained, then the IRB must use its discretion in deciding whether to inform potential subjects of this issue.

Privacy and Confidentiality Protections

Privacy and confidentiality are closely related concepts, although not identical. Confidentiality refers to maintaining the integrity of information shared by a subject within the professional relationship. The subject has a right to expect that personal information that he or she provides will only be shared with designated investigators or staff affiliated with the research. In contrast, privacy can be breached through the generation of *new* information about the subject without his or her consent. Therefore the analysis of a linked tissue sample to reveal the subject's risk status for a disease without the explicit consent of the subject would constitute a breach of privacy, whether or not the results were communicated outside the project. Indeed, telling subjects information about themselves that they did not want to know constitutes a breach of privacy.

As discussed above, privacy and confidentiality can be protected through a process of unlinking data and samples from individual identifiers. With linked samples, privacy risks can be addressed by explicitly discussing the extent of the research to be conducted with the sample. If identifiable specimens are to be retained in a repository, subjects might be offered a choice about the nature of research to be conducted with their tissue. If specimens are acquired primarily for research involving cancer, for example, it will be appropriate to offer a choice to make the tissue available only for cancer research, or for research addressing other health problems as well, assuming that prospect is anticipated by the investigators. If the consent process focuses exclusively on cancer research, then an IRB may not permit the sample to be used for noncancer-related work.

Recontacting Subjects for Consent

There remains some controversy over whether subjects should be asked to provide blanket consent for future research on linked samples. The American Society of Human Genetics Statement on Informed Consent for Genetic Research (1996) concludes: "It is inappropriate to ask a subject to grant blanket consent for all future unspecified genetic research projects on any disease or in any area if the samples are identifiable in those subsequent studies." The National Bioethics Advisory Commission (1999) in its Recommendation 9 outlined six options that investigators might include in consent forms. Among these were the following (using NBAC's outline letters and text):

(c) permitting coded or identified use of their biological materials for one particular study only, with no further contact permitted to ask for permission to do further studies;

(d) permitting coded or identified use of their biological materials for one particular study only, with further contact permitted to ask for permission to do further studies;

(e) permitting coded or identified use of their biological materials for any study relating to the condition for which the sample was originally collected, with further contact allowed to seek permission for other types of studies; or

(f) permitting coded use of their biological materials for any kind of future study.

One commissioner, Alexander Capron, objected to options (e) and (f), stating that subjects cannot provide a truly informed consent to future, unspecified studies. Since the risks and benefits of such studies are unknown, Capron does not believe it is appropriate for subjects to agree to the use of their coded samples without being recontacted for discussion and explicit consent. A second commissioner and NBAC Chair, Dr. Harold Shapiro, also objected to option (f), concurring with Capron's analysis of this provision.

This is a critical debate for the protocol development for a household survey with sample collection. Ultimately, an IRB will determine whether recontacting the subject for consent is necessary for specific applications to use the samples. The IRB will determine whether the new proposed use is consistent with the original consent and whether the proposed use entails risks that require a new discussion with subjects. For example, we can imagine a repository that is established for investigators to seek new genetic markers for susceptibility to a number of diseases of older age, including, say, cancer, stroke, and osteoporosis. An investigator who approaches the repository with a proposal to do an exploratory search for markers for basal cell carcinoma on linked (or unlinked) samples may not be required by the IRB to recontact subjects. However, if the investigator would like to screen all tissue samples first for BRCA1/2, FAP and p53 mutations (established tests that reveal an increased risk for cancer), then the IRB is likely to require recontacting the subjects for detailed consent. Of course, the investigator may not know the identities of the tissue sources, but the repository does, and it would be left with a dilemma if the investigator reports to the repository that she found subjects who are mutation carriers on clinically valid tests to which the subject did not consent.

A potential solution to the problem of recontacting subjects for consent is to unlink samples that are distributed to investigators. This may limit their scientific value since investigators cannot re-access the survey database to expand their knowledge of the tissue sources. In addition, some members of the NIH/CDC Workshop (Clayton, 1995) expressed concern about unlinking samples since (1) recontacting subjects for consent is possible before the samples are unlinked, and (2) unlinking eliminates the ability to get back to subjects if clinically valuable information is generated in the research. In addition, unlinking samples does not avoid the risk of group or community harms to which subjects may object even if the samples are anonymous. In contrast, the College of American Pathologists recommends that a simple consent be considered sufficient for the subsequent research use of unlinked samples.

Withdrawal from Protocol

Federal guidelines require that the consent process include a statement that "participation is voluntary, . . . and the subject may discontinue participation at any time without penalty or loss of benefits." In the context of a household survey in which there may be only a single contact with the subject, the definition of withdrawal from research is ambiguous. Certainly the investigators may choose the cleanest definition of withdrawal in this context by eliminating the subject's data from the database and destroying the specimen and any samples that have been distributed, assuming they are identifiable. However, if analyses of the data or specimens have occurred prior to subject withdrawal, it is unclear whether withdrawal requires destruction of the research results derived from the individual. Particularly in genetic research, results from specific individuals may be key to analyzing genetic patterns in whole kindreds, so the loss of results from single individuals can be damaging to large projects.

If specimens or data are unidentified or unlinked, then subjects should be informed that these cannot be expunged or destroyed if a subject withdraws from the project. A potential option, subject to IRB approval, is to inform subjects that should they withdraw from the research, their data, specimens, and results to the time of withdrawal will be rendered unidentified (anonymous) but will continue to be used. This issue has not been the subject of commentary by the organizations that have developed guidelines on stored tissues.

Commercial Use of Specimens

Academic medicine and public agencies have an increasingly complex relationship with biotechnology companies that may seek to use resources developed for research or public health activities for the development of commercial products. Legal ownership of specimens collected for research remains unclear (Grizzle et al., 1999). Tissues cannot be sold by subjects or investigators, but they can be given away. In one of the few legal cases to address this issue, Moore v. the Regents of the University of California (1990), the court decided that tissues that have been transformed through the expertise of the investigators were no longer the property of the tissue donor. The College of American Pathologists' statement concludes that professional products such as slides and tissue blocks created from subject specimens "can fairly be claimed as the property of the entity that produced them" (Grizzle et al., 1999). Whether specimens retained as frozen whole blood, urine, or cheek swabs would be considered the legal property of the investigators is unclear. In the Moore case, the court found that the subject did not have a right to share in the commercial rewards derived from use of his tissues, but that investigators had an obligation to inform potential subjects when commercial products might result from their participation in research. Subjects who participate in research for altruistic reasons may decline participation if commercial enterprises are involved. It now is common for IRBs to require disclosure to potential subjects when commercial products might result from use of tissues and that, generally, subjects will not be provided a share of any profits from commercial use of their tissue.

Consent for Family Contact

If identifiable specimens are going to be retained and used for a prolonged period of time, investigators may wish to ask subjects to name a family contact who could be notified of results after the death or incapacity of the subject. If it is conceivable that the projects will pursue research with clinical relevance to family members (primarily blood relatives such as siblings and offspring), obtaining consent from subjects to contact a specified family member with information in the future may be beneficial to the family. We can imagine a scenario in which research identifies a new mutation for cancer susceptibility in a subject who has expired from cancer prior to the research results. If the name of a relative and a contact number have been provided by the subject, the relative can be contacted and provided with information about the research results and the implications for family members. Without a contact name and number, contacting family members may be difficult or impossible, and it may be unclear whether the subject would have consented to communication of his research results.

INCLUSION OF VULNERABLE SUBJECTS IN RESEARCH

Because children and mentally impaired individuals cannot provide informed consent for their participation in research, they are considered vulnerable populations. Specific federal regulations apply to children (Department of Health and Human Services, 1991). In brief, research involving no greater than minimal risk (as defined above) is permissible with the permission of the parents and assent of the older child (generally meaning about 7-9 years of age, at the discretion of the IRB). Research involving greater than minimal risk is permissible if:

(1) there is a prospect of direct benefit to the individual subject (that is, therapeutic research);
(2) there is no prospect of direct benefit to the child, but the research is

a minor increase over minimal risk and will yield vital, generalizable knowledge about the subject's disorder or condition; or

(3) there is no prospect for benefit but the research offers to prevent, alleviate or understand a serious problem affecting the health of children and the project is approved by the Secretary of Health and Human Services after consultation with a panel of experts.

Option (1) is not relevant to survey research and option (3) is pursued only rarely, if ever. Option (2) also is a poor fit for household survey research since such surveys typically do not target children with specific health disorders or conditions. Therefore a key question is whether research involving the acquisition of tissue samples involves greater than minimal risk. NBAC (1999:v) concluded: "IRB's should operate on the presumption that research on coded samples is of minimal risk to the human subject if (a) the study adequately protects the confidentiality of personally identifiable information obtained in the course of research, (b) the study does not involve the inappropriate release of information to third parties, and (c) the study design incorporates an appropriate plan for whether and how to reveal findings to the sources of their physicians should the findings merit such disclosure." However, the NIH/CDC Working Group (Clayton et al., 1995:1790) stated: "As is true for adults, research using linkable or identifiable tissue samples from children, particularly to search for mutations that cause specific diseases, usually poses greater than minimal risk." The NIH/CDC Working Group proceeds to conclude that when the research involves more than minimal risk for children, permission of the parents and assent of the child is sufficient to allow the research to proceed. While this is true for therapeutic research, the regulations indicated that nontherapeutic research on healthy children should entail no more than minimal risk. Therefore an IRB's interpretation of the minimal risk criterion will be critical for the inclusion or exclusion of children in such projects.

Particular concern has been expressed about genetic testing of children for adult onset conditions. The American Society of Human Genetics in collaboration with American College of Medical Genetics (ASHG, 1995), and the American Academy of Pediatrics (in press) have published statements that advise forgoing genetic testing for adult onset disorders unless there are measures that must be taken in childhood to reduce the morbidity or mortality of the condition. Children may be especially vulnerable to social stigma and discrimination based on predictive test results. Therefore any household survey research that included testing of linked specimens of children for serious adult onset disorders probably would be considered greater than minimal risk. Less sensitive information could be generated on children without superceding the minimal risk threshold, although, of course, this determination ultimately must be made by an IRB. However, investigators will have to be cognizant of the burdens of tissue sampling itself for some children. For many children between the ages of about 1 to 6 years, a blood draw can cause substantial anxiety and may be considered greater than minimal risk. Alternative approaches to tissue sampling might be considered for this sensitive age group. With the new impetus at the federal level to include children in research, there is no reason in principle why children could not be participants in household surveys with the collection of biological specimens.

Inclusion of individuals who have lost decision making capacity, perhaps such as those with Alzheimer disease or stroke, might provide a valuable resource for research on these common problems. Federal guidelines for research involving mentally impaired subjects are less explicit than those for children. Recognizing mentally impaired persons as a vulnerable population, the Common Rule directs IRBs to include "additional safeguards . . . to protect the rights and welfare" of these subjects (NBAC, 1998:Appendix I). The Common Rule permits a mentally impaired subject's "legally authorized representative" to give consent for the subject's participation in research, but as the NBAC noted in its 1998 report on research with mentally impaired subjects, the Common Rule "provides no definitions of incapacity, no guidance on the identity or qualifications of a subject representative beyond 'legally authorized' and no guidance on what ratio of risks to potential benefits is acceptable" (NBAC, 1998:Appendix I). Therefore, under existing federal guidelines, inclusion of mentally impaired subjects in a household survey would require only the consent of a legally authorized representative of the subject, as interpreted and approved by an IRB. However, a number of states have legislated prohibitions on research with mentally impaired subjects that would have to be carefully evaluated in a national survey (NBAC, 1998:note 280). The National Bioethics Advisory Commission's 1998 recommendations would not change these general guidelines if the research is deemed of minimal risk. However, if the research was considered to have greater than minimal risk without prospects of benefit to the subject, NBAC's recommendations would require the protocol to be approved by a Special Standing Panel at the Department of Health and Human Services developed to address research issues with mentally impaired individuals. A Special Standing Panel for this purpose has not been established at the time of this writing.

FORMAT FOR CONSENT FORMS

Given the variety of choices that might be offered subjects in research involving tissue storage, a check-box format is coming into use. This means a mini menu is provided to potential subjects on the consent form to allow them to pick and choose options about how their tissues will be used. Providing a variety of options is not necessary, but it has the advantage of being explicit about what the subject wants and may enhance recruitment of subjects who want only limited involvement. The National Heart, Lung and Blood Institute (1997) recommends the extensive use of this format. Of course, the problem with offering many choices is that it creates a complex stratification of subjects that is unlikely to be random. There also are significant administrative burdens to tracking what kinds of projects can be done with different samples.

Using this approach on a more limited basis, investigators might offer choices (documented on the form) including:

- Acquisition of a biological sample and use in research;
- Retention of specimens in an identified or unidentified form;
- Whether research can be conducted using the subject's specimen for health issues beyond the primary focus of the initial project;
- Whether the subject permits recontact for additional survey data or consent for use of linked specimens for studies beyond the primary focus of the initial project; and
- Consent to provide results to a designated family member if the subject is deceased or incompetent.

CONCLUSIONS

The concept of informed consent often has a poor reputation among clinicians and investigators. Consent may been seen as a perfunctory exercise in response to a litigious society, and/or as a futile effort to quickly educate laypersons in complex medical concepts. Indeed, subjects often have a poor recollection of basic research facts, and may even forget that they are involved in research (Advisory Committee on Human Radiation Experiments, 1995). Whether this reflects the inherent impossibility of achieving an ideal informed consent, or whether it reflects the inadequacies of our efforts to obtain informed consent is unclear. Current regulations and standards, while burdensome, are based on clear episodes of abuse of subjects in research. There is often an inherent conflict between the welfare of subjects and the pursuit of knowledge. Thoughtful guidelines and careful peer review are essential. More importantly, subjects should be viewed and treated as collaborators in the research endeavor. To the best of the investigator's ability, and to the limit of the subject's interest and understanding, the ideal is that conversations about projects should proceed as between collaborators, albeit with very different roles to play. Additional research on how subjects view all of these issues is essential.

The preceding points to consider are lengthy and occasionally complex, but they reflect a contemporary sensitivity to risks associated with powerful new technologies. Many of the risks of stigma and discrimination may prove to be overstated, and excessive caution now may slow the progress of research. Nevertheless, the alternative to caution risks generating useless samples through insufficient planning or, worse, a breach in public trust that will impair the integrity of the research enterprise and only further delay the substantial benefits this work offers.

REFERENCES

Advisory Committee on Human Radiation Experiments
    1995   *Final Report of the Advisory Committee on Human Radiation Experiments.* Washington, DC: U.S. Government Printing Office.

Allen, A.L.
    1997   Genetic privacy: Emerging concepts and values. Pp. 31-59 in *Genetic Secrets: Protecting Privacy and Confidentiality in the Genetic Era*, M.A. Rothstein, ed. New Haven: Yale University Press.

American Academy of Pediatrics, Committee on Bioethics
    in   Ethical Issues with Genetic Testing in Pediatrics.
    press

American College of Medical Genetics
    1995   Statement on storage and use of genetic materials. *American Journal of Human Genetics* 57(6):1499-1500.

American Society of Human Genetics
    1996   Statement on informed consent for genetic research. *American Journal of Human Genetics* 59:471-474.

American Society of Human Genetics, American College of Medical Genetics
    1995   Points to consider: Ethical, legal, and psycho-social implications of genetic testing in children and adolescents. *American Journal of Human Genetics* 57:1233-1241.

Andrews, L.
    1997   The genetic information superhighway: Rules of the road for contacting relatives and recontacting former patients. Pp. 133-143 in *Human DNA: Law and Policy: International and Comparative Perspectives*, B.M. Knoppers, C.M. Laberge, and M. Hirtle, eds. Boston: Kluwer Law International.

Annas, G.J.
    1993   Privacy rules for DNA databanks: Protecting coded "future diaries." *Journal of the American Medical Association* 270:2346-2350.

Annas, G.L., L.H. Glantz, and P.A. Roche
    1995   Drafting the genetic privacy act: Science policy, and practical considerations. *Journal of Law, Medicine and Ethics* 23:360-365.

Caplan, A.
    1992   When evil intrudes (In a series "Twenty years after: The legacy of the Tuskegee syphilis study"). *Hastings Center Report* 22(6):29-32.

Clarke, J.T.R., and P.N. Ray
    1997   Look-back: The duty to update genetic counselling. Pp. 121-132 in *Human DNA: Law and Policy: International and Comparative Perspectives*, B.M. Knoppers, C.M. Laberge, and M. Hirtle, eds. Boston: Kluwer Law International.
Clayton, E.W., K.K. Steinberg, M.J. Khoury, E. Thomson, L. Andres, M.J.E. Kahn, L.M. Kopelman, and J.O. Weiss
    1995   Informed consent for genetic research on stored tissue samples. *Journal of the American Medical Association* 274:1786-1792.
Coombs, M.
    1999   A brave new crime free world? Pp. 227-242 in *Genetics and Criminality: The Potential Misuse of Scientific Information in Court*, J. Botkin, W. McMahon, and L. Francis, eds. Washington, DC: The American Psychological Association Press.
Department of Health and Human Services
    1991   Code of federal regulations. Title 45, Part 46: Protection of human subjects. *Federal Register* 56:28003. June 18.
Foster, M.W., D. Bernsten, and T.H. Carter
    1998   A model agreement for genetic research in socially identifiable populations. *American Journal of Human Genetics* 63:696-702.
Freedman, W.
    1998   The role of community in research with stored tissue samples. Pp. 267-301 in *Stored Tissue Samples: Ethical, Legal and Public Policy Implications*, Robert Weir, ed. Iowa City: University of Iowa Press.
Fuller, B.P., M.J.E. Kahn, P.A. Barr, L. Biesecker, E. Crowley, J. Garber, M.K. Mansoura, P. Murphy, J. Murray, J. Phillips, K. Rothenberg, M. Rothstein, J. Stopher, G. Swergold, B. Weber, F.S. Collins, and K.L. Hudson
    1999   Privacy in genetic research. *Science* 285:1359-1361.
Grizzle, W., W.W. Grody, W.W. Noll, M.E. Sobel, S.A. Stass, T. Trainer, H. Travers, V. Weedn, and K. Woodruff
    1999   Ad Hoc Committee on Stored Tissues, College of American Pathologists. Recommended policies for uses of human tissue in research, education and quality control. *Archives of Pathological Laboratory Medicine* 123(4):296-300
Holtzman, N.A., and M.S. Watson, eds.
    1997   Promoting safe and effective genetic testing in the United States. *Final Report of the Task Force on Genetic Testing.* NIH-DOE Working Group on Ethical Legal and Social Implications of Human Genome Research, National Institutes of Health. Bethesda, MD.
Kipnis, K.
    1998   DNA banking in the military: An ethical analysis. Pp. 329-344 in *Stored Tissue Samples: Ethical, Legal and Public Policy Implications*, Robert Weir, ed. Iowa City: University of Iowa Press.
Lapham, V., et al.
    1996   Genetic discrimination: Perspectives of consumers. *Science* 274:621-624.
McEwen, J.E.
    1998   Storing genes to solve crimes: Legal, ethical, and public policy considerations. Pp. 311-328 in *Stored Tissue Samples: Ethical, Legal and Public Policy Implications*, Robert Weir, ed. Iowa City: University of Iowa Press.
Moore v. the Regents of the University of California
    1990   793 P2d 479 (Cal 1990).

Murray, T.H.
  1997 Genetic exceptionalism and "future diaries": Is genetic information different from other medical information? Pp. 60-73 in *Genetic Secrets: Protecting Privacy and Confidentiality in the Genetic Era*, M.A. Rothstein, ed. New Haven: Yale University Press.
National Bioethics Advisory Commission (NBAC)
  1998 Research involving persons with mental disorders that may affect decision making capacity. [Online]. Available: http://bioethics.gov/capacity/TOC.htm.
  1999 Research involving human biological materials: ethical issues and policy guidance. [Online]. Available: http://bioethics.gov/pubs.html.
National Heart, Lung and Blood Institute
  1997 Report of the Special Emphasis Panel: Opportunities and Obstacles to Genetic Research in NHLBI clinical Studies. [Online]. Available: http://www.nhlbi.nih.gov/meetings/workshops/opporsep.htm.
National Human Genome Research Institute
       http://www.nhgri.nih.gov/Policy_and_public_affairs/Legislation/insure.htm
Office for Protection from Research Risks (OPRR), National Institutes of Health
  1997 Issues to consider in the research use of stored data or tissues. November 7. [Online]. Available: http://www.nih.gov/grants/oprr/human subjects/guidance/reposit.htm.
Steinberg, K.K., E.J. Sampson, G.M. McQuillan, and M.J. Khoury
  1998 Use of stored tissue samples for genetic research in epidemiologic studies. P. 83 in *Stored Tissue Samples: Ethical, Legal and Public Policy Implications*, Robert Weir, ed. Iowa City: University of Iowa Press.
Wallace, R.B.
  1997 The potential of population surveys for genetic studies. Pp. 234-244 in *Between Zeus and the Salmon: The Biodemography of Longevity*, K.W. Wachter, and C.E. Finch, eds. Washington DC: National Academy Press.

13

Ethical and Social Issues in Incorporating Genetic Research into Survey Studies

Sharon J. Durfy

The promise of genetic studies for improvements in human health has been widely espoused (for example, Hood, 1992; Fears and Poste, 1999; National Bioethics Advisory Commission, 1999), and genetic studies have achieved added significance as the end point of the Human Genome Project approaches (Pennisi, 1999). There is the strong sense that everyone at some point in the not too distant future will be affected by genetic research, and that medicine in general is undergoing a transformation to "molecular medicine," in which knowledge of individual genomes will aid in disease treatment and prevention.

In a recent report, *Research Involving Human Biological Materials*, the National Bioethics Advisory Commission (NBAC) emphasized that, in order to obtain improvements in human health, it will be crucial to collect biological samples from persons who are also willing to provide ongoing clinical information about themselves (NBAC, 1999). The potential for learning more about health and the human condition by linking ongoing and planned population surveys with genetic research is a topic of intense interest.

Others in this book and elsewhere (e.g., Wallace, 1997) have described existing population survey studies, enumerated the potential applications of population surveys for genetic study, and suggested means by which existing population surveys could be modified to render them more applicable for use in genetic studies. The purpose of this chapter is to provide an overview of the ethical and social issues associated with broadening existing household surveys to include biological sampling and associated genetic studies. The chapter provides some background on the historical consideration of ethical and social issues associated with genetic research, and discusses the particular features of genetic information and samples that give rise to these issues. Four general categories of ethical and social issues in genetic research studies are considered, including privacy, access and ownership of genetic information and materials, psychosocial risks of participating in genetic research studies, and potential group-related harms. In each of these sections, an overview of the relevant concerns associated with genetic research is provided and any special issues particular to survey studies are discussed. This chapter ends by suggesting that three general themes be incorporated into discussions about whether to include biological sampling and/or genetic research in ongoing and planned survey studies. The important topic of informed consent in genetic research is covered by Botkin elsewhere in this volume.

BACKGROUND

Several reports over the last 25 years have concerned, at least in part, ethical issues associated with molecular biology and/or genetic research. A list of selected reports appears in Table 13-1, and includes several from Presidential Commissions, most recently, *Research Involving Human Biological Materials: Ethical Issues and Policy Guidance* from the National Bioethics Advisory Commission (1999). In addition, other governmental agencies and working groups, such as the National Research Council, the Office of Technology Assessment, the Office for Protection from Research Risks (OPPR), and the Task Force on Genetic Testing have considered ethical, social, and policy issues associated with genetic research (see Table 13-1). Thus, there are many existing resources from diverse sources and perspectives to draw from when considering the issues associated with incorporating genetic research into survey studies.

Although not new, the discussion of ethical issues associated with genetic research seems to have intensified in the last 10 years. This likely is due to several factors. The U.S. Human Genome Project (HGP) officially began in 1990, and since that time rapid developments in gene discovery and technical and molecular capabilities have occurred due to the influx of funding to these areas of research. In addition, the HGP directs about 5 percent of its yearly budget into researching ethical, social, and legal issues associated with developments in genetics, attracting increased attention to these issues (Meslin et al., 1997). Also, the increasing investment of commercial interests in genetics and the burgeoning biotechnology industry have focused attention on the adequacy of regulations applicable to genetic technologies and tests and the responsibilities of biotechnology concerns in introducing those technologies to the market

TABLE 13-1 Selected Institutional Reports Including Reference to
Ethical, Social, and/or Policy Issues Related to Genetic Research

Date	Report Title	Institution
1975	Genetic Screening: Programs, Principles and Research	Committee for the Study of Inborn Errors of Metabolism, Division of Medical Sciences, Assembly of Life Sciences, National Academy of Sciences
1982	Splicing Life: A Report on the Social and Ethical Issues of Genetic Engineering with Human Beings	President's Commission for the Study of Ethical Problems in Medicine and Biomedical and Behavioral Research
1983	Screening and Counseling for Genetic Conditions: A Report on the Ethical, Social, and Legal Implications of Genetic Screening, Counseling, and Education Programs	President's Commission for the Study of Ethical Problems in Medicine and Biomedical and Behavioral Research
1988	Mapping and Sequencing the Human Genome	Committee on Mapping and Sequencing the Human Genome, Board on Basic Biology, Commission on Life Sciences, National Research Council
1988	Mapping Our Genes. Genome Projects: How Big, How Fast?	U.S. Congress, Office of Technology Assessment
1993	Human Genetic Research	Office for Protection from Research Risks
1994	Assessing Genetic Risks: Implications for Health and Social Policy	Committee on Assessing Genetic Risks, Division of Health Sciences Policy, Institute of Medicine
1997	Promoting Safe and Effective Genetic Testing in the United States: Principles and Recommendations	Task Force on Genetic Testing of the NIH-DOE Working Group on Ethical, Legal and Social Implications of Human Genome Research
1997	Evaluating Human Genetic Diversity	Committee on Human Genome Diversity, Commission on Life Sciences, National Research Council
1999	Research Involving Human Biological Materials: Ethical Issues and Policy Guidance	National Bioethics Advisory Commission

(Task Force on Genetic Testing, 1997; Holtzman, 1999). Other features of the current time, such as increasing public concern about the privacy of medical records, increasing concerns about access to health care, and increased attention to research ethics issues in general and gene therapy research in particular (Moreno et al., 1998; Ellis, 1999; Woodward, 1996; Marshall, 2000), have increased the attention to social and ethical issues associated with genetic information and genetic research.

IS GENETIC INFORMATION SPECIAL?

Part of the debate surrounding ethical issues in genetics research turns on a discussion of whether genetic information and research are different from other forms of medical information and research, and the implications any differences may have for protecting participants in genetic research protocols. Some have argued that genetic information is not inherently different from other types of sensitive medical information (Murray, 1997). Other forms of medical information may show strong correlation with various diseases or health states. The analogy of viral transmission has been invoked to illustrate how other forms of medical information have direct implications for individuals other than the infected person (Mehlman et al., 1996; NBAC, 1999).

To others, however, genetic information has certain features that render it distinct from other forms of medical information. These include its familial nature, coupled with its unique identifying characteristics (Annas, 1993; Institute of Medicine, 1994; Jonsen et al., 1996; American Society of Human Genetics Social Issues Subcommittee on Familial Disclosure, 1998). With the exception of identical twins, a person's DNA is unique to them, but at the same time, knowledge of genetic information about a person can reveal information about directly identifiable others, including their relatives and even larger groups of individuals. Another distinguishing feature of genetic information may be its predictive capabilities and the potential relevance of this information to persons other than the individual from whom this information was obtained (Institute of Medicine, 1994). Other important considerations relate to the DNA molecule itself. DNA mutations do not change over the course of an individual's lifetime (NBAC, 1999). Also, the DNA molecule is very stable. Although some information can be derived from the molecule at this time, with completion of the Human Genome Project and the deciphering of the entire DNA code, the capacity to extract information will greatly increase (Annas et al., 1995). The wealth of information in a particular DNA molecule is enormous, and in many cases DNA may provide information about predisposition to health conditions that are not yet manifesting, and some of this information may be extremely sensitive. Thus it will be possible for researchers to extract genetic information (health-related or otherwise) from stored samples at times well removed from sample collection. This information may be unknown to the person from whom the sample was taken and may be of a very sensitive nature (Annas, 1993).

These characteristics of genetic information and of DNA molecules raise concerns about genetic research that may be grouped into four general categories: privacy of genetic information, access and ownership of genetic information and samples, psychological risks, and potential group-related harms. Considerable scholarly attention has been directed to each of these areas. The following sections of the chapter provide an overview of the issues to consider in planning and executing genetic research studies in each of these four categories, and directly relate these considerations to incorporating genetic research into survey studies.

PRIVACY OF GENETIC INFORMATION IN RESEARCH STUDIES

Paramount in the conduct of genetic studies is concern about protecting the privacy of potentially sensitive genetic information generated about research participants. A number of groups have offered recommendations for protecting the privacy of study participants' genetic information (for example, Annas et al., 1995; Fuller et al., 1999; NBAC, 1999). Privacy concerns arise because many individuals, institutions, and/or organizations may have an interest in knowing a person's genetic status, and such knowledge has the potential to result in stigmatization, discrimination, and other adverse effects.

Potential Societal Stigmatization and Discrimination

Examples of insurance (e.g., auto, health, and life) and employment discrimination related to genetic information have been reported by consumers and by genetic counselors and nurses in genetics (U.S. Congress, Office of Technology Assessment, 1992; Geller et al., 1996; Lapham et al., 1996). These cases also reveal that difficulties with other societal agencies and institutions such as blood banks, adoption agencies, the military, and schools may be possible (Geller et al., 1996). It has been suggested that educational and legal institutions may have an interest in genetic status for identifying learning problems (Geller et al., 1996; Fuller et al., 1999) and deciding custody and paternity disputes (Fuller et al., 1999). Medical benefits reportedly have been denied to retirees with illnesses determined to have a known genetic basis (Fuller et al., 1999), an issue that may be particularly relevant to incorporating genetic sampling and studies into demographic studies of aging populations.

Despite these studies, the extent of the risk of genetic discrimination in health insurance and other societal institutions has been difficult to pin down. Examples of genetic discrimination, such as those included in the studies referred to above, resulted in legislation in many states and at the federal level, through the Health Insurance and Portability and Accountability Act (HIPAA) (for overviews see Fuller et al., 1999; Hall and Rich, 2000). However, current policies and existing laws to protect the privacy of genetic information are limited in number and nature and vary according to state, while comprehensive federal protections do not exist. A recent study aimed to assess the effectiveness of laws prohibiting health insurers' use of presymptomatic genetic information (Hall and Rich, 2000). The study used a variety of approaches to collect information from representatives of various groups, including genetic counselors, state departments of insurance, and health insurers. Similar data were collected from seven different states with and without laws prohibiting health insurers' use of presymptomatic genetic information. After a lengthy analysis, researchers were unable to document any substantial degree of genetic discrimination by health insurers. They were also unable to document a difference in insurers' actions between states with and without genetic-specific laws or before and after enactment of state laws in a particular state. However, they did discover that insurers were well aware of the existence and content of such laws, and suggest that the existence of such laws has served to heighten insurers' awareness of the "social legitimacy" of using presymptomatic genetic information.

In addition to genetic-specific laws and regulations, protection of participants in federally funded research is addressed by a two-pronged approach, that is, review by an institutional review board (IRB) and execution of an informed consent process. Most institutions that receive some federal funds require that nonfederally funded projects be reviewed by their IRB as well. The critical importance of the informed consent process in describing the privacy-associated risks of genetic research studies and the mechanisms in place to protect participants is discussed in detail by Botkin in this volume, as well as elsewhere (Institute of Medicine, 1994; Clayton et al., 1995; American Society of Human Genetics, 1996). For federally sponsored research, the IRB is responsible for ensuring that participants' risks are minimized, their rights and welfare are protected, and their consent to the research protocol is informed and voluntarily given (Fuller et al., 1999; Department of Health and Human Services, 1991). IRBs also consider issues related to the confidentiality of research records and how these protections are communicated to study participants. Specific suggestions about considering these issues within the context of genetic research studies are offered in the IRB Guidebook (OPRR, 1993). However, as noted elsewhere, research on current practices to protect confidentiality of research data, including genetic data, is limited, and best practices have not yet been developed (Fuller et al., 1999).

One option that may be available to genetic researchers is to obtain a federal Certificate of Confidentiality. Certificates of Confidentiality may apply to certain types of genetic research (see Earley and Strong, 1995; Fuller et al., 1999). Originally developed to provide protections for research into illegal or very sensitive activities, such as illegal behavior, sexual practices, and alcohol or drug use, Certificates of Confidentiality protect federally and privately funded institutions from being compelled to reveal identifying information about participants in a research study (OPRR, 1993). However, as noted by Fuller et al., these Certificates do not protect research participants from being compelled to reveal research data or information.

Another option available to investigators is to work with anonymous or unlinked samples, i.e., samples that cannot be linked to any identifying information. It is often difficult in genetic studies to work with unlinked samples, since matching DNA sequences with medical histories or pedigree information is integral to the research process. In addition, it may still be desirable for individuals to be able to exert some control over how their samples are used, even if the samples have had all identifying information removed (see below; Clayton et al., 1995; Botkin, this volume). However, if unlinked samples can be used, this affords protection from many privacy concerns (Clayton et al., 1995; NBAC, 1999).

A further privacy concern arises when investigators are ready to publish their research results and/or discuss their results in public, either at conferences or, increasingly, with the media. Many genetic conditions are extremely rare, and concern has been expressed that research participants can be identified by presentation of data such as pedigree data in reporting research results (Powers, 1993). Depending on the nature of the sampling and genetic research that might be linked to survey studies, this might or might not be an issue for such studies. The degree to which reporting of pedigree data is truly a risk to the privacy of research participants is a matter of some controversy and experts disagree on what, if anything, should be done to address these potential risks (Powers, 1993; Botkin et al., 1998; Byers and Ashkenas, 1998). However, most agree that researchers and IRBs should consider how study results will be reported, and should communicate any plans for publication to study participants as part of the informed consent process (OPRR, 1993; Powers, 1993).

When considering adding genetic studies to existing household demographic surveys, privacy-related concerns should be considered in light of the fact that at least some data from a number of current longitudinal U.S. household surveys are publicly available. For example, data from the Health and Retirement Study (HRS) are for public use and are available by registering at a World Wide Web site or from the principal investigators, although certain sensitive data may be restricted and proposals for use of sensitive data must be reviewed by an IRB (Willis, 1999). A publicly available, population-based database including information such as economic status and health status coupled with genetic or biological information and/or samples would be an extremely powerful and attractive resource to many investigators. However, policies on what constitutes sensitive data will need to be revisited and mechanisms of data and sample collection and sharing will need to be developed. These policies must also be clearly articulated to study participants as part of the informed consent process. Finally, existing database protections and operating procedures will need to be reexamined in light of collecting biological samples for genetic studies and sharing genetic information and/or samples. Issues associated with exploiting the accessibility of the Internet, and potential electronic security risks associated with genetic data that retains identifiers, are discussed in more detail elsewhere (National Research Council, 1997).

Protecting Individual Privacy Within Families

Protecting the privacy of sensitive genetic information also involves protecting an individual's privacy within the family unit. Family members may have an interest in knowing each other's genetic status. For example, in some genetic research studies, such as studies to identify genetic predispositions to disease, it may be necessary to first identify a gene mutation in a family member who has the disease of interest. Then, researchers can ask whether another family member with no symptoms carries a similar genetic marker. In general, this approach requires that family members cooperate and that the symptomatic family member receive genetic information about himself or herself and share it with the presymptomatic family member(s). Family members may or may not want to participate in such studies (Green and Thomas, 1997) and may or may not want to share their genetic status with each other. Recruitment methods must be carefully considered to protect the privacy of the individual participant in a genetic study (OPRR, 1993).

Recently, the question of who the individual is that needs to be protected, that is, who is the human subject in a particular genetic research study, has come under scrutiny. In a widely publicized case, the OPRR was contacted by a father whose twin daughter had been mailed a questionnaire as part of a genetic research study being conducted at Virginia Commonwealth University (VCU). The questionnaire included questions about parents' and siblings' histories of depression, infertility, alcoholism, and mental illness. Upon opening his daughter's questionnaire, the father complained to the OPRR about the contents and expressed his concerns about the violation of privacy associated with collection of such sensitive information about him when he had not consented to participate in the research study (Brainard, 2000). The OPRR launched an investigation into this and other research studies at VCU and subsequently suspended the research trials (approximately 1,500) at the university. The OPRR agreed with the father and has ruled that the local IRB should have considered this potential risk to family members in the design of the research study (Brainard, 2000). The American Society of Human Genetics has responded to this ruling by issuing an alert discussing the relevant federal regulations concerning waivers of informed consent (American Society of Human Genetics Executive Committee, 2000). This alert also supports the need for further discussions that the Society hopes will be directed toward developing better regulations that will protect study participants without unduly restricting human genetic and genetic epidemiology research studies. In the context of a household survey, IRBs will have to carefully consider whether the acquisition of data on other family members makes those family members human subjects and whether informed consent must be obtained from them.

ACCESS TO AND OWNERSHIP OF GENETIC INFORMATION AND SAMPLES

Biological samples from participants in a population-based survey may be an important repository of interest to many researchers and may allow previously challenging research questions to be addressed. It would be in keeping with the current policy of some U.S. demographic studies to make genetic data and/or samples generated in association with household surveys publicly accessible to all researchers. In addition to the privacy issues outlined above, issues of ownership of samples and/or genetic information and data need to be addressed in considering the collection of biological samples and the addition of genetic research to survey studies.

Commercial Interests

Issues of ownership and access are becoming increasingly prominent in the area of genetic research, especially as the international Human Genome Project nears its goal of a complete, publicly available sequence of the human genome. In one widely discussed example, the private Iceland company deCODE Genetics has been granted permission from the Icelandic parliament to create a health database for the entire population of Iceland (Enserink, 1999; Annas, 2000; Gulcher and Stefansson,

2000). This database, combined with collection of biological samples for genetic analysis, is expected to be a very powerful tool in the search for the genetic contributions to disease, including common diseases such as cancer and heart disease. However, the project has been the target of national and international concerns regarding the mechanism of consent utilized, privacy issues, and questions regarding the desirability of a private company holding exclusive rights to a database containing information about an entire country's gene pool (Enserink, 1999; Annas, 2000; Gulcher and Stefansson, 2000).

A second recent example of commercial interest in genetic research may be especially relevant to incorporating genetic research into household survey studies. Boston University (BU), sponsor of the Framingham Heart Study, has entered into an agreement with venture capitalists to create Framingham Genomic Medicine, Inc. (FGM), a for-profit company in which BU will have a 20 percent interest. According to one report, the company will use the study's voluminous collection of data, which includes genetic, clinical, and behavioral components, to create an electronic database which biotechnology and pharmaceutical companies may access after paying an annual fee. In addition to data of varying types, approximately 5,000 blood samples have been collected from study participants. Negotiations are currently under way to sort out issues of ownership and access, and include representatives of BU, FGM, and the National Heart, Lung and Blood Institute, the governmental agency that has funded a considerable proportion of the research (Rosenberg and Kowalcyzk, 2000).

It may be very instructive for those involved in survey studies to follow the Framingham discussions because of the similarities between the Framingham Heart Study and household surveys. Some household survey studies collect vast amounts of data on participants over long periods of time. The survey studies and corresponding databases this volume is concerned with are or will be established with federal funds. Similar to the Framingham study, some of the survey studies have had a longstanding policy of public availability of the data. Both deCODE and FGM are founded on the belief that biotechnology and pharmaceutical firms will have considerable interest in a population-based repository of biological samples coupled with an extensive health-related database. Policies will need to be developed regarding who and what entities should have access to what information and/or samples collected in association with survey studies. Others have discussed issues related to ownership and financial interests in research of this type (e.g., National Research Council, 1997; Knoppers et al., 1999; Annas, 2000). All of these policies must be clearly communicated to study participants as part of the informed consent process.

Study Participants

Issues of ownership of genetic information and/or samples also reside at the level of the individual study participant. The deCODE example has focused attention on the rights of study participants to opt out of participation in the database. In the deCODE example, informed consent has been waived. Unless an Icelandic citizen specifically requests their information not be included, their information can be submitted to the database. The argument supporting this approach is that obtaining informed consent from all 270,000 Icelanders would not be feasible, and in order to create a database with the desired power for health-related research, inclusion of data from as many Icelanders as possible is required. Compelling reasons must be presented to waive informed consent in genetic studies, and it does not appear that adding genetic research studies to survey studies would automatically qualify for a waiver, although this will depend very much on the nature of the genetic research under consideration. Specific situations in which waiver of consent for genetic studies might be possible have been discussed elsewhere (NBAC, 1999; American Society of Human Genetics, Executive Committee, 2000).

Once a study is ongoing, some individuals, for whatever reason, decide they no longer want to participate. In certain types of genetic studies, particularly those in which family and pedigree data are critical to the analysis, it may be very difficult scientifically to have a key participant decide to no longer continue in a study. Researchers must develop a plan, communicated to study participants prior to their enrollment in the study, regarding how the biological sample and any data generated from that sample or information provided by the participant will be handled should they decide to withdraw from the study (Clayton et al., 1995; Botkin, this volume).

Because deCODE is at the initial stage of developing the database and negotiating the licensing agreement with the Icelandic government, the published discussions surrounding deCODE's plans for gene discovery using the database information do not yet include what will be done if clinically relevant genetic information is discovered. Of course, what happens in Iceland, a country with a comprehensive national health insurance system, may be very different from what happens in the United States. But an important question for genetic research in general is that of the nature of clinically relevant information and what access study participants can expect to have to such information throughout the course of a study.

Experts have discussed policies for sharing research results with study participants and some of these discussions have considered genetic research results in particular (NBAC, 1999). Some think that all research results should be shared with study participants (Veatch, 1981). Others believe that serious harms could result from sharing unconfirmed findings and that unconfirmed findings do not constitute "information" (MacKay, 1984; Fost and Farrell, 1989). In general, the consensus of opinion is that genetic research results must be scientifically valid and confirmed prior to their provision to study participants (Task Force on Genetic Testing, 1997; Fuller et al., 1999; NBAC, 1999).

This may be complicated in genetic research studies, because in general, genes, mutations, and their relationship to disease(s) are always more complex than first presumed. Even so-called "simple" Mendelian conditions, such as cystic fibrosis (CF) and Huntington disease (HD) have proven to be more complicated than originally understood. For example, cystic fibrosis, a Mendelian inherited recessive condition, has been shown to have hundreds of mutations that cause effects ranging from infertility in men, without other effects, to the classically understood symptoms of life-threatening lung and pancreatic disease (Welsh et al., 1995). Huntington disease, thought to be a clear example of an autosomal dominant neurological disorder, demonstrates anticipation, in that successive generations within a family sometimes show earlier onset of disease symptoms, particularly if the mutation is transmitted through the paternal line (Ranen et al., 1995). In addition to complexity of disease mechanism within a gene, genetic factors and genetic conditions have been shown to have unexpected associations, such as that of apolipoprotein E (APOE) alleles and Alzheimer's disease (American College of Medical Genetics/American Society of Human Genetics Working Group on APOE and Alzheimer Disease, 1995). Thus, investigators can expect both complex and unexpected findings and associations between genes and other factors (both genetic and nongenetic) to occur, which may pose challenges in communicating results to study participants.

As genetic research progresses, it can be expected that susceptibilities or inherited characteristics with much less import for disease than the examples above will be identified. For example, it is already possible in juvenile (type 1) diabetes to use genetic markers at the HLA locus to screen and identify children with an increased risk for this form of diabetes (i.e., a risk of approximately 1/80 vs. the general population risk of 1/300). Is this information relevant to study participants in any way, should it be provided, and if so, how? One solution to communicating very complicated genetic information of uncertain value that is generated in the context of a research proposal is to be very clear, in policy and communication with study participants, that interim results will not be provided to research participants.

Even if researchers do not plan to provide study participants with interim research results, circumstances may occur to cause them to reconsider this decision. Researchers may feel compelled to act on any information they discover (expected or unexpected) with clinical relevance. Also, participants may approach researchers asking for information for various reasons. While searching for a gene for susceptibility to breast and ovarian cancer, University of Michigan researchers were approached by a study participant at risk to carry a gene mutation who had scheduled a prophylactic mastectomy. She inquired of researchers if there were any new developments prior to having her surgery. According to their research results, she did not carry the gene mutation and researchers were suddenly faced with a decision about what interim information to convey to her and how to convey it (Biesecker et al., 1993; Breo, 1993).

Therefore, in planning genetic research studies, researchers must consider the following questions: What is the role of study participants in deciding about the use of their samples for research? What research results are of interest to study participants? Which, if any, research results will be provided to study participants and when will these results be provided? If future research studies generate information of potential interest to study participants, will this information be provided? How will genetic information be provided to study participants? Who will provide the information and what support will be offered to study participants in understanding the information? Researchers need to think through these questions as much as possible and have a plan in place to address them (OPRR, 1993; Clayton et al., 1995; NBAC, 1999). Some of these issues can be addressed in the informed consent process in which the agreement between researchers and study participants about what information will or will not be provided and when is clarified (Botkin, this volume). Other recommendations involve putting mechanisms in place to ensure that the information provided to research participants is valid and replicable, and having support systems for research participants in place to minimize any potential psychological risks associated with receipt of genetic information (see, e.g., Institute of Medicine, 1994; Task Force on Genetic Testing, 1997; Fuller et al., 1999).

PSYCHOLOGICAL RISKS OF PARTICIPATION IN GENETIC RESEARCH STUDIES

Many studies have documented psychological effects associated with receipt of genetic information. For genetic studies that plan to provide genetic information to participants as part of the study, these effects must be considered. Familial relationships and dynamics may be altered when family members receive genetic information and preconceptions of genetic status and risk are directly supported or refuted (for example, Bloch et al., 1992; Fannos and Johnson, 1995a; 1995b). Individual psychological effects of receipt of genetic information have been documented and likely vary depending on the nature of the disorder in question, among other features (Bloch et al., 1992; Marteau et al., 1992; Wiggins et al., 1992; Lerman and Croyle, 1996). A number of studies have shown depression and/or anxiety to be associated, to varying degrees, with discovery of gene mutations (for example, Wiggins et al., 1992; Lerman et al., 1996). Along with these anticipated results, unexpected effects of providing genetic information have been described (Huggins et al., 1992).

Depending on the status of the research, not all participants in a genetic study will necessarily receive informative results. This is because in the early phases of gene discovery, mutations are identified through linkage analysis and/or gene mutations have not been fully characterized and the information may be difficult to interpret. Therefore some individuals who may have expected to have their genetic risk clarified as a result of participation in a genetic study will not receive this benefit and may experience psychological effects associated with the continued uncertainty.

In addition to possible effects due to provision of genetic information generated by the study itself, investigators may also discover information with significant impact for individuals and families, such as nonpaternity, adoption, abortion, and other biological and/or social information. Concerns about psychological effects on individuals and families also extend to recruitment for genetic studies. One ongoing discussion includes whether IRBs should be concerned with how to avoid familial coercion to participate in a genetic research study (Parker and Lidz, 1994). This might become an issue in the context of demographic studies if any proposed research targets family members of the original demographic study participants.

Discussing these possibilities with study participants is an important component of the informed consent process for applicable genetic studies. As much as is possible, investigators must articulate plans to address such possibilities, and IRBs evaluating these research studies must be aware of these potential risks associated with genetic study participation and evaluate the study procedures accordingly (OPRR, 1993).

In general, if results of a clinically significant nature are to be provided, appropriate resources, including genetic or other sources of counseling, information, and/or support, must be available to study participants in order to minimize the potential for psychological risks (Institute of Medicine, 1994; Fuller et al., 1999; NBAC, 1999). For some studies, this may be a prohibitive undertaking: one estimate places the cost of counseling before and after a genetic test for 10,000 study participants at approximately $500,000 (Fuller et al., 1999). The Health and Retirement Study includes 12,600 participants (Wallace, 1997).

Finally, it is notable that the types of psychological risks described above can be used to understand the potential benefits associated with participation in genetic research studies. For some people, knowledge of genetic status can contribute to feelings of well being, can provide relief from uncertainty or anxiety (regardless of the results), can positively affect familial relationships, may help people obtain needed social benefits and/or health care, and can aid in future financial and life planning (see, e.g., Bloch et al., 1992; Wiggins et al., 1992; Biesecker et al., 1993; Breo, 1993; Holloway et al., 1994; Mitchell et al., 1996). In addition to the potential for psychological harm, the informed consent process should also allow potential study participants the opportunity to consider the possible benefits of participation in genetic research.

Both the potential psychological benefits and risks of participating in genetic research studies are not yet well documented, and further research is required to understand these effects for research participants. Survey studies (both ongoing and proposed) that follow individuals over long periods of time may be well positioned to contribute to this effort if genetic research studies are added to them. Some of these studies already maintain the infrastructure necessary to collect information regarding health-related decisions and life planning issues over extended periods of time. Questions specifically addressing the effects of participation in genetic research studies and knowledge of genetic information could be added to existing instruments and/or data collection methods. Assessing the impact of genetic information on individuals and their families in terms of the life decisions they make over extended periods of time would greatly enhance the informed consent process both in genetic research studies and in clinical genetic testing.

GROUP-RELATED HARMS OF PARTICIPATION IN GENETIC RESEARCH STUDIES

Privacy, access, ownership, and psychological risks of genetic information all must be considered within the context of cultural views of genetic and medical information and scientific research. American society as a whole places a great deal of value on information in and of itself and strongly supports research into health-related concerns. Overlaying the value we place on personal health-related information is the special regard in which we seem to hold genetic information. We seem to view it as uniquely predictive and powerful, with the ability to predict the future and to profoundly shape and affect one's life. We use genetic information to explain all kinds of behaviors and circumstances, both health-related and other (Nelkin and Lindee, 1995). The importance of genetic contributions to understanding human behavior will only increase as the entire genome is decoded and researchers begin work to understand all the genes identified.

We also relate genetic information to groups of people, raising the potential for stigmatization and discrimination of individuals who belong to those groups, as well as the possible stigmatization of the group as a whole (National Research Council, 1997). The concern is that genetic explanations might be used to support racial, gender, and other stereotypes. Thus research designed to study disease or other characteristics of a particular group may result in labeling of all members of that group, even those who did not participate in the research. This is one reason that some argue that study participants may want some control over how their biological samples are used, even if the study protocol uses samples that are completely anonymous (Clayton et al., 1995; Botkin, this volume).

The complex questions of how groups define themselves, how researchers define groups to study, and the implications of determining how or if the genetic characteristics of a group align with the socially defined characteristics of the group, have been discussed in detail elsewhere (National Research Council, 1997; Juengst, 1998; Reilly, 1998). These questions will arise if genetic research is incorporated into survey studies. Because the large demographic studies currently being conducted in the United States are representative of the population as a whole, they will include individuals for whom group-related issues may be very important. Second, researchers may be particularly interested in studying subsets of individuals from the larger population-based sample that belong to a particular group defined by the researcher. Third, a consideration of whether the elderly constitute a "group," and the potential for group-related harms to the elderly, may arise. One goal of some current survey studies is to understand the health-related needs of the U.S. population as it ages (Wallace, 1997). The potential for stigmatization and discrimination of the elderly in our society is real, particularly as the population continues to age and the costs of health care associated with conditions of age continue to increase. These questions of identification of populations and groups are directly relevant to demographers and identify an intersection between genetic research and demography that bears further research and analysis.

A thoughtful consideration of mechanisms to address potential group-related harms will be important if genetic research is incorporated into survey studies. The report "Evaluating Human Genetic Diversity" by the Committee on Human Genome Diversity, National Research Council (1997), made a number of recommendations for conducting research studies on human genetic variation in a multinational, multicultural setting that can be extrapolated to genetic research within survey studies. The Committee made recommendations relevant to considering genetic research studies in general as well as recommendations that specifically address group-related harms. The latter include the importance of accurate identification of populations through consultation with local communities and other experts, processes for handling "community withdrawal from a genetic study," and a discussion of individual vs. group consent to research processes.

The issue of individual and group consent for participation in genetic research focuses on the informed consent process and the necessity, desirability, and/or practicality of obtaining group or population consent for the genetic research in question (Foster et al., 1998; Juengst, 1998; Reilly, 1998). Clearly the nature of the population or group under consideration dramatically affects how one approaches the informed consent process, and this aspect of research proposals must be considered on a case-by-case basis.

Consultation with members of the group to be studied is a crucial component of designing research studies that has been used in genetics research in the past—for example, in providing Tay-Sachs screening programs (Beck et al., 1974)—as well as recently. Consultation with the Ashkenazi Jewish community in the Baltimore-Washington area was an important part of planning the anonymous testing research directed at determining the frequency of mutations in BRCA1 and BRCA2 (breast cancer genes) in that population (Hartge et al., 1999). An example of community consultation in a genetic research study on diabetes in a Native American population has been described in detail (Foster et al., 1998). Community consultation allows the views of the group and its individuals about privacy, the body, bodily substances, genetic information, and research in general to be identified and incorporated into research designs. It also allows groups to express their interests, financial or otherwise, in the genetic information, samples, and/or gene sequences that are generated with their research participation. The diabetes study referenced above describes an approach to sharing of financial proceeds with the tribe (Foster et al., 1998). Community consultation is an approach of increasing importance in genetic research as well as in research with human subjects in general.

NEW DIRECTIONS

Coupling ongoing and planned survey studies with biological sampling for genetic studies holds considerable potential to contribute to our understanding of human diseases, conditions, and aging. In considering how to best utilize these potential resources and at the same time effectively address the specific issues itemized in this chapter, three general themes should infuse discussions of the issues.

Research Participants as Research Partners

Genetic research is causing us to rethink the relationship between the researcher and the study participant. Henry Greely (1998) has suggested that participants in genetic research be regarded as "somewhat limited" partners in that research. Several observations indicate that, at least in genetic research, there is a move toward more of a partnership between these two roles. First, there is now a presumption in favor of providing to research participants more detailed information about all facets of the study and the researchers involved. The chapter by Botkin in this volume documents this phenomenon.

Second, support groups and patient advocacy groups have become more involved in the research process in genetics. For example, the Alliance of Genetic Support Groups has produced a brochure on informed consent for participation in research studies, entitled *Informed Consent: Participating in Genetic Research Studies* (1993). This brochure advises potential study participants on the areas they should consider and the questions they should ask prior to agreeing to participate in a research study. In a second example of the involvement of research participants in the research process, the National Institutes of Health (NIH) is recommending, although not yet requiring, that its institutes include patient advocates in their research study sections (Agnew, 1999). Several institutes have implemented this recommendation already, and this is a model that has been used by the Department of Defense to review applications for its breast cancer research funding (Agnew, 1999).

Other observations I have made come from my participation as coinvestigator in NIH-funded studies to examine how best to offer testing for inherited susceptibility to breast cancer. In 1994, these studies formed a group called the Cancer Genetic Studies Consortium (CGSC). Representatives of the National Breast Cancer Coalition (NBCC) have been involved in cancer genetic research in several ways. These include: authoring and publishing in a prominent journal a position statement on whether such genetic susceptibility testing should be offered clinically or only under research protocols (Visco, 1996); participating in NIH CGSC meetings (at which the advocate representative sat at the head table with NIH representatives); and coauthoring (with NIH investigators, including Francis Collins, head of the U.S. Human Genome Project) papers that describe issues associated with genetic research in general and research on genetic susceptibility to breast and ovarian cancer in particular (Clayton et al., 1995; Burke et al., 1996; Geller et al., 1997). Most recently, NBCC representatives coauthored a paper on privacy issues in genetic research (Fuller et al., 1999).

There is room right now for discussion of how a new relationship between researchers and participants in genetic research should look, a discussion that should involve both parties. Incorporating genetic research into survey studies may provide an opportunity to engage the general population in this discussion. Rethinking the relationship between the parties in genetic research will also force examination of the researcher-participant relationship in general, and will require a reexamination of the nature of genetic information and research and how they are similar to or different from other types of medical information and research.

Responding to Change

In genetics, the one constant seems to be change. What is understood about genes and the genetic mechanisms of disease changes over time with further research. Data regarding the potential risks and benefits associated with participating in genetic research change. Laws affecting access to insurance and other social goods change. Federal regulations affecting genetic tests and patent decisions change. The capacity for clinical intervention in various diseases changes. Some sort of mechanism is needed to respond to these changes and to provide advice to researchers and participants in genetic studies.

It is unrealistic to expect the IRB system, with its current level of support, to bear the responsibility for responding to the constantly shifting sands of genetic research. Others have recommended that a national advisory committee on genetic testing be formed (Institute of Medicine, 1994; Task Force on Genetic Testing, 1997). As a result, the Secretary's Advisory Committee on Genetic Testing (SACGT) was recently established, and provides recommendations to the Secretary of Health and Human Services on genetic testing and research issues. The SACGT may address "the development of guidelines, including criteria regarding the risks and benefits of genetic testing, to assist Institutional Review Boards in reviewing genetic testing protocols in both academic and commercial settings" (http://www4.od.nih.gov/oba/sacgt.htm). As policy makers and investigators consider adding a genetic component to existing and planned demographic studies, they should look to the recommendations of this body and others. For large household surveys with already existing advisory committees, one way to do this would be to expand committee membership to include people who are familiar with ethical, legal, and social issues associated with genetic research. The advisory body could then provide oversight and advice on the collection of samples; the informed consent process; privacy and confidentiality issues; and the interplay of various study procedures and ethical, legal, and social issues.

A Research Agenda

This chapter has described various areas in which further research would help define the best protocols by which to conduct genetic research in association with household surveys. The need for research on how best to conduct genetic research cannot be understated, and is a current focus of the federal HGP (Collins et al., 1998; http://www.nhgri.nih.gov/98plan/elsi/). Many of the presumed risks and benefits associated with genetic research have only limited data to support them as either risks or benefits. For example, the limited and conflicting nature of data on insurance discrimination against people with genetic diagnoses or predispositions has been noted. There are very few data on the impact of genetic testing and research on the family unit. The lack of data poses challenges for the informed consent process in genetic research studies because it makes it difficult to give potential study participants good information about the true nature of the risks and benefits associated with their participation in a given study. Little is known about how potential study participants perceive these risks and benefits or about their motivation for participation in genetic studies. Little is known about the effectiveness of the informed consent process for genetic studies.

Survey studies that consider including a genetic component have an exciting opportunity to address some of these questions. Pilot studies of attitudes toward including a genetic component in household surveys would provide information about attitudes toward genetic research and research in general, and about motivations for participation in research. Informed consent forms could be piloted with study participants and would provide important data about the informed consent process for genetic research. Educational methods and materials could be developed to help the general population, in its ethnic and cultural diversity, understand genetic studies. Many survey studies have the infrastructure in place to follow participants over long periods, affording an opportunity to assess the experience of being in a genetic research study and potentially receiving genetic information over an extended time. In addition, given the nature of the information collected by some of these surveys, participant reports of effects of receiving genetic information can be correlated with other information independently obtained, such as various economic and/or health data.

A recent analysis of the Ethical, Legal and Social Implications (ELSI) Program of the HGP has identified a number of areas in which the ELSI program could strengthen its research portfolio. Specifically, the ELSI Research Planning and Evaluation Group recommended that ELSI "encourage activities that employ new theoretical perspectives . . . that promote cross-fertilization between ELSI research and other areas of the social sciences, law, and the humanities," and that investigators be recruited "from a broader array of disciplines, such as economics, anthropology" (ELSI Research Planning and Evaluation Group, 2000). It seems that the time is ripe for a merging of the many disciplines, approaches, and resources that would be involved if genetic studies were appended to survey studies. If approached in a thoughtful and systematic fashion, expanding survey studies to include a genetic component has the potential to address many questions directly relevant to the introduction of genetic information and genetic services to the population as a whole.

REFERENCES

Agnew, B.
  1999   NIH invites activists into the inner sanctum. *Science* 283:1999-2001.
Alliance of Genetic Support Groups
  1993   *Informed Consent: Participating in Genetic Research Studies.* Chevy Chase, MD: Alliance of Genetic Support Groups.
American College of Medical Genetics/American Society of Human Genetics Working Group on ApoE and Alzheimer Disease
  1995   Statement on use of apolipoprotein E testing for Alzheimer disease. *Journal of the American Medical Association* 274:1627-1629.
American Society of Human Genetics
  1995   Statement on informed consent for genetic research. *American Journal of Human Genetics* 59:471-474.
American Society of Human Genetics, Executive Committee
  2000   Membership Alert: Family History and Privacy Advisory.
American Society of Human Genetics, Social Issues Subcommittee on Familial Disclosure
  1998   Professional disclosure of familial genetic information. *American Journal of Human Genetics* 62:474-483.
Annas, G.J.
  1993   Privacy rules for DNA data banks. Protecting coded 'future diaries'. *Journal of the American Medical Association* 270:2346-2350.
  2000   Rules for Research on Human Genetic Variation—Lessons from Iceland. *New England Journal of Medicine* 342:1830-1833.
Annas, G.J., L.H. Glanz, and P.A. Roche
  1995   Drafting the Genetic Privacy Act: Science, policy and practical considerations. *Journal of Law, Medicine and Ethics* 23:360-366.
Beck, E., S. Blaichman, C.R. Scriver, and C.L. Clow
  1974   Advocacy and compliance in genetic screening. Behavior of physicians and clients in a voluntary program of testing for the Tay-Sachs gene. *New England Journal of Medicine* 291:1166-1170.
Biesecker, B.B., M. Boehnke, K. Calzone, D.S. Markel, J.E. Garber, F.S. Collins, and B.L. Weber
  1993   Genetic counseling for families with inherited susceptibility to breast and ovarian cancer. *Journal of the American Medical Association* 269:1970-1974.
Bloch, M., S. Adam, S. Wiggins, M. Huggins, and M.R. Hayden
  1992   Predictive testing for Huntington disease in Canada: The experience of those receiving an increased risk. *American Journal of Medical Genetics* 42:499-507.

Botkin, J.R., W.M. McMahon, K.R. Smith, and J.E. Nash
  1998   Privacy and confidentiality in the publication of pedigrees. *Journal of the American Medical Association* 279:1808-1812.

Brainard, J.
  2000   Father's complaint contributes to suspension of university's research trials. *Chronicle of Higher Education* (online). June 13, 2000.

Breo, L.
  1993   Altered fates—counseling families with inherited breast cancer. *Journal of the American Medical Association* 269:2017-2022.

Burke, W., M.J.E. Kahn, J.E. Garber, and F.S. Collins
  1996   "First do no harm" also applies to cancer susceptibility testing. *Cancer Journal from Scientific American* 2:250-252.

Byers, P.H., and J. Ashkenas
  1998   Pedigrees—publish? Or perish the thought? *American Journal of Human Genetics* 63:678-681.

Clayton, E.W., K.K. Steinberg, M.J. Khoury, E. Thomson, L. Andrews, M.J.E. Kahn, L.M. Kopelman, and J.O. Weiss
  1995   Informed consent for genetic research on stored tissue samples. *Journal of the American Medical Association* 274:1786-1792.

Collins, F.S., A. Patrinos, E. Jordan, A. Chakavarti, G. Gesteland, and L. Walters
  1998   New goals for the U.S. Human Genome Project: 1999-2003. *Science* 282:682-689.

Department of Health and Human Services
  1991   Code of federal regulations. Title 45, Part 46: Protection of Human Subjects. *Federal Register* 56:28003. June 18.

Earley, C.L., and L.C. Strong
  1995   Certificates of confidentiality: A valuable tool for protecting genetic data. *American Journal of Human Genetics* 57:727-731.

Ellis, G.B.
  1999   Keeping research subjects out of harm's way. *Journal of the American Medical Association* 282:1963-1965.

Ethical, Legal and Social Implications Program (ELSI), Research Planning and Evaluation Group
  2000   A review and analysis of the ethical, legal, and social implications (ELSI) research programs at the National Institutes of Health and the Department of Energy. February 10, 2000.

Enserink, M.
  1999   Iceland OKs private health databank. *Science* 283:13.

Fannos J.H., and J.P. Johnson
  1995a Barriers to carrier testing for adult cystic fibrosis sibs: The importance of not knowing. *American Journal of Medical Genetics* 59:85-91.
  1995b Perception of carrier status by cystic fibrosis siblings. *American Journal of Human Genetics* 57:431-438.

Fears, R., and G. Poste
  1999   Building population genetics resources using the U.K. NHS. *Science* 284:267-268.

Fost, N., and P.M. Farrell
  1989   A prospective randomized trial of early diagnosis and treatment of cystic fibrosis: A unique ethical dilemma. *Clinical Research* 37:495-500.

Foster, M.W., D. Bernsten, and T.H. Carter
  1998   A model agreement for genetic research in socially identifiable populations. *American Journal of Human Genetics* 63:696-702.

Fuller, B.P., M.J.E. Kahn, P.A. Barr, L. Biesecker, E. Crowley, J. Garber, M.K. Mansoura, P. Murphy, J. Murray, J. Phillips, K. Rothernberg, M. Rothstein, J. Stopher, G. Swergold, B. Weber, F.S. Collins, and K.L. Hudson
  1999 Privacy in genetics research. *Science* 285:1359-1361.

Geller, G., J.R. Botkin, M.J. Green, N. Press, B.B. Biesecker, B. Wilfond, G. Grana, M.B. Daly, K. Schneider, and M.J.E. Kahn
  1996 Genetic testing for susceptibility to adult-onset cancer. The process and content of informed consent. *Journal of the American Medical Association* 277:1467-1474.

Geller, L.N., J.S. Alper, P.R. Billings, C.I. Barash, J. Beckwith, and M.R. Natowicz
  1995 Individual, family, and societal dimensions of genetic discrimination: A case study analysis. *Science and Engineering Ethics* 2:71-88.

Greely, H.T.
  1998 Genomics research and human subjects. *Science* 282:625.

Green, R.M., and A.M. Thomas
  1997 Whose gene is it? A case discussion about familial conflict over genetic testing for breast cancer. *Journal of Genetic Counseling* 6:245-254.

Gulcher, J.R., and K. Stefansson
  2000 The Icelandic Healthcare Database and informed consent. *New England Journal of Medicine* 342:1827-1830.

Hall, M.A., and S.S. Rich
  2000 Laws restricting health insurers' use of genetic information: Impact on genetic discrimination. *American Journal of Human Genetics* 66:293-307.

Hartge, P., J.P. Struewing, S. Wacholder, L.C. Brody, and M.A. Tucker
  1999 The prevalence of common BRCA1 and BRCA2 mutations among Ashkenazi Jews. *American Journal of Human Genetics* 64:963-970.

Holloway, S., M. Mennie, A. Crosbie, B. Smith, S. Raeburn, D. Dinwoodie, A. Wright, H. May, K. Calder, L. Barron, and D.J.H. Brock
  1994 Predictive testing for Huntington disease: Social characteristics and knowledge of applicants, attitudes to the test procedure and decisions made after testing. *Clinical Genetics* 46:175-180.

Holtzman, N.A.
  1999 Are genetic tests adequately regulated? *Science* 286:409.

Hood, L.
  1992 Biology and medicine in the twenty-first century. In *The Code of Codes. Scientific and Social Issues in the Human Genome Project*, Daniel J. Kevles and Leroy Hood, eds. Cambridge MA, London, England: Harvard University Press.

Huggins, M., M. Bloch, S. Wiggins, S. Adam, O. Suchowersky, M. Trew, M. Klimek, C.R. Greenberg, M. Eleff, L.P. Thompson, J. Knight, P. MacLeod, K. Girad, J. Theilmann, A. Hedrick, and M.R. Hayden.
  1992 Predictive testing for Huntington disease in Canada: Adverse effects and unexpected results in those receiving a decreased risk. *American Journal of Medical Genetics* 42:508-515.

Institute of Medicine
  1994 *Assessing genetic risks: Implications for health and social policy.* Committee on Assessing Genetic Risks, Division of Health Sciences Policy. Washington, DC: National Academy Press.

Jonsen, A.R., S.J. Durfy, W. Burke, and A.M. Motulsky
  1996 The advent of the "unpatients": The ethics of molecular medicine. *Nature Medicine* 2:622-624.

Juengst, E.T.
1998 Group identity and human diversity: Keeping biology straight from culture. *American Journal of Human Genetics* 63:673-677.
Knoppers, B.M., M. Hirtle, and K.C. Glass
1999 Commercialization of genetic research and public policy. *Science* 286:2277-2278.
Lapham, E.V., C. Kozma, and J.O. Weiss
1996 Genetic discrimination: Perspectives of consumers. *Science* 274:621-624.
Lerman, C., and R.T. Croyle
1996 Emotional and behavioral responses to genetic testing for susceptibility to cancer. *Oncology* 10:191-195, 199.
Lerman, C., S. Narod, K. Schulman, C. Hughes, A. Gomez-Caminero, G. Bonney, K. Gold, B. Trock, D. Main, J. Lynch, C. Fulmore, C. Snyder, S.J. Lemon, T. Conway, P. Tonin, G. Lenoir, and H. Lynch.
1996 *BRCA1* testing in families with hereditary breast-ovarian cancer. A prospective study of patient decision making and outcomes. *Journal of the American Medical Association* 275:1885-1892.
MacKay, C.R.
1984 Ethical issues in research design and conduct: Developing a test to detect carriers of Huntington's disease. *IRB* 6:1-5.
Marshall, E.
2000 Gene therapy on trial. *Science* 288:951-957.
Marteau T.M., M. van Duijn, and I. Ellis
1992 Effects of genetic screening on perceptions of health: A pilot study. *Journal of Medical Genetics* 29:24-26.
Mehlman, M.J., E.D. Kodish, P. Whitehouse, A.B. Zinn, S. Sollitto, J. Berger, E.J. Chiao, M.S. Dosick, and S.B. Cassidy
1996 The need for anonymous genetic counseling and testing. *American Journal of Human Genetics* 58:393-397.
Meslin, E.M., E.J. Thomson, and J.T. Boyer
1997 The Ethical, Legal, and Social Implications research program at the National Human Genome Research Institute. *Kennedy Institute of Ethics Journal* 7:291-298.
Mitchell, J.J., A. Capua, C. Clow, and C.R. Scriver
1996 Twenty-year outcome analysis of genetic screening programs for Tay-Sachs and B-Thalassemia disease carriers in high schools. *American Journal of Human Genetics* 59:793-798.
Moreno, J., A.L. Caplan, P.R. Wolpe, and Members of the Project on Informed Consent, Human Research Ethics Group
1998 Updating protections for human subjects involved in research. *Journal of the American Medical Association* 280:1951-1958.
Murray, T.
1997 Genetic exceptionalism and future diaries: Is genetic information different from other medical information? Pp. 60-73 in *Genetic Secrets*, M. Rothstein, ed. New Haven, CT: Yale University Press.
National Academy of Sciences
1975 *Genetic Screening. Programs, Principles and Research*. Committee for the Study of Inborn Errors of Metabolism. Division of Medical Sciences, Assembly of Life Sciences. Washington, DC: National Academy of Sciences.
National Bioethics Advisory Commission (NBAC)
1999 *Research Involving Human Biological Materials: Ethical Issues and Policy Guidance. Volume I: Report and Recommendations of the National Bioethics Advisory Commission.* Rockville, MD: National Bioethics Advisory Commission.

National Research Council
 1997 *Evaluating Human Genetic Diversity*. Committee on Human Genome Diversity. Board on Biology, Commission on Life Sciences. Washington, DC: National Academy Press.

Nelkin D., and M.S. Lindee
 1995 *The DNA Mystique. The Gene as a Cultural Icon.* New York, NY: W.H. Freeman and Company.

Office for Protection from Research Risks (OPRR)
 1993 *Protecting Human Research Subjects: Institutional Review Board Guidebook.* Washington, DC: U.S. Government Printing Office.

Parker, L.S., and C.W. Lidz
 1994 Familial coercion to participate in genetic family studies: Is there cause for IRB intervention? *IRB* 16:6-12.

Pennisi, E.
 1999 Academic sequencers challenge Celera in a sprint to the finish. *Science* 283:1822-1823.

Powers, M.
 1993 Publication-related risks to privacy: Ethical implications of pedigree studies. *IRB* 15:7-11.

Ranen, N.G., O.C. Stine, M.H. Abbott, M. Sherr, A-M. Codori, M.L. Franz, N.I. Chao, A.S. Chung, N. Pleasant, C. Callahan, L.M. Kasch, M. Ghaffari, G.A. Chase, H.H. Kazazian, J. Brandt, S. Folstein, and C.A. Ross
 1995 Anticipation and instability of IT-15 (CAG)$_N$ repeats in parent-offspring pairs with Huntington disease. *American Journal of Human Genetics* 57:593-602.

Reilly, P.R.
 1998 Rethinking risks to human subjects in genetic research. *American Journal of Human Genetics* 63:682-685.

Rosenberg, R., and L. Kowalcyzk
 2000 Heart study will sell patient data for profit. *Boston Globe*, June 16, p. A01.

Struewing, J.P., D. Abeliovich, T. Peretz, N. Avishai, M.M. Kaback, F.S. Collins, and L.C. Brody
 1996 The carrier frequency of the BRCA1 185delAG mutation is approximately 1 percent in Ashkenazi Jewish individuals. *Nature Genetics* 11:198-200.

Task Force on Genetic Testing (NIH-DOE Working Group on Ethical, Legal and Social Implications of Human Genome Research)
 1997 *Promoting Safe and Effective Genetic Testing in the United States. Principles and Recommendations.* Bethesda, MD: National Institutes of Health.

U.S. Congress, Office of Technology Assessment
 1992 *Genetic Counseling and Cystic Fibrosis Carrier Screening*: Results of a Survey—Background Paper, OTA-BP-BA-97. Washington, DC: U.S. Government Printing Office.

Veatch, R.M.
 1981 *A Theory of Medical Ethics.* New York, NY: Basic Books.

Visco, F.M.
 1996 Commentary on the ASCO statement on genetic testing for cancer susceptibility. *Journal of Clinical Oncology* 14:1737.

Wallace, R.B.
 1997 The potential of population surveys for genetic studies. Pp. 234-244 in *Between Zeus and the Salmon: The Biodemography of Longevity*, K.W. Wachter and C.E. Finch, eds. Washington, DC: National Academy Press.

Welsh, M.J., L-C. Tsui, and A.L. Beaudet
    1995   Cystic fibrosis. Pp. 3799-3876 in *The Metabolic Basis of Inherited Disease*, xth ed.,
           C.L. Scriver, A.L. Beaudet, W.S. Sly, and D. Valle, eds. New York, NY: McGraw-
           Hill.
Wiggins, S., P. Whyte, M. Huggins, S. Adam, J. Theilmann, M. Bloch, S.B. Sheps, M.T.
Schechter, M.R. Hayden, for the Canadian Collaborative Study of Predictive Testing
    1992   The psychological consequences of predictive testing for Huntington's disease.
           New England Journal of Medicine 327:1401-1405.
Willis, R.J.
    1999   Personal communication, August 19.
Woodward, B.
    1996   Challenges to human subject protections in U.S. medical research. *Journal of the
           American Medical Association* 282:1947-1952.

14

Biosocial Opportunities for Surveys

Kenneth W. Wachter

Biological indicators are nothing new to social surveys. Two such indicators, height and weight, tabulated by social class, were already being collected during the reign of Queen Victoria by the British Association for the Advancement of Science. Its President for 1885, Francis Galton, invented linear regression in the course of his analysis of heights. Height turns out to be a many-faceted biological indicator of health and standards of living and a sensitive probe of social differentials. The intellectual lineage that leads from Galton through Robert Fogel and his research partners is a major source for the present wide interest in biological indicators among social scientists.

In three other respects, the example of height is a good precedent for biological indicators in general. In the first place, height is the quintessential expression of an interaction between genes and the social and economic environment. Each child's height is determined to a considerable extent by the genes of its parents, and yet observed differences across time and between groups and populations mainly reflect environmental influences associated with nutrition, physical effort, and disease. In the second place, the study of height is interwoven with the study of the social dimensions of health, successfully bridging the biomedical, economic, and demographic research communities. In the third place, from the very beginning, analysis of data on height has required and given birth to new statistical methods, from the fitting of normal distributions and linear regression onwards. All three observations are central to the new interest in biological indicators in social surveys: the primacy of gene-environment interactions, the bridging of research communities, and the imperative for new statistical approaches.

As individuals, we know so much, but only so much, about ourselves. Self-reports as the mainstay of social surveys have taken us a long way, but now survey research is stretching itself to move beyond them. One sign of the change is the increasing investment in linking survey data to administrative data, for instance to earnings records or medical expenditure claims. Secure data facilities are being established to protect respondents' confidentiality while facilitating flexible research. Another sign of the change is the panoply of initiatives treated in previous chapters involving the collection of genetic, anthropometric, endocrinological, cognitive, and physiological markers in conjunction with socioeconomic measures and demographic histories.

This volume is meant, first and foremost, to address the question of what we stand to learn, early on, from the inclusion of biological indicators in social surveys. The future will be changing rapidly and probably unforeseeably, but sensible first steps are within view.

When I think about the immediate value of including genetic and physiological indicators in social surveys, I find that I want to speak in praise of negative results. I fear that over the next decade we are likely to see a crude biological determinism trying to gobble up the social sciences. Envision streams of television and internet announcements of "the gene for X" and "the gene for Y"—the gene for math, the gene for lying, the gene for winning elections, the gene for millionairehood, the double-gene for billionairehood, the gene behind early retirement, early childbearing, early divorce, depression, satisfaction, long life, joy, and luck. One effect of the new genetics on the popular imagination will likely be the reinforcement of beliefs that complex outcomes have simple causes. The appeal of hidden variable theories of behavioral mechanics is doubled when the hidden variables take the name of genes and submit themselves to decoding.

If such claims were all silly, our problem would be media relations and public communication of science. But some such claims will not be silly. There may well be significant genetic determinants of some social behaviors. Sifting the valid from the spurious is a critical role for social science in the coming decade. It is particularly important because some claims may carry with them troubling political and ethical baggage. I am speaking "in praise of negative results," because the most important priority may be the ability to say on firm evidence that a false claim is false, that a purported effect just isn't there.

The social science community needs to be prepared to evaluate the efficacy of ostensible determinants of behaviors, basing its investigations on data that are representative at the population level and include appropriate control variables. Much of what has come out of genetic searches for genes figuring in diseases derives from studies of highly selected samples of individuals with little in the way of controls for demographic and behavioral covariates. Early announcements of findings generally overstate the strength of the effects that would be seen at the level of whole populations. Such announcements tend to exaggerate the simplicity of the genetic pathways themselves. Social scientists will not be in a position to evaluate claims and speak with authority unless the capability to analyze genetic indicators is already at hand in data sets which contain the relevant sociological, economic, and behavioral responses. If, in each case, we have to wait three years while we go out and collect new data, we will have excluded ourselves from the scientific debate. These stories, when they happen, play out quickly.

Summing up this line of argument, I believe it is a matter of urgency for us to have biological material collected by some of our leading social surveys as a resource ready to allow timely careful testing of new claims. This means we need to solve problems of appropriate safeguards and informed consent sufficiently well to have stored blood that can be used to type for new candidate genes as they come into the limelight of scientific debate. For a variety of reasons, among them imprecisely defined phenotypes and sparse coverage of family members and relatives, social surveys are not usually suited for hunting candidate genes associated with conditions and outcomes. But once candidate genes have been identified by geneticists and epidemiologists, the role of social surveys in confirmatory analysis becomes paramount. This role can only be realized with the creation of the required data resources in advance. Many of us are believers in preventive medicine. We also need preventive social science.

I turn now to the kinds of questions that the inclusion of biological indicators in social surveys would help us to address. A prime question, asked from a social scientist's perspective: How pleiotropic is the world? How typical is it for a given gene or set of genes to be related to multiple phenotypic outcomes? Are the genes that will be discovered to have biological impacts on health also going to turn out to be associated with socioeconomic characteristics and choices? Will such alleles mostly be randomly distributed across subgroups or concentrated in particular subgroups? This is no simple question, considering the large number of dimensions along which population subgroups may be defined.

We are at a point where genetic epidemiologists are beginning to identify genes with alleles that are strongly enough associated with health outcomes to affect mortality rates at national levels. Apolipoprotein E is the prize example so far. Douglas Ewbank's chapter in this volume cautions us against expecting large numbers of alleles with unambiguous effects. But studies are already underway looking for alleles that are concentrated among survivors to extreme ages, and they will be bringing to attention a potpourri of genes whose behavioral associations would be ripe for testing. Studies of quantitative trait loci (QTLs) will similarly be identifying candidate regions of the genome associated with biological outcomes whose behavioral correlates will merit study. Will we start discovering a rich web of genetically grounded crosswise connectivity between our biological and our social life-course trajectories? Or will correlations typically wash out? Between the biomedical and the social sphere, has the genome opted for division of labor or entanglement?

Our conceptualization of the overall health impacts of genetic determinants is going to be very different if alleles with strong biomedical effects typically also bring along propensities for a whole set of ancillary behaviors. Genetic configurations may turn out to be associated—causally or through the accidents of genealogy—with risk-taking or health-promoting behavior, with choices about insurance or about human capital investment. They may be associated with propensities for caregiving, with familial stability, or with commitment to the maintenance of kinship networks. Or, in the end, there may be very little here to find. Such a discovery would also be liberating.

Genetic epidemiologists may already have the ingredients for answers to some of the questions about which demographers and sociologists are wondering. The divergent interests of the disciplines make communication tricky. Opportunities to work on common data sets can help create a common language, and the inclusion of biological markers in social surveys is a logical step. An attractive alternative is to include social science modules in future waves of ongoing surveys already replete with biological indicators. The National Health and Nutrition Examination Survey (NHANES) is a promising example. To reap the benefits, conditions for access to the genetic and biological variables would need to be made practicable for specialists outside the health sciences. Social science modules in health surveys would be limited in scope compared to the social surveys that currently collect full employment histories; components of income, assets, and transfers; or family and kinship constellations. Nonetheless, for many purposes, full detail is not essential, and modest social data linked to biological variables would open new horizons. A step-by-step approach is reasonable.

Drawing on ideas expressed by many of the authors represented in this volume, I have my own personal list of issues that I am anxious to see illuminated. Many of these involve anthropometric or physiological indicators rather than genetic markers. First in my mind is an issue of the different meanings of self-reported and measured responses. There is already a lot of work in this area. Survey responses about diagnoses ever communicated by a physician are being compared to on-the-spot survey measurements of conditions. Self-reports of difficulties in activities of daily living are being compared to measured performance at specified tasks. Self-reports of earnings are being compared with linked earnings histories. Self-reports of expectations about one's own future survival are being compared against life table projections.

Inclusion of a range of biological markers in social surveys would greatly enhance the range of comparisons available to study. The subject is important because motivation, risk assessment, frustration, or a sense of well-being are as much potential causal factors as cortisol, bank balances, and muscle tone. Furthermore, what we know about ourselves and what we say about ourselves to ourselves and to others is a component of life that is of thematic interest in its own right in this "information age." What do people hear when they listen to their doctor or watch a pollution special on television? What is the personal probability calculus that people wield for their own decision-making, from youth through age? Coupling self-reports with measured and monitored outcomes is a clear next step toward understanding.

Several of the authors in this book look forward to a time almost upon us when unobtrusive monitoring devices will be able to collect extensive individual data on environmental exposures, activity levels, and physiological responses. I am told that there will be computers woven into my scarf, controlled by the twiddling of my fingers in thin air, and devices in my belt buckle capable of reporting to the survey researcher more about my movements and environmental encounters than I think I ever want to know. Experience with the more modest world of small numbers of carefully pretested biological markers in social surveys will help us prepare to keep our bearings in the face of technological opportunities.

A fairly specific research area in which the juxtaposition of biological and demographic variables will be critical is the interpretation of correlations between educational attainment and outcomes in the realm of health, disability, and mortality. What will help resolve the tension between the camp of researchers who believe that education has content that is causal and the camp who see mainly a drama of selectivity and social classification? Sets of intermediate physiological outcome variables gathered within the framework of longitudinal social surveys may be a key contributor. Current work with the Wisconsin Longitudinal Survey shows the promise of this line of research.

There is some possibility that genetic markers, hormonal assays, or related measurements might prove valuable as instrumental variables in statistical attempts to untangle arrows of causation. Such uses would involve variables whose values were unknown or only known after the fact to an individual. A related idea was highlighted by Robert Willis at the workshop leading to this volume. Obligations to inform survey participants of the outcomes of biological measurements turn surveys more explicitly than ever before into interventions. If they are carefully and appropriately designed, longitudinal studies in the course of which test results are communicated to participants could aid understanding of how specific pieces of personal medical knowledge affect subsequent behavior.

One strand of research already in progress that may be a good guide to future opportunities is the set of studies focused on the concept of allostatic load, described briefly with references in the chapters by Crimmins and Seeman and by Weinstein and Willis. Allostatic load is a term for the long-range cumulative effects of the body's physiological accommodations to stress, which can include changes that are adaptive in the short term, but which may also be injurious in the long run. Some researchers have operationalized allostatic load using a composite variable constructed from various biological measurements including systolic and diastolic blood pressure, cholesterol ratios, and cortisol levels. Viewed biomedically, the concept is far from simple. Evolution has equipped organisms with a wide variety of homeostatic mechanisms to cope with stresses whose presence may be bound up with biological success. Cumulative effects may be positive as well as negative, reflecting health rather than depletion. So far, however, as used in demographic applications, allostatic load is predominantly associated with waning health and gradually diminishing prospects for survival.

Going beyond specific applications, the concept of allostatic load suggests a certain philosophical stance about the nature of aging, a view summed up for me in lines from Matthew Arnold's poem "The Scholar Gypsy":

> For what wears out the life of mortal men?
> 'Tis that from change to change their being rolls:
> 'Tis that repeated shocks again, again,
> Exhaust the energy of strongest souls
> And numb the elastic powers.

Studies of allostatic load are among the most successful forays so far into the world of biological indicators in longitudinal social surveys. Certain features of this work may be important considerations for the field as a whole. One is the demand placed on the development of new statistical and demographic methods. As a measure of cumulative stress, allostatic load should be determined by cumulative processes. New statistical models are being devised which take whole sequences of life-course events or experiences as predictor variables, in place of the one-by-one predictor variables familiar in linear regression. Patterns of challenge and recovery rather than the presence and absence of specific positive or negative factors are treated as determinants in these new models. The approach makes heavy demands on sample size, but it has the advantage of coming closer to our intuitive sense of the cumulative longitudinal processes of development and aging.

The construction of the prevailing operational measure of allostatic load is itself interesting from a statistical point of view. It is an example of "dimensionality reduction," a leading principle of multivariate statistical analysis. The measure of allostatic load is a composite index, a nonlinear function of ten variables. Instead of using all ten variables separately, a single index is created. The formula for this index was developed from theoretical considerations. Statistical methods are also available for constructing such indices automatically by searching for combinations of a given set of variables which capture as much as possible of the multi-dimensional variability in the data significant for some particular purpose defined by the researcher.

In the case of allostatic load, dimensionality reduction takes us from ten variables down to one index. It could take us from thousands of variables down to a handful. Statisticians are rapidly developing non-linear search methods for dimensionality reduction taking advantage of available computing power. Such methods will only give useful results if some strong underlying relationship is actually present, hidden by its highly multidimensional character, and if the researcher can define what constitutes significant variability in a strategic way. The technology for checking thousands of genetic markers for each individual in a longitudi-nal survey at low cost may soon be ready. New techniques for obtaining other biological indicators may also provide thousands of variables. The challenge then will be to invent analytic strategies that can make meaning-ful use of the overwhelming riches of data. Sample sizes in longitudinal surveys will not grow in pace with the numbers of variables. Just as the opportunities of data on heights transformed the field of statistics a cen-tury ago, so the opportunities provided by biological indicators in social surveys will demand whole new forms of dimensionality reduction and nonlinear statistical analysis.

The words "allostatic load" prompt one more reflection. There is an allostatic load on every social scientist. Cumulative stress bears down on all of us. As biological indicators come to be included in social surveys, old kinds of expertise will become obsolete, new kinds of expertise will become mandatory, circles of collaboration will have to expand. Stress will increase.

It is pointless to provide for including biological indicators in social surveys unless we can provide for the researchers who can make intelli-gent use of them. The changes are too rapid for us to wait to grow a new generation with the needed skills and interpersonal connections. How do we ease transitions by established researchers into this interdisciplinary territory? Training is part of the picture, but not the whole of the picture. We are talking about life-course transitions for researchers, with an interplay of intellectual, psychological, social, and physiological challenges. These are themselves examples of the kinds of processes we seek to study with biosocial surveys. As we study allostatic load, we need to learn to manage allostatic load and, borrowing Matthew Arnold's words, renew the "elastic powers."

Suggested Readings

G iven the diverse range and specificity of subject matter in this volume, the identification of key references from among the hundreds of citations in the individual chapters is difficult at best. The following references were singled out by the authors and editors of this volume as especially useful to the interested reader.

Abecasis, G.R., L.R. Cardon, and W.O.C. Cookson
    2000   A general test of association for quantitative traits in nuclear families. *American Journal of Human Genetics* 66:279-292.

Adler, N.E., M. Marmot, B.S. McEwen, and J. Stewart, eds.
    1999   *Socioeconomic Status and Health in Industrial Nations. Social, Psychological and Biological Pathways.* Annals of the New York Academy of Sciences, 896. New York: New York Academy of Sciences.

Brown, P.O., and D. Botstein
    1999   Exploring the new world of the genome with DNA microarrays. *Nature Genetics* 21:33-37.

Clayton, E.W., K.K. Steinberg, M.J. Khoury, E. Thomson, L. Andres, M.J.E. Kahn, L.M. Kopelman, and J.O. Weiss
    1995   Informed consent for genetic research on stored tissue samples. *Journal of the American Medical Association* 274:1786-1792.

Crabbe, J.C., J.K. Belknap, and K.J. Buck
    1994   Genetic animal models of alcohol and drug abuse. *Science* 264:1715-1723.

Glass, T.A.
    1998   Conjugating the "tenses" of function: Discordance among hypothetical, experimental, and enacted function in older adults. *Gerontologist* 38:101-112.

Khoury, M.J., T.H. Beaty, and B.H. Cohen
    1993   *Fundamentals of Genetic Epidemiology.* New York/Oxford: Oxford University Press.

Lander, E.S., and N.J. Schork
  1994   Genetic dissection of complex traits. *Science* 265:2037-2048.
Lapham, E.V., C. Kozma, and J.O. Weiss
  1996   Genetic discrimination: Perspectives of consumers. *Science* 274:621-624.
McClearn, G.E., and D.J. Vandenbergh
  2000   The structure and limits of animal models: Examples from alcohol research. *ILAR Journal* 41(3):144-152.
Miller, R.A.
  1997   When will the biology of aging become useful? Future landmarks in biomedical gerontology. *Journal. American Geriatrics Society* 45:1258-1267.
  1999   Kleemeier award lecture: Are there genes for aging? *Journal of Gerontology: Biological Sciences* 54A:B297-B307.
Modelmog, D., S. Rahlenbeck, and D. Trichopoulos
  1992   Accuracy of death certificates: A population-based, complete-coverage, one-year autopsy study in East Germany. *Cancer Causes and Control* 3:541-546.
National Bioethics Advisory Commission
  1999   *Research Involving Human Biological Materials: Ethical Issues and Policy Guidance.* Volume I: Report and Recommendations of the National Bioethics Advisory Commission. Rockville, MD: National Bioethics Advisory Commission. [Online at http://bioethics.gov/pubs.html]
National Institutes of Health
  1999   Innovative study designs and analytic approaches to the genetic epidemiology of Cancer. *Monographs of the Journal of the National Cancer Institute,* 26. Bethesda, MD: National Institutes of Health.
Nelkin D., and M.S. Lindee
  1995   *The DNA Mystique. The Gene as a Cultural Icon.* New York: W.H. Freeman and Company.
Reuben D.B., L.A. Valle, R.D. Hays, and A.L. Siu
  1995   Measuring physical function in community-dwelling older persons: A comparison of self-administered, interviewer-administered, and performance-based measures. *Journal. American Geriatrics Society* 43:17-23.
Ridley, Matt
  1999   *Genome: The Autobiography of a Species in 23 Chapters.* New York: Harper Collins Publishers.
Risch, N.J., and K. Merikangas
  1996   The future of genetic studies of complex human diseases. *Science* 273:1516-1517.
Rothman, K.J., and S. Greenland
  1998   *Modern Epidemiology.* Second Edition. Philadelphia: Lippincott-Raven Publishers.
Task Force on Genetic Testing (NIH-DOE Working Group on Ethical, Legal and Social Implications of Human Genome Research)
  1997   *Promoting Safe and Effective Genetic Testing in the United States. Principles and Recommendations.* Bethesda, MD: National Institutes of Health.
Thoits, P.A.
  1995   Stress, coping, and social support processes: Where are we? What next? *Journal of Health and Social Behavior* (extra issue):53-79.
Vaupel, J.W., J.R. Carey, K. Christensen, T.E. Johnson, A.I. Yashin, N.V. Holm, I.A. Iachine, V. Kannisto, A.A. Khazaeli, P. Liedo, V.D. Longo, Y. Zeng, K.G. Manton, and J.W. Curtsinger
  1998   Biodemographic trajectories of longevity. *Science* 280(5365):855-860.
Wallace, R.B.
  1997   The potential of population surveys for genetic studies. Pp. 234-244 in *Between Zeus and the Salmon: The Biodemography of Longevity,* K.W. Wachter and C.E. Finch, eds. Washington, DC: National Academy Press.

Glossary

Many of the following definitions pertaining to genetics are taken from a glossary developed and maintained by the National Human Genome Research Institute (NHGRI). The NHGRI glossary may be accessed at http://www.nhgri.nih.gov/DIR/VIP/Glossary/pub_glossary.cgi

ADLs. Activities of daily living; measures of basic functional status (e.g., bathing, dressing, toileting, continence, feeding, transferring). Sometimes referred to as BADLs (basic activities of daily living).

Allele. One of the variant forms of a gene at a particular locus, or location, on a chromosome. Different alleles produce variation in inherited characteristics, such as hair color or blood type.

Allostatic load. A composite measure of the body's accommodation to stress from the wear and tear resulting from chronic overactivity or underactivity of physiological systems.

Amino acid. Any of a class of 20 molecules that combine to form proteins in living things. The sequence of amino acids in a protein and hence protein function are determined by the genetic code.

Antagonistic pleiotropy. Multiple gene effects such that alleles that improve fitness in early life have detrimental effects later in life.

APOE. The apolipoprotein E gene, which instructs the body to make a protein that ferries cholesterol through the bloodstream. One variant (allele) of APOE (APOE e4) is associated with increased risk of certain diseases, notably heart disease and Alzheimer's.

Apoptosis. Programmed death of cells during embryogenesis and metamorphosis or during cell turnover in adult tissues.

Assortive mating. A process by which individuals select mates on the basis of one or more phenotypic characteristics.

Bacterial artificial chromosomes (BACs). Large segments of DNA (100,000 to 200,000 bases) from another species cloned into bacteria. Once the foreign DNA has been cloned into the host bacteria, many copies of the DNA can be made.

Base pair. Two complementary nucleotides in double-stranded DNA.

Base sequence. The order of nucleotide bases in a DNA molecule.

Biodemography. An emerging field of research that seeks to integrate and translate findings from a variety of disciplines (e.g., demography, evolutionary and molecular biology, genetics, epidemiology, ecology) into their effects on population health status and individual/social behavior.

Bioindicators. In biology and ecology, living organisms that respond in a clear way to a change in the environment. Increasingly used in health and social sciences to refer to measurable properties of organisms that are associated with the manifestation of, or susceptibility to, disease processes.

Biomarkers. Observable properties of an organism that can be used in four general ways: (1) to identify the organism's presence, (2) to estimate prior exposure to an exogenous agent, (3) to identify changes in the organism, and (4) to assess underlying susceptibility.

Biomarkers of aging. Age-related biological parameters, the absolute values or rates of change of which might estimate, for example, subsequent life expectancy.

BRCA1/BRCA2. The first breast cancer genes to be identified. Mutated forms of these genes are believed to be responsible for about half the cases of inherited breast cancer, especially those that occur in younger women.

Candidate gene. A gene, located in a chromosome region suspected of being involved in a disease, whose protein product suggests that it could be the disease gene in question.

cDNA. A DNA sequence copied in the laboratory from a messenger RNA sequence.

Contamination effect. In the context of ongoing surveys, the possibility that a respondent's behavior will be affected by information revealed by the survey (e.g., if a study team discovers that an individual has a disease and relays that information to the individual, his/her subsequent behavior likely will be less representative of the larger population and more reflective of the intervention of the study itself).

Crossing over. The exchange of parts between homologous chromosomes during meiosis; recombination.

DNA. Deoxyribonucleic acid: the molecular basis of heredity.

DNA sequencing. Determining the exact order of the base pairs in a segment of DNA.

Enzyme. A protein that catalyzes or accelerates specific biochemical reactions.

EPESE. Established Populations for Epidemiologic Studies of the Elderly. Ongoing studies, initiated by the National Institute on Aging in 1982, of randomly sampled community-dwelling men and women aged 65 years or older. Major findings have focused on biomedical and psychosocial predictors of health and functioning in older cohorts.

Epigenetic changes. A broadly used term that historically described changes in gene expression or phenotype that were not the result of a mutation or other change in the DNA sequence of a gene. The term now includes specific changes (e.g., methylation of DNA bases) that can modify gene expression.

Epistatic effect. The suppression of gene expression by one or more other genes.

Exon. The region of a gene that contains the code for producing the gene's protein. Each exon codes for a specific portion of the complete protein. In some species (including humans), a gene's exons are separated by long regions of DNA called introns (or sometimes "junk DNA") that have no apparent function.

F_1 generation. Offspring, from the mating of individuals of two different strains, that are heterozygous for all loci for which their parental strains differed in allelic configuration.

Founder effect. The introduction of a certain gene variant into a population such that the variation spreads in the absence of competition, which leads to fixation of the characteristics of that variant.

Gamete. An egg or sperm cell; a germ cell.

Gene. The functional and physical unit of heredity passed from parent to offspring. Genes are pieces of DNA, and most genes contain the information for making a specific protein.

Gene mapping. Determination of the relative positions of genes on a DNA molecule and of the distance, in linkage units or physical units, between them.

Genetic drift. Genetic changes in populations caused by random phenomena rather than by selection.

Genetic marker. A segment of DNA with an identifiable physical location on a chromosome whose inheritance can be followed. A marker can be a gene, or it can be some section of DNA with no known function.

Genome. The total inventory of heritable nucleic acids, usually DNA, including chromosomal DNA in cell nuclei (nuclear genome) but also mitochondrial and chloroplast DNA.

Genotype. The genetic inventory of an individual organism that may not be revealed by outward (observable) characteristics.

Gerontogene. A gene that affects longevity either by reducing (e.g., as a result of antagonistic pleiotropy) or increasing average life span.

Germ cell. A reproductive (i.e., egg or sperm) cell.

Health and Retirement Survey (HRS). A longitudinal study begun in 1992 of 12,600 persons aged 51-61, plus their spouses, to which additional cohorts and age groups have been added in subsequent years. See http://www.umich.edu/~hrswww/

Heritability. The proportion of the variation in the distribution of a quantitative trait that is explained by inherited genes.

Homeostasis. The maintenance of normal internal stability in an organism by coordinated responses of organ systems that automatically compensate for environmental changes.

Homocysteine. An amino acid, formed by the liver after ingestion of another amino acid (methionine), that participates in metabolic pathways for certain vitamins.

Homologous. Corresponding in structure and position; allelic chromosomes are homologous. Also refers to structures or processes that have the same evolutionary origin though their functions may vary widely.

Human Genome Project (HGP). An international research project to map each human gene and to completely sequence human DNA.

IADLs. Instrumental activities of daily living; measures of an individual's ability to maintain an independent household (e.g., shopping for groceries, driving or using public transportation, using the telephone, meal preparation, housework, handyman work, laundry, taking medications, handling finances). Many community-based services (e.g., homemaker, meals-on-wheels) are aimed at providing IADL services and thereby permitting disabled older persons to remain in their homes.

Isoforms. For genes, isoforms can refer to alternatively spliced forms of the same gene. For proteins, isoforms can refer to members of a family of closely related proteins coded by different genes that evolved from a shared single ancestral gene.

Linkage. The association of genes and/or markers that lie near each other on a chromosome. Linked genes and markers tend to be inherited together.

Locus (pl. loci). The set of homologous parts of a pair of chromosomes that may be occupied by allelic genes; the locus thus consists of a pair of locations (except in the X chromosome of males).

LOD score. "Likelihood of odds" score; a statistical estimate of whether two loci are likely to lie near each other on a chromosome and are therefore likely to be inherited together.

Longevity genes. Genes that promote survival. Most fixed genes are presumed to be of this type.

Meiosis. Two consecutive special cell divisions in developing germ cells, characterized by the pairing and segregation of homologous chromosomes. The resulting germ cells (gametes) will have reduced chromosome sets.

Messenger RNA (mRNA). A variety of RNA that serves as a template for protein structure and synthesis. The sequence of a strand of mRNA is based on the sequence of a complementary strand of DNA.

Microarray. A recently developed technology based on computer chips for examination of hundreds to thousands of genes at the same time. The data may inform how the cell regulates batteries of genes simultaneously. Sometimes referred to as a gene chip.

Mitochondria. The subcellular particles (organelles) that make the ATP (energy) used for most cell activities. Mitochondria have a small number of their own genes.

Monogenic diseases. Diseases caused by mutation in a single gene.

Monozygotic twins. Identical twins, who share all their genetic material because they came from a single egg that separated into two embryos after fertilization by a single sperm.

Morphogens. Molecules that function as pattern organizers in evolving tissues (e.g., in embryos), signaling and directing gene activity in their target cells.

NHANES. The National Health and Nutrition Examination Survey; an ongoing program of studies conducted by the National Center for Health Statistics and designed to assess the health and nutritional status of adults and children in the United States. See http://www.cdc.gov/nchs/nhanes.htm

Nucleotide. One of the structural components of DNA and RNA. A nucleotide consists of a base (one of four chemicals: adenine, thymine, guanine, and cytosine) plus a molecule of sugar and one of phosphoric acid.

Oligogene. Also called a major gene, thought to have moderate-to-large effects on a given phenotypic trait.

Oligonucleotide. A short sequence of single-stranded DNA or RNA often used as a probe for detecting complementary DNA or RNA because it binds readily to its complement.

Pedigree. A recorded or known line of descent. In humans, this may be a diagram of family genealogy that shows family members' relationships to each other and how a particular trait or disease has been inherited.

Phenotype. The physical manifestation of gene function; the observable traits or characteristics of an organism (e.g., hair color, weight, the presence or absence of a disease). Phenotypic traits can be influenced by the environment.

Phyletic. Of, or pertaining to, a phylum or to an evolutionary line of descent.

Pleiotropy. Multiple effects of one gene; the capacity of a gene to affect several aspects of the phenotype.

Polygenic. Relating to a normal characteristic or hereditary disease controlled by the added effects of genes at multiple loci.

Polymerase chain reaction (PCR). A widely used and convenient technique for using enzymes to make an unlimited number of copies of any piece of DNA. Sometimes called "molecular photocopying."

Polymorphism. A gene variation (allele) present in at least 1 percent of the population.

Positional cloning. Identification of a gene by virtue of its location in the genome rather than by its biochemical function.

Probands. People who have the disorder under investigation in a family history study.

Proteomics. The study of the entire protein set that can be produced by a given genome; also understood more broadly as the large-scale experimental analysis of proteins.

Quantitative trait. A trait for which phenotypic variation is continuous (rather than discrete).

Quantitative trait locus (QTL). One of a group of genes specifying any particular quantitative trait.

Recombinant. A composite DNA molecule resulting from insertion into the original sequence (by chemical, enzymatic, or biologic means) of a new sequence; an offspring that has received chromosomal parts from different parental strains.

Recombination. Reshuffling of parental genes during meiosis due to crossing over. Recombination also may be induced in a test tube by enzymes.

RNA. Ribonucleic acid, a single-stranded string of cytocine, guanine, adenine, and uracil bases.

Senescence. Deterioration in performance seen later in the adult life span, associated with increasing mortality rates.

Short tandem repeat (STR). A tandem repeat in which the repeat units are 2-7 base pairs. Also referred to as a microsatellite.

Single nucleotide polymorphism (SNP). A single-base variation in the genetic code, the most common form of polymorphism.

Somatic cells. All cells in the body except for the germ-line cells that make eggs or sperm.

Stochastic. Random; involving chance or probability.

Syntenic. Denoting the linkage of a group of genes that is found in related species.

Tandem repeat. Multiple copies of the same base sequence on a chromosome; used as a marker in physical mapping.

T-cell. Also called t-lymphocyte, a white blood cell that is essential in the immune system.

Telomere. A specialized repeated DNA sequence found at the end of a chromosome.

Variable number of tandem repeats (VNTRs). Repeating units of a DNA sequence.

Zygote. The cell resulting from the union of a male and female gamete until it divides; the fertilized ovum.

Zygotic twins. Nonidentical (fraternal) twins, who on average share 50 percent of their genes (similar to ordinary siblings).

Index

B

Baby-boom cohorts, 252
Backcross groups, 223
Bacterial artificial chromosomes (BACs), 139, 340
Balance, 18
Baltimore Longitudinal Study of Aging, 162
Bangladesh, 271
Base pairs, 137, 139, 340
Base sequence, 340
Basic activities of daily living (BADLs), 168, 258
Behavioral genetics
    in addictions, 45, 50, 78n.11, 86, 102, 116
    association studies, 86
    community-based studies, 241-242
    and demographic analysis, 76, 78n.11, 85-87, 100
    generalizability of findings, 100
    psychiatric disorders, 86
    research opportunities, 330-331
    twin studies, 45, 48, 68, 86
Beta amyloid precursor protein, 140-141, 150
Beta secretases, 141
Between-population differences, in gene—environment interactions, 85, 90, 95
Bias
    in adoption studies, 44
    in case-control studies, 142, 240
    environment-disease association studies, 237-238
    in genetic epidemiology, 235
    in linear regression, 77-78
    in logistic regression, 78
    population stratification, 239
    in risk assessment, 255
    sampling, 86, 98, 111, 150, 239, 253
    selection, 246, 267
    in twin studies, 44, 117-118
    type I errors, 237
Biodemography, 340
Bioindicators. *See also* Biomarkers
    advantages in social surveys, 4-6, 254-265
    allostatic load, 25-26, 339
    antioxidant profiles, 20, 24
    appropriateness, 9
    blood samples as, 171-172, 254
    of cardiovascular system, 18, 19, 20, 21, 22
    changes over time, 256

cholesterol as, 15, 19, 22, 25, 254
cognitive function, 21, 22, 23, 24, 25
collaborative research opportunities, 272
defined, 340
in demographic approach, 14-16, 94
environment-health linkages from, 259-263
fertility, 15
gene expression data and, 207, 208
height and weight as, 329-330
historical context, 329
HPA axis, 20, 22-23, 25, 29
for inclusion in household surveys, 17-26, 31, 254
liabilities in social surveys, 265-266
lung function, 19, 20, 24, 28, 54, 161-162, 174
of metabolic processes, 19-21, 161
physiological, 18-19, 21
renal function, 19, 20, 24, 159, 161, 170, 172
and representativeness of nonclinical data, 254-256
risk factors, 15, 19
self-report calibration with, 256-259
SNS activity, 19, 20, 23, 25, 29
symptoms, 15
value of, 330-336
Biological determinism, 320
Biological pathways, 16
Biological specimens. *See also* Blood samples; Collection of biological specimens; DNA samples/sampling; Pathology samples; Repository specimens; Urine samples
    and association studies, 236
    from autopsies, 149-150
    genetic specimen sources, 149-150, 245-246, 276
    for hypothesis testing, 208
    transport and storage, 244-245, 268
    uses of data from, 9, 276
Biomarkers. *See also* Bioindicators
    of coagulation processes, 20, 21-22, 161
    defined, 184, 340
    of diabetes, 172, 184-185
    in epidemiologic studies, 17
    of inflammation processes, 19, 20, 21-22, 25
    of neuronal cells, 137

U

V

W

X

Y

Z